THE THIRD REVOLUTION

THE THIRD REVOLUTION

XI JINPING AND THE NEW CHINESE STATE

ELIZABETH C. ECONOMY

A Council on Foreign Relations Book

OXFORD
UNIVERSITY PRESS

OXFORD
UNIVERSITY PRESS

Oxford University Press is a department of the University of Oxford. It furthers
the University's objective of excellence in research, scholarship, and education
by publishing worldwide. Oxford is a registered trade mark of Oxford University
Press in the UK and certain other countries.

Published in the United States of America by Oxford University Press
198 Madison Avenue, New York, NY 10016, United States of America.

CIP data is on file at the Library of Congress
ISBN 978–0–19–086607–5

3 5 7 9 8 6 4 2

Printed by Edwards Brothers Malloy, United States of America

For David, Alexander, Nicholas, and Eleni

CONTENTS

———◆◆———

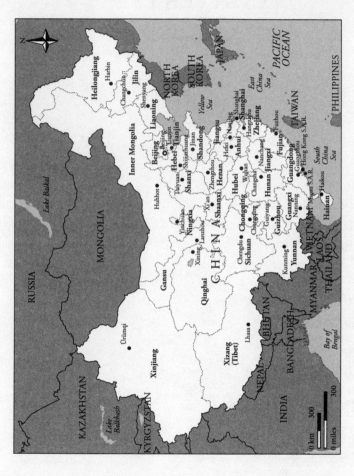

Map of China and Its Provinces
Credit: mapsopensource.com

PREFACE

———⟡———

China's rise on the global stage has been accompanied by an explosion of facts and information about the country. We can read about China's aging population, its stock market gyrations, and its investments in Africa. We can use websites to track the air quality in Chinese cities, to monitor China's actions in the South China Sea, or to check on the number of Chinese officials arrested on a particular day.

In many respects, this information does what it is supposed to do: keep us informed about one of the world's most important powers. From the boom and bust in global commodities to the warming of the earth's atmosphere, Chinese leaders' political and economic choices matter not only for China but also for the rest of the world; and we can access all of this information with a few strokes on our keyboards.

Yet all these data also have the potential to overload our circuits. The information we receive is often contradictory. We read one day that the Chinese government is advancing the rule of law and hear the next that it has arrested over two hundred lawyers and activists without due process. Information is often incomplete or inaccurate. In the fall of 2015, Chinese officials acknowledged that during 2000–2013, they had underestimated the country's consumption of coal by as much as 17 percent; as a result, more than a decade of reported improvements in energy efficiency and greenhouse gas emissions were called into question. We are confused by dramatic but often misleading headlines that trumpet China's every accomplishment. More Americans believe (incorrectly), for example, that China, not the United States, is the world's largest economic power. It is a country that often confounds us with contradictions.

The challenge of making sense of China has been compounded in recent years by the emergence of Xi Jinping as Chinese Communist Party general secretary (2012) and president (2013). Under his leadership, significant new laws and regulations have been drafted, revised, and promulgated at an astonishing rate, in many instances challenging long-held understandings of the country's overall political and economic trajectory. While previous Chinese leaders recognized nongovernmental organizations from abroad as an essential element of China's economic and social development, for example, the Xi-led government drafted and passed a law to constrain the activities of these groups, some of which Chinese officials refer to as "hostile foreign forces." In addition, contradictions within and among Xi's initiatives leave observers clamoring for clarity. One of the great paradoxes of China today, for example, is Xi Jinping's effort to position himself as a champion of globalization, while at the same time restricting the free flow of capital, information, and goods between China and the rest of the world. Despite his almost five years in office, questions abound as to Xi's true intentions: Is he a liberal reformer masquerading as a conservative nationalist until he can more fully consolidate power? Or are his more liberal reform utterances merely a smokescreen for a radical reversal of China's policy of reform and opening up? How different is a Xi-led China from those that preceded it?

I undertook this study to try to answer these questions for myself and to help others make sense of the seeming inconsistencies and ambiguities in Chinese policy today. Sifting through all of the fast-changing, contradictory, and occasionally misleading information that is available on China to understand the country's underlying trends is essential. Businesses make critical investment decisions based on assessments of China's economic reform initiatives. Decisions by foundations and universities over whether to put down long-term stakes in China rely on an accurate understanding of the country's political evolution. Negotiations over global climate change hinge on a correct distillation of past, current, and future levels of Chinese coal consumption. And countries' security policies must reflect a clear-eyed view of how Chinese leaders' words accord with their actions in areas such as the South China Sea and North Korea.

As much as possible, I attempt to assess the relative success or shortcomings of the Chinese leadership's initiatives on their own merits. In other words, I ask, what is the Chinese leadership seeking to accomplish with its policy reforms and what has it accomplished? I begin with Xi Jinping himself and lay out his vision for China and its historical antecedents. I then dive into six areas the Xi government has identified as top reform priorities—politics, the Internet, innovation, the economy, the environment, and foreign policy. In some cases, there are competing interests and initiatives to tease out. Nonetheless, taken together, these separate reform efforts provide a more comprehensive picture of the arc of Chinese reform over the past five years and its implications for the rest of the world. I conclude the book with a set of recommendations for how the United States and other countries can best take advantage of the transformation underway to achieve their own policy objectives.

ACKNOWLEDGMENTS

Writing a book is both a solo and a collective endeavor. For over two decades, I have been privileged to call the Council on Foreign Relations a second home. For this, I thank both Leslie A. Gelb, who hired me as a newly minted PhD and nurtured me through my first decade, and Richard Haass, who has supported me ever since by giving me the room to make mistakes, learn from them, and find my voice in the process. My colleagues have been an integral part of my intellectual journey as well—Adam Segal, always my best sounding board, but also Max Boot, Irina Faskianos, Shannon O'Neil, Micah Zenko, and my terrific Asia Studies colleagues, Alyssa Ayres, Jerome Cohen, Yanzhong Huang, Josh Kurlantzick, Ely Ratner, Sheila Smith, and Scott Snyder. All of them set a high standard of quality and productivity that I strive to meet. Amy Baker, Nancy Bodurtha, and Patricia Dorff also all provided important support in the process of writing the book. Outside the Council on Foreign Relations, Winston Lord and Orville Schell, two outstanding leaders in U.S.–China relations, inspire me both for their intellectual integrity and their generosity of spirit. Arthur Kroeber read part of the manuscript and provided invaluable advice.

The actual process of writing this book was facilitated by many people. Certainly, I owe an enormous debt to those Chinese scholars, activists, businesspeople, and officials who took the time to meet with me and share their perspectives. In some cases, our conversations spanned a decade or more. I am fortunate as well that two outside reviewers, as well as CFR Director of Studies James Lindsay and President Richard Haass took the time to read the manuscript carefully and pushed me to make it better. Their contributions cannot be overstated. I am grateful to David McBride for his support and guidance throughout the publication process. The Starr Foundation also has my deepest gratitude for providing the financial support that enabled me to research and write this book. My two research associates, Rachel Brown and Gabriel Walker, provided invaluable research assistance and brought intellectual rigor and an attention to detail that aided me throughout the process of research and writing. I was fortunate that when they went off to graduate school, two more outstanding research associates, Maylin Meisenheimer and Viola Rothschild, stepped into their shoes and helped me complete the process of fact-checking and proofreading. Natalie Au, who interned during the final editing stages, also provided critical support. All translations and any mistakes, of course, are my own.

Last, but never least, I would like to thank my family. My parents, James and Anastasia Economy; my siblings, Peter, Katherine, and Melissa; and above all my husband, David; and our children, Alexander, Nicholas, and Eleni. They all remind me on a daily basis what really matters in life.

Elizabeth C. Economy
New York City

THE THIRD REVOLUTION

I

Introduction

IN MID-NOVEMBER 2012, THE World Economic Forum hosted a breakfast in Dubai for several dozen prominent Chinese scholars, businesspeople, and government officials.[1] The Chinese had traveled there to discuss pressing global matters with their counterparts from around the world. I was one of a few non-Chinese citizens at the breakfast and soon noticed that the attention of most of the participants was not on climate change or youth unemployment but instead on the dramatic news from home. After months of suspense, the Chinese Communist Party (CCP) had just revealed the membership of the Politburo Standing Committee (PBSC)—the seven men selected to lead the country for the next five years.

Strikingly, most of the Chinese at the breakfast could say little about the new leaders. In contrast to the American and other democratic political systems, which are designed to strip bare the political and personal inclinations of public officials, the selection of Chinese leadership takes place almost entirely behind closed doors. It combines a bargaining and bartering process among former top leaders with a popularity contest among the two hundred or so members of the Communist Party who comprise the powerful Central Committee.

The run-up to this particular selection process had been particularly fraught. It was the first time in two-and-a-half decades that the general secretary of the CCP had not been hand-picked by Deng Xiaoping, the transformative leader of the country from the late 1970s until his death in 1997. Deng had led China out of the turmoil of the Cultural

Revolution and set the country on its historic path of economic reform and opening up. Since the mid-1980s, he had anointed each of
the CCP's previous four general secretaries: Hu Yaobang, Zhao Ziyang,
Jiang Zemin, and finally Hu Jintao. Without Deng's imprimatur, the
selection process appeared not only opaque but also at times chaotic.
One top contender, Bo Xilai, the charismatic head of Chongqing and
son of one of China's original revolutionary leaders, Bo Yibo, had
fallen in scandal during spring 2012, eventually landing under arrest
for corruption. Xi Jinping, the heir-designate and eventual winner in
the political sweepstakes, had disappeared for a period of two weeks in
September, giving rise to a raft of rumors concerning his fate. Until the
group of seven men walked onto a stage in the Great Hall of the People
in Beijing shortly before noon on November 15, 2012, the Chinese
people could not state with complete certainty who would be leading
their country.

When I asked the Chinese at my table what they made of the new
PBSC members, they pointed out that, overall, they appeared to represent the older, more conservative element within the party. Sixty-
six-year-old former Guangdong Party Secretary Zhang Dejiang, for
example, possessed a degree in economics from North Korea's Kim Il-
Sung University and was known above all for his poor handling of the
early 1990s SARS epidemic and his repressive approach to the media.
In contrast, fifty-seven-year-old Wang Yang, Zhang's dynamic and
reform-oriented successor in Guangdong, was left waiting in the wings.
(He was selected for the still prestigious, but less powerful, Politburo.)
Beyond such generalities, however, my Chinese colleagues could say
little. Indeed, Xi Jinping, who at fifty-nine years of age now stood at the
apex of the Communist Party as general secretary and would just four
months later become president of the country and head of the military,
was largely an unknown quantity. Despite three decades of government
service, Xi's accomplishments, temperament, and leadership qualities
remained a question mark.

The Xi Vision

The new general secretary did not leave the Chinese people or the rest
of the world wondering for long. Speaking at a press conference shortly

after the new leaders made their appearance at the Great Hall of the People, Xi outlined his priorities. He spoke of the need to address the endemic corruption that plagued the Communist Party and to ensure that the party served the people. Fighting corruption would soon become the signature issue of his first years in office.

The essence of Xi Jinping's vision, however, was his call for the great revival or rejuvenation of the Chinese nation. Reflecting on China's five thousand years of history, Xi referenced the country's "indelible contribution" to world civilization.[2] At the same time, he acknowledged that efforts by successive Chinese leaders to realize the great revival of the Chinese nation had "failed one time after another."[3] The rejuvenation narrative is a well-understood and powerful one in China. It evokes memories of the country as the Middle Kingdom demanding tribute from the rest of the world; China as a source of innovation, creating paper, gunpowder, printing, and the compass; and China as an expansive, outward-facing power, with Ming dynasty Admiral Zheng He commanding a naval fleet of more than three hundred ships and sailing throughout Asia to the Horn of Africa and the Red Sea. Left out of the rejuvenation narrative, but etched deeply into the minds of many Chinese, are those periods of Chinese history that evoke shame, such as the one hundred years of humiliation (1849–1949), when China was occupied and invaded by foreign powers, or the periods that remain the black holes of contemporary Chinese history, in which the Chinese people suffered at the hands of their own government, such as the Great Leap Forward, the Cultural Revolution, and the Tiananmen Square massacre.

During his tour of "The Road toward Renewal" exhibition at the National Museum of China just two weeks later, Xi again underscored the theme of China's rejuvenation, calling it "the greatest dream for the Chinese nation in modern history."[4] The site of Xi's speech at the National Museum was not accidental. While much of Chinese history is marked by revolutions, political and social upheaval, and discontinuities in leadership and political ideologies, the museum celebrates the ideal of continuity in Chinese history. Quoting from both Mao and ancient Chinese poets, Xi used the museum as a backdrop to make clear the linkages between an imperial China and a China led by the Communist Party.

In the following months, Xi elaborated further on his vision for the country. He equated his call for rejuvenation with the "Chinese Dream" (*Zhongguo meng*, 中国梦). For Xi, the Chinese Dream was premised on the attainment of a number of concrete objectives: China should double its per-capita GDP from 2010 to 2020; it should have a military "capable of fighting and winning wars"; and it should meet the social welfare needs of the people. There also should be no doubt concerning the country's ideological future: Xi declared, "The selection of path is a life-or-death issue for the future of the CPC. We should unswervingly uphold socialism with Chinese characteristics . . . the superiority of our system will be fully demonstrated through a brighter future."[5] To this end, a robust Communist Party at the forefront of the political system was of paramount importance. Xi was also careful to distinguish the Chinese Dream, rooted in collective values, from the more individualistic American Dream, noting that the great rejuvenation of the Chinese nation "is a dream of the whole nation, as well as of every individual," and that "only when the country does well, and the nation does well, can every person do well."[6]

Not all Chinese shared Xi Jinping's particular understanding of the Chinese Dream. Some argued that the Chinese Dream was a dream of political reform or constitutionalism, in which the Communist Party would not be above the law but instead would be bound by it. Others said that it was a dream to better Chinese society through improvements in food safety or the quality of the environment. And still others, drawing on the American Dream, called for individual dreams and pursuits to be respected. Over the course of his first year in office, Xi began to incorporate some of these other elements, such as opportunities for better education, higher income, and a cleaner environment, into his dream narrative.[7] Yet it remained at heart a call for a CCP-led China to reclaim the country's ancient greatness.

Xi is not the first modern Chinese leader to use the theme of rejuvenation to remind the Chinese people of past glories in an effort to bind them to modern China. Deng Xiaoping talked about the "invigoration of China,"[8] and his successors Jiang Zemin and Hu Jintao both called for the "great rejuvenation of the Chinese nation."[9] Over the course of more than three decades as China experienced a dizzying period of economic and political reform and opening up to the outside world, all of

China's modern leaders sought to build a China that could reclaim its place as a global power.

Yet in seeking to realize this common vision, Xi and the rest of the Chinese leadership have parted ways with their predecessors. They have elected a way forward that largely rejects the previous path of reform and opening up: instead there is reform without opening up. In a number of respects, the leadership has embraced a process of institutional change that seeks to reverse many of the political, social, and economic changes that emerged from thirty years of liberalizing reform. The Chinese leaders have also shed the low-profile foreign policy advanced by Deng Xiaoping in favor of bold initiatives to reshape the global order.

These dramatic shifts reflect in large measure a belief on the part of Xi Jinping that China at the time of his ascension was at an inflection point. The post-Mao era of reform and opening up had yielded significant gains: double-digit growth for more than two decades, and international admiration for China's economic and other achievements. Yet as Xi rose up through the party ranks, he also had a front-row seat to the mounting challenges facing the country: the Communist Party had become corrupted and devoid of an ideological center, the provision of public goods had fallen dramatically behind society's needs, and even the economy needed a new infusion of reform. In the eyes of Xi, nothing less than dramatic, revolutionary change could save the party and the state and propel China forward to realize its full potential as a great power.

Xi's Inheritance

By the time of Mao's death in 1976, the Chinese leadership had just begun the process of recovery from the political strife, social upheaval, and economic impoverishment that marked much of his quarter-century tenure. Xi Jinping himself had experienced some of the worst of Mao's excesses. In the early 1960s, his father, a leading revolutionary figure and former vice-premier of the government, was branded a traitor and jailed for his bourgeois background. Soon after, fifteen-year-old Xi was "sent down" to a remote village where he labored for several years on an agricultural commune. Rather than feel bitter toward the

Communist Party for his family's difficulties, Xi became determined to join the party, applying for membership multiple times before finally being accepted in 1974. And in 1975, when Premier Zhou Enlai set out the Four Modernizations (agriculture, industry, science and technology, and military) to begin the process of revitalizing China's economy and society, Xi Jinping began his own journey alongside that of the country. He returned to Beijing that same year as a worker-peasant-soldier student to study chemical engineering at Tsinghua University, one of China's most prestigious academic institutions. Xi's university education during this time, however, was still shaped by Mao's revolutionary impulses, with significant periods of time devoted to learning from farmers and the People's Liberation Army, as well as studying Marxism-Leninism. (Only in 1977, with the reintroduction of exams for university entrance, did academics begin to reclaim a more dominant place in Chinese university life.)

The deaths of Mao Zedong and Zhou Enlai in 1976 were followed by a brief and bloodless power struggle that resulted, by 1978, in the ascension to power of Deng Xiaoping. Deng and his supporters cemented the Four Modernizations as the direction of the country and initiated a wholesale reform of the country's economic and political system—a transformative process that Deng would later call "China's Second Revolution." In the early 1980s, the Chinese leadership began to relax the tight state control that, in one way or another, had defined China's economic and political system since the 1950s. In the economic realm, this signaled the beginning of a transition from a command to a more market-driven economy. Deng devolved significant economic authority to provincial and local officials, removing political constraints on their economic activities and diminishing Beijing's ability to influence the development and outcome of these activities. China also invited participation from the international community in China's economic development through foreign direct investment and trade. By 1984, the government had opened up fourteen port cities along China's coast to foreign investment in special economic zones. In the mid-to-late 1990s, the state began in earnest to dismantle many of the state-owned enterprises, which had been the foundation of the urban economy, to encourage the expansion of private and cooperative ventures, and to energize the rural economy through the development of smaller scale township and village enterprises. The result was dramatic: average growth rates that exceeded 8 percent annually for more than two decades—elevating hundreds of millions of Chinese out of poverty, and earning China significant respect internationally.

Jiang Zemin, who assumed the position of general secretary of the Communist Party in 1989 and president of the country in 1993,[10] further elevated the role of the private sector in the Chinese political system, actively welcoming successful businesspeople into the party for the first time. China's turn outward to the rest of the world also expanded. China joined the World Trade Organization in 2001, and Jiang, along with Premier Zhu Rongji, encouraged the country's state-owned enterprises and other economic actors to "go out" in search of natural resources to fuel China's continued economic growth. Hundreds of thousands of Chinese relocated throughout the world for work and study. By 2008, China's reputation as an economic heavyweight was established and further burnished by its strong standing in the midst of the global financial crisis.

Changes in the economic realm were matched by reforms in the political sphere. A collective leadership and more institutionalized succession process replaced the highly personalized nature of governance at the top of the political system; significant political authority was devolved from central to local officials; and China embraced assistance, policy advice, and financial support from the international community. Moreover, as the government retreated from the market, it also retreated from its traditional role as social welfare provider, encouraging private, nonstate actors to fill the gap in areas such as education, medical care, and environmental protection; in the mid-1990s, Beijing allowed the establishment of formally approved and registered nongovernmental organizations (NGOs), enabling the rapid development of civil society. The advent of the Internet also elevated the role of civil society in Chinese governance. Despite maintaining controls over certain types of political content, by the mid-to-late 2000s, the web had become a virtual political space, with greater transparency, political accountability, and rule of law (in which Chinese citizens used the Internet to investigate crimes, seek justice for victims, and even push to overturn wrongful convictions) than existed in the real political system.

The era of President Hu Jintao and Premier Wen Jiabao (2002–2012) also marked the beginning of a more concerted public diplomacy effort. The leadership proclaimed China's "win-win" philosophy and worked hard to reassure Beijing's neighbors and the rest of the world that China's rise would be peaceful and, as its fortunes grew, so too would those of its partners. In summer 2008, Beijing hosted a world-class Olympic Games that earned accolades internationally and cemented the reputation inside Chinese political circles of the senior official who oversaw preparations for the games, new Politburo member and rising political star Xi Jinping.

The continued strength of the Chinese economy throughout the global financial crisis also introduced a new element into the country's foreign policy. Increasingly there were calls within China for the country to assume its rightful place on the global stage as a world leader, capable of shaping international norms and institutions. As the United States struggled to climb out of economic recession, senior Chinese economic, military, and foreign policy officials argued that the decline of the United States and the rise of China—long predicted to occur at some time during the twenty-first century—had begun. China's military, the beneficiary of double-digit budget increases for more than a decade, started to grow its ambitions alongside its capabilities. By the late 2000s, the Chinese leadership had progressed from rhetorically staking its claims to maritime sovereignty in the East and South China Seas to using its military prowess to realize them. Sitting at the helm of a small group of senior officials overseeing these moves in the South China Sea was Xi Jinping.

China's economic and foreign policy triumphs notwithstanding, by the time of Xi's ascension to power, there was also a growing sense within the country that significant contradictions had emerged in the political and economic life of China. The Communist Party had lost its ideological rationale and, for many of its more than 80 million members, the party served as little more than a stepping-stone for personal political and economic advancement. Corruption—an issue that Xi put front and center as he moved up the party ranks—was endemic throughout the party and the economy. And while three decades of "go-go" economic growth had brought significant economic benefits to the Chinese people, Beijing had failed to attend to the need for public

goods such as environmental protection and healthcare. The social welfare net, dismantled along with many of the state-owned enterprises,
had not been fully replaced, and, critically, distribution of social welfare benefits had not kept up with changing work patterns: more than
200 million migrant workers, who toiled in the city's factories or construction sites, could not legally live, receive medical care, or educate
their children in the cities in which they worked. The number of popular protests in the country rose to more than 180,000 by 2010. Even
the Chinese economy, while still posting growth rates well beyond
those of any other country, began to slow. A few outlier economists in
China and the West sounded alarm bells about structural weaknesses.
Investment-led growth was taking its toll, contributing to skyrocketing
levels of public and corporate debt. And for all its impressive economic
gains in low-cost manufacturing, China had little to show in the way
of innovation or the development of the service sector, the markers
of the world's advanced economies. By the time of Xi's ascension to
the top job, despite a number of noteworthy economic and foreign
policy achievements, the Hu Jintao era had become known as the "lost
decade." Xi Jinping took power determined to change China's course.

Charting a New Course

In a 2000 interview in the Chinese journal *Zhonghua Ernu*, Xi Jinping
then governor of Fujian Province, shared his perspective on leadership.
A new leader, he stated, needed to "continue working on the foundations" laid by his predecessor but at the same time "come in with his
own plans and set an agenda during the first year." He likened leadership to a relay race, in which a successor has to "receive the baton prop-
erly" and then "run it past the line."[11] More than a decade later at his
first press conference in 2012, Xi reiterated the baton analogy, stating
that the responsibility of the party leadership is to "take over the relay
baton passed on to us by history" to achieve the "great renewal of the
Chinese nation."[12]

In receiving the baton, however, Xi and his team have set out to
run the race differently from their predecessors—with a distinctive
new strategy and at an accelerated pace. They have moved away from
a collective leadership to elevate Xi as the preeminent leader, deepened

the role of the Communist Party and state in society and in the economy, and sought to elevate China's role in world affairs. Not everything is new. Some of the initiatives, such as the heightened attention to corruption within the Communist Party and more assertive behavior in the South and East China Seas, reflect impulses and tendencies that emerged during the latter stages of Hu's tenure (2007–2012) or even before. Yet Xi and the rest of the Chinese leadership have amplified these efforts in ways that have transformed China's domestic political landscape and its role on the regional and global stage. (While provocative actions by China and other claimants in the South China Sea were commonplace, for example, Beijing's massive land reclamation and militarization of the islands in the South China Sea did not begin until 2014.) In describing China today, dean of Peking University's School of International Relations, Jia Qingguo, suggested to me that Xi Jinping had ushered in the third, thirty years of contemporary Chinese history—crystallizing my sense that Deng's "second revolution" had drawn to a close. Xi Jinping's "third revolution" was underway.

The Revolution Has Begun

The ultimate objective of Xi's revolution is his Chinese Dream—the rejuvenation of the great Chinese nation. As noted earlier, however, Xi's predecessors shared this goal as well. What makes Xi's revolution distinctive is the strategy he has pursued: the dramatic centralization of authority under his personal leadership; the intensified penetration of society by the state; the creation of a virtual wall of regulations and restrictions that more tightly controls the flow of ideas, culture, and capital into and out of the country; and the significant projection of Chinese power. It represents a reassertion of the state in Chinese political and economic life at home, and a more ambitious and expansive role for China abroad.

Over the course of Xi Jinping's tenure as CCP general secretary and president, he has accrued progressively more institutional and personal power. Unlike his immediate predecessors, he has assumed control of all the most important leading committees and commissions that oversee government policy; demanded pledges of personal loyalty from military and party leaders; eliminated political rivals through a sweeping anticorruption campaign; and adopted the moniker of "core" leader, which signifies his ultimate authority within a traditionally collective leadership. By many accounts, Xi is the most powerful leader since Mao Zedong.

Xi and the rest of the Chinese leadership have also expanded the role of the state in society and increased the power of the organs of party and state control. Writing in 2000 about the transition from Mao Zedong to Deng Xiaoping, China scholar David Shambaugh noted, "If one of the hallmarks of the Maoist state was the penetration of society, then the Dengist state was noticeable for its withdrawal. The organizational mechanisms of state penetration and manipulation were substantially reduced or dismantled altogether."[13] The current Chinese leadership, however, has launched an aggressive set of reforms that augments rather than diminishes the party's role in political, social, and economic life. For example, while the government welcomes NGOs that help fulfill the objectives of the Communist Party, advocates for change or those who seek a greater voice in political life, such as women, labor, or legal rights activists, increasingly risk detention and prison. Moreover, while promising a continued opening up of China's market, the Chinese leadership has nonetheless moved to support and strengthen the role of the party and state in the economy.

This enhanced party control also extends to efforts to protect China's society and the economy from foreign competition and influence. Xi Jinping has increasingly constrained the avenues and opportunities by which foreign ideas, culture, and, in some cases, capital can enter the country by building a virtual wall of regulatory, legal, and technological impediments. Yet the wall is selectively permeable. While progressively less is permitted in, more goes out. Xi has pushed, for example, to enhance significantly the flow of ideas and influences from China to the outside world, through the Chinese media, Confucius Institutes (Chinese government–sponsored language and cultural centers), and think tanks. Similarly, the Xi government encourages capital targeted at specific sectors or countries to flow out of China (although at times restricting the flow of capital to other sectors or countries).

And finally, Xi Jinping's call for the rejuvenation of the great Chinese nation has accelerated the nascent shift begun during Hu Jintao's tenure to move away from a commitment to maintaining a low profile in international affairs to one that actively seeks to shape global norms and institutions. He has established China's first overseas military logistics base; taken a significant stake in strategic ports in Europe and Asia; championed China as a leader in addressing global challenges, such as climate change; and proposed a number of new trade and security institutions. Xi seeks to project power in dramatic new ways and reassert the centrality of China on the global stage.

Many elements of these reforms—the strong drive of the current Communist Party leadership to control the flow of information or to exert control over economic actors, for example—and Beijing's efforts to be more proactive internationally are hallmarks of various periods throughout Chinese history. Nonetheless, they run counter to *recent* Chinese history. Xi seeks his own model of politics and foreign policy: a uniquely Chinese model that he believes will deliver his Chinese Dream and perhaps become a standard bearer for other countries disenchanted with the American and European models of liberal democracy.

The Third Revolution Takes Hold

To understand the nature and magnitude of the People's Republic of China (PRC)'s third revolution, I took a journey through scores of Xi Jinping's speeches and commentaries to understand how he prioritized his agenda for change. The next six chapters, outlined below, reflect the range of his reform priorities, beginning with the political and cyber arenas, continuing to a set of economic concerns—innovation, state-owned enterprises, and the environment—and concluding with a broad look at Xi's foreign and security policies. Each chapter explores how the Chinese leadership has moved forward to advance its objectives, as well as the intended and unintended consequences of its new approach. The final chapter lays out a set of recommendations for the United States and the international community to cooperate or coordinate with and—when necessary—confront this transforming and transformative power.

Chapters 2 and 3 explore the centralization of power and the growing presence of the Communist Party in political life. Chapter 2 focuses on the real-world applications of Xi Jinping's transformation of political institutions and processes—the elevation of his personal power, the use of mass campaigns, and the adoption of legal reforms, among others. Chapter 3, in turn, looks at the parallel world of state–society relations in the context of the Internet. Over the course of the 2000s, the Internet became a virtual political world, offering the opportunity for the blossoming of civil society, wider political commentary, and enhanced transparency and accountability within the political system. The current Chinese leadership, however, has used new technological advances, pressure on Internet companies, and a cyber-army to control content—both generated domestically and produced outside China. These measures, along with new Internet regulations, have sharply diminished the vibrancy of China's Internet as a political space.

Chapters 4, 5, and 6 explore three areas at the heart of Xi's drive to modernize the economy—state-owned enterprises, innovation, and air quality. In the economic arena, the Xi-led government earned plaudits internationally for the bold and extensive reform agenda it outlined in November 2013 at the Third Plenum of the 18th Party Congress. While publicly advocating greater market reform and integration with the international economy, the Xi-led government is nonetheless maintaining and even enhancing the role of the party in the economy. It is intervening aggressively to protect the economy from the vicissitudes of the market, shielding it from foreign competition, and more actively intervening in economic decision-making at the firm level. Chapter 4 looks explicitly at the fate of state-owned enterprise (SOE) reform and reveals that far from reducing the role of SOEs in the economy and the party's role in SOEs, the state has elevated their importance as national champions and intensified the role of the party in SOE decision-making.

Innovation, a top priority for the Chinese government, reflects a more mixed reform picture with both state and market forces playing important roles. Chapter 5 explores the Chinese government's efforts to support the development of an indigenous electric car market and finds that despite calls for greater competition, the government continues to protect the industry from foreign competition and to prevent the market from determining winners and losers through initiatives such as Made in China 2025. While political and economic support for targeted strategic industries, such as electric cars, provides valuable time for nascent industries to develop and capture market share, it also puts at risk the economic efficiencies and drive to innovate that emerge from true competition. Even in China's booming start-up technology sector, intervention by local governments threatens to keep weak actors alive while crowding out investment opportunities for potentially stronger technologies.

Growing societal pressure has vaulted environmental protection to the top of the Chinese leadership's agenda. Chapter 6 looks at China's economic reform effort through the lens of the leadership's efforts to reconcile its desire for continued rapid economic development with the popular demand for clean air and improved public health. The leadership has adopted a multifaceted program including traditional top-down campaigns to control pollution, institutional reform within the legal and environmental systems, and controlled access for civil society through participation in environmental NGOs or other forms of popular activism. The result has been a mix of success and failure, with success for some parts of the country earned on the backs of others. Ultimately, the government's efforts are hindered in significant measure by a continued priority on economic growth, poor implementation of top-down initiatives, and the relaxation of environmental regulations to accommodate the competing priority of economic development.

Chapter 7 assesses both the form and substance of China's growing international political, economic, and security presence, exploring the new initiatives and institutions put forth by the Chinese leadership to help transform the country into a global leader. Even as it has worked to seal off China's borders from foreign ideas and competition, it has sought to project Chinese power internationally and to assert itself as a champion of globalization. It has launched the grand-scale Belt and Road Initiative (BRI), which, if successful, will link countries in every region of the world through infrastructure, digital communications, finance, and culture. In the process, it has the potential to transform not only trade and investment relations but also international relations more broadly. It has also promoted a "go out" strategy for Chinese media, think tanks, and overseas language and cultural institutions to enhance Chinese soft power. Ultimately, chapter 7 finds that while the Chinese leadership has adopted policies and established institutions that have the potential to transform China into a global leader, the content of these initiatives lags behind. Moreover, Xi Jinping's efforts to seal off China's borders from foreign ideas and economic competition have engendered criticism in the international community and further undermined the country's ability to lay claim to global leadership.

The final chapter explores several implications of Xi Jinping's reform efforts for the United States. It proposes recommendations for how the United States can best advance its interests in the era of Xi Jinping's China, including strengthening the economic and political pillars of U.S. policy toward Asia, leveraging Xi Jinping's ambition, adopting standards of reciprocity, coordinating policies with allies, and ensuring China lives up to its stated commitments to international leadership, among others.

Broader Lessons of the Third Revolution

Taken together, these chapters provide a deeper understanding of how Xi's model is taking root and transforming Chinese political and economic life. They also offer several broader insights into the changes underway and their implications for the rest of the world.

First, the Xi-led leadership is playing a long game. The government's preference for control rather than competition—both in the economic and political realms—often yields policy outcomes that appear suboptimal in the near term but have longer strategic value. By enhancing the role of the state and diminishing the role of the market in the political and economic system, as well as by seeking to limit the influence of foreign ideas and economic competition, the leadership has deprived itself of important feedback mechanisms from the market, civil society, and international actors. Xi's centralization of power and anticorruption campaign, for example, while affording him greater personal decision-making authority, have actually contributed to slower decision-making at the top, increasing paralysis at local levels of governance, and lower rates of economic growth. Yet, Chinese leaders tolerate the inefficiencies generated by nonmarket activity—such as a slow-processing Internet or money-losing SOEs—not only because they generally contribute to their political power but also because they afford them the luxury of longer-term strategic investments. Thus, the government encourages SOEs to undertake investments in high-risk economies (that no other country or multinational would support) in support of its BRI. Decisions that may appear irrational in the context of liberal political systems and market-based economies in the near term thus often possess a longer-term strategic logic within China.

Second, Xi's centralization of power and growing control over information mean it is difficult to assess the degree of real consensus within China over the leaders' policy direction. While less robust than during previous times, wide-ranging debate within the Chinese scholarly and official circles over the merits of many of the regime's current policies continues. A significant drop in the amount of foreign direct investment flowing into the country—attributed by a number of Chinese scholars at least in part to the anticorruption campaign—for example, has contributed to consternation in policymaking circles and calls for change in the nature of the anticorruption drive. The growing penetration of the state in economic and political life has raised concerns among many of China's wealthiest and most talented, prompting them to seek refuge for their capital and families abroad. Even Xi's signature BRI has produced critical commentary from Chinese scholars and business leaders, who are concerned about the lack of economic rationale for many of the proposed investments. More dramatically, there are indications of dissent within the top echelons of the Communist Party. In the lead-up to the 19th Party Congress in October 2017, at which Xi Jinping was formally re-selected as CCP general secretary, rising political star Sun Zhengcai was purged on grounds of corruption and then accused of plotting against Xi personally. It is also plausible that the bold—or in some cases extreme—nature of Xi's initiatives may over time produce an equally strong opposition coalition within China calling for a moderation of his policies.

Third, Xi's ambition for China to reclaim its greatness on the global stage offers both new opportunities for collaboration and new challenges for the outside world. In some cases, Chinese interests and those of the rest of the world largely overlap. Thus, a number of China's initiatives, such as the BRI and Asian Infrastructure Investment Bank, offer important opportunities for Chinese businesses, while providing significant new public goods for the rest of the world. Moreover, there is a clear opportunity for actors in and outside China to leverage Xi's ambition for greater Chinese leadership to do more than it might otherwise. On issues as wide-ranging as Ebola, climate change, and proliferation, Xi Jinping's desire for China to be a leader in a globalized world has required the country to undertake a greater degree of political and often financial commitment than it has previously assumed. In other words, the rest of the world can challenge China to match its rhetorical commitment to globalization and international leadership with its actions on the ground.

At the same time, a more ambitious China is also producing greater potential for conflict in areas such as operations in the South China Sea or over the sovereignty of Taiwan. As China proposes and establishes new international institutions and plays a larger role in established organizations, how it will exercise its growing influence also becomes a question of central importance. Thus far, the results are mixed: in some cases, China appears to uphold traditional norms, while in others it seeks to pervert or even break with established precedent to realize its own advantage.

Finally, the greatest emerging challenge—and the one least well understood—exists at the intersection of China's dual-reform trajectories. China is an illiberal state seeking leadership in a liberal world order. The importance of China's domestic political and economic system for the rest of the world has never been greater. At one time, the international community might have viewed Chinese human rights practices as a primarily domestic political issue—albeit one that many observers cared deeply about; now, however, issues of Chinese governance are front and center in the country's foreign policy. China exports not only its labor and environmental practices through investment but also its political values through a growing foreign media presence, Confucius Institutes, and—in some cases—government-affiliated student organizations. Yet China sharply constrains opportunities for foreign cultural, media, and civil society actors to engage with Chinese citizens. With its growing economic and political power, China increasingly takes advantage of the political and economic openness of other countries while not providing these countries with the same opportunities to engage within China. Even as its SOEs take majority stakes in mines, ports, oil fields, and electric grids across the world, it prohibits other countries' multinationals from doing the same in China. Addressing this particular challenge requires understanding the new China model within the context of a globalized world. It is a combination that provides China with new levers of influence and power that others will have to learn to exploit and counter in order to protect and advance their own interests.

Will Xi Succeed?

Does Xi's third revolution have staying power? There is no compelling evidence that Xi's revolution is in danger of being reversed, and the outcomes of the 19th Party Congress suggest that his consolidation of power and mandate for change have only been strengthened. Xi's theoretical contribution to the socialist canon—"Xi Jinping Thought on Socialism with Chinese Characteristics for a New Era"—was enshrined in the Constitution in a manner previously granted only to Mao Zedong; both Xi's name and the word "thought" were attached to his ideas. Xi also avoided naming his successor as general secretary; this marked a break in a twenty-five-year CCP tradition and was widely interpreted as leaving open the possibility that Xi would be reselected as general secretary in 2022. Finally, Xi filled the top positions in the Communist Party—the PBSC and the Politburo—with his supporters. By one count, as many as four of the seven members of the PBSC, not including Xi Jinping himself, and eighteen of the twenty-five Politburo members are allies of Xi.[14]

An air of triumphalism also permeated Xi's three-and-a-half-hour Party Congress speech as he reported on the accomplishments of the previous five years, noting that China was at a "new historic juncture." He asserted that China has "stood up, grown rich, and is becoming strong." For the first time, Xi also raised the prospect that China could serve as a model of development for other countries by utilizing "Chinese wisdom" and a "Chinese approach to solving problems."[15]

In fact, Xi has made significant progress toward achieving his Chinese Dream: doubling incomes by 2020 and recapturing China's historic centrality and greatness in the international system. And the priorities he has laid out for his next five-year term are overwhelmingly the same he has pursued to date: fighting corruption, addressing environmental challenges, pressing forward on economic reform and growth, and ensuring that the party and its ideals are fully and deeply embedded in Chinese political and economic life.

Nonetheless, as the next chapters illuminate, all of his reform priorities face significant and, in some cases, growing contradictions. We should be alert to the potential of discontent coalescing into a significant political challenge. Certainly, comparative history is not on Xi Jinping's side. Despite a rollback of democracy in some parts of the world, all the major economies of the world—save China—are democracies.

The primary message of this book, however, is that we must deal with China as it is today. The strategic direction of Xi's leadership is evident and is exerting a profound impact on Chinese political and economic life and on the country's international presence. Much of the world remains ill-prepared to understand and navigate these changes.

2

Heart of Darkness

IN JANUARY 2013, GUANGDONG Province propaganda head Tuo Zhen took his censor's pen to the annual New Year's editorial of *Southern Weekend* (*Nanfang Zhoumo,* 南方周末). The newspaper is renowned as one of the two or three most investigative and forward leaning in the country,[1] and the editorial, "China's Dream, the Dream of Constitutionalism" (*Zhongguo meng, xianzheng meng,* 中国梦, 宪政梦) was a clever play off of the new CCP General Secretary Xi Jinping's Chinese Dream narrative. Instead of calling for a robust Communist Party at the forefront of the political system, however, it advocated political reform and constitutionalism. There was little chance that Tuo would approve such a title. Although he had been an award-winning journalist in his earlier years, he had long traded in his investigative eye in favor of a political career. He had risen through the ranks first of the *Economic Daily* (*Jingji Ribao,* 经济日报) and later of the state-run Xinhua news service before assuming the position in Guangdong, earning a reputation for toeing the party line along the way.[2] In fact, by the time the editorial reached Tuo's desk, the title of the piece had already undergone a significant edit: *Southern Weekend*'s editor had preemptively softened the title to read "Dreams Are Our Promise of What Ought to Be Done" (*Mengxiang shi women duiying ran zhi shi de chengnuo,* 梦想是我们对应然之事的承诺).[3] But Tuo, reflecting the new mood in Beijing, changed the title yet again to "We Are Closer Than Ever Before to Our Dreams" (*Women bi renhe shihou dou geng*

20

*jiejin mengxiang,*我们比任何时候都更接近梦想) and removed all references to any politically sensitive topics.[4]

As news of Tuo's censorship spread online, students at Guangdong Province's prestigious Sun Yat-sen University drafted a petition that read: "Our yielding and our silence has not brought a return of our freedom. Quite the opposite, it has brought the untempered intrusion and infiltration of rights by power."[5] The protest went viral, and several popular national personalities adopted the cause. Well-known race car driver and cultural blogger Han Han wrote: "They grab you by your collar, clamp you by the neck, yet at the same time encourage you to run faster, sing better, and win them more honor." Fashion and media mogul Hung Huang spread the word to her millions of microblog followers that Tuo's actions undermined the reformist credibility of the new Communist Party leadership. The virtual protest also assumed a physical reality, with a few hundred protestors demonstrating in front of *Southern Weekend*'s owner, the Southern Media Group, calling for freedom of speech and criticizing censorship.[6] In retaliation, party officials fired several *Southern Weekend* journalists and editors and closed their microblog accounts.[7]

Censors in Beijing were facing a similar problem. *China through the Ages* (*Yanhuang Chunqiu,* 炎黄春秋), the monthly Beijing-based journal, had also published a New Year's article attacking the party for not adhering to the principles of freedom of speech and an independent judiciary—rights, the editorial argued, enshrined in the Chinese constitution.[8] The journal had a degree of political protection. Over the course of its more than twenty-year history, many former senior party officials and intellectuals had used it as a forum to publish pieces calling for political reform. Moreover, the journal's deputy publisher, Hu Dehua, was the son of Hu Yaobang, the renowned political reformer and CCP general secretary from 1982 until 1987, when he was forced to resign.[9] Its political pedigree notwithstanding, within days, the journal's editors were notified that the Ministry of Industry and Information Technology had taken away the license for its website.[10]

The censors' crackdowns on *Southern Weekend* and *China Through the Ages* were among the first signs of a shifting political wind. The new Chinese leadership was on the cusp of launching a set of far-reaching political reforms designed to strengthen the role of the Communist

Party and party values throughout the Chinese polity. In the fight to reclaim the legitimacy of the party, there was no room for alternative voices and perspectives, particularly those that reflected Western ideals. Leading the charge was CCP General Secretary Xi Jinping, who left little doubt that he planned to set a new political tone and agenda for the country. His message of change—like those that would later sweep through parts of Europe and the United States—was imbued with a nationalist fervor that diminished the value of foreign ideas and influences and a populist call to action that promised to advance the interests of the broader citizenry against the entitled elites. Implicit in his message was also the idea that Xi alone was suited to lead China on the path to reclaim its greatness. What soon emerged was a full-scale onslaught on the country's formal and informal political institutions: top-down campaigns to root out corruption, to reaffirm the core values of the CCP in party members, and to eliminate the influence of Western ideas in Chinese society, as well as efforts to reform the legal system to serve the party's interests more effectively. One of the new general secretary's first orders of business, however, was breaking free of the bonds of China's system of collective leadership and establishing himself as the preeminent Chinese leader.

Xi at the Core

In September 2016, I jokingly suggested to a visiting Chinese scholar that perhaps Xi would stay in office beyond 2022, informally understood as the preordained end date of his tenure. While the scholar at first rejected the notion, he then laughingly noted that such a situation might in fact come to pass as Xi had "learned a lot from Mao Zedong," the implication being that Xi, like Mao, would not allow himself to be constrained by party rules or practice. Xi's decision at the 19th Party Congress to avoid designating a clear successor as party general secretary, as many had anticipated, suggests that it may not be far from the truth. Although Xi prefers to view himself in the mode of Deng Xiaoping, the revered patron of China's reform and opening up, others in China are quick to make analogies between Xi's governing style and that of Mao, the ruthless revolutionary, who launched a continual stream of political campaigns to cleanse the party and systematically and relentlessly punished his political adversaries in the name of serving the people.

Xi has emerged as the descendant of both Mao and Deng. Like both these revolutionary leaders—and unlike his immediate predecessors Hu Jintao and Jiang Zemin—Xi has amassed significant authority over virtually all policy. Pushing aside decades of institutionalized collective decision-making that acknowledged the general secretary of the CCP and president of the country as first among equals, Xi Jinping, like Mao before him, has established himself as simply first. He has used political institutions and political culture to centralize power in his own hands.[11] Institutionally, he has created and assumed the chairmanship of several new, small leading groups and commissions within the top leadership, including leading groups on "Comprehensively Deepening Reform," cybersecurity,[12] and military reform,[13] as well as a National Security Commission,[14] among others. These leading groups and commissions allow him to manage and coordinate the overall direction of the most important policy arenas. In addition, each leading group has its own staff, providing Xi a powerbase distinct from that of the broader governmental bureaucracy. In some instances, such as that of the leading group on deepening reform, his chairmanship directly circumvents the power of other top officials, in this case Premier Li Keqiang, who is nominally in charge of economic policy for the country.[15]

Xi's emerging institutional power is complemented by his elevation in status in October 2016 to the core, or *hexin* (核心), of the political leadership.[16] Beginning in January 2016, mentions of Xi as the core became more frequent, as one provincial leader after another began to refer to Xi as the core, and party newspapers began to raise the issue of "emulative consciousness" with reference to Xi.[17] In Sichuan Province, for example, the party secretary hosted a meeting of the provincial standing committee in which emphasis was placed on protecting the core leadership position of Xi Jinping.[18] In late October 2016, at the Fifth Plenum of the 18th Party Congress, the most notable announcement was that, moving forward, Xi Jinping would be recognized as the core of the Communist Party. The enshrinement of "Xi Jinping Thought on Socialism with Chinese Characteristics for a New Era" at the 19th Party Congress one year later further enhanced Xi's standing by granting his ideas the same status as those of Mao in the party constitution.

The CCP's Propaganda Department—or Publicity Department, as it is sometimes called—and state-run media have also cultivated a political image of Xi as both admirable and approachable. A song-writer captured Xi's visit to a pork bun restaurant—where he displayed his common person characteristics by waiting in line with everyone else—in a Peking-opera-style verse.[19] Articles referred to Xi as Xi Dada (translated as "Uncle Xi" or "Big Daddy Xi") and a video, "Xi Dada loves Peng Mama" highlighted Xi's relationship with his wife Peng Liyuan,[20] while another song advised, "If you want to marry, marry someone like Xi Dada" (yao jia jiu jia xi dada zheyang de ren,要嫁就嫁习大大这样的人).[21] Stories of Xi's selfless service during his time in a small village in the Cultural Revolution and pictures of his return there after becoming president of the country cemented his image as a powerful leader, who nonetheless is a man of the people.[22] As one Western observer noted, Xi is portrayed as a "tireless, self-sacrificing servant of the people and of their revolutionary project."[23] Some older Chinese, however, are wary of the intense adulation of Xi. It reminds them of the personality cult that developed around Mao. As Beijing-based commentator Zhang Lifan said, "Xi is directing a building-god campaign, and he is the god."[24]

One frequently offered rationale for Xi's consolidation of power is that it is necessary to clean up the party and push economic reform. Jinan University professor Chen Dingding argues along these lines: "Who has power is less important than who can accomplish what with power. There is nothing wrong with one leader holding multiple titles as long as this leader can get things done. And President Xi is getting things done in China."[25] Outside China as well, analysts suggest that Xi's centralization of power is beneficial to the reform effort, contending that too much decentralization has allowed the provinces to pursue unsustainable fiscal policies and that corruption has created networks of officials and businesspeople unwilling to implement reforms. From that perspective, Xi is trying to address the challenges these networks pose to China's future economic growth, and once Xi finishes cleaning up the system, China will be on the right path.[26] Xi's public support and power consolidation could also help him in other areas. China scholar Cheng Li believes that Xi's backing among the military and elsewhere will allow him to focus on economic reform at home and put aside foreign disputes or tensions that might develop alongside the rise of ultra-nationalism in the country.[27] Li's prediction, however, may be overly optimistic. China's often fractious relations with its neighbors such as Japan, Vietnam, South Korea, and India offer little indication that Xi Jinping has adopted a more compromising approach to regional security affairs in order to focus his attention on domestic economic concerns.

Many Chinese reject such an analysis, believing that Xi's centralization of power is in good measure a self-serving one. Moreover, they argue, it raises several challenges for the Chinese policy process. Advisors have reported that bottlenecks in decision-making are frequent. As one senior official commented, "No decisions can be made when Xi Jinping travels, and Xi travels a lot." Even more telling is the warning by Deng Xiaoping in 1980 concerning the dangers of too great a concentration of power: "Over-concentration of power is liable to give rise to arbitrary rule by individuals at the expense of collective leadership . . . There is a limit to anyone's knowledge, experience, and energy. If a person holds too many posts at the same time, he will find it difficult to come to grips with the problems in his work and more important, he will block the way for other more suitable comrades to take up leading posts."[28]

Make New Friends but Keep the Old

Xi's institutional power at the very top of the political hierarchy is important for his ability to set the political and economic agenda for the country. It does not, however, automatically grant him the personal loyalties or the broad-based institutional or popular support he needs to realize his ambitions. Like all Chinese leaders, he has tried to strengthen his hold on power by promoting officials he trusts to important positions. Most significantly, at the 19th Party Congress, Xi successfully maneuvered three trusted allies—his de facto chief-of-staff Li Zhanshu, his top foreign policy strategist and advisor on Party Theory Wang Huning, and head of the organization department (responsible for personnel appointments) Zhao Leji—into three of the seven places on the PBSC.

Xi has also moved many of his associates from his days as party secretary in Zhejiang into important positions. Several now serve on the staffs of the central leading groups that Xi chairs.[29] Others, such as Huang Kunming, who serves as the Publicity Department's executive deputy director,[30] Chen Min'er, who is party secretary in powerhouse Chongqing, and Li Qiang, who serves as party secretary in Jiangsu Province,[31] have become powerful leaders in their own right. Along with Xi Jinping's top economic advisor Liu He, whom Xi knew from a young age,[32] all three of these Zhejiang associates were promoted into the Politburo (the political body immediately subordinate to the PBSC) at the 19th Party Congress.

Xi also has undertaken significant reform of the People's Liberation Army (PLA), altering traditional power bases in the process. He transformed four powerful general departments into fifteen functional departments (including the original four). The General Office of the Central Military Commission (CMC)—a commission that Xi heads—is the most prominent and gives Xi more direct control over the military.[33] He also raised the stature of the air force and navy, making them bureaucratically equal to the army, and separated the rocket force and strategic support force from the army.[34] While there is an undeniable security logic to elevating the air force and navy given China's far-flung trade and economic interests—as well as its claims to the vast maritime domain in the East and South China Seas—the creation of new commands enabled Xi to elevate his allies. Many of those promoted to newly created leadership positions after the military reforms were directly linked to Xi Jinping.[35]

One of Xi Jinping's most significant efforts to stack the political deck in his favor was his attack on the Communist Youth League (CYL), the institution that has given rise to many of his political competitors. The CYL, which boasts 87 million members ages fourteen to twenty-eight, has long served as a training ground for the party's elite who are not "princelings" (the descendants of high-ranking revolutionary Chinese leaders such as Xi Jinping himself). Top leaders Li Keqiang and Wang Yang, for example, are both products of the CYL. (Often understood as more politically open than Xi and his supporters, neither has typically been considered closely aligned with Xi Jinping.) In 2016, a two-month inspection by the Central Commission for Discipline Inspection (CCDI) of the

CYL concluded with criticism of the Youth League for its "aristocratic tendencies."[36] The party moved to reduce the Youth League's budget to less than half that of the previous year,[37] and closed the undergraduate division of the CYL-directed China Youth University of Political Studies.[38]

Xi's efforts to establish his allies in significant political positions and to reform institutional pillars of political power initially considered outside his grasp, such as the PLA and CYL, demonstrate his growing political influence. At the same time, these moves, while critically important, are dwarfed in magnitude by his push to reform the entirety of the CCP and its relationship to the Chinese people. This reform of the CCP is the centerpiece of Xi's first five years in office, and he has launched a number of campaigns, including the well-publicized anti-corruption campaign, to develop a more "virtuous" class of party officials that is both loyal to the Communist Party and more responsive to the Chinese people.

"Virtues Are Central, Punishment Supplements Them" (*dezhuxingfu*, 德主刑辅)

> —Xi Jinping quoting Han dynasty political philosopher Dong Zhongshu[39]

The corruption of government officials is deeply embedded in Chinese political culture. It has appeared throughout Chinese history as a source of significant public resentment and a contributing factor to the decline and collapse of many Chinese dynasties.[40] New emperors often began their reign preaching the need for clean governance and taking steps to root out the corruption of their predecessors. Imperial governments adopted legal codes and systems of penalties to deter corruption: During the Western Zhou dynasty (1046–771 BCE), for example, the Criminal Code of the Duke of Lü included punishment for taking bribes; the Tang code introduced penalties for a range of official abuses, such as "robbery, larceny, taking bribes and perverting the law, taking bribes without perverting the law, receiving tribute from subordinates and people in one's jurisdiction, and receiving improper gifts from people out of one's jurisdiction"[41]; and during the Qing dynasty—in which the sale of offices became a significant problem[42]—the imperial rulers attempted to improve the moral quality and competency of bureaucrats through meritocratic exams, a system other dynasties had also pursued.[43] As Yin Huiyi, the Qing governor of Henan between 1737 and 1739, proclaimed, "an official who has been appointed to a post should, first and foremost, remain pure . . . No matter whether his rank is lofty or humble, in the end, incorruptibility should be his most precious jewel."[44] When all else failed, emperors might also rely on a vast system of internal surveillance to keep officials in line.[45]

Despite such efforts, corruption blossomed. Officials enforced legal standards selectively, when it was politically expedient to do so. The prosecution of an official was often "less a function of 'justice' than it was of politics."[46] Oftentimes, too, the officials who were responsible for enforcing anticorruption laws instead participated in corrupt practices.

Little changed with the advent of communist rule in 1949. Corruption—and the Communist Party's attempts to address it through anticorruption campaigns—became a staple of political life in the People's Republic of China from the inception of the new state. Mao Zedong's first anticorruption campaign, launched in 1951, netted 107,830 charges against government or party officials for embezzlement of amounts over 1,000 yuan.[47] Mao launched repeated, often unpredictable, anticorruption campaigns in search of "tigers" (those who were engaged in highly lucrative corruption), as well as "fleas" (lower-level corrupt officials). He stated famously: "The more graft cases that are exposed, the happier I am. Have you ever caught fleas on your body? The more you catch, the more pleased you are."[48]

Subsequent CCP leaders continued to try to address the challenge through additional campaigns, as well as through new regulations and laws, including the Criminal Law of 1979 and a revised version in 1997.[49] Yet the Chinese political system was ill-equipped to follow through on the promise of the laws. It lacked the transparency and independence from political influence that effective law enforcement typically demands. And as Claremont McKenna professor Minxin Pei has illuminated in his study of crony capitalism, an entrenched network of personal political and economic ties among officials and businesspeople provided little hope that the problem would be adequately addressed.[50] Communist Party General Secretary Hu Jintao, in a July 2011 speech at the CCP's ninetieth anniversary, offered a stark assessment of the state of corruption in the Communist Party: "If corruption does not get solved effectively, the party will lose the people's trust and support."[51] He also warned that unchecked corruption could "deal a body blow to the party and even lead to the collapse of the party and country."[52]

Corruption Takes Center Stage

There was little to distinguish Xi Jinping's call to fight corruption from that of his predecessors, at least initially. Upon his selection as general secretary, Xi echoed Hu Jintao's remarks concerning the significant threat corruption posed to the future of the party and suggested a renewed and reinvigorated effort to address the challenge.[53] Yet Xi brought something more to the table. From 2008 to 2012, he had led the effort within the top leadership to strengthen the party;[54] he had a demonstrated commitment to fighting corruption; and he knew better than most the extent of the challenge.[55] The campaign Xi launched at the outset of his tenure was thus more personal, more profound, and more political than that of any previous general secretary since Mao Zedong.

As Xi Jinping rose through the ranks of the party, no issue seemed to command more heartfelt attention and comment from Xi than corruption. He raised the issue directly during his time as an official in Fujian Province in the late 1990s and early 2000s, stating in an interview in 2000 with a party newspaper:

If you go into politics to make a career, you must give up any thought of personal advantages. That is out of the question. An official may not through a long career have achieved very great things, but at least he has not put something up his sleeve. He is upright. In a political career you can never go for personal advantages or promotion. It is just like that. It can't be done. These are the rules . . . you should not go into politics if you wish to become wealthy. In that case you will inevitably become a corrupt and filthy official. A corrupt official with a bad reputation who will always be afraid of being arrested, and who must envisage having a bad posthumous reputation.[56]

As party secretary in Zhejiang Province, his signature issue was anticorruption;[57] and in 2007, Xi's selection as Shanghai party secretary to replace Chen Liangyu—who was at the center of a pension fund scandal involving hundreds of millions of dollars—was widely believed to be a testament to Xi's incorruptibility.[58] As general secretary, Xi's selection of the highly respected and talented vice-premier Wang Qishan to lead the first five years of the campaign through the CCDI further underscored the importance of the campaign to Xi.[59]

The all-encompassing nature of the anticorruption campaign Xi has undertaken also distinguished his effort from those that preceded it. With more than 800,000 full- and part-time officials committed to working on the campaign,[60] Xi has sought to eliminate through regulation even the smallest opportunities for officials to abuse their position. Regulations now govern how many cars officials may own, the size of their homes, and whether they are permitted secretaries.[61] Other rules cover the number of days officials are permitted to travel and the number of courses that may be served at a business dinner. Golf club memberships are now banned.[62] The campaign has also left no part of the Chinese bureaucracy and economy untouched. More than 170 senior officials,[63] including a former member of the PBSC, Zhou Yongkang; a top aide to President Hu Jintao, Ling Jihua; top military officials;[64] senior SOE executives in the energy, resources, media,[65] and railways industries;[66] as well as ministers, such as the former minister of railways[67] and head of the National Bureau of Statistics,[68] have been detained, formally arrested, and/or prosecuted and jailed.

Nor has the campaign waned after the first year or two. Anticorruption campaigns directed by previous Chinese leaders typically concluded within a year or two of their inception and then relaunched after a period of a year or more. Xi Jinping signaled a different intent almost immediately upon assuming office: "The key is to repeatedly stress the fight against corruption and make a long-term commitment. We must solidify our resolve, ensure that all cases of corruption are investigated and prosecuted, and that all instances of graft are rectified." He pressed further: "The issue of working style is in no sense a small one. If misconduct is not corrected but allowed to run rampant, it will build an invisible wall between our party and the people. As a result, our party will lose its base, lifeblood and strength."[69] Five years later, in his speech before the 19th Party Congress, he reinforced his commitment to the anticorruption campaign claiming: "The people resent corruption most; and corruption is the greatest threat our Party faces." He further indicated that the party would take the fight to "people's doorsteps" with a new system of discipline inspection for local party committees.[70]

The numbers suggest that the current anticorruption campaign has not faltered (see figure 2.1). In the first year alone, the number of punishments jumped by approximately 37 percent compared with the annual average from the previous five years.[71] Between the start of the campaign and the end of 2014, over 400,000 officials were disciplined and more than 200,000 prosecuted in courts.[72] In 2015, the anticorruption campaign disciplined more than 300,000 officials, 200,000 of whom were given "light punishment" and an additional 80,000 who received harsher punishment.[73] In 2016, the number of cadres disciplined for graft exceeded 400,000. The conviction rate for those prosecuted remained steady—around 99 percent.[74]

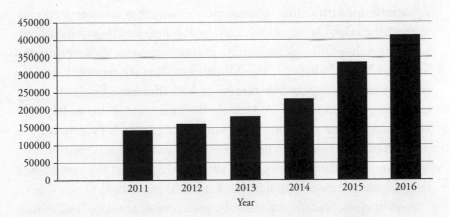

FIGURE 2.1 Number of Party Cadres Disciplined for Graft from 2011 to 2016

Source: Central Commission for Discipline Inspection Annual Reports

Xi Jinping also has drafted the international community to assist in his anticorruption campaign through "Operation Foxhunt" and "Operation Skynet." Under the auspices of Operation Foxhunt, Beijing sent over fifty police teams abroad to work in conjunction with Chinese overseas missions and domestic law enforcement in various countries.[75] Other countries have generally been supportive of China's efforts, although Australia and the United States complained in 2015 when they discovered that China had been deploying undercover Chinese agents without their permission. Operation Skynet, launched in 2015, targets not only fugitives from China but also the people and organizations that assist them. It represents a combined effort by the Ministry of Public Security (MPS), the Supreme People's Procuratorate, the People's Bank of China, and the Central Organization Department of the CCP (the last helps with overseeing officials' private passports).[76] By the end of its first year, the Skynet campaign had returned an impressive 1,023 Chinese businesspeople and repatriated $461.5 million in assets;[77] and in 2016, an additional 1,032 fugitives were returned along with $347 million in assets.[78] Nonetheless, these numbers represent a small fraction of the estimated 18,000 officials and $120 billion in assets that fled China from 1990 through 2011.[79]

Campaign Contradictions

By several measures, the anticorruption campaign has been very effective. The sale of luxury items, such as watches, jewelry, leather goods, and liquor, has fallen dramatically, as have expenses for catering and high-end hotels.[80] In 2015, the Ministry of Finance reported that the government underspent the budget it had allotted officials for overseas travel, entertainment, and cars.[81] The campaign is also widely popular among Chinese citizens. That same year, the CCDI received more than 2.8 million tips from the Chinese public concerning corruption.[82] Moreover, Chinese public opinion surveys suggest that the campaign is a significant source of popular support for Xi himself. [83]

Nonetheless, the campaign has also given rise to a range of both short- and long-term challenges. At one level, it raises questions concerning the very essence of the party's system of *nomenklatura*, the process by which officials are selected and promoted. Prominent Chinese venture capitalist Eric X. Li argues that the party succeeds above all because it is meritocratic. In his estimation, the Organization Department of the CCP is able to cull the cream of the crop from the party's more than 80 million members by continuously evaluating officials' performance, interviewing other officials and people, and so forth, to ascertain who are the most talented and competent. Somewhat provocatively, Li asserted, "A person with [U.S. President] Barack Obama's pre-presidential professional experience would not even be the manager of a small county in China's system."[84] Li claims that the CCP's adaptability, system of meritocracy, and legitimacy with the Chinese people will enable the country to meet its challenges with "dynamism and resilience."[85] He suggests that when policies do not work, as in the cases of the Great Leap Forward and Cultural Revolution, the party self-corrects as it did with Deng Xiaoping's economic reforms.

Yet as MIT professor Yasheng Huang notes in his critique of Li's argument, the narrative is not as seamless as Li portrays. Of the six top leaders of the CCP during 1949 to 2012, two were pushed out, and one fell from power and served fifteen years under house arrest until his death. In addition, the self-correction to which Li refers in the cases of the Great Leap Forward and the Cultural Revolution happened only after the deaths of millions of Chinese citizens at the hands of the party.[86] Moreover, the rampant corruption within the party that Xi is attempting to address includes the widespread buying and selling of offices in the National People's Congress (NPC), as well as a demonstrable willingness on the part of local officials to flout laws and regulations for personal profit, suggesting that a system of meritocracy is not yet well entrenched.

Somewhat paradoxically, Chinese opinion surveys suggest that while the anticorruption campaign is popular, it also enhances the sense among the Chinese people that corruption is a deep and endemic problem.[87] The more the party focuses its attention and resources on the challenge, the greater the concern of the Chinese people. In addition, removing corrupt high-level officials, while popular in the short run, does little to address the real issue for many in China, which is improving the lives of the poor by tackling issues such as price levels, wealth distribution, and educational opportunities. Thus, the campaign may well not achieve a central objective of Xi, which is to legitimize the Communist Party.[88]

The political nature of the campaign also affects the degree of legitimacy the campaign ultimately achieves within the Chinese public. During December 2012 through 2014, more than twenty of the forty-four officials at the vice-ministerial level or higher whom the CCDI had removed had close ties or financial connections with Zhou Yongkang, considered one of Xi's most formidable political adversaries.[89] Moreover, according to one study, very few officials from Zhejiang and Fujian Provinces, where Xi has spent much of his career, have been targeted for corruption.[90] A 2016 quantitative study of corruption in China by John Griffin, Clark Liu, and Tao Shu further found that firms where top officials attended the same universities as national leaders have a decreased likelihood of being investigated.[91]

The potential for a political backlash is yet another cause for concern for Xi and his supporters. The campaign has produced pockets of highly discontented officials: retired leaders whose power has been diminished, officials and businesspeople who are frustrated with new spending restrictions,[92] and legal officials and political reformers who are concerned about the lack of transparency and the rule of law in the way the anticorruption campaign is being prosecuted.[93]

Strikingly, the campaign may not be addressing some of the more significant sources of corruption. Griffin, Liu, and Shu's research also demonstrates that among the 150 firms (including 130 SOEs) they investigated, of ten measures of possible firm corruption, only one—business entertainment expenditure—demonstrated any significant change after the onset of the anticorruption campaign.[94]

Of greatest concern to Chinese officials, however, are the costs the campaign may exact on political efficacy and economic growth. In March 2015, the Shanxi party secretary announced that the province had yet to replace nearly three hundred officials who had been removed as a result of graft investigations.[95] In a similar vein, the head of a well-known multinational headquartered in Shanghai commented to me that as one official after another was arrested in the energy sector, it was often unclear whom he should contact for business.[96] Officials who remain in power are often paralyzed by their concern that green-lighting new projects or undertaking new reforms will draw unwanted attention. Some have reportedly started avoiding entrepreneurs and are refusing to move forward on projects,[97] even stopping bidding for projects midstream. Officials are uncertain about the changing rules and restrictions and fear that they will be caught on the wrong side of a new regulation.[98] One of China's leading corruption researchers, Beihang University professor Ren Jianming, noted, "Many local government officials are reluctant to do their jobs at the moment, afraid of being punished for making wrong decisions."[99] Premier Li Keqiang has acknowledged that many big projects and investment initiatives are not being completed and has admonished local officials for their inaction: "Some officials are taking a wait-and-see attitude, being reluctant to implement major policies of the central government, and not caring about their own political achievements."[100] Overall, this slowdown in economic activity, when coupled with the clampdown on luxury goods and activities, cost China an estimated 1 to 1.5 percent of its annual GDP during 2014 and 2015.[101]

Despite the costs, reforms to the anticorruption campaign are underway that suggest the campaign will only grow in scope, including a new network of supervisory commissions that will oversee anticorruption charges against not just party members but all state employees. And while party officials tout the planned introduction of a new detention system *liuzhi,* which they claim will avoid the abuses of the previous secretive *shuanggui* system, critics claim that the continued denial of legal representation to the accused means that the new system is unlikely to result in a more transparent or fair process for corruption suspects.[102]

Down to the Masses

The anticorruption campaign is only one of several campaigns Xi has launched to strengthen the party and deepen the party's relationship to Chinese society. He has mobilized the party to fortify the moral character of party members, inculcate socialist values, and reject Western cultural and ideological influences. The campaign model of political change is particularly attractive to Xi. Campaigns enable Xi to place a priority on transforming the Chinese people rather than the political institutions that make up the state. The result is that the one-party state remains intact, and Xi has avoided any significant political institutional reform that would challenge his authority or that of the Communist Party.[103]

Such campaigns are a staple of Communist Party politics. Without elections, a robust civil society, and an open media, the party must police itself. Mao began such campaigns during the Yan'an period in the mid-1940s, even before the establishment of the People's Republic of China. During the Yan'an Rectification campaign, for example, party members were asked to make self-criticisms and were invited to study Mao's writings and offer their thoughts. Those that did not support Mao were isolated and criticized.[104] Mao used this process of criticism and self-criticism not only to try to ensure ideological rectitude but also to eliminate enemies. Deng Xiaoping,[105] Jiang Zemin, and Hu Jintao all conducted rectification campaigns designed to promote ideological steadfastness and enhance party discipline.[106] Jiang Zemin's "Three Stresses" campaign (*sanjiang*, 三讲), for example, called on the CCP to "stress study, stress politics, and stress rectitude" (*jiang xuexi, jiang zhengzhi, jiang zhengqi,* 讲学习, 讲政治, 讲正气). Officials were required to participate in discussion and self-criticism sessions in their offices and author anonymous critiques of their superiors.[107]

The current Chinese leadership has followed suit. In June 2013, the Politburo began a year-long Mass Line campaign (*qunzhong luxian,* 群众路线) to improve relations between party members and the public. In announcing the campaign, Xi echoed his rhetoric from the anticorruption campaign: "Winning or losing the people's support is an issue that concerns the CPC's survival or extinction."[108] The campaign was designed to improve the process for evaluating cadres,[109] reduce officials' propensity to undertake vanity projects,[110] such as constructing large government office buildings, and encourage officials to undertake community service to demonstrate their ties to the people.[111] Practical administrative issues, such as too many meetings and too much paperwork, were also targeted for reform.[112] Officials were called upon to "watch from the mirror, groom oneself, take a bath and seek remedies"—in other words, consider their own behavior and fix any problems.[113]

Party officials participated in "democratic meetings" in which they offered self-criticisms that were written down and reviewed by supervisory bodies.[114] The teams sent to supervise the process were tasked with writing final reports, and the meetings were expected to continue after the Mass Line campaign wrapped up.[115] The campaign formally ended on October 8, 2014, coinciding with the 80th anniversary of the

Long March.[116] The symbolism of the date was clear. The Long March, in which communist revolutionaries experienced great hardship at the hands of an advancing Kuomintang army during 1934–1935, stands as one of the Communist Party's most important markers of self-sacrifice and commitment to communist ideals, as well as the birthing ground for the leadership of Mao Zedong. More campaigns have followed, each emphasizing the need of the party to rectify itself.

Dissenting voices have also made themselves heard. Party theorist Li Haiqing, who almost a decade earlier had published an article arguing that ideology was critical to mobilizing people's enthusiasm for collective action and sacrifice,[117] penned an article in 2013 suggesting the Mass Line was not an effective alternative to democratic processes.[118] Others echoed the necessity of institutional reform. Hu Xingdou of the Beijing Institute of Technology noted: "Such a campaign is still of significance at a time when vested interests are getting in the way of political reform. But officials could fundamentally make themselves accountable to the masses via a democratic system."[119]

As with the anticorruption campaign, Xi's rectification efforts have had mixed results. On the one hand, they have achieved several of their intended objectives: a decline in the number of meetings, a significant reduction in the number of unnecessary official buildings, and a drop in the amount of public expenditures on official receptions.[120] Yet for some senior party members, who have experienced many such rectification campaigns, there is unlikely to be a change in behavior. One party member told me: "We sit around a table and perform self-criticisms, and then everyone else says, 'No, no, you are a good party member.' It is all a big joke." A renewed commitment to the party, he suggested, will require something more around which party members could unite. For Xi Jinping, at least one element of the unification narrative appears to be establishing Western liberal values as an existential threat to the party and its principles.

Us against Them

In April 2013, the Communist Party circulated the *Communiqué on the Current State of the Ideological Sphere*, later referred to as Document 9 because it was the ninth such communiqué sent out that year. The document painted the CCP as in the midst of an intense struggle with Western liberal values that had begun to take hold in certain sectors of Chinese society. These values included constitutionalism, universal values, civil society, neoliberalism and market economics, freedom of the press, reassessing China's history, and suggesting that China's reform and opening up should be evaluated according to Western standards. The authors of the document also underscored the role of Western anti-China forces and internal dissidents "actively trying to infiltrate China's ideological sphere."[121] Over time, Document 9 has become known as advancing the "seven no's" or seven perils: universal values, press freedom, civil society, citizens' rights, the party's historical aberrations, the "privileged capitalistic class," and the independence of the judiciary.[122] It represents both a confirmation and an expansion of the "five no's" that then NPC Standing Committee Chairman Wu Bangguo articulated in 2011: no multiparty politics, no diversification of the party's ideology, no separation of powers, no privatization, and no federal system of government.[123]

While some observers initially suggested that the document might reflect only the perspective of one conservative faction within the party as opposed to the views of the central leadership,[124] evidence soon mounted that Document 9 signaled the onset of a significant new campaign against Western values. This campaign differentiates Xi from his predecessors who demonstrated a much greater tolerance for the expression of liberal ideas.[125]

Xi's first target was universities. Even before he became Communist Party general secretary, Xi called for party branches in universities to play a stronger role in guiding students and ensuring that their education inculcated socialist values.[126] Ideological education soon became a hallmark of Xi's leadership. In May 2013, the Ministry of Education, along with several departments of the CCP, issued a document that called for enhancing the role of ideology in universities. In an interview regarding the document, officials from the Ministry of Education noted, "A few young college teachers are confused or vague about their political ideologies, and their work ethic and emotions are fading."[127] Allegedly, universities were also to observe the "seven taboos of higher education," which corresponded with the "seven no's," or perils, in Document 9.[128] A CCP-affiliated magazine, *Liaoning Daily*, in November 2014 also sent journalists to universities and reported on professors who purportedly supported Western political ideals or were otherwise critical of the Chinese government. The paper's editors argued that the professors and students suffered from a lack of "three identities": theoretical identity with CCP history and ideology, political identity with the CCP, and emotional identity with the CCP and its policies.[129] In December 2014, Xi called for enhancing ideological control over China's universities.[130]

In January 2015, the party issued Document 30, a summary of various speeches by Xi, in which he again called for strengthening the party's influence on universities and enforcing ideological education. The Ministry of Education soon followed with calls to restrict the use of Western textbooks that advocated Western political values. Professors submitted books published abroad or not originally written in Chinese for review of their ideological content.[131] According to at least one prominent Chinese political science professor, however, as long as he does not tell the university he will be using a Western text, he will not get in trouble. If he asks for permission, he will certainly be denied.[132] Still, the government continues to try to find new ways to ferret out nonbelievers. The Ministry of Education announced in 2016 that university hires would have to pass not only a written exam but also a political correctness interview; and universities were further given the right to conduct investigations into applicants' political stances in their hometowns.[133]

A second target of Xi's campaign against Western values was the Chinese Academy of Social Sciences (CASS). In 2014, CCDI official Zhang Yingwei criticized CASS for ideological problems such as "using the internet to promote theories that played into the hands of foreign powers," permitting "undue foreign influence in sensitive issues," and fostering "illegal collusion" between CASS experts and their foreign counterparts.[134] In early February 2016, after months of investigation by inspectors,[135] the CCDI made public a wholesale indictment of CASS, concluding, "The party's leadership had weakened, the guiding place of Marxism in some academic disciplines had been marginalized, and there existed erroneous ideological tendencies." The inspectors also criticized some CASS institutes for emphasizing research and underemphasizing party building, noting, "The life of the party leadership group is not robust."[136] As one former CASS institute director described the situation to me, the inspection was reminiscent of the Maoist period, with inspectors knocking on the door of one institute director at night and grilling her about specific statements she had reportedly made in the past.[137]

In 2016, the party further expanded the scope of its education effort to target members of the party who were promoting Western values or had "wavering confidence" in socialism.[138] No part of the Chinese bureaucracy has been immune to the hunt for nonbelievers, including the military and the propaganda apparatus itself. The CCDI in June 2016 criticized the propaganda apparatus as having inadequate "depth in its research into developing contemporary Chinese Marxism," not being "forceful enough in coordinating ideological and political work at universities," and not succeeding on the Internet "to implement the principle of the party managing the media."[139] According to a high-ranking CCDI official, investigations found that "the damage done by political indiscipline is far greater than that caused by corruption."[140] The CCDI has leveled similar criticisms against state-owned firms, such as CITIC, claiming officials there were "talking about business too much while seldom talking about the Party" and spending too much time on the golf course.[141]

Xi Jinping has also moved to enhance the role of the party in the media. In summer 2013, Xi proclaimed, "Politicians [should] run the newspapers."[142] In 2017, China ranked 176 out of 180 in the World Press Freedom Index,[143] and the Committee to Protect Journalists reported that China ranked second in the world, behind only Turkey, for the number of journalists in prison.[144] In early 2016, after visiting a number of Chinese news outlets and telling newsroom staff that the Chinese media "must love the party, protect the party, and closely align themselves with the party leadership,"[145] Xi went so far as to claim that the media "must be surnamed party" (*bixu xing dang,* 必须姓党).[146]

The Chinese leadership's efforts to restrict media content extend well beyond articles and programs that engage sensitive political issues. In March 2016, the State Administration of Press, Publication, Radio, Film, and Television issued a new set of rules that banned shows—either television or online—that depicted "the dark side of society," or promoted a "luxurious lifestyle." The rules, which include more than forty banned topics, reflected a dramatic increase from the original

2010 rules, which were limited to a ban on content that harmed China's image or unity, was pornographic, or encouraged criminal behavior.[147]

One of the most significant initiatives to limit the impact of foreign ideas and values within China was the adoption in January 2017 of the Law on the Management of Foreign Nongovernmental Organizations. The government solicited input from a wide range of government and nongovernmental actors, and the law was subjected to an extraordinarily high level of discussion and debate during its drafting stages, both among Chinese actors and between Chinese actors and their foreign counterparts. The law stipulates that all foreign NGOs must be registered with the MPS (previously NGOs were overseen by the Ministry of Civil Affairs); that they are formally affiliated with a Chinese government entity that holds oversight responsibility for their projects, personnel, and so forth; and that they cannot raise money within China, among other restrictions. Early signals suggested an almost complete breakdown in the registration process. According to one source, fewer than one hundred foreign NGOs out of several thousand had been accepted for registration within the first six months. (Without such registration, NGOs are required to obtain temporary permits to operate, a difficult bureaucratic process.) Among those accepted were a batch of prominent NGOs that already worked closely with the government on important energy and economic issues, such as the World Economic Forum, the Paulson Institute, and the Energy Foundation—all of which received affiliation with the powerful National Development and Reform Commission (NDRC).

Despite the slow start, when I sat down in June 2017 with the head of the Beijing representative office for one foreign NGO, she was surprisingly positive about her experience. The process, while onerous, had not been as contentious as she had anticipated. The key was doing things "the Chinese way," which meant using connections to facilitate the process. In this case, Tsinghua University's philanthropy group proved to be the savior for a number of foreign NGOs. Beginning in late January, in the immediate aftermath of the law's adoption, the Tsinghua team not only organized workshops to explain the registration process but also took it upon itself to play matchmaker among a select group of NGOs, the Public Security Bureau, and a prominent Chinese government-organized NGO, which could serve as the foreign

NGOs' official partner (despite the NGOs having no experience with that partner). Although state security had in recent years often harassed the NGO and its workers, the Public Security officials responsible for the foreign NGO registration were welcoming of the NGO's application. Her NGO, as well as at least two others assisted by Tsinghua, received approval for registration in early July 2017.

There is, however, a price to be paid for registration. The nature of foreign NGOs' work and the range of their activities will be more scrutinized and circumscribed. Organizations that previously focused on governance issues, such as the rule of law within China, are already discussing using their expertise to facilitate better Chinese governance practices outside the country, such as corporate social responsibility within the context of the BRI. The new programming direction, while important and beneficial to China and other countries, ensures that foreign NGOs will no longer directly engage with sensitive issues of governance or Western political values and ideals within China.

The Value Proposition

Xi Jinping's effort to prevent foreign ideas and influences from permeating Chinese society and his campaigns to inculcate a stronger moral code within the party both reflect a singular weakness in the CCP's leadership: the ability to project an attractive and compelling ideology. In 2002, scholars from the Ningxia Party School published the results of a survey among urban residents in Ningxia: roughly "25 percent did not believe in the cause of socialist construction any more, 50 percent doubted the CCP's role as vanguard of the working class . . . and 79 percent had lost their close emotional ties to the party."[148]

Xi recognizes the enormity of the task before him. In August 2013, while speaking at the National Propaganda and Ideology Work Conference, he reiterated several times the lack of belief among party members in Marxism and socialism, pointing out: "The disintegration of a regime often starts from the ideological area, political unrest and regime change may perhaps occur in a night, but ideological evolution is a long-term process. If the ideological defenses are breached, other defenses become very difficult to hold."[149]

Xi has attacked the challenge with a vengeance. He is attempting in the first instance to develop a continuous historical narrative for the party in order to diminish the potential for ideological divisions that could weaken the party. In January 2013, he articulated the "two undeniables": the Maoist period before Deng cannot be used to deny the Deng reforms, while the Deng reform period cannot be used to deny the Maoist period.[150] He has also legitimized Confucius as part of China's political culture, drawing on Confucius's beliefs in virtuous rule and the necessity of meeting the needs of the people. Speaking before the International Confucian Association in September 2014, Xi promoted the CCP as the successor to traditional Chinese culture.[151]

Xi has also reinforced the idea that the Chinese political system is oriented toward achieving concrete goals that meet the needs of the Chinese people, such as those embodied in his Chinese Dream: developing a prosperous society,[152] building a military capable of fighting and winning wars,[153] and reclaiming China's place as a global power. Xi's Four Comprehensives—a set of political and economic objectives announced in 2015 and defined as building a moderately prosperous society, deepening reform, governing the nation according to law, and strictly governing the party—underpin the Chinese Dream and further buttress the sense that Xi has a clear vision for where he wants to lead the party and the country.[154]

And finally, Xi has sought to instill a common understanding of the party's values and its right to lead. At the time of his ascension to the position of CCP general secretary, the party announced twelve ideals that reflected core socialist values (*shehui zhuyi hexin jiazhiguan,* 社会主义核心价值观)—prosperity, democracy, civility, harmony, freedom, equality, justice, the rule of law, patriotism, dedication, integrity, and friendship.[155] And in January 2013, he promoted the "three confidences" (*sange zixin,* 三个自信): confidence in the path of socialism with Chinese characteristics, confidence in the theory, and confidence in the current political system. A fourth confidence was added later: confidence in China's culture. Xi has attempted to instill these ideals into party members, as well as to introduce them to the broader Chinese public not only through traditional means, such as school and media propaganda, but also through (relatively) more creative and engaging approaches. For example, a city in Jiangsu Province held speech competitions on "family morality," and officials in Sichuan Province put the core socialist values in riddle form.[156]

To the extent that Chinese officials and scholars are more aware of the limits of free expression of ideas and public debate, Xi's campaign has been a success. Yet the effort to enforce ideological uniformity among Chinese officials has also contributed to tensions within the party. An article published by a CCDI-managed newspaper titled "A Thousand Yes-Men Cannot Equal One Honest Advisor," for example, called for more open debate. The piece, written in an allegorical form lauding the Emperor Taizong, who was known for his tolerance of criticism, noted, "The ability to air opinions freely and to accept suggestions frequently determined the rise or fall of an empire . . . . We should not be afraid of people saying the wrong things; we should be afraid of people not speaking at all."[157] And as we will see in the following chapters, behind closed doors and in some cases openly, Chinese scholars and officials continue to debate government policy on a wide range of economic and foreign policy issues.

The Expanding Limits of the Law

Fall party plenums are held annually in October or November and bring together the most senior leadership of the Communist Party—the over two hundred full members of the Central Committee—for discussion of important party matters.[158] They are also occasions for the general secretary and the PBSC to articulate their political and economic priorities and establish the benchmarks by which their legacy will be evaluated. For Xi Jinping, the Fourth Plenum of the 18th Party Congress in October 2014 represented an opportunity to stake out his views on the rule of law in China.[159]

Early in his tenure, Xi hinted that he would bring a fresh understanding to the meaning and significance of the rule of law. In a 2012 speech, he noted that problems in the legal system—including abuse of power and dereliction of duty for personal gain—were a source of significant popular discontent.[160] Importantly, in his December 2012 speech marking the thirtieth anniversary of China's Constitution, he claimed: "In essence, the rule of law is rule by the Constitution; the key to law-based governance is Constitution-based governance."[161]

Vice-President of the Supreme People's Court Jiang Bixin wrote one week later in the *People's Daily* that Xi's words—"ruling in accordance with the Constitution"—"open a new era of rule of law."[162] Previous understandings of the relationship between the party and the Constitution held that the party exerted ultimate authority over the Constitution, not that the party was subordinate to the Constitution. Xi's words appeared to signal an important shift.

Some legal reformers found further cause for hope in the appointment of Zhou Qiang, the former governor and later party secretary of Hunan Province, as head of the Supreme People's Court in March 2013.[163] Zhou, unlike his predecessor who was a police officer,[164] was formally trained as a lawyer; a reform-oriented legal scholar referred to Zhou as possessing "political courage" and being unique among provincial party secretaries for advancing the rule of law.[165] While in Hunan, Zhou became known for spearheading a critical advancement in Chinese law. Prompted by a 2006 World Bank report that ranked five of Hunan's cities in the bottom ten in China for "investment friendliness," Zhou pushed through the country's first draft comprehensive regulation of administrative procedure. The provisions not only created and strengthened important restrictions on official conduct—including that of the security and police apparatus—but also served as a legislative experiment for the entire country.[166]

The Fourth Plenum did, in fact, affirm some of the optimism of the legal scholars. Three reforms stood out in the party's "Decision on Several Important Issues Regarding the All-Around Promotion of Ruling the State According to Law": Beijing would establish circuit courts with jurisdictions separated from local governments; any intervention by party officials in the judicial process would be recorded; and the system of judges would be professionalized so that all of them would be trained as lawyers or law professionals.[167] (Traditionally, like Zhou's predecessor, many judges were retired party or military officials without any legal training.)[168] Taken together the reforms added up to a more professional legal system and one less subject to political intervention.

Additional reforms in the sector also appeared promising. China law scholar Neysun Mahboubi has suggested that revisions to the administrative litigation law, along the lines initiated by Zhou Qiang, which enhance the power of the court to review cases against the government, are particularly noteworthy. Mahboubi suggests that the reform is already having an important impact: the number of administrative litigation cases almost doubled from about 150,000 to around 250,000 during 2014–2015.[169]

The limitations of legal reform under Xi, however, have also come into sharper focus. In January 2014, Xi announced that all judicial, procuratorial, and public security departments needed to uphold definitively the leadership of the party,[170] and further that they must "vindicate the authority of the party's policies and the state's laws."[171] As political scientists Zheng Yongnian and Shan Wei note, there is a stark difference between the understanding of the rule of law in the West and that in China. In the West, the rule of law was developed as a means of restraining arbitrary actions by those in power. There is no person or group above the law. In China, however, the rule of law is equated with rule by law or ruling the country according to law. The law is an instrument with which the Communist Party can ensure the continued dominance of the party itself.[172] Zheng argues convincingly that Xi's approach to the law's relationship to the Communist Party is deeply rooted in China's historical political culture, in which the emperor stood above the law; legalism was simply a means of achieving government efficiency and there was virtually no gap between the judiciary and the state.[173] In this vein, as University of Nottingham scholar Samantha Hoffman argues, Xi Jinping has created a "more coherent legal framework to enforce preservation of the party state."[174]

The unprecedented crackdown on lawyers during Xi's tenure also raises questions about how the rule of law should be understood in the current context. Perhaps the most significant event, was the 709 crackdown—so named because it began on July 9, 2015—which resulted in the harassment and detention of over three hundred human rights lawyers and activists over the course of several months, and the later arrest of some held in detention.[175] The Beijing-based Fengrui law firm, alone, saw thirty-eight of its lawyers and staff arrested.[176] Trials were conducted behind closed doors (although government-approved media were allowed), and in many instances the detained lawyers were barred from seeing family members,[177] some of whom were taken away themselves.[178] In August 2016, after a year being held without any contact with family members or lawyers,[179] a number of the lawyers appeared on Chinese television to confess their crimes, including "being used" by foreign forces to harm the Chinese government, making "improper" comments to foreign journalists,[180] and working to overthrow the Communist Party.[181] Zhou Shifeng, the head of the Fengrui law firm, who received a seven-year sentence, perhaps ironically thanked Xi Jinping on television in his trial's closing statement, stating: "Xi Jinping's rule of law has made China ever stronger."[182]

In light of such incidents, King's College London scholar Eva Pils supports Hoffman's assessment that Xi Jinping is using legal reform to strengthen the coercive power of the state and outlines the steps the party has taken to institutionalize this power. Even as the Chinese government has created laws and legal institutions, she notes, it ignores the fundamental contradiction between "a party that exacts unconditional obedience to centrally made decisions . . . and a legal system that purports to limit public power."[183] Pils points to the provisions on surveillance in the revised Criminal Procedure Law as one example. In certain types of cases, the new law suspends the protections that a suspect should have in the ordinary criminal process. The result is that the law provides the opportunity for "torture and terror" of public interest lawyers, women's rights activists, labor activists, and journalists. Pils describes it as a "zone of exception from legality."[184] In effect, the law enables practices such as forced disappearances, which once happened secretly, to be part of the system and carried out in accordance with the law.[185] The recorded and public confessions further serve to create a climate of "unlimited, in principle arbitrary and all the more fearful, state power."[186]

Even before the spate of high-profile televised confessions in August 2016, leading legal figures in China were speaking out against the more repressive tactics of the Xi government. At the March 2016 annual meeting of the Chinese People's Political Consultative Conference (CPPCC) and NPC, the Deputy Chairman of the All-China Lawyers Association Zhu Zhengfu criticized the rising number of pre-trial confessions on television. He told the *Beijing News*: "The possibility is too high that a suspect will plead guilty against his will and in spite of the facts . . . Forcing people to confess on TV means saddling them with a high presumption of guilt."[187] His views were later echoed by the chief judge of Henan Province's High People's Court Zhang Liyong who told *Wall Street Journal* reporters that no one outside of a court, including the police, prosecutors, and especially not the media, is qualified to determine someone's guilt.[188]

Chinese lawyers represent a small but potent force pushing back against the direction of the current reforms. They are not the only Chinese citizens resisting Xi Jinping's efforts to narrow the boundaries of acceptable political discourse and action. Even as opportunities for public debate are closed off, activists in and outside China continue to articulate contrary views and push for change.

Dissenting Voices

By summer 2016, the three-decade-old *Southern Weekend* was a shadow of its former self. The paper suffered mass departures and positions were reportedly filled with conservative writers.[189] The transformation of *Yanhuang Chunqiu* was even starker. On July 19, 2016, the editors announced that the journal had ceased publication after virtually all the members of the editorial committee were removed or demoted by the Ministry of Culture's Chinese National Academy of Arts—the oversight organization for the journal. The magazine's executive editor stated that the closure of the magazine was a reflection of the full-scale purging of reformist voices within the party.[190] (The magazine has since been revived but is under CCP control.) And in October 2016, I received a brief email note from a friend of the publisher of *Consensus Net*, an online chat room for liberal reform thinking and debate, noting that its temporary closure would likely be permanent.[191]

Yet dissenting voices continue to make themselves heard. Not everyone is comfortable with the direction in which Xi is moving the country. Many push within the system. At the March 2016 meeting of the Chinese People's Political Consultative Conference—a legislative advisory body to the NPC that consists of members of China's democratic parties—several representatives also called for greater political openness. Well-known CCTV anchor Bai Yansong, for example, argued for increased freedom of the press, claiming that if China wants to address social ills such as environmental pollution, the government must "give media the green light." In an interview with *Caixin*, Shanghai University of Finance and Economics professor Jiang Hong promised to speak about freedom of speech at the meeting, and commented, "As for affairs within the Communist Party, I am an outsider. I have no right to criticize or make irresponsible remarks. But as a citizen, [my] freedom of expression must be protected." (The interview was later deleted from *Caixin's* website by the Cyberspace Administration of China.)[192] In an earlier speech, Jiang had noted, "To permanently cure corruption, we need political reform to put power into the cage of a system and to fundamentally clear the soil that creates corruption." He proposed that every legal citizen be allowed to participate in elections and to compete to be elected.[193] Moreover, on narrower political issues, CPPCC members can exert significant influence. In one case, a vice-chairman of the CPPCC complained to then PBSC member Liu Yunshan about a set of new restrictions on travel for scholars and think tank analysts—pointing out that it was difficult for Chinese think tanks to "go global" and promote China's messages abroad if, in fact, scholars were not permitted to travel freely and were only permitted five day stays in other countries.[194] Liu concurred, and the regulations were modified to allow for greater ease of travel.

While most of Xi Jinping's detractors attack his policies, some are more directly personal in their approach. While the congress was underway, an anonymous letter calling for the resignation of Xi was published on *Wujie News*, a website backed by the government of Xinjiang and the SEEC media group, which also owns the influential financial news magazine *Caijing*.[195] (The Internet behemoth Alibaba also reportedly backed *Wujie News*, but in the wake of the letter's appearance denied any formal affiliation.) While the letter acknowledged Xi's efforts to clean up the party and his popularity among the Chinese people, it criticized him for moving away from most of the guiding principles of Deng Xiaoping's domestic and foreign policy, including the principle of collective leadership, keeping a low profile internationally, supporting one country-two systems, presiding over the stock market crash of 2015–2016 and real estate bubble, growing conflict with North Korea, and creating a cult of personality. The letter, which disappeared quickly from the Internet, also called for Xi's resignation in order to ensure "safety for you and your family."[196] As many as twenty people were reportedly linked to the letter and later detained.[197] And in October 2017, at the time of the 19th Party Congress, chairman of the China Securities Regulatory Commission Liu Shiyu suggested that a number of former senior officials had attempted to overthrow Xi Jinping, including Sun Zhengcai, who only a few months earlier had been considered a potential successor to Xi as general secretary.[198]

While debate may continue behind the largely closed doors of official China, the world of independent activists has become a far more difficult and, in some cases, dangerous one under Xi Jinping. Some activists have been forced to modify their behavior in order to continue to push for change. When I sat down in July 2016 with Li Fan, a prominent scholar and political activist who has received international attention for his work training independent candidates to compete in local Chinese elections, he was measured in his assessment of how much his work has changed since Xi took office. Certainly, he tells me, his efforts to train independent candidates have ceased. There is no room for such independent political thinking and activity in the current political environment. (He nonetheless continues to travel the world to observe and learn from democratic elections.) Instead, he is focusing his attention on his other passion: working at the local level to expand transparency in the budget process. Such work is much easier, he says, because it fits in well with the government's current emphasis on official accountability. Still, Li argues that despite the more repressive political environment, liberal intellectuals such as himself continue to fight; their platform has simply shifted to the Internet.

Yet for many Chinese rights activists, there is simply no political space in which to operate in Xi's China, except that which exists outside the country. While Li has managed to navigate the new political terrain successfully, many of China's most outspoken reform voices have gone silent—in some cases imprisoned or forced to leave the country. In Xi's first few years in office, more than five hundred activists were detained or arrested. Famed civil rights lawyer Teng Biao fled China in 2014 and has since taken up residence at various American universities, including Harvard, and New York University (NYU), as well as the Institute for Advanced Study in Princeton. Teng began his professional life as an academic dedicated to promoting the rule of law but transformed into an activist in 2003 with the Sun Zhigang case, in which a twenty-seven-year-old college graduate and factory worker was beaten to death, while being detained for not possessing the appropriate residency permit. (The resulting public outcry and legal case resulted in the abolition of the custody and repatriation system.) Together with other young lawyers, Teng gained international acclaim for his work advocating on behalf of Chinese civil rights, beginning in 2003 with the Open Constitution Initiative (*Gongmeng*, 公盟) and later through the New Citizens' Movement (*Zhongguo Xingongmin Yundong*, 中国新公民运动). When I caught up with Teng in late spring 2017 at NYU Law School, he described the change in China's political openness in the aftermath of Xi's accession to power as dramatic—a shift from "maintaining stability" to "wiping out any critics." Just before Xi's ascension to power in 2012, the New Citizen's Movement, of which Teng was a founder, was in its heyday. The movement was dedicated to bringing online activism to the ground. Dinner gatherings took place on the last Saturday of every month in as many as thirty cities with participants discussing broad concerns around human rights, as well as local cases of civil rights abuses. Full of enthusiasm, many of the participants posted pictures on Sina Weibo (a Chinese microblogging platform) and Twitter, and members of the movement traveled to different cities to meet other activists. In some cities, such as Guangzhou, Beijing, or Shenzhen, there might be more than one hundred people at a dinner. The movement, Teng says, was modeled on Internet guru Clay Shirky's book *The Power of Organizing without Organizations*. In 2014, however, the arrest of Xu Zhiyong, Teng's friend and his co-founder of both the New Citizen's Movement and the Open Constitution Initiative, dampened the energy of the movement. While some groups continue to meet, many of the members now participate only online.

Teng's activism came at great personal cost. Before leaving China, he was suspended from teaching three times, disbarred, forcibly disappeared, detained, and tortured. It is a fate, he says, that many of his fellow activists have shared. Teng himself is now burdened by the harsh fate of many he left behind, saying that he suffers from "survivor's guilt." Nonetheless, he remains undaunted. He has co-founded, along with several other Chinese political activists, a new NGO, the China Human Rights Accountability Center, which is designed to collect information on Chinese human rights abusers with an eye toward having the U.S. government sanction them. He is also active in speaking on behalf of Hong Kong activists, testifying before the U.S. Congress on Chinese human rights concerns, and raising money for Chinese activists. He may live outside China, but his life is consumed with efforts to advance the cause of political change within the country.

Nowhere are dissenting voices louder, however, than in regions Beijing oversees, such as Hong Kong, or claims as sovereign territory, such as Taiwan. Xi Jinping has moved aggressively to enforce greater political discipline in both regions. Over the past several years, Xi has sought to tighten the mainland's political control over Hong Kong by arresting booksellers who sell politically sensitive books, pushing for schools to adopt curricula that stress patriotic education, and passing a law criminalizing disrespect of the Chinese national anthem, among other initiatives. Frequent mass demonstrations by Hong Kong citizens in support of democracy and against such increasing political encroachment by Beijing are met with an increasingly hard-line stance by Beijing and additional efforts to narrow the political space between Hong Kong and the mainland.

In Taiwan, as well, in the wake of the 2016 election of Tsai Ingwen as president, Xi Jinping has sought to use Beijing's political and economic leverage to pressure Tsai to recognize the '92 Consensus,[199] a political accord signed by a previous leadership that acknowledges Taiwan is part of China—a claim to which Tsai and her political party, the Democratic Progressive Party, do not subscribe. Her resistance to supporting the consensus has led Beijing to cut back tourism to Taiwan by almost 20 percent, threaten Taiwan with the presence of an aircraft carrier, and break off formal talks between Beijing and Taipei. Despite the fact that only 14.9 percent of Taiwanese favor unification with the mainland,[200] Xi has made it clear that he believes that reunification between Taiwan and the mainland under one country, two systems is "historical inevitability."

Conclusion

Over the course of Xi Jinping's first five years in office, he has made significant progress in transforming the institutions that govern political life. He has weakened the principle of collective leadership and amassed political power through the use of traditional political institutions such as leadership of small groups, the principle of the core leader, and a series of political campaigns and initiatives designed both to strengthen the party and eliminate political adversaries. His decision not to designate a successor as general secretary of the Communist Party leaves open the possibility that Xi himself will remain in that position beyond his expected retirement in 2022. He has also moved to reverse the trend of reform and opening up that has characterized much of the previous almost four decades by deepening the role of the party in civil society, the educational system, and the media. At the same time, he has worked to prevent the influx of foreign ideas and influences in education and the media, as well as to limit the influence of foreign NGOs through a new registration system.

Advocates for liberal political reform—as defined by individual freedoms and the institutions that serve them—increasingly find the space for debate and dissent narrowing. Xi Jinping has identified such ideas as hostile to the well-being of the Communist Party and Chinese people. The educational and legal systems, as well as the media, have become tools through which the party can exercise greater political control. In such an environment, political activists must choose among three unsatisfying options: constraining their voice and actions within acceptable parameters, facing an increased likelihood of incarceration, or abandoning their homeland entirely.

Some of the contradictions inherent in Xi's efforts have become clear, such as the negative impact of the anticorruption campaign on economic growth, and the bottleneck in decision-making incurred as a result of Xi's centralization of power. Other costs are likely to emerge over time. Efforts to limit the ability of the Chinese people to engage with ideas from outside the country may simply result in more Chinese seeking to study abroad. The clampdown on rights lawyers and activists may hinder the ability of the Chinese government to realize a justice system that effectively redresses societal wrongs. And at a more fundamental level, the sheer depth of party intrusion into the moral and cultural fabric of society sits in direct opposition to the outward facing trend of Chinese society, in which more than 120 million Chinese travel abroad annually and as many as 750 million people use the Internet.

As the next chapter explores, however, the Chinese leadership appears more than willing to accept such costs. Not content to limit itself to reform in traditional governance structures, it is bringing the same principles of increasing party penetration and rejection of outside ideas and forces to shape political life on the Internet. Despite Li Fan's optimism, the party leadership sees little distinction between the real and virtual worlds.

3

Chinanet

JING ZHAO, OR AS he is known in the West, Michael Anti, does not mince words. A Chinese journalist, he also became a globally renowned Internet activist. The Internet, in Anti's view, is a battlefield, not only between the government and the people but also between corporations and the government. Ultimately, argues Anti, a free Internet depends on who controls the technology. Speaking at the Oslo Freedom Forum in 2014, he called on "all the geeks of the world and the freedom fighters" to unite in the cause of a free Internet.[1] His call to arms reminds me of something he said a few years earlier over lunch in Beijing about his role as a blogger: "I am a bridge, and my message to the Chinese people is: the government is not the only player—you are the future." Although in his speeches Anti often raises challenges to Internet freedom in Russia and even the United States, it is clear that his primary target is China. In Anti's words, China doesn't have the Internet, it has a "Chinanet," and that is not a legacy he wants to leave for the next generation of Chinese.

Anti's university studies and early career choices did not preordain his life as a voice for Internet freedom. Born in the 1970s, at the tail end of the Cultural Revolution, Anti graduated from Nanjing Normal University in 1995 with a degree in industrial automation, but he began by working as a receptionist in a hotel in far-off Wuxi. His primary motivation for taking the job was to gain some independence from his mother. After one year, he left his job to become an online bulletin board system (BBS) product manager for a travel company. By

1999, he had become a chat room master,[2] and two years later, he was a commentator for the English-language *China Times*. At that point, his career took off. He spent time as a journalist in Iraq, worked for the *Washington Post* and *New York Times*, studied at Cambridge, earned a Nieman Fellowship to study journalism at Harvard, and finally landed back in China, teaching journalism and earning a reputation as a well-known blogger and commentator.[3] His international profile received a significant bump when he delivered a 2012 TED talk that was viewed well over one million times.

While Anti's forthright approach to sensitive political issues is viewed favorably by his admirers, it has occasionally landed him in hot water. In 2011, Facebook removed his profile, ostensibly because he used the pseudonym Michael Anti instead of the official name on his Chinese identity card. Since "nonreal" name registration was common among Chinese Facebook users—as it is in the United States—most observers believe Anti was targeted as part of Facebook's broader campaign to get back in the Chinese government's good graces. Beijing blocked Facebook in 2009 after protestors in Xinjiang used Facebook to communicate.

The Facebook censure only reinforced Anti's commitment to push for greater Internet freedom in China. Still, he is not immune to the current unfavorable political winds. In 2012, when we met, he was full of confidence about the Internet and its role as an agent for change in China's political future. He told me that while the previous generation was waiting for reform to happen within the government, his generation doesn't care what happens in the government; they know that CCP rule will eventually end. He is particularly enamored of Twitter with its capability to inform and build communities around ideas instantaneously. Despite the ban on Twitter in China, Anti sees it as an important platform. He points to a Twitter dialogue with the Dalai Lama as engendering a profound shift in the way that many netizens referred to him—no longer calling him by the disrespectful CCP term of Dalai but rather using his full title of Dalai Lama.[4] When I saw him again in the summer of 2015 at a conference in Colorado, however, he was less optimistic, talking about China's "new normal" and the new constraints faced by Chinese netizens. When I asked him about the current state of Internet openness in China, he made it clear that

Internet policy depends above all else on the top leader and that Xi Jinping does not welcome participation by civil society via the Internet. Any opening, he implies, will have to wait for the next leader.

Two years later when I sat down for tea with Anti in Beijing in the summer of 2017, he had all but forsaken his role as Internet activist. Instead, he reveled in his new role as head of global news for *Caixin*. In this capacity, he is enthusiastic about China's BRI and the opportunity to help Chinese companies better understand the local interests and cultures of the countries where they want to invest. When I asked Anti whether he was still concerned about issues related to Internet freedom, he replied that he did not see much point at the time—not only because of Xi Jinping's efforts but also because the election of President Trump in the United States in November 2016 signaled to him a change in American priorities away from human rights and Internet freedom. Without U.S. leadership on these issues, he argued, there is no hope; there is no one who will stand up on behalf of the Chinese rights community.

Anti is not alone in his relatively dismal assessment of Internet life in China and the potential for change. The consensus among Chinese domestic and foreign elite is that the Internet in China is no longer the vibrant virtual political space it was in the pre–Xi Jinping period. The Chinese leadership has dramatically expanded the technological capacity and human capital devoted to controlling content on the Internet. Government policies have contributed to a dramatic fall in the number of postings on the Chinese blogging platform Sina Weibo (similar to Twitter) and have silenced many of China's most important voices for political reform and opening up on the Internet. However, that does not mean that civil society has simply accepted the "new normal." The Internet continues to serve as a powerful tool for those bent on advancing social change and human rights. The game of cat and mouse continues, and there are many more mice than cats.

Xi Jinping's Internet Vision

Thousands of tech entrepreneurs, analysts, and even a sprinkling of heads of state from around the world listened carefully as Chinese president Xi Jinping outlined his vision for China's Internet future. They had traveled to Wuzhen, a small city in the southern part of China, to attend the country's second World Internet Conference in December 2015. Xi clearly conveyed his point: "We should respect the right of individual countries to independently choose their own path of cyber development, model of cyber regulation, and Internet public policies . . . . No country should pursue cyber hegemony, interfere in other countries' internal affairs, or engage in, connive at, or support cyber activities that undermine other countries' national security."[5] No one was surprised by what they heard. Xi had already established that the Chinese Internet would in many respects be a world unto itself, with its content closely monitored and managed by the Communist Party.

To accomplish Xi's vision requires recalibrating the state's relationship with society, as well as its relationship with the outside world. While Chinese history is replete with efforts to control the flow of information both within the country and from outside it, in the years immediately preceding Xi's ascension to power, the Internet brought the Chinese people an unprecedented level of transparency and ability to communicate with one another. New authoritative business and political voices, like Michael Anti's, advocated social reform and even political opening, and commanded tens of millions of followers on China's blogging sites. Chinese citizens who wanted forbidden content from outside the country tapped into virtual private networks (VPNs) that gave them access to blocked websites and other information. Citizens banded together online to hold authorities accountable for their actions—through both virtual petitions and physical protests. In 2010, a survey of three hundred officials conducted by the *People's Daily Online*, Tencent, and the People's Forum Online revealed that 70 percent were anxious about whether mistakes or details about their private life might be leaked through the Internet with negative ramifications for their careers and personal lives. Of the almost six thousand Chinese citizens who were also surveyed, 88 percent believed it was good for officials to be anxious about the power of the Internet.[6]

For Xi Jinping, however, there is no distinction between the virtual world and the real political world: both should reflect the same political values, ideals, and standards. There is limited room for competing voices and content. To this end, the Chinese leadership has directed significant time and energy to investing in technological upgrades to increase the state's already potent capacity to monitor and prevent undesirable content from entering and circulating throughout the country. The government has passed new laws and regulations designed to define more narrowly what constitutes acceptable content, and it has aggressively punished those who defy the new restrictions. Under Xi's guidance, foreign content providers have also found their access to China shrinking. They are being pushed out by both Xi's ideological war and his desire that Chinese companies dominate the country's rapidly growing Internet economy.

At home, Xi paints the West's version of the Internet, which prioritizes freedom of information flow, as anathema to the values of the Chinese government. Abroad, he asserts China's sovereign right to determine what constitutes harmful content on the Internet, aligning China with other nations that share his perspective, such as Russia. Rather than acknowledging that efforts to control the Internet are a source of embarrassment—a sign of potential authoritarian fragility—Xi is trying to turn his vision of a "Chinanet" into a model for other countries.

The challenge for Xi and the rest of the Chinese leadership, however, is maintaining what they perceive as the benefits of the Internet—advancing commerce and innovation—while at the same time protecting against the potential political downsides of uncontrolled information flow. They know that the world of global trade and finance relies on the rapid transmission of information via the Internet. Their dream of transforming the country into an innovation powerhouse similarly depends on access to the world of thought outside the country, as well as the free flow of information within the country. And the Chinese people have become accustomed to the virtual life of the Internet, not only for shopping and gaming but also for news and a shared sense of community. What Xi wants to avoid is the Internet as a political change accelerator—speeding up the transmission of political information and enabling large political demonstrations. Yet in the process, there are costs to China in terms of economic development, creative expression, government credibility, and the development of civil society. Xi and his supporters appear willing to bear these costs to create and maintain the Internet as a Chinanet. Many Chinese citizens, however, are less prepared to make the same sacrifice.

Historical Legacy

Xi's drive to control the information Chinese people can access is not a new one. Chinese leaders from imperial times to the present have lived with the constant threat of mobilized political discontent undermining their legitimacy and ability to rule. Most of Chinese history reflects a desire by the country's rulers to shape the social and political world of the citizens they govern, through censorship and limits on access to information, as well as through more proactive efforts, such as propaganda, to affect public discourse.[7]

China's first emperor, Qin Shi Huang (213 BCE–206 BCE), for example, was concerned about the potential of scholars to use history to compare his reign with that of the past—a concern that continued through successive Chinese dynasties. This resulted in an order to ban and then burn all Confucian texts,[8] and more than four hundred scholars who owned these forbidden books were subsequently buried alive. He also established a system of codes and laws that subsequent dynasties then used to codify censorship provisions, amending them along the way.[9] The Tang Code, which was drafted and amended during 624–653 CE,[10] included a regulation that prohibited any item that could be used for prognostication, as well as the republication of specific books, religious texts, and government documents.[11] The code of the Song dynasty (960–1279 CE) further mandated that local officials review publications by printers before they were published. Banned publications included "government and military documents, the classics, writings that inappropriately used the names of members or ancestors of the royal family, and pornography." The code also restricted religious freedom and speech.[12] The Ming dynasty banned texts with pictures of past leaders, books on astronomy, and any "texts which ought to be banned";[13] the Qing dynasty, then fearing a threat from their Ming predecessors, also censored any literature that they believed might undermine their leadership.[14] Even after the transformation of China from a dynasty to a republic, Chinese leaders continued to censor the media, concerned about the threat posed by opposition forces.

The rise to power of Mao Zedong and the communists in 1949 ushered in a new era of censorship. Throughout the 1960s and 1970s, popular access to foreign literature and media was heavily restricted and often only accessible to party elites.[15] No academic journals were published for over six years, and many publishing houses closed.[16] As the political system became increasingly insular—with information from the outside world and within China carefully controlled—Mao, like his imperial predecessors, also tried to contain rumors. In closed regimes, rumors have the potential to undermine social stability by spreading nonsanctioned ideas.[17] Reflecting just such a concern, in 1962, the MPS released a document on the "prevention and suppression of rumor," designed to counter various rumors of a poor economy, war, and superstitions.[18]

Mao also used culture and the media to promulgate socialist values, arguing that "the politicians must run the newspapers" (*zhengzhijia banbao*, 政治家办报).[19] His deputy, Lin Biao, put it even more forcefully: "A gun barrel, a pen barrel, seizing power depends on these two barrels, and consolidating power depends on these two barrels."[20] Ever fearful of subversion, the government required that artists, writers, and others engaged in creative professions "reflect proletarian values."[21]

Modern Chinese history has not been without its periods of open debate and creative expression. Proponents of the New Culture Movement in the mid-1910s and 1920s, for example, argued that China's traditional Confucian culture had kept it weak relative to Japan and Western nations and advocated adopting Western values such as science and democracy.[22] Among the most influential publications during this period was the *New Youth* journal, which published pieces by many budding radicals including Mao Zedong.[23] Additionally, during the Hundred Flowers Campaign in 1956–1957, the CCP briefly allowed scholars and intellectuals to write and speak without fear of retribution. During the mid to late 1980s, as well, increasing numbers of Chinese students and scholars began to study and do research in the West, shaping a new generation of thinkers who had exposure to political values inherent in democracies, such as freedom of speech and the rule of law.[24] In 1989, Beijing and other cities erupted with calls for improved economic well-being and expanded political rights. For several months, students, reporters, and other protestors occupied Beijing's central Tiananmen Square and communicated with each other and with the outside world via fax machines.[25] Yet none of these periods of greater openness or intellectual ferment took root. Instead, they ended in violence and were followed by a period of intense political repression.

The arrival of the Internet in China in the late 1980s held the promise of breaking the traditional dynamic of control between the rulers and the ruled. It introduced a new level of transparency and connectivity into Chinese political, social, and economic life, allowing Chinese citizens to communicate across geographic and socioeconomic boundaries. Yet from the outset, the Chinese government understood the underlying threat to its authority that unfiltered access to information would present. Chinese netizens pushed boundaries and explored the virtual world, presenting new challenges to the control of the Communist Party, and seeking ways around the obstacles the government placed in front of them. The Chinese government, while occasionally able to foresee the challenge, generally chased after the netizens, trying to determine which activities posed a genuine threat and how best to respond.

You've Got Mail

The very first e-mail in China was sent in September 1987[26]—sixteen years after American Ray Tomilson sent the first e-mail in the United States.[27] It broadcast a triumphal message: "Across the Great Wall we can reach every corner in the world."[28] For the first several years, the government reserved the Internet for academics and officials. But once Beijing opened Internet service to the general public in 1995,[29] it celebrated its arrival with great enthusiasm: with only 150,000 Chinese people connected to the Internet, the government deemed 1996 the "Year of the Internet," and Internet clubs and cafes sprouted everywhere in China's largest cities.[30]

Yet as enthusiastically as the government proclaimed its support for the Internet, it also took steps to assert its control over the new technology, issuing a temporary set of regulations, mandating that all Internet connections would be channeled through international ports established and maintained by the government.[31] As Oxford scholar Rogier Creemers noted, "as the Internet became a publicly accessible information and communication platform, there was no debate about whether it should fall under government supervision, only about how such control would be implemented in practice."[32] By 1997, Beijing had enacted its first Internet laws (following interim regulations in 1996[33]) criminalizing Internet postings that it believed were designed to hurt national security, the interests of the state or of a group, or to disclose state secrets,[34] and, by July of that year, Chinese police were searching for advanced filtering software at a conference in Hong Kong.[35]

China's leaders were right to be worried. Their citizens quickly realized the political potential inherent in the Internet. In 1998, thirty-year-old software engineer Lin Hai forwarded thirty thousand Chinese e-mail addresses to a U.S.-based pro-democracy magazine. Lin was arrested, tried, and ultimately sent to prison in the country's first known trial for a political violation committed completely via the Internet.[36] A more troubling event for the country's leaders occurred the following year, when the spiritual organization Falun Gong used e-mail and cell phones to organize a silent demonstration of more than ten thousand followers around the party's central compound, Zhongnanhai, to protest their inability to practice freely. The gathering, which had been arranged without the knowledge of the government, served as a wake-up call for officials, and precipitated an ongoing hunt and persecution of Falun Gong practitioners, as well as a new determination to exercise control over the information that flowed through the Internet.[37]

Nailing Jello to the Wall

The man who emerged to lead the government's effort to control the Internet on the technological front was Fang Binxing. Fang, who earned his PhD in computer science at the Harbin Institute of Technology during the tumult of the 1989 Tiananmen Square demonstrations, began working on homegrown software to manage Internet content in 1999, just at the time of the Falun Gong demonstration. As deputy chief engineer at the state-run National Internet Emergency Response Center,[38] Fang worked on developing the "Golden Shield"—transformative software that enabled the government to inspect any data being received or sent and to block destination IP (Internet protocol) addresses and domain names.[39] Fang's work was rewarded by a swift rise up the political ladder. He became chief engineer and director of the center one year later, and eventually rose to become president of Beijing's University of Posts and Telecommunications.[40] By the 2000s, Fang had earned the moniker the "Father of the Great Firewall" and, eventually, the enmity of hundreds of thousands of netizens for his ongoing efforts to control their access to information.[41]

Technology alone, however, was not enough to prevent a burgeoning number of Chinese netizens from expanding their virtual worlds. Throughout the early 2000s, the Chinese leadership supplemented Fang's technology with a set of new regulations designed to ensure that anyone with access to China's Internet—either domestic or foreign—played by Chinese rules. In September 2000, the State Council issued Order No. 292, which introduced new content restrictions that required Internet service providers to make sure that the information sent out on their services adhered to the law and that domain names and IP addresses were recorded for providers engaged in media or online bulletin boards.[42] Two years later, Beijing blocked Google for the first time.[43] (In 2006, Google introduced Google.cn, a censored version of the site.[44]) That same year, the government also increased its emphasis on self-censorship with the Internet Society of China's "Public Pledge on Self-Discipline for China's Internet Industry," which established four fundamental principles for Internet self-discipline: patriotic observance of law, equitableness, trustworthiness, and honesty.[45] Over one hundred companies, including U.S. information-technology leader Yahoo! Inc., signed the pledge.[46] In addition, the Ministry of Information Industry and General Administration of Press and Publishing outlined a set of restrictions governing Internet content, banning any material that might harm national unity and sovereignty, reveal state secrets, damage the reputation of the state, or contribute to social unrest.[47]

Perhaps the most significant development during this period, however, was a 2004 guideline on Internet censorship issued by the Ministry of Education and CYL that called for Chinese universities to recruit politically trustworthy Internet commentators who could write and publish posts that would guide Internet discussions in politically acceptable directions. Local party officials soon followed suit, organizing training programs for commentators who could shape online conversation and report on comments that did not follow Chinese law. These commentators became known as *wu mao dang* (五毛党), or "fifty-cent party," for the *wu mao*, or roughly seven cents that they earned as a bonus to their regular salary for each post.[48] Over time, the posts of these content monitors have become fodder for netizens' humor and sarcasm.

With each new challenge, the government added to its toolbox. In spring 2005, for example, Beijing and Shanghai residents used the Internet to organize large-scale anti-Japanese protests. Some analysts called these protests "a wakeup call for the government's censors."[49] Several months later, the Chinese leadership held a meeting in the northeast city of Qingdao to discuss methods for managing the Internet.[50] The result of the protests was improved keyword filtering systems and a set of new regulations mandating what constituted an Internet news service organization and what such groups could publish.[51]

Even as the government worked to enhance its capacity to limit Chinese citizens' access to information, however, the netizens were making significant inroads into the country's political world—both virtual and real. Their primary target was addressing the corruption and abuses perpetrated by local officials.

A Virtual Political System

In February 2009, in the southwest province of Yunnan, a twenty-four-year-old farmer, Li Qiaoming, who had been imprisoned on charges of illegal logging, was found dead. According to officials, while a prisoner, he had been playing a game of *duo maomao* (躲猫猫) or "elude the cat"—a game similar to Marco Polo, in which a person is blindfolded and attempts to find others through the sound of their voice. Reportedly, during the course of the game, Li incurred a fatal head injury.[52] The incident sparked outrage among netizens, who assumed that the local police had beaten him to death. "Elude the cat" quickly became an Internet buzzword,[53] and over seventy thousand posts were made regarding the case on QQ.com, a popular Chinese bulletin board.[54] As posts on the topic mounted, the media also started questioning the official report.[55] A poll on Sina.com found that 87 percent of online respondents did not trust the government's "eluding the cat" story.[56] Ultimately, after a committee made up of both officials and citizens investigated the incident, three other prisoners and two policemen were convicted and sent to jail.[57]

That same year, Deng Yujiao, a young woman working in a hotel in Hubei Province, stabbed a party official to death after she rejected his efforts to pay her for sex and he tried to rape her. Police initially committed Deng to a mental hospital.[58] A popular blogger, Wu Gan, with more than thirty thousand Twitter followers, however, publicized her case. Using information gathered through "human flesh searches" (*ren rou sousuo*, 人肉搜索), in which netizens collaborate to identify and reveal the identity of a specific individual or organization, Wu wrote a blog describing the events and actions of the party officials involved.[59] In an interview with the *Atlantic* magazine at the time, he commented, "The cultural significance of flesh searches is this: In an undemocratic country, the people have limited means to get information. Information about [the activities of] public power is not transparent and operates in a black box, [but] citizens can get access to information through the internet, exposing lies and the truth."[60] Strong public support for Ms. Deng's case took shape on and offline, with young people gathering in Beijing with signs reading: "Anyone could be Deng Yujiao."[61] The court ruled that Deng had acted in self-defense.[62]

The latter years of Hu Jintao's tenure witnessed a remarkable rise in the use of the Internet as a mechanism by which Chinese citizens held their officials accountable. Most cases were like those of Li Qiaoming and Deng Yujiao: lodged and resolved at the local level. A very few, however, reached central authorities in Beijing. On July 23, 2011, a high-speed train in China derailed in Wenzhou, a coastal city renowned for its entrepreneurial spirit, leaving at least 40 people dead and 172 injured.[63] In the wake of the accident, Chinese officials told journalists to use only information "released from authorities," banning them from investigating, commenting, or reflecting on the crash. However, local residents who arrived at the scene quickly snapped photos of the wreckage being buried instead of being examined for evidence. The photos went viral and heightened the impression that the government's main goal was not to seek the true cause of the accident.[64] A Sina Weibo poll—later blocked—asked Internet users why they thought the train wreckage was buried: 98 percent (61,382) believed it represented destruction of evidence.[65] Dark humor spread among Chinese netizens: "How far are we from heaven? Only a train ticket away," and "The Ministry of Railways earnestly requests that you ride the Heavenly Party Express."[66]

The popular pressure resulted in a full-scale investigation of the crash, and in late December, the government issued a report blaming poorly designed signal equipment and insufficient safety procedures. As many as fifty-four officials faced disciplinary action as a result of the crash.[67]

The Internet also provided a new sense of community for Chinese citizens, who mostly lacked the robust civil society organizations found in more open political systems. In July 2012, devastating floods in Beijing led to the evacuation of more than sixty-five thousand residents and the deaths of at least seventy-seven people. Damages totaled an estimated $1.88 billion. Local officials failed to respond effectively: police officers allegedly kept ticketing stranded cars instead of assisting residents, and the early warning system did not work. Yet the real story was the extraordinary outpouring of assistance from Beijing netizens, who volunteered their homes and food to stranded citizens and even drove to the airport to help the eighty thousand or more stranded passengers.[68] In a span of just twenty-four hours, an estimated 8.8 million messages were sent on Weibo regarding the floods and 520,000 were posted to help organize netizens to pick up people who were stranded. Of course, many also used Weibo as a forum to complain about inadequate infrastructure.[69] The story of the floods became not only one of government incompetence but also one of how an online community could transform into a real one.

The Party Goes Online

While the Chinese people explored new ways to use the Internet, the Chinese leadership also began to develop a taste for the new powers the Internet offered. Enhancing the accountability of local governments was one important new direction. The 2010 State Council Information Office's white paper "The Internet in China," for example, called on governments at every level to address all the problems reported by the Chinese people via the Internet.[70] In this way, the Internet soon became a popular mechanism for the government to learn about official corruption.[71]

In addition, party leaders recognized that the Internet could serve as a transmission belt for government views to be disseminated to the people. As early as 2004, the Chinese government began to stress the influence that the Internet could have on public opinion.[72] In July 2007 following a scandal in which children were found working at a Shanxi brick kiln, the government provided guidance to major Internet sites, stating that "[websites must] intensify public opinion guidance and management on the Internet of the Shanxi Kiln Affair . . . . [Websites must] regularly release positive and authoritative information, and regularly report information about related people receiving medical treatment and being safely relocated, leading to a favorable online public opinion. Internet opinion must cool off rapidly."[73] The MPS also actively promoted the use of microblogs by officials, and by 2013, government bodies operated approximately sixty thousand Weibo accounts.[74]

The government also viewed the Internet as an opportunity to assess the opinions and concerns of the Chinese people. Harvard University professor Elizabeth Perry points to the use of social media and technology by the propaganda arm of the Jincheng Coal Group in Shanxi Province during the company's privatization process. The company gathered the thoughts of workers via blogs and e-mail and used the information to help smooth the process of privatization.[75] In another case, authorities in Xiamen undertook an online poll to assess public antipathy toward a planned PX plant in 2007 that thousands had protested.[76]

China's leaders appreciated the ability of the Internet to enhance their understanding of citizens' concerns, shape public opinion, and improve local governance. Yet as the Internet increasingly became a vehicle for organizing local protests, concern within the leadership mounted that the Internet might be used to mobilize a large-scale political protest—one that crossed provincial boundaries and threatened the legitimacy of the central government as opposed to challenging the authority of local officials.

An Internet Revolution

In 2008, the *People's Daily* opened a Media Opinion Monitoring Office to report on and analyze online comments and send reports to government officials on the prevailing attitudes toward controversial topics on a daily and weekly basis.[77] It also reported on the ability of local governments to respond to Internet-based mass incidents.[78] While the Chinese government may not have liked criticism of its policies and actions, what triggered the greatest concern and most censorship was the potential for large-scale mobilization. A 2013 study of censorship on Chinese social media by a group of Harvard University scholars revealed that criticism of the state was less likely to be censored than comments that contributed to spurring collective action.[79] The incidents cited by the report included a number of protests between 2011 and 2013 that involved citizens organizing behind causes related to environmental quality, law enforcement, and natural disasters, among other topics.

As uprisings spread throughout the Middle East during the early months of 2011, the government's concern appeared prescient. A few Chinese citizens and expatriates started to call for their own "Jasmine Revolution." Like their African and Middle Eastern counterparts, the Chinese activists used the Internet to try to organize people to protest in support of political change. Chinese security forces rapidly locked down sites for the proposed demonstrations and arrested individuals suspected as sources of possible unrest. The protests ultimately proved ephemeral, with police far outnumbering demonstrators. However, the massive deployment of public security forces showed both the strength of the country's security apparatus and the leadership's acute insecurities, particularly regarding the ability of the Internet to facilitate organized opposition.[80] The word for "jasmine" (*moli*, 茉莉) was blocked on the Chinese Internet and in text messages.[81]

The Chinese leadership considered protests that crossed provincial boundaries particularly threatening. In Shifang, Sichuan Province, in July 2012, for example, thousands of people rallied to oppose a proposed $1.6 billion molybdenum-copper alloy refinery because of its potential environmental and health risks.[82] The protests received considerable attention on Weibo: nearly 5.25 million posts with the word "Shifang" appeared between July 1 and July 4, 2012, and nearly 400,000 images related to the protests circulated online.[83] On one day, "Shifang" was the most searched Weibo term,[84] although coverage in traditional media was almost nonexistent. As a result of the protests, the plans for the factory were ultimately scrapped.[85] The Shifang protests, however, also inspired similar protests in other parts of China,[86] demonstrating the ability of the Internet to be used in cross-provincial protests, and lending credibility to Beijing's concern.

Beijing Fights Back

By 2011, as the voices of Chinese netizens grew louder and their demands proliferated, the Chinese government took notice. A June 2011 article in the *China Youth Daily* written by two scholars, Ye Zheng and Zhao Baoxian from the PLA's Academy of Military Sciences, expressed concern about the way outside forces could use the Internet to influence public views. They wrote, "The targets of psychological warfare on the Internet have expanded from the military to the public." They noted the "domino effect" that had occurred via the Internet during the Arab Spring and saw the United States as contributing to the problem:[87] "Of late, an Internet tornado has swept across the world . . . massively impacting and shocking the globe. Behind all this lies the shadow of America."[88]

Beijing sought new ways to tamp down the enthusiasm, expectations, and the growing sense of power that netizens were deriving from their online activism. Officials launched a campaign against "rumor-mongering," pressured social media sites to remove postings with unfavorable allegations,[89] and banned reporters from using information from the Internet that the authorities considered unverified. An article published by *Xinhua* in November 2011 argued: "Like all forms of vice and iniquity, Internet rumors are extremely infectious" and can result in "poisoning the social environment and impacting social order."[90] The government also reinforced its 2002 guideline requiring Sina Weibo users to register with either their cell phone numbers or their identity cards, and called on the company to review the posts of any user who had more than a hundred thousand followers, deleting any posts that are harmful to "national interests" within five minutes.[91] That same month, the official news service Xinhua reported that Sina Weibo and Tencent had both been punished for allowing rumors, particularly those of a potential coup in March 2012, to spread on their sites.[92] The commenting function on Sina Weibo was also suspended for three days during this period.[93] A 2012 study from Carnegie Mellon that reviewed content censorship in Weibo posts based on keywords discovered that of 57 million posts collected between June and September 2011,[94] over 16 percent of the posts were deleted nationwide.[95] For posts originating in Tibet, the deletion rate was as high as 53 percent.[96]

Internet activism in China exploded during the final years of Hu Jintao's tenure. The Chinese people logged on to engage in lively political social discourse, to gain access to the world outside China, and to organize themselves to protest against perceived injustices. The Chinese government responded with a stream of technological fixes and political directives to contain what they viewed as the most dangerous behavior; yet the boundaries of Internet life continued to expand.

The advent of Xi Jinping and a new Chinese leadership, however, brought a new determination to move beyond sounding warning bells, deleting posts, and passing regulations. Instead, Beijing began to seek to ensure that Internet content more actively served the interests of the Communist Party. Within the virtual world, as in the real political world, the Communist Party moved to silence dissenting authoritative voices, to mobilize the party in support of CCP values, and to prevent the influence of foreign ideas from seeping into Chinese political and social life.

@XiJinping

Early in his tenure, Xi Jinping embraced the world of social media. According to one Chinese scholar, President Xi saw WeChat, a popular mobile messaging app, and Weibo as important assets in the party's ongoing anticorruption drive.[97] Xi also used the Internet to develop a personal following. One Weibo fan group, "Fan Group to Learn from Xi," appeared in late 2012 much to the delight of Chinese propaganda officials. (Many Chinese suspected that the account was directed by someone in the Chinese government, although the account's owner denied any connections).[98] Xi allowed for a visit he made to Hebei to be live-blogged on Weibo by government-affiliated press,[99] and his 2015 New Year Address paid homage to the importance of social media, when he noted, "I would like to click the thumbs-up button for our great people."[100] The government even ignores its own regulations, by using Facebook, which is banned, to promote Xi's international profile, tracking his visits abroad on a Facebook page with infographics and scenic pictures.[101] The page has over 2,750,000 likes.[102] Videos about Xi, including a viral music video called "How Should I Address You" based on a trip he made to a rural mountain village, have become popular on social media and demonstrate the government's increasing skill at creating propaganda for the digital age.[103] Yet in late 2017, the government also displayed the limits of its openness to social media when it banned all references and images of the character Winnie the Pooh, which had begun popping up in 2013 as a popular stand-in for President Xi.

The Chinese government also recognizes the economic benefits of the Internet, and Xi's tenure has witnessed a dramatic expansion in the number of Chinese Internet users. In 2012, there were approximately 573 million Internet users. Four years later, there were over 720 million.[104] Chinese spend a significant portion of their leisure time—roughly one-third—on the Internet, particularly on mobile devices.[105] Most of the time is spent watching online videos or on social networks, while search, e-commerce, and news make up much of the rest of the average Chinese netizen's online time.[106] The American consulting firm McKinsey and Company estimates that sales in China's e-commerce market reached $760 billion in 2016, larger than those in the United States. More than one-third of Chinese citizens order online at least once per week.[107]

Yet whatever value the Chinese leaders may discern from a vibrant Internet is more than matched by the dangers they perceive. In a leaked speech from the National Propaganda and Ideology Work Conference in August 2013, Xi articulated a dark vision: "The Internet has become the main battlefield for the public opinion struggle."[108] With this in mind, he moved quickly to assert his personal control over the political institutions governing the cyber world. In February 2014, Xi assumed the chairmanship of the Central Internet Security and Informatization Leading Group,[109] also known as the Central Leading Group for Cyberspace Affairs (*Zhongyang Wangluo Anquan he Xinxihua Lingdao Xiaozu*, 中央网络安全和信息化领导小组), which had previously been headed by the premier.[110] Xi also elevated the political stature of the largely moribund State Internet Information Office, transforming it into the Cyberspace Administration of China. The two organizations are closely linked—the Leading

Group's administrative office is housed within the CAC[111]—providing Xi with not only broad directional oversight for Internet policy but also a more direct path to the actual bureaucracy responsible for formulating policy.

The official tasked with directing the Leading Group's office and heading the newly formed and powerful CAC during Xi's first years in office, Lu Wei, brought significant experience to the position. He had most recently served as minister of the State Council Information Office, but previously had a long career as a journalist and then an official for the Xinhua news agency.[112] Lu was a fierce proponent of Internet sovereignty and strong party control over content. While still vice president of Xinhua, Lu penned a July 2010 essay in *Seeking Truth*, the CCP's top political magazine, in which he argued that China should strengthen its control over information technologies, noting that "without information security, there is no financial security, there is no economic security, and there is no national security in the truest sense."[113] Lu proved a formidable political talent serving as both domestic Internet watchdog and the public face of China's international Internet diplomacy until his removal as CAC head in July 2016[114] and subsequent detention on charges of corruption in November 2017.

The Cyber Octopus

The optics could not have been better for Beijing. A smiling Facebook CEO Mark Zuckerberg stood beside a beaming Chinese Internet czar Lu Wei, with a carefully positioned copy of Chinese president Xi Jinping's collection of speeches and interviews, *The Governance of China*, sitting on a nearby desk.[115] No matter that Facebook had been banned in China since 2009,[116] Zuckerberg was doing everything he could to find a way into Beijing's good graces, and he knew that Lu Wei held one key to China's vast cyber world. However much he may have enjoyed his personal Silicon Valley tour, Lu demonstrated no interest in welcoming Facebook back to China. As he commented in response to a press query about Facebook's absence: "China has always been warm and hospitable, but I have a choice about who comes to be a guest at my home. I can say that I have no way of changing you, but I have a right to choose my friends."[117]

Lu's fingerprints were also all over the highly restrictive first draft of the cybersecurity law issued in July 2015 by the NPC.[118] Many aspects of the draft encoded into law policies or rights that the government already exercised and clarified previously gray areas.[119] For example, Article 50 (later Article 56 in the 2016 revised draft law) states, "To fulfill the need to protect national security and social public order, and respond to major social security incidents, the State Council, or the governments of provinces, autonomous regions and municipalities with approval by the State Council, may take temporary measures regarding network communications in certain regions, such as restricting it." This would put into law the ability that the Chinese government has previously exercised in cutting off the Internet in certain areas (such as Xinjiang and Sichuan[120]) during times of unrest. The law would also allow censors to delete and block content that violated Chinese laws and regulations.[121] For foreign firms, the draft law promised stringent requirements concerning data localization and restrictions on the transfer of "important data" overseas for business purposes.[122] The final law, which came into effect on June 1, 2017, mandated that a vast range of businesses—almost all that manage their own e-mail or other data networks—must allow access to their data, along with "technical support" to Chinese security officials upon the latter's request. One of the most onerous requirements for foreign firms was a measure that permits Beijing to access computer program source code, which is considered highly sensitive intellectual property. In addition, the requirement that all Chinese citizens' personal information gathered by companies be stored only in China reduces efficiency and increases costs for multinationals, which otherwise might store all their information on cloud data centers outside China.

Technology Is Our Friend

Xi Jinping's tenure has also been marked by technological innovation that has enabled the government to exert far greater control over the Internet. In January 2015, the Chinese government blocked many of the virtual private networks (VPNs) that citizens had used to circumvent the Great Firewall, such as Golden Frog, StrongVPN, and Astrill.[123] The nationalist newspaper *Global Times* attributed the change to an effort to upgrade the Great Firewall to enhance cyberspace sovereignty.[124] The clampdown was surprising to many outside observers. Most believed that given the role of VPNs in the Chinese economy—supporting multinationals, banks, and retailers among others—China would not crack down.[125] But, Beijing had even more technology to control the Internet at its disposal. In late March and April 2015, it launched the Great Cannon. Unlike the Great Firewall, which has the capacity to block traffic as it enters or exits China, the Great Cannon is able to adjust and replace content as it comes through the Internet.[126] One of its first targets was the U.S. coding and software development site GitHub. The Chinese government used the Great Cannon to levy a distributed denial of service attack against GitHub, overwhelming the site with traffic redirected from Baidu (a search engine like Google).[127] The attack focused on two sites in particular, the Chinese version of the *New York Times* and GreatFire.org, a popular VPN that helps people circumvent Chinese Internet censorship.[128] The University of Toronto's Citizen Lab called the Great Cannon a "significant escalation in state-level information control."[129]

Beijing frequently deploys its censorship technology during times of heightened political sensitivity. During July and August 2014, the government blocked a number of chat apps, such as Line, Talkbox, and Kakao Talk, ostensibly because they were permitting terrorism-related content.[130] More likely, however, the apps were blocked because of the pro-democracy protests in Hong Kong. Indeed, the beginning of Line service disruptions in China coincided with the anniversary of the date Hong Kong was returned to mainland China.[131] During the pro-democracy Umbrella Revolution protests in Hong Kong in September and October 2014, a number of social media platforms were censored. The government prevented mainland WeChat users from seeing certain pictures posted by Hong Kong–based accounts; interrupted Instagram service; and deleted a greater number of posts on Weibo than usual.[132]

After the crackdown on Sina Weibo in 2012–2013, many netizens preferred using Tencent's WeChat platform, which is driven by information exchanged among smaller groups of people who are mostly known to one another. The State Council's China Internet Information Center reported that 37 percent of users who left Weibo in 2013 began using WeChat instead.[133] Some WeChat accounts gained hundreds of thousands of followers, providing those account holders with an influential platform. However, even these accounts are not immune to suspension.[134]

What Is Okay and What Is Not

Xi Jinping's most noticeable gambit has been to constrain the nature of the content available on the Internet. For better or worse, he has provided greater clarity as to what is acceptable content. In August 2013, the Chinese government issued a new set of regulations: the "Seven Baselines" (*qitiao dixian,* 七条底线)—the Baseline of Laws and Regulations, of the Socialist System, of National Interests, of Citizens' Legal Rights and Interests, of Public Order, of Morality, and of Information Accuracy.[135] The baselines were intended to reflect the inviolable core interests of the party. An article supportive of the Seven Baselines in the *Southern Daily* stated, "While the Internet provides people with a convenient, fast and diverse experience, it has also become an important place for the spreading of rumors and the breeding of false information."[136] The reaction by Chinese Internet companies was immediate. Sina, for example, shut down or "handled" 100,000 Weibo accounts found to not comply with the new rules.[137]

Reminiscent of imperial Chinese leaders' ban on rumors, the government soon adopted tough restrictions on Internet-based rumors. In September 2013, the Supreme People's Court and Supreme People's Procuratorate ruled that authors of online posts that deliberately spread rumors or lies, and were either seen by over five thousand individuals or shared over five hundred times, could face defamation charges and be sentenced to up to three years in jail.[138] Following massive flooding in Hebei Province in July 2016, for example, the government detained three individuals accused of spreading "false news" via social media regarding the death toll and cause of the flood. One activist speculated on the government's fear that true details would come out saying, "I [think] it's the officials who are spreading rumors [in state-media reports], and the people should detain them instead."[139] Some social media posts and photos of the flooding, particularly of drowning victims, were also censored; unsurprisingly, state media reports highlighted the official account of events.[140]

An article in *Xinhua* defending the ban argued, "The newly unveiled rules offer answers for the lingering problem of unclear sentencing criteria for illegal Internet activities in China. As the Internet has grown into an easily accessible platform for the Chinese public, an increase in crimes such as defamation and blackmail has occurred online over the past few years."[141] Others were critical, however. Professor of law at the Beijing Institute of Technology Xu Xin argued that the ruling "violates the principles of criminal law."[142] Or as Chinese journalist Cheng Yizhong simply put it, "Rumors are the penalty for lies."[143]

In addition to lowering the bar for what is considered unacceptable content, one of the Xi-led government's most significant policy innovations was to target particular individuals who have large social media followings. These individuals, referred to as "big Vs" for their "verified" status, are capable of shaping and driving public discourse, at times in ways that directly challenge the authority of the Communist Party. Reining them in has been a priority for the Chinese leadership.

Kill the Chicken to Scare the Monkey

Billionaire real estate mogul, party member, and former PLA soldier Ren Zhiqiang boasted almost 38 million followers on Sina Weibo as of early 2016. His outspoken opinions earned him the moniker "cannon Ren," and his posts often seemed to skate right along the invisible red line of political acceptability.[144] In February 2015, for example, he wrote, "If our own value systems are superior to Western value systems, if China wishes to see the world accept our value system, then why can't the two systems be allowed to compete on the same platform publicly? Why is it necessary to fear the Western value systems?"[145] And on October 1, 2015, the sixty-sixth anniversary of the founding of the PRC, he posted, "This festival is not a celebration for the founding of a nation, but rather a celebration for a new government." Offline he was just as provocative. While giving a speech at Peking University, Ren called for the students to "push over the wall" and to rebuild a social-democratic society.[146] And speaking at the 2015 Annual Meeting of the China 50 Forum, a collection of leading Chinese economists, Ren gave voice to what many scholars and businesspeople said in private: "The government puts too much emphasis on guns and knives, and opposes Western ideals. The winds of the Cultural Revolution are starting to blow."[147]

One year later, however, Ren skated across the line. Criticizing Xi Jinping's mandate that the media needed to mirror the views of the party and act on behalf of the party, he posted, "When did the 'People's Government' turn into the 'Party's Government?'" In a later post, he wrote, "Once all the media is part of one family and stops representing the interests of the people, then the people will be cast aside and left in some forgotten corner."[148] For his comments, the CAC ordered Ren's blog account deleted; Beijing's propaganda bureau publicly attacked him for having "lost his party spirit" and "opposing the party"; and the Communist Party placed him on a one-year probation.[149] The party attack on Ren Zhiqiang did not go unanswered. Fellow business leaders, scholars, and media officials spoke out against the decision to silence Ren.[150] Nonetheless, the punishment held, and his blog went silent.

Ren's punishment was the latest in a series of attacks by Beijing on the country's most popular bloggers, many of whom used their platforms to push for greater political openness and most of whom had upward of 10 million followers. The party initially tried to coopt these influential figures. In August 2013, Lu Wei advised a group of social media celebrities that it was their responsibility to ensure that their commentary was positive and to promote values such as virtue and trust.[151] It soon became apparent, however, that the bloggers had little interest in toeing the party line. Throughout the fall, a number of the most prominent Chinese web influencers, including Internet consultant Dong Rubin, cartoonist Wang Liming, venture capitalists Xue Biqun (Charles Xue) and Lee Kai-Fu, and real estate mogul Pan Shiyi were detained or forced to "confess" their crimes on television, or in some cases virulently attacked in the Chinese media. The restrictions on big V users beginning in 2013 represented an important turning point in China's Internet life. Discussions began to move away from political topics to focus more on personal and less sensitive issues.[152] The impact on Internet traffic on Sina Weibo was dramatic: Coupled with the crackdown on Sina Weibo more broadly, web traffic on the platform dropped precipitously. According to a study of 1.6 million Weibo users commissioned by the UK newspaper the *Telegraph,* by 2013, the number of Weibo posts fell by 70 percent from 2011.[153]

The Moral Imperative

While the Chinese leadership has directed the majority of its energy in Internet governance to controlling both the nature of and people's access to content, it is also in the midst of exploiting the power of the Internet to launch a vast social experiment: the development of a social credit system. Designed for both companies and individuals, the objective of the social credit system is to monitor, rate, and shape the behavior of participants in a way that advances ethical behavior.[154] The government's plan is to collect data on individuals and corporate behavior via the Internet and develop a rating system that will provide benefits for good behavior and penalize bad behavior, such as not repaying debts or traffic violations.

The backbone of the system is the National Credit Information Sharing Platform, which was established in 2015. The platform collects data from local and central governments and from sectoral social-credit systems, and will—in the future—utilize data from commercial credit-rating companies. Since August 2015, the NDRC and People's Bank of China have authorized a total of forty-three pilot cities and districts to test social-credit systems.[155] Eight Chinese companies, such as Alibaba, Tencent, and Baidu, are also involved in the process. Sesame Credit—a government-designed program that is offered via Alibaba-affiliated Ant Financial—uses data provided by Alibaba's Alipay and provides a score to willing Alipay users. Alipay automatically collects data on users' shopping preferences but also offers them the opportunity to provide other information such as their legal and educational records. It then assigns users a score based on personal information, ability to pay, credit history, social networks, and behaviors. People who are labeled "trustbreakers" may be penalized in terms of job promotions or the right to own a house. Those Chinese with high-credit scores, however, may be rewarded with benefits such as fast-track airport security or greater ease in accessing loans. Despite the fact that the program is still in its pilot phase, the Supreme People's Court has maintained a list since 2013 of long-term debtors—a number that has reached almost 7 million—and has sought to ban them from air and high-speed rail travel.[156]

Some Chinese express concern about the totalitarian nature of the social-credit program. In an interview with the *Washington Post*, well-known novelist Murong Xuecun argued, "This is like Big Brother, who has all your information and can harm you in any way he wants."[157] Much as they did in the first decades of Chinese communist life, some neighborhood committees in Shanghai collect information on residents' behavior; yet today they contribute it to a computerized database. One of the first pilot projects—initiated in 2010 before the government-wide initiative—was launched in Suining County in Jiangsu Province. The pilot delved deeply into citizens' personal lives, penalizing them, for example, for failing to take care of elderly relatives or participating in demonstrations that blocked government offices. The local citizens protested, and the program was modified.

Yet other Chinese support the government's efforts. When I conducted an informal poll of fifteen Beijing citizens during a trip there in summer 2017, the results were striking: two were completely unaware of the social-credit system, while the rest were largely favorably inclined. As one said, "there is a lack of trust among people in China; the social-credit system will help to fix that." Many young Chinese, in particular, appear enamored of the system, using the social-credit scores as a screening mechanism for dates. Part of their comfort may stem from the system's familiarity. All Chinese citizens have a *dang'an*, or dossier, that begins when they enter school and includes information such as their educational background, grades, workplace assessments, health records, and any potential political liabilities. In many respects, the Chinese leadership has simply developed an expanded online version of this already well-entrenched system.

The Push for Internet Sovereignty

Xi's Internet policy is also distinguished by its efforts to control Chinese access to websites outside China. In November 2014, more than one thousand attendees, including a number of major international and domestic tech companies such as Microsoft, Amazon, Alibaba, Tencent,

Baidu, and Apple, gathered at China's first annual World Internet Conference.[158] At the end of the conference, Lu Wei led an effort, ultimately unsuccessful, to persuade attendees to sign a declaration that included a provision on "Internet sovereignty," which stated: "We should respect each country's rights to the development, use and governance of the Internet, refrain from abusing resources and technological strengths to violate other countries' Internet sovereignty, and build an Internet order for equality and mutual benefit."[159] Although the phrase "Internet sovereignty" was introduced in the 2010 State Council white paper on the Internet,[160] it has gained traction under Xi as a statement of China's position vis-à-vis foreign companies and countries in a broader context of international negotiations over global Internet governance.

Earlier Chinese censorship had been more clearly delineated based on what was domestic and what was international. The domestic issues were largely the remit of the Propaganda Department (also known as the Publicity Department), while the international issues (including the Internet) were under the authority of the State Council Information Office.[161] The CAC, with Lu Wei at the helm, however, fused the internal and the external. Speaking at a spring festival banquet in February 2015, Lu Wei stated, "We live in a common online space . . . this online space is made up of the Internets of various countries, and each country has its own independent and autonomous interest in Internet sovereignty, Internet security, and Internet development. Only through my own proper management of my own Internet, [and] your proper management of your own Internet . . . can the online space be truly safe, more orderly, and more beautiful."[162]

Internet sovereignty also reflects a desire on the part of the Chinese government to ensure that Chinese Internet companies dominate the Chinese market. Much in the way that the Chinese government has learned about market economics from the West and adapted and modified those principles for China, the leadership has embraced the Internet but shaped it to fit the needs of the Communist Party. It is a policy, as Michael Anti has put it, of "Block and Clone."[163] China blocks Facebook, Twitter, and YouTube, and hinders Google's search operations, which run through Hong Kong, while supporting homegrown Internet companies such as Baidu, Tencent, Renren (a Facebook emulator), Youku and Tudou (YouTube twins owned by one parent company), and Sina. The government's ability to ensure that its political restrictions—controlling content that comes in, is transmitted, and goes out—are followed is far greater with Chinese companies than multinationals. In addition, Xi Jinping has increased the challenge for foreign media and Internet companies to gain access to the Chinese public. In February 2016, the government announced a new set of restrictions banning any company that is even partly foreign-owned from publishing online media, games, and other creative content unless it has approval from the State Administration of Press, Publication, Radio, Film and Television.[164] The Ministry of Commerce is responsible for monitoring compliance with the new regulations, and any product that contains prohibited information will be banned.

Beijing's Cyber Army

The strength of the Communist Party's control over the Internet rests above all on its commitment to prevent information containing values and ideals it finds dangerous from spreading through the Chinese public. It has also adopted sophisticated technology, such as the Great Firewall and the Golden Shield, in service of its objectives.[165] Perhaps its most potent source of influence, however, is in the cyber-army it has developed to implement its policies.

Overall the number of people employed to monitor opinion on the Internet and censor content (deemed euphemistically "Internet public opinion analysts") is estimated to be 2 million according to the *Beijing News* in 2013. They are employed across government propaganda departments, private corporations, and news outlets.[166] One Harvard study reviewed a cache of almost 44,000 posts by China's fifty-cent party, in one district of a city in Jiangxi Province and discovered that over 99 percent of those posts originated from government employees. Overall, the authors estimate that the Chinese government fabricates and posts approximately 488 million comments on social media annually.[167] A considerable amount of censorship is conducted through the manual deletion of posts and an estimated 100,000 people are employed by both the government and private companies just to do manual censorship.[168]

Policies are implemented on both the national and local levels. Local officials also may invest in their own specially tailored monitoring systems; they are particularly concerned about the potential for local unrest to embarrass them.[169] More often, however, the various agencies involved in Internet supervision and regulation issue new laws and regulations that then flow down through the various levels of government.[170] Additionally, many government departments have Internet divisions of their own. Each major ministry has divisions that focus on how to collect and interpret information gathered on the Internet, allowing them to monitor online chatter.[171]

Private companies also play an important role in implementing and facilitating Internet censorship in China. As the state has become more supportive of private enterprises, particularly Internet and technology companies, the government has demanded that these companies adhere to censorship regulations. Few businesspeople publicly rebel or complain against this as the business opportunities are too valuable. As the CEO of Youku Tudou, Victor Koo, said, "there's no incentive for us to be a force for unrest."[172] Since commercial Internet content providers play such a large role in censoring the content on sites that they host, Internet scholar Guobin Yang argues, "It may not be too much of a stretch to talk about the privatization of Internet content control. Through privatization, the party-state delegates part of the responsibility of control to private firms."[173] The process is made simpler by the fact that several major technology entrepreneurs also hold political office. For example, Robin Li of Baidu is a member of the advisory legislature the CPPCC; Lei Jun, founder and CEO of cell phone giant Xiaomi, and Pony Ma, Tencent founder, are both representatives of the NPC.[174] In addition, in October 2017, the government announced that it planned to acquire special management shares equivalent to a 1 percent stake in companies such as Tencent and Youku Tudou in exchange for a position on the companies' boards.

The MPS further ensures compliance by Internet companies by placing "network security officers" at important Internet sites and firms.[175] The deputy minister of the MPS has stated that the practice, which was implemented in August 2015, was designed to "catch criminal behavior online at the earliest possible point."[176]

There are clear signs that the increased effort by Xi Jinping and the rest of the Chinese leadership to gain greater control over the Internet is making gains: important voices have been silenced; foreign entertainment content has been diminished; and a wider range of content is subjected to censorship. Such actions are not without cost, however. The country's reputation, scientific innovation, and economic development all are hampered by the growing technological and political constraints placed on Chinese netizens. Moreover, the Chinese people continue to engage politically via the Internet, protesting unpopular decisions and policies both online and in the real world.

People Power Persists

In early March 2015, just days prior to International Women's Day, five Chinese women's rights activists were detained, the first such incident since 1913.[177] The group, which became known as the "Feminist Five," had previously protested domestic violence by wearing blood-stained wedding dresses and engaging in occupations of men's rest rooms to advocate for larger women's bathrooms. On the day they were detained, they were planning a multi-city protest against sexual harassment. They were held for over a month without formal charges filed; eventually the police accused them of "gathering crowds to disturb public order."[178]

Online support for the group erupted. A petition circulated the Internet advocating an end to their detention, and other feminist activists launched digital campaigns and established new social media accounts to post updates about the case. One Chinese netizen writing on Weibo expressed surprise at the cause of their detention: "Who knew a few young women opposed to groping on public transportation could frighten the authorities this much?" Pictures and messages tracking the length of the women's detention appeared online. Well-known Chinese human rights activist Zeng Jinyan wrote in the *Guardian* that there were a variety of digital tools at the activists' disposal: "WeChat and Weibo could be used to educate or increase support among broader audiences while encrypted mobile applications that changed when the government caught on could be used for more sensitive discussions about strategy."[179]

The government tried to contain the online outrage by censoring key terms such as the names of the group's members paired with "women's rights" or "release." Yet the group had already become an international cause célèbre. The hashtag #FreeTheFive became popular on Twitter, Facebook, and other forms of social media. The online conversation translated into on-the-ground action as well. In Chinese cities such as Beijing and Guangzhou, as well as in cities outside China, such as New York and New Delhi, people marched to protest the detention. Some went so far as to wear masks featuring the five women's faces. Particularly challenging for the government was the fact that Xi Jinping was co-hosting a meeting at the United Nations on women's rights while the five were under detention. Even former U.S. Secretary of State Hillary Clinton—who had two decades earlier attended the first UN women's conference in Beijing—joined in, retweeting a post about the detention and adding, "Xi hosting a meeting on women's rights at the UN while persecuting feminists? Shameless."[180] In the face of both domestic and international pressure, the five were released thirty-seven days after their original detention. Since then, they have continued to push for women's rights; for example, they raised money via crowd-funding to place an ad in a Guangzhou metro station warning about sexual harassment on trains.[181]

While the regime fears the overt challenge posed by online and real-time protests, such as that of the Feminist Five, there are other less obvious—but potentially equally concerning—costs to Beijing that flow from its desire to control so tightly the flow of information to its people. Innovation, economic growth, and government credibility all suffer.

Innovation Damper

The Chinese leadership, as we will see in chapter 5, is expending extraordinary economic and human capital to become a global leader in innovation. Part of its commitment is to expand the role of the Internet throughout the economy. Yet creativity and innovation thrive in an environment in which information is transparent and easily accessible. Interference with VPNs, for example, affects a range of people from "graphic designers shopping for clip art on Shutterstock" to "students submitting online applications to American universities."[182] Many Chinese businesspeople and academics argue that the loss of access to VPNs limits their ability to be innovative. As one young Chinese news editor said, "I feel like we're like frogs being slowly boiled in a pot."[183] Indeed, the restrictions on the Internet, as well as other lifestyle factors, may make some young Chinese who are educated abroad less interested in returning to China to work. In considering their plight, University of Pennsylvania professor Avery Goldstein writes, "If they aren't able to get the information to do their jobs, the best of the best might simply decide not to go home."[184]

Scientific innovation, particularly prized by the Chinese leadership, may also be at risk. After the VPN crackdown, a Chinese biologist published an essay that became popular on social media entitled "Why Do Scientists Need Google?" In the essay, he referred to the importance of Google Scholar and wrote:

> If a country wants to make this many scientists take out time from the short duration of their professional lives to research technology for climbing over the Great Firewall and to install and to continually upgrade every kind of software for routers, computers, tablets, and mobile devices, no matter that this behavior wastes a great amount of time; it is all completely ridiculous. To say nothing of the fact that this country says that it wants to respect and develop science. Science is done by people and this kind of sealing off is not engaging in respect for scientists.

He added that because of the restrictions on access to information, a generation of young people will grow up not understanding the knowledge that they don't possess and will not develop some of the traits necessary to become scientists.[185] Another scientist, Zheng Wan, publishing in *Nature,* shared his frustration with the Chinese government's censorship and lack of access to reliable data. He explained, "With no access to Google Scholar—which I prefer over other search engines, because it combines books, papers, theses, patents and technical reports— I have to keep track of trends by individually searching the databases operated by publishers that are still accessible."[186] Since the restrictions prevent many scientists from accessing their Google Scholar pages, this not only hurts their own access to information, but it also reduces their ability to disseminate their research and improve China's image in the scientific world.

Constricting the Internet, Constricting Growth

There are also real, measureable economic costs to an Internet that either does not work efficiently or limits access to information. Notoriously unreliable and slow, China's Internet ranks ninety-first in the world in speed.[187] As *New Yorker* writer Evan Osnos queried in discussing the transformation of the Chinese Internet during Xi's tenure, "How many countries in 2015 have an Internet connection to the world that is worse than it was a year ago?"[188]

A 2016 survey conducted by the European Chamber of Commerce in China found that 26 percent of European companies felt that slow Internet speeds and restrictions on access were harmful to their business, and 23 percent said that they could not access information and undertake necessary research as a result of China's Internet restrictions. Even more telling, 22 percent believed that Internet restrictions cost their companies the equivalent of 10 percent of annual revenues or more; this represented an increase from 13 percent the year before.[189] While Beijing may be willing to tolerate such economic losses, changing Internet regulations also affected the fortunes of national champions. Fanfou.com, a Twitter clone, for example, was completely shut down for more than a year as a result of the Xinjiang protests in 2009.[190] And Sina's revenues may have been hurt by the crackdown on big V Weibo users, which contributed to a loss in users and the advertising money that accompanies them. The same censorship likely also decreased the valuation of Weibo during its initial public offering (IPO) in 2014.[191]

Costs to Credibility

More difficult to gauge is the cost the Chinese leadership incurs to its credibility within the broader population, as well as among significant segments of the educated elite. Netizens criticizing the Great Firewall have used puns to mock China's censorship system. Playing off the fact that the phrases "strong nation" and "wall nation" share a phonetic pronunciation in Chinese (*qiangguo*), some began using the phrase "wall nation" to refer to China, even going so far to modify the phrase "strong nation dream" with a "wall nation dream."[192] Those responsible for seeking to control content are particularly subjected to popular derision. Fang Binxing, creator of the Great Firewall, is a case in point. Fang has been the target of thousands of attacks—most of them via the Internet—but some in real space as well. When Fang opened an account on Sina Weibo in December 2010, he quickly closed the account after thousands of online users left "expletive-laden messages" accusing him of being a government hack. Censors at Sina Weibo blocked "Fang Binxing" as a search term; one Twitter user wrote, "Kind of poetic, really, the blocker, blocked."[193] And Michael Anti commented, "We Chinese have now become second class citizens in the Internet age. A whole generation is suffering from the lack of freedom of information, and definitely, Fang should be blamed for this."[194] When Fang delivered a speech at Wuhan University in central China in 2011, a few students pelted him with eggs and a pair of shoes. Posts on Weibo after the incident mocked Fang with messages such as "Fang Binxing, you have forgotten to block my shoe!"[195] Fang's retirement speech from his position as president of Beijing University of Posts and Telecommunications in June 2013 earned yet another round of attacks from angry Internet users.[196] Yet in the face of widespread popular criticism, Fang remains defiant, claiming in a February 2011 *Global Times* interview, "I regard the dirty abuse as a sacrifice for my country. . . . They can't get what they want so they need to blame someone emotionally."[197]

In addition, as we saw in the cases of the Wenzhou train crash, Chinese netizens have little patience for government efforts to cover up disasters. They widely criticized efforts by Beijing to control the narrative surrounding the August 12, 2015, blasts at a Tianjin warehouse that killed more than 170 people and injured as many as 700. Many Chinese complained online that the local television station was broadcasting movies and soap operas and that CNN reporting was obstructed by people yelling, "Don't let foreigners report on this." In the first day after the blasts alone, Weibo posts on the topic received more than 590 million views. A few days later, Weibo posts about the explosion had over 1.4 billion views, and "#Tianjin Tanggu massive explosion"

(#*Tianjin tanggu da baozha,* #天津塘沽大爆炸) received 3.32 billion Weibo views and more than 3.6 million comments.[198] One censored message asked, "Who will take responsibility?! Why would a warehouse full of dangerous materials be located right near residential areas?! The Tianjin city press conference this afternoon was like not having one at all."[199] This comment touched on two of the most sensitive topics for censors: references to the decisions surrounding chemical storage, and criticism of how the disaster was being handled by officials. The CAC punished a number of websites for their coverage of the blast: thirty-two were temporarily blocked and eighteen were shut down indefinitely.[200] Residents also used social media applications such as WeChat and QQ to communicate among themselves concerning compensation schemes—over 17,000 residences were damaged or lost. When the government's plan proved less than satisfactory, they protested. When the government released its report on the disaster in February 2016, it promised to punish 123 government workers. Compensation for those that lost their homes, however, reached only 16 percent of the price of the home along with some additional living expenses. The majority of the families affected elected not to return to the site.[201]

Conclusion

Xi Jinping and the rest of the Chinese leadership make no real distinction between the virtual and real political worlds and the threats inherent in each. They have moved aggressively to deepen the party's control over the Internet, adopt new censorship technologies, expand the number of regulations governing content on the Internet, increase the number of people assigned to monitor and report on violations of Internet protocol, and eliminate popular authoritative blogging voices. They have also worked to construct a Chinanet to prevent the influx of harmful foreign ideas.

There are significant costs to the government's Internet policy. The Communist Party's unwillingness to permit the free flow of information hurts its credibility among Chinese netizens, many of whom resent their inability to have access to a full range of information. CCP control impedes innovation by preventing scientists from participating fully in the international scientific community through Google scholar and reducing efficiency for businesses—both Chinese and foreign—because of slow and undependable service, as well as the intermittent or permanent blocking of important news and websites. China's staunch support of Internet sovereignty also costs it support in the international community.

At the same time, the relatively relaxed attitude of the Chinese people to many of the changes underway as a result of the social-credit system suggests they have a greater tolerance for government penetration of their lives and management of their personal information than others outside the country. Their political history has long engaged a deeper level of government access to information about their personal lives. Moreover, many Chinese appear to view the proposed system as a means of building trust in a society that has a serious trust deficit.

For the international community, Beijing's cyber policy is representative of the challenge that a more powerful China presents to the liberal world order, which prioritizes political values such as freedom of speech, as opposed to China's effort to constrain the range of ideas on the Internet. It also reflects the paradox inherent in China's efforts to promote itself as a champion of globalization, while simultaneously advocating a model of Internet sovereignty and closing its cyber world to information and investment from abroad. As the following chapters illuminate, it is a pattern that is replicated in the relationship between its economic reforms at home and its trade and investment behavior abroad.

4

The Not-So-New Normal

EVERYONE LOVES A SUREFIRE bet. And for more than a year, the Chinese stock market appeared to be just that. Over the course of 2014, the Shanghai Composite Index, which tracks all stocks traded on the Shanghai Stock Exchange, jumped 50 percent. The government was the market's biggest cheerleader. The Chinese state-run newspaper the *People's Daily* inked columns that hyped "4,000 is just the beginning." A sign outside a Shanghai bank proclaimed: "Keep in step with policy and seize market trends! Selling red hot: SOE reform, New Silk Road, the most bullish concept stocks!"[1]

It was not a hard sell. The Chinese people had become accustomed to the real estate market serving as their default investment, and with real estate an overleveraged and overbuilt sector, the government viewed the stock market as an attractive alternative. Rising corporate debt, particularly in the SOE sector, also contributed to the government's efforts to boost the Shanghai market: a rising stock market would allow indebted companies to raise new capital and help pay off their mounting loans, relieving some of the burden on the state banking sector.[2]

Cautionary voices were few. Independent Beijing-based economist Chen Long raised concerns about leverage in the system at the end of 2014. Nearly 5 million Chinese investors possessed margin accounts, meaning that they were borrowing from their brokers to buy stocks. And *Quartz* economic journalist Gwynn Guilford suggested "the madness is official," noting that while Chinese data in December 2014 indicated that demand for Chinese products both in and outside the country was weaker than expected, the Shanghai Composite Index continued to rise.[3]

Six months after these warning bells sounded, the bottom fell out. After reaching a seven-year high on June 12, 2015, the bubble burst and the value of the Shanghai stock market fell by nearly one-third.[4] And it wasn't only the Shanghai stock exchange. The smaller Shenzhen Composite was equally battered. Together they lost $3.4 trillion in the value of shares traded.[5]

The government intervened to prevent the market from a complete rout. The Chinese Security Regulatory Commission (CSRC) pledged almost $20 billion to be distributed among twenty-one brokerages to stabilize the market; at the same time, these firms promised not to sell any of their own proprietary equities. The government also permitted pension funds to invest up to 30 percent of their net assets in equities.[6] The state-supported Asset Management Association of China told investors to look upon the 20 percent drop as an "investment opportunity."[7] The Chinese leadership halted trading for shares equivalent to 40 percent of the stock market's capitalization and ceased IPOs. Beijing also mandated that state-owned brokers continue to buy stocks until the index reached a higher level and banned shareholders who held more than 5 percent of a company's stock from selling for six months.[8] By September, the Chinese government had spent an estimated $236 billion in its efforts to bolster the stock market.[9]

Most analysts understood the crash as a risk inherent in a too-frothy, overleveraged market. Some Chinese media and officials, notably chairman of the state-owned aviation behemoth Aviation Industry Corporation of China (AVIC) Lin Zuoming, however, blamed foreigners for the stock market collapse. Lin claimed the nation was under attack: "This short-selling directly challenged the ruling position of the Communist Party of China, testing the party's ability to manage the economy. The short-selling powers tried to use the plunge to make China's economy slump and its society to become unstable, even to mobilize a color revolution."[10]

Despite the government's best efforts, uncertainty continued. In January 2016, the CSRC introduced a new system of circuit breakers for the stock market: if indices fell 5 percent (from the previous close), trading would pause; if they dropped 7 percent, trading would cease for the day. The first day they were operational, the breakers went into action, halting trading, and causing a panic among investors. Day four brought a repeat performance, with the result that the CSRC abandoned the circuit breaker system on Friday, January 8.[11] By February, CSRC Chairman Xiao Gang was out of a job.[12]

Making Money

By themselves, the stock market travails might have been chalked up to a singular, rather spectacular, case of financial mismanagement. However, as the government moved to rescue the stock market, it was also creating uncertainty elsewhere. In comments before the International Monetary Fund (IMF) in April 2015, People's Bank of China (PBOC) Chairman Zhou Xiaochuan stated that China had learned a lesson from the global financial crisis and would establish its own path for managing its currency: "The capital account convertibility China is seeking to achieve is not based on the traditional concept of being fully or freely convertible . . . . China will adopt a concept of managed convertibility."[13] In August, the PBOC announced a 1.9 percent devaluation of the Chinese currency and indicated that, rather than have the daily rate be set primarily and arbitrarily by the PBOC itself, the rate would now be set based on the previous day's closing rate on the onshore renminbi (RMB) market combined with other factors in the currency market.[14] This moved the Chinese government one step closer to a market-based rather than government-determined value for its currency. This was a move that China's most reform-oriented economists and the international financial community had advocated but that the government had resisted; it did not want to lose its ability to use the currency as an economic lever for accomplishing other economic goals, such as boosting exports by devaluing the RMB. Driving this decision to enhance the role of the market in managing China's currency was, in part, the government's desire to see the renminbi join the dollar, pound, euro, and yen in the IMF's strategic drawing rights (SDR) basket of reserve currencies. While the practical significance of having the renminbi in the basket was small, the reputational value was significant. It would, along with the growth in the RMB's use in trade between China and other countries, be a marker of equality for China's currency along-side other global currencies, in particular the dollar. When the IMF indicated it would accept the RMB into the SDR, it did so with the understanding that Beijing would continue to make progress on making the value of the RMB more market driven.[15]

The devaluation, however, was initially interpreted as a signal that the government had possibly reverted to a more interventionist policy. Thus, for many outside observers, it induced further confusion over Chinese government policy. It also had the unfortunate side effect of adding to another economic pressure Beijing was confronting. Chinese businesses and individuals had been accelerating their investments abroad because of concerns over the stability of the Chinese economy and attractive opportunities overseas. Chinese foreign currency reserves were being rapidly depleted as a result, causing consternation within the government. According to economist Mark Williams, the currency announcement had the effect of signaling to investors that the PBOC did not know what it was doing.[16] To stem the outflows, the Chinese government took steps to limit the ability of multinationals in China to repatriate their earnings, and the State Administration of Foreign Exchange limited foreign ATM withdrawals using Chinese UnionPay cards to around $7,860 (50,000 RMB) through the end of 2015. For 2016, the annual amount was set at approximately $15,700 (100,000 RMB).[17] One wealthy Chinese businessperson commented to me that whenever she seeks to transfer money outside the country, she receives calls from bank officials asking the purpose of the transaction. The government was also forced to spend significant amounts of its foreign currency reserves to prop up the RMB. From June 2014 to the end of 2015, Chinese foreign currency reserves experienced more than a $500 billion dollar drop from $3.993 trillion to $3.33 trillion.[18] By early 2016, the central bank had reverted to a mixed form of currency management: in some cases setting the RMB's value in reference to a basket of currencies, and in others pinning it to the dollar; in all cases, however, with reference to maintaining economic and political stability.[19]

Chinese President Xi Jinping's outward disposition through the turmoil in the Chinese markets was calm. He claimed that the economy would "stay on a steady course with fairly fast growth," and argued that the stock market had entered a "phase of self-recovery" after a period of ups and downs.[20] But the more than year-long tumult in the Chinese economy had taken its toll, costing the leadership credibility and raising questions about the future of the Chinese economy.

The Economic Reform Imperative

With the exception of the anticorruption drive, no issue is as central to the Chinese leadership's legitimacy as ensuring rising income levels. Doubling Chinese income levels from 2010 until 2020 is one of the tenets of Xi's Chinese Dream. Chinese public opinion polls suggest that more than absolute GDP growth, rising income levels are a significant source of popular support—and by extension of political stability—for the Chinese leadership.[21] China's economic success is also at the heart of China's rise as a major power. Double-digit economic growth and lifting hundreds of millions of people out of poverty are China's international calling cards, and a growing economy is essential for Beijing's ability to project its influence, whether through military or financial means.

On the face of it, Chinese President Xi Jinping and Premier Li Keqiang have little to worry about. Their predecessors Hu Jintao and Wen Jiabao achieved a series of high-growth markers: China became the world's second-largest economy, the world's largest exporter, and the world's largest construction site, operating half of the world's cranes. Chinese companies were also laying down markers globally at an impressive rate; in the cement industry, for example, they commanded more than 50 percent of the world market. And China was developing a reputation as a global financial power, pushing to increase its voting power in international financial institutions, such as the IMF, and seeking to promote the RMB as an internationally tradable currency on par with the dollar. The Chinese people were also growing wealthier. During 2001–2011, China's middle class expanded by 203 million people.[22]

Yet the country's economic model had also reached an inflection point. To compete at the next level, alongside the United States, Germany, and Japan, as well as other advanced economies, the country's leadership needed to shift from an economy reliant on low-cost, low-end manufacturing and exports to one supported by innovation, high-end manufacturing, and services. In addition, Chinese investment in heavy industry and infrastructure—an important source of GDP growth throughout the 1990s and 2000s—was allocated inefficiently. State-directed investment produced significant overcapacity in critical areas, such as cement, steel, and coal, and contributed to mounting corporate and local government debt. As China responded to the global financial crisis with another round of state-led investment in the domestic economy, local government debt doubled from 2009 to 2012.[23] Although the debt remained below that of other large economies, such as the United States, Japan, and Germany, some observers voiced concerns about the rate of the increase. The investment was also highly inefficient. A 2016 study of Chinese transport infrastructure by a group of Oxford University professors, for example, suggests that while Chinese projects are completed faster than the global average for advanced economies, average cost overruns are as high as 30 percent.[24]

Domestic consumption also remained far below that of both the world's more advanced economies, such as the United States, in which consumer spending accounts for almost 70 percent of GDP, and even that of some less developed countries, such as India, in which consumption makes up almost 60 percent of GDP. A consumption-based economy is more sustainable than one reliant on investment and exports; it signals higher consumer confidence and serves as an important indicator of people's preferences and allocation of resources. Yet Chinese consumption declined from 52 percent of GDP in 1985 to 37 percent in 2014.[25] As the government retreated from managing all aspects of the Chinese economy during these years, the social welfare net dissolved. Housing, medical care, education, and retirement all depended increasingly on the individual. Personal savings skyrocketed as Chinese citizens sought to ensure that they could meet their basic welfare needs.

The new Chinese leadership also confronted demographic challenges. Unlike the development trajectories of the world's wealthiest countries, China was in danger of becoming old before it became rich. The number of working-age Chinese was falling, while the number of retirees was rising. The implications were stark: fewer workers means higher wages, while a larger share of older workers means lower productivity and higher pension payouts. According to one Chinese expert, Beijing will have a funding gap of more than $12 trillion between what is being paid into the pension system and what the government will have to pay out. Already by 2015, twenty-two out of thirty provinces were calling on Beijing for help to meet pension shortfalls of more than $50 billion.[26]

Thus despite the much vaunted success of more than three decades of economic reforms, China's new leaders recognized that moving the economy to the next level of performance required a reboot. After taking office, Chinese President Xi Jinping almost immediately signaled his commitment to launching a new round of economic reform.

Early Promise

The message could not have been more clearly delivered. In mid-December 2012, just one month after assuming the position of general secretary, Xi Jinping traveled south to Shenzhen and Guangzhou, replicating the 1992 trip made by Deng Xiaoping. Deng's "southern tour" had heralded a renewed push for market-oriented economic reform, and two decades later, Xi appeared to be signaling a similar intent. Pictures in the Chinese media reinforced such an impression. Xi appeared planting a banyan tree—the same type of tree Deng planted during his tour—and placing a wreath of flowers at the foot of a statue of Deng.[27] There were also reports that Xi visited with several retired officials who had accompanied Deng in 1992. And in his remarks before a group of officials and entrepreneurs in Guangdong, Xi took pains to underscore his commitment to reform: "The reforms will not stop and the pace of opening up will not slacken."[28]

Xi's southern trip was soon followed by a number of official pronouncements that reinforced the impression of a reinvigorated commitment to economic reform. In a September 2013 speech, newly appointed Premier Li Keqiang outlined a number of critical reform objectives: dramatically reducing the role of government stimulus to boost the Chinese economy, deleveraging the financial system, and undertaking structural reform—including liberalizing interest rates, tax reform, and spending more on social welfare and public goods.[29] Li, who holds a PhD in economics, also focused attention on urbanization as a central element of China's economic reform process. Even before becoming premier, Li had stressed the importance of bringing rural Chinese into the cities, noting in a 2012 article that urban residential consumption is 3.6 times that of rural consumption, and therefore urbanization was at the heart of boosting domestic demand.[30] He advocated reforming the *hukou* system (the system of residency permits that defines where a Chinese citizen can work and earn social welfare benefits) in order to advance urbanization and the development of the middle class. A group of economists from Barclays bank branded China's potential new economic strategy "Likonomics."[31]

The most important signal of the leadership's intentions, however, was the economic reform agenda released at the Third Plenum of the 18th Party Congress in November 2013.[32] The agenda encompassed dozens of areas of reform and represented an ambitious roadmap for China's future economic development.[33] Foreign observers heralded the plan, calling it "one of the most detailed and potentially far reaching reform plans in China's modern history" and compared its scope to that of the 1978 Third Plenum of the 11th Party Congress that set in motion China's economic reform and opening up.[34]

The 2013 Third Plenum promised something for everyone. There were long-awaited financial reforms, such as liberalizing exchange and interest rates, land reform, and tax reform. The formal decision that emerged in the wake of the plenum also addressed broader issues of development such as relaxing the one-child policy, reforming the *hukou* system to enable a smoother and more equitable process of urbanization for migrant workers, and ensuring that China's growth was sustainable from an energy and environmental standpoint.[35]

The plenum was also noteworthy for introducing two new institutions to oversee economic policymaking: the Central Leading Group for Comprehensively Deepening Reform (which is responsible for reform in six broad areas, including economic, political, cultural, social, environmental, and party building), and a new Commission for National Security (which brings together domestic and foreign security concerns such as cybersecurity and terrorism).[36] The logic behind these new groups was straightforward: to streamline and rationalize coordination of economic and security decision-making. And, beginning to cement a pattern that became clear over the next several years, Xi Jinping assumed the chairmanship of each these new central oversight bodies.

The most important takeaway from the Third Plenum for a number of financial and other analysts was the apparent commitment to grant the market the "decisive role" in the Chinese economy. Traditionally, the market had occupied only a "basic" role in resource allocation. These analysts heralded the new direction. Stephen Roach, former chairman of Morgan Stanley Asia, said that the shift was "indicative of a strong commitment" to market reform.[37] Longtime China-watcher Bill Bishop stated that Xi had "clearly articulated resolve and vision for reform" and had enhanced his credentials as a "Dengist" as opposed to a "Maoist."[38]

Still, several analysts were less sanguine about the prospects for market-driven reform. They pointed to other language in the plenum's communiqué that suggested a less significant shift: "We must unswervingly consolidate and develop the public economy, persist in the dominant position of public ownership, give full play to the leading role of the state-owned sector, and continuously increase its vitality, controlling force, and influence."[39] How, some wondered, could the market be decisive when the communiqué also promised the continued commitment of the government to the leading role of the state-owned economy?[40] American Enterprise Institute resident scholar Derek Scissors was particularly skeptical, suggesting, "The only solution is a return to market-driven, politically difficult reform. Such reform must be focused primarily on rolling back the state sector."[41]

Questions regarding the capacity of the state to enforce its objectives also arose. Political analyst Alastair Newton, for example, noted that addressing challenges in policy implementation would be essential.[42] After all, "vested interests," including local officials, SOE heads, and even ministers of government agencies tied to economic planning and development, were unlikely to welcome radical reform that would diminish their role and importance. And there was confusion over the lines of authority in economic decision-making. The quality of the Chinese economic team was undisputed. Many of the most senior officials, such as Xi's top economic advisor Liu He, lead central banker Zhou Xiaochuan, and Finance Minister Lou Jiwei, were well-known and highly respected figures in the international business community. They had ably steered China through the global financial crisis, and there was general consensus that this was a group well suited to navigating the challenges of economic reform. However, Xi's assumption of leadership of the new commissions raised the specter of competition both between party and government entities and between Xi Jinping and Li Keqiang.

Underpinning the skeptics' analysis was also an understanding of Chinese history. The role of the state was deeply entrenched in the Chinese economy. For many periods in China's history, leaders had approached both the market and foreign trade with suspicion. Even if the new leadership were wholly committed to fundamental structural reform, there would be strong countervailing pressures and deeply ingrained beliefs concerning the importance of the state in managing the economy to overcome.

The Historical Legacy

Expanding the role of the market in China's economy is a tall order. The state has long played a significant, even dominant, role in managing the country's economic affairs. Imperial Chinese rulers often exerted a strong influence over the distribution of natural resources and foreign trade. At times they maintained a monopoly on valuable commodities, both to enrich the state and to help ensure social stability.[43] During the Yuan dynasty (1271–1368), officials supported robust overseas trade but took 70 percent of the profit. They also made the state the only legal entity engaged in foreign trade, before eventually adding restrictions on merchants trading abroad.[44] Rulers also worried that China might become too dependent on foreign actors and that foreign ideas, knowledge, and technology could "undermine the essence of what it meant to be Chinese."[45] Different rulers during the Ming dynasty (1368–1644) reflected widely disparate impulses: at first adopting an open and curious approach to the outside world, seeking to become an important seafaring power under the leadership of Admiral Zheng He, but later destroying the naval fleet and largely sealing off China's borders from foreign trade.[46] While the Qing dynasty (1644–1912) loosened the state's hold on trade, it nonetheless attempted to control the monetary benefits of trade through four maritime customs offices and the establishment of a steep tariff on foreign goods.[47] In addition, cultural factors came into play. The Qing discouraged some wealthy people from participating in the market, for example, because they believed that it would prevent them from living the "virtuous, moral life of the Confucian ideal."[48]

The weighty role of the state in the Chinese economy also limited institutional and other innovation. Chinese leaders failed to develop the institutions of a modern economy, such as a well-functioning banking or tax system. Innovation suffered from lack of incentive and competition; as economist Arthur Kroeber has noted, despite the fact that China was the world's largest economy in 1800, its global influence fell well short of Europe because it failed to embrace technological change.[49]

The Republican period (1912–1949) largely retained the central role of the state in economic development. As early as 1912, China's first Republican leader Sun Yat-sen argued: "All major industries in our country, such as railroads, electricity, and waterways ought to be owned by the state, so that no private individuals will be able to reap all the profits [from these undertakings]."[50] His successor Chiang Kai-shek established two commissions to oversee the development of the economy and foster plans for long-term economic development and nation building: the National Reconstruction Commission, and the National Economic Commission.[51] Between 1936 and 1945, the National Resources Commission founded or assumed partial or complete control over 130 heavy industry enterprises, including those in metallurgy, machinery, electrical equipment, chemicals, mining, energy, and services.[52] Deputy Director Qian Changzhao stated, "We should not repeat the mistake of capitalist countries in offering unlimited encouragement to private enterprise. There are not very many big capitalists in China today and consequently we may not have an urgent need to regulate capital. When the time for regulating capital finally arrives, however, we cannot afford to be excessively liberal about it."[53] And in 1942, Wu Bannong, a well-known Chinese economist, set out the "ten principles of state ownership," arguing that the state should own a significant subset of all industry including mining, metallurgy, machines, transportation, communication, national defense industries, public utilities, enterprises critical to the country's economy and individual's livelihoods, large-scale enterprises, and those with significant political and cultural value. Most enterprises outside of those should be managed by private parties."[54] The foundations for Chinese state control of the economy were thus established well before the CCP assumed power.

After the 1949 revolution, Mao Zedong and the CCP leadership only strengthened the role of the state in managing the economy. They argued that markets enabled wealthy capitalists to repress citizens and prevent economic equity. They adopted elements from the Soviet economic system that removed many of the market elements of supply and demand. Even as China moved away from the highly centralized Soviet model and toward a more decentralized system in the 1960s, the market remained virtually absent from the Chinese economy. Communes and commune brigades were entrusted to run smaller scale firms.[55] The lack of market mechanisms, however, remained a barrier to the efficient allocation of resources, and the egalitarian income distribution stunted the motivation, productivity, and creativity of farmers, workers, and firms.[56] By this time, the economy had evolved, through policy missteps and productivity inconsistencies, into a distinctively Maoist incarnation of the socialist command economy.[57]

Mao Zedong's death in 1976 provided the impetus for a rethinking of China's economic model. In 1978, Deng Xiaoping proposed a starkly contradictory approach to economic development, turning Mao's approach on its head. His plan encouraged some regions, firms, and workers to get rich based on their productivity, fostering an economic world that valued efficiency over egalitarianism.[58] Within a year, economic reform policies that liberalized prices, fostered competitive markets, and attracted foreign investment began to take root. Household farming returned, and the commune system was abolished in the early 1980s.[59] Small-scale township and village enterprises were permitted to produce and sell according to market demand. Special Economic Zones in many of China's coastal provinces drew foreign capital, boosted exports, and enabled China to reintegrate with global markets.[60]

Throughout the 1980s and 1990s, new policies emerged that further decentralized economic decision-making, encouraged citizens to become entrepreneurs, and permitted certain coastal cities to experiment with free market reforms.[61] While the state still remained the dominant force in planning core sectors of the economy, such as energy, raw materials, and defense, Deng's innovative approach unleashed the entrepreneurial energy of the Chinese people, as well as the benefits of international investment and expertise, that had been suppressed throughout most of Mao's tenure. Under the guidance of Premier Zhu Rongji in the 1990s, the government also consolidated state planning agencies, elevated the status of regulatory agencies, and took ambitious steps to reform China's inefficient SOEs.[62] Zhu also ushered in a new era of market reforms by spearheading China's World Trade Organization (WTO) accession in 2001.[63] By joining the WTO, China signaled its willingness to lower trade barriers, discourage unfair trade practices, and affirm the importance of the markets.

As noted earlier, the era of Hu Jintao and Wen Jiabao reflected a rapidly expanding Chinese economy that was more firmly integrated into the global economy than at any time in the country's history. At the same time, it produced a raft of economic and social challenges, and economic growth slowed. While China's growth rate had averaged 10 percent in the thirty years leading up to 2011—and indeed ran as hot as 12 to 14 percent in the mid-2000s—by the end of the Hu and Wen era, the government was struggling to maintain a rate of 8 percent.[64]

The Chinese leadership recognized the challenges the economy confronted, and the twelfth Five-Year Plan (2011–2015) reflected their understanding of the change necessary to move the economy forward. The plan called for transforming China into a more innovative economy, with a focus on strategic industries such as clean energy, new materials, and biotechnology; rebalancing the economy away from its reliance on exports and investment to increase the role of consumption; and ensuring that growth was environmentally friendly and sustainable.[65] In many respects the plan was a harbinger of the Third Plenum reforms.

Yet the Third Plenum, with its tantalizing reference to "the decisive role of the market," appeared to promise more. For the outside world, of particular interest was the implicit promise of reform of the SOE sector. The twelfth Five-Year Plan focused almost exclusively on strengthening SOEs to become national champions, capable of competing internationally and delivering large-scale domestic projects in areas such as power, rail, and communications at global standards.[66] The Third Plenum reform embraced by the new leadership appeared to offer a far greater commitment to structural reform of the sector. In broad terms, the plan proposed separating the state from direct management of enterprises, enabling and encouraging bankruptcy where necessary (both for SOEs and other enterprises), deregulating prices for energy and other resource inputs, inviting private investment into state-run firms, and reforming structures for pay and promotion. The international community, in particular, welcomed the initiatives as a sign that China's desire to increase the competitiveness of the sector would translate into a more level playing field for foreign firms.

Loud Thunder, Small Raindrops

Gao Xiqing speaks his mind. In his estimation, economic reform, particularly SOE reform, has stalled. Gao is in a position to know. Since the early 1990s, he has occupied senior roles in a number of China's most important economic agencies, including the China Securities Regulatory Commission, the National Council for Social Security Fund, and sovereign wealth fund China Investment Corporation. Retired in 2014 at the age of sixty, Gao now spends his time teaching at Tsinghua University and promoting Chinese innovation.

Certainly Gao is full of enthusiasm for the reform orientation of the Third Plenum. He believes it represents a move to cut the power of the government, to streamline state control, to reform SOEs, and to deal with the issue of overcapacity in a number of different respects. Yet sitting in New York before a packed audience at the Council on Foreign Relations two-and-a-half years after the plenum, Gao's assessment of the government's accomplishments to date and the likelihood of success moving forward is bleak.

Nowhere is stasis more evident than in efforts to reform the system of SOEs. Not only has there not been progress, Gao argues, but in a number of respects reform is moving backward. He notes that in several industries, monopolies that had been broken up during the days of Zhu Rongji have now reconstituted themselves.[67] Gao is not alone in his assessment. Ji Xiaonan, who heads the Supervisory Committee of Key Large-Sized SOEs within the State-Owned Assets Supervision and Administration Commission (SASAC) (the government oversight agency for the ninety-eight central and most powerful SOEs, such as China National Nuclear Corporation and the State Grid Corporation of China) reflected in a 2016 interview with Chinese media, "Progress on SOE reform is slow, and the focus and timeliness is clearly lacking. Now many scholars and members of the public are discussing its various aspects, and everyone has high hopes for reform . . . but the gap between reform and people's expectations is pretty large."[68]

Reforming the vast, entrenched system of SOEs is a herculean task. The process began at the outset of economic reform in 1978, when future Party General Secretary Zhao Ziyang enacted a pilot reform in Sichuan Province that permitted six SOEs to keep a portion of their profits and use them to invest in production, innovation, or workers' welfare. At that time, the state sector generated almost 80 percent of industrial output.[69] Six years later, SOEs began to sell their excess production for up to 20 percent more than the official price. Concerns over weak competitiveness prompted another round of reform in 1992–1993, in which SOEs could be leased or sold to the Chinese public or employees. The 1993 Company Law allowed SOEs to become corporatized, with a corporate board, and establish joint stock companies. The last significant effort began in the mid-1990s through early 2000s.[70] At that time, the Chinese leadership began privatizing all but the largest SOEs in a movement termed "grasping the large, letting go of the small" (*zhua da fang xiao*, 抓大放小).[71] As a result, employment in the SOE sector dropped by almost half from 70 million in 1997 to around 37 million in 2005.[72] Hu Jintao and Wen Jiabao, however, took steps to return SOEs to a position of centrality in the Chinese economy. In 2003, they established SASAC, which serves as both a shareholder and a regulator of nonfinancial SOEs, and initiated a crackdown on privatization through management buyouts. The 2009 stimulus—in the midst of the global financial crisis—further enhanced the strength of the SOEs because most stimulus funds were routed through them.[73] Successive reforms were smaller in nature and tended to increase rather than diminish the power of the state in the SOE structure. In 2009, for example, several ministries enforced a salary cap in which the senior-most SOE officials could earn no more than twenty times what the average employee did.[74] With these initial reforms, SOEs remained one of the pillars of the Chinese economy. Together, approximately 150,000 SOEs control over $21 trillion in assets and employ over 40 million people.[75] Some still play a significant role in social welfare, providing for the housing, education, medical, and other needs of their workers. In addition, except in rare circumstances, working for the Chinese state, whether in the government or in an enterprise, means a job for life. Chinese SOEs also make up the vast majority of the largest firms in China and are heavily represented in all capital-intensive sectors,[76] such as mining and energy. The central government controls roughly half of all SOE assets, while provincial and municipal governments manage the rest.[77] Whatever the level of government management, SOEs receive preferential interest rates when they borrow money, lower tax rates, and privileged access to resources, such as land. In 2015, SOEs were responsible for the purchase of 80 percent of all "land kings," plots of land that sold for record-breaking prices.[78]

Despite such advantages, or perhaps because of them, SOEs are notorious for overburdening the state and underperforming relative to private firms. Xiao Yaqing, who in early 2016 assumed leadership of SASAC, has stated that the competitive spirit of many SOEs "isn't strong."[79] Indeed, Xiao is likely understating the challenge. The list of SOEs' financial and other sins is a long one.

First, private firms consistently outperform SOEs on a number of measures including profit margins, cash flows, and return on assets.[80] Excluding financial institutions, SOEs earned a return on assets of 2.4 percent in 2014 compared with 6.4 percent for U.S. firms and 3.1 percent for Chinese companies listed on the stock exchange. Locally owned SOEs boast an even poorer return on assets of around 1.5 percent.[81] Despite this, private companies have a much more difficult time accessing capital and are assessed much higher interest on their loans: In the second quarter of 2016, they paid an average annual interest rate of 9.9 percent on loans—approximately 6 percentage points above the rate for SOEs.[82]

State-owned enterprises are also poor generators of new jobs. In early 2016, the State Administration for Industry and Commerce announced that single-owner and private companies accounted for roughly 90 percent of all new urban jobs.[83]

In addition, SOEs are a significant source of government debt. The outstanding debt of SOEs outside the financial sector is already nearly 120 percent of GDP.[84] In contrast, the debt level of SOEs in Japan and South Korea stands at around 30 percent of GDP.[85] Moreover, SOE debt represents roughly 75 percent of China's overall corporate debt. From 2011 until 2016, all forms of debt as a percentage of GDP—corporate, household, and government—grew significantly (see figure 4.1). This debt is the source of mounting concern both within Beijing and in the international financial community. According to the IMF, a rapid increase in debt often precipitates a financial crisis,[86] and China's increase is among the highest in recent history.[87]

Moreover, SOEs are major contributors to overcapacity. As the Chinese economy has slowed, overcapacity has become a particularly acute problem. Since SOEs typically do not pay dividends (except to the state and much of those are returned to the SOEs), they use the dividends to expand capacity and keep employment levels up. In the steel sector, for example, in 2015, China had 336 million tons of overcapacity and contributed 46 percent of the world's overcapacity.[88]

Finally, SOEs are prone to waste significant funds through misappropriation and fraud. In 2016, China's National Audit Office discovered that seventy subsidiaries related to ten large central SOEs spent over 1 billion RMB (around $150 million) on activities and goods, including luxury cars, fancy dining services in office, and travel to tourist sites. In some cases, SOEs paid senior officials "illicit allowances," even as the anticorruption campaign was underway.[89]

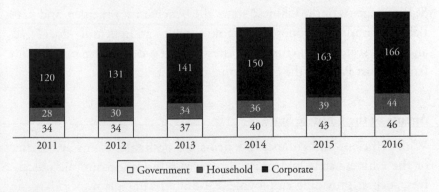

FIGURE 4.1 China's Debt-to-GDP Ratio by Sector (Percentage of GDP) from 2011 to 2016

Source: Bank for International Settlements; http://www.bis.org/statistics/tables_f.pdf

Reform Context

Despite the urgency conveyed by the Third Plenum, SOE reform did not begin in earnest until almost two years later in August 2015,[90] when the government released the "Guiding Opinions on Strengthening and Reform of State-Owned Enterprises," which was followed in December 2015 by a set of implementing guidelines,[91] and then again by another set of more specific reorganization guidelines for various aspects of SOE operations in July 2016.[92] Over the course of the year, from August 2015 to August 2016, SOE assets and liabilities both expanded,[93] placing greater pressure on Chinese decision-makers to move aggressively on their reform program.

The roadmap that emerged stressed partial privatization of SOEs, personnel incentives that are tied to firm performance, consolidation of SOEs, and relaxed state control over SOE management, especially for SOEs not in strategic sectors.[94] According to Zhang Xiwu, vice-chairman and deputy secretary of SASAC, 345 enterprises are targeted for reorganization or closure within three years, with coal and steel in particular targeted for a reduction of 10 percent of capacity over two years.[95] In each of five core areas of SOE policy reform—the role of the SOE in the Chinese political system, SOE management, SOE efficiency and competitiveness, the role of privatization, and the tolerance for SOE failure—however, the picture of reform suggests marginal rather than transformational change. The Chinese leadership has maintained its commitment to the dominant role of the state as opposed to the market. This commitment is reflected in the continued use of SOEs as agents of the Chinese state; the penchant for mergers and partial privatization as opposed to bankruptcy to address individual SOE and SOE sectoral structural weaknesses; and a deepening role for the Communist Party in the SOE management structure.

Agents of the Chinese State

While efficient and competitive firms are desirable, SOEs are agents of the Chinese state and must also serve other noneconomic objectives, such as providing employment, fulfilling strategic imperatives, or acting as brand ambassadors for the country. Xuan Xiaowei, a research fellow at the State Council's Development Research Center, noted in an interview that SOEs were established originally as a "big brother" to the Chinese working class, providing guaranteed lifetime employment.[96] And as independent economist He Qinglian has commented, the guidelines make very clear the primary purpose of SOEs: "SOEs are owned by the people as a whole . . . and are an important material base and political foundation for the development of our party and state."[97]

While the number of workers employed in Chinese SOEs is not overwhelmingly large relative to the overall workforce (about 40 million Chinese work in SOEs in a workforce of about 800 million), their influence is oversized in the Chinese political psychology and system.[98] Their jobs represent an implicit promise from a socialist state of guaranteed employment, and Chinese SOEs have long been holding pens for excess manufacturing labor. Productivity per person at Chalco, which used to be the largest aluminum producer in China, for example, is one-seventh of its private competitor Hongqiao.[99]

Initially, Chinese officials suggested that for SOE reform to be successful, excess labor would have to be cut. In February 2016, the minister of Human Resources and Social Security outlined a cut of 1.8 million workers, including 1.3 million from the coal industry and about 500,000 from the state sector.[100] The next month, Chinese officials suggested that as many as 5–6 million workers might be laid off by 2019.[101]

The specter of social unrest looms large. From 2014 to 2016, labor protests in China almost doubled to reach 2663.[102] Li Keqiang has therefore insisted that while excess labor has to be cut, firms need to transfer the workers to new jobs instead of laying them off,[103] and SASAC head Xiao Yaqing has said that restructuring should not come at the expense of social stability. At a press conference around the edges of the fourth session of the twelfth NPC in March 2016, Xiao stated, "Protecting the interests of SOE employees will be a major task in the next step." The message was transmitted through the Chinese media: the current round of SOE reform will not lead to the types of layoffs experienced during the 1990s round of SOE reform,[104] and the state media reported that the reform would mainly be pushed forward through mergers and acquisitions instead of bankruptcies.[105]

In addition to providing a safe haven for Chinese workers, SOEs also serve Beijing's broader strategic objectives. For almost two decades, China has advanced a "going out" strategy, in which the government and the SOEs work hand in hand to achieve both economic and political objectives in areas such as natural resource exploitation and infrastructure development. As Xiao Yaqing noted in a June 2017 piece he penned for *Study Times*, the CCP's theoretical journal, SOEs must be the "most trustworthy force for the party," and a "major force" for realizing "going out" and the BRI.[106]

In one case, as former Rio Tinto executive Michael Komesaroff describes, Beijing used the state-owned mining company Chinalco to control the global price of iron ore. According to Komesaroff, China's NDRC ordered Chinalco to purchase a significant share of Rio Tinto to block a merger between the Anglo-Australian firms BHP Billiton and Rio Tinto, which the Chinese were concerned would lead to control of one-third of the world's iron ore and drive up the price by seven to eight times. To counter the potential merger, the NDRC held a "beauty pageant" to determine which of the major iron ore companies—Shenhua, Chinalco, or Baosteel—would "carry the Chinese flag." The Chinese government provided Chinalco, which was then headed by current SASAC head Xiao Yaqing, with the money necessary to block the bid. Xiao spent $14 billion to take a 12 percent stake in Rio Tinto, leading BHP Billiton to withdraw. In the end, Chalco, of which Chinalco is the parent company, ended up with a $10 billion loss; however, as Komesaroff argues, China's "national interests paid off."[107] Moreover, as Xiao Yaqing indicated, and as we will see in chapter 7, Xi Jinping's BRI, which includes plans to link the world's nations through new highways, railroads, pipelines, and ports, only enhances the importance of SOEs in realizing Beijing's broader political and strategic objectives.

Big Is Beautiful

"We are in the business of growing bigger and better," stated Xiao Yaqing at a press briefing on the sidelines of China's annual legislative session in March 2016.[108] Merging SOEs is not a new strategy; it has been underway since the 1990s. Since 2012, however, the pace of such mergers has accelerated, jumping from 275 mergers in 2012 to 481 in 2014.[109] One senior SASAC official indicated that the number of central government-controlled SOEs would eventually be consolidated into forty mega SOEs.[110] For Xiao, consolidation via mergers and acquisitions comes naturally; under his leadership, Chinalco expanded continuously through acquisition of other firms, purchasing offshore mining assets, and taking stakes in other foreign mining companies.[111]

Such mega-mergers are already underway. China Ocean Shipping (Group) Co. and China Shipping Group combined to form China COSCO Shipping Corp. in late 2015, and in August 2016, the State Council announced the merger of two of the country's largest cement makers, China National Building Materials Group Corp. and China National Materials Group Corp. Ltd.[112] Mergers were also conducted at the two largest state-owned railroad rolling stock firms and two large government power-generating companies.[113]

The consolidation or merger of SOEs can bring efficiency gains; however, many economists have also pointed to additional priorities for the Chinese government that make such gains doubtful. Unlike bankruptcy, mergers avoid the pain of mass worker layoffs and thus the potential of labor unrest. They also contribute to the Chinese desire to establish national champions—companies that can compete with world-renowned multinationals. As early as 2007, then SASAC chairman Li Rongrong called for the development of thirty to fifty national champions.[114] Chinese commentators refer to companies such as Bombardier, Siemens, and Airbus as models of national champions that have achieved significant success in global markets.[115] China is already well on its way. Fortune's 2016 Global 500 list boasted eighty-three SOEs. Although Walmart topped the list, State Grid, China National Petroleum Corp, and Sinopec—all SOEs—earned second, third, and fourth place, respectively.

As Li Keqiang made clear in his report at the twelfth NPC in March 2015, one of the government's objectives is to speed up the implementation of the "going out" strategy in areas such as railroads, electric power, automobiles, aircraft, electronics, and communications[116]—the majority of these are sectors in which China has significant SOE participation. Already a global powerhouse in overseas acquisition of resources and infrastructure development for well over a decade, Beijing is now encouraging its companies to go out in search of investment opportunities that will help reduce overcapacity in areas such as cement or low-cost manufacturing, showcase China's strength in areas such as high-speed rail, or assist in China's technological advancement through the acquisition of foreign technology firms. In the third quarter of 2015, China's outbound investment surpassed its inbound investment for the first time,[117] a trend that accelerated during 2016.

While Chinese leaders refer to consolidation of firms as a means of both increasing efficiency and creating powerhouse global competitors, many economists and senior business officials doubt the efficiency and economic gains of these SOE mergers, arguing that they are unlikely to reduce the distortionary role of the state. Sheng Hong, one of the founders of the independent Chinese thinktank Unirule Institute of Economics, argues that efforts to enlarge SOEs will only "further reinforce their illegitimate monopolies, squeezing out what remains of private businesses. . . . After the consolidation of central SOEs, the difficulty will be even higher if the central government wants to regulate them."[118] Komesaroff concurs, commenting that although Beijing believes the consolidation process will strengthen its control over the economy, he argues instead, it will impinge on efforts to enhance economic efficiency and "slow productivity improvements that are required to rationalize excess capacity." Moreover, Komesaroff claims that if consolidation is to be successful, it has to introduce new efficiencies unavailable to an individual SOE, such as economies of scale, the sale of unprofitable subsidiaries, or downsizing through worker layoffs.[119] To date, the skepticism of Sheng and Komesaroff has borne out. While the government has repeatedly pledged to cut millions of jobs in the coal and steel sectors, the numbers reported thus far are only in the hundreds of thousands.

Partial Privatization Is Preferable

In 2015, a Xinhua News Agency headline summed up the leadership's view: "We Must Unequivocally Oppose Privatization."[120] While mixed ownership is prized, complete privatization of SOEs that would remove virtually all the state's direct influence is not on the table.[121] From the perspective of the Chinese leadership, the value of mixed ownership is twofold. First, it brings in private capital, thereby marginally reducing the burden on state banks to support SOEs. Second, it offers private actors the opportunity to deploy their capital in some of China's largest and most strategic enterprises and perhaps place pressure on SOEs to improve their economic performance. The policy does not, however, move China along the path to full privatization.

Beijing can already point to some examples of success in piloting projects at the provincial level. In Shanghai, a number of private equity firms have acquired minority shares in local SOEs. For example, the Chinese private equity firm Hony Capital bought a 12.4 percent share in state-owned Shanghai Jinjiang International Hotels. Shandong Province is transferring shares—as much as 30 percent—in selected local SOEs to its social security fund to support the fund and put pressure on SOEs to perform. And Jiangxi and Guangdong Provinces both have indicated that they plan to let private investors invest in over 70 percent of the firms they manage.[122]

Veteran Beijing-based economic analyst Anne Stevenson-Yang is skeptical, however, that the reform will have much impact. She notes that all SOEs are "on assignment" to get non-bank infusions to reduce the pressure on the state-bank sector—even though such infusions are unlikely to make a significant difference in the overall capitalization of the SOEs. In her assessment, SOE reform is not about privatization but rather about politics.[123] Other researchers also suggest that the impact of the reform will be limited because much of the new investment will come from other state actors. Citing the case of Jiangxi Salt, which was opened to private investment in 2015, a Gavekal Dragonomics research study notes that three of the new investors are administered by provincial or central SASACs and the one with the largest stake—Cinda Asset Management Company—is controlled by the Ministry of Finance. Thus, there is little reason to expect that the involvement of new state players will generate greater productivity or efficiencies.[124] Other instances of mixed ownership suggest a similar reliance on state actors. The Chinese energy conglomerate Sinopec sold 30 percent of its distribution unit in 2014, but only 10 percent went to private investors while other SOEs and financial institutions captured the rest.

Yet the government continues to tout such deals. In 2017, the NDRC, which holds responsibility for managing mixed-ownership experiments, concluded a much-heralded deal for a subsidiary of China Unicom, one of China's state-owned telecommunications companies in which private companies Tencent, Alibaba, Baidu, and JD all took stakes in the company. Yet a deep dive into the deal by Gavekal analyst Xie Yanmei revealed that effective state ownership will still be 58 percent. Moreover, the stakes taken by the technology firms appear to be overwhelmingly individual—by the firms' founders or senior managers—so as not to risk their companies' funds. Xie concludes that mixed ownership is not designed to use privatization to accomplish efficiency and profitability gains but instead "provides a way for the state to direct private capital to serve national development and political priorities."[125]

The benefits for private companies to invest—outside of generating political goodwill from the government—are thus not likely to be immediately apparent to many potential investors. As a Mercator Institute report notes, the effort is designed to expand opportunities for private capital in the state sector, while at the same time ensuring that private investors retain only a minority stake.[126] Wanda Group Chairman Wang Jianlin, whose portfolio includes a number of foreign acquisitions such as AMC Theatres, Legendary Entertainment, and Sunseeker International, raises this same point directly: "If I'm going to 'mix,' the private company definitely needs to have a controlling share, or at least I want relative control . . . . If the SOE has the controlling share, isn't that the same as me helping out the SOE by giving it money? Wouldn't that be crazy of me to do? I can't do that kind of thing."[127] Chinese analyst Xin Liu perhaps sums up the sentiment of many observers when he suggests that the idea of mixed ownership means that the SOE reform is likely to be "another fantasy for the Chinese economy."[128]

The Zombie Attack

While consolidating SOEs and infusing them with outside capital are the favored approaches for reforming the SOE sector, the Chinese leadership nonetheless continues to stress the importance of allowing firms to fail. In December 2015, Premier Li Keqiang stated, "For those 'zombie enterprises' with absolute overcapacity, we must ruthlessly bring down the knife."[129] (According to China's State Council, zombie enterprises

are those firms which incur three years of losses, cannot meet environmental and technological standards, do not align with national industrial
policies, and rely heavily on government or bank support to survive.[130])
And in May 2016, he reiterated that SOEs needed to "lose weight and
get fit."[131] One signal of the leadership's intent to move in this direction
is likely the ongoing effort to establish bankruptcy courts.[132]

Yet evidence of real commitment to structural reform through
enterprise failure remains an open question. The State Council's efforts to reduce overcapacity in the steel industry bring the challenge into sharp relief. China boasts nearly 50 percent of the world's
global steel supply and pledged in 2015 to cut production capacity
by 100 to 150 million tons over five years—both because foreign
competitors claimed it was dumping cheap exports and because the
industry was inefficient and demand was weak.[133] The government
initially appeared on track, and some smaller steel producers closed
their doors. Nonetheless, in 2017, China's overall steel output rose.
While officials from the NDRC claimed the Chinese firms were
merely responding to market demand, the chairman of Angang
Steel hinted otherwise, calling for Beijing to "pay close attention to
those mills that are supposed to be eliminated but have restarted."[134]
Gao Xiqing raised another concern about the government's plan.
While Beijing initially sought to close down the most inefficient
steel enterprises, it then called for every province simply to reduce
its capacity by 13 percent or so. He shared that the message from
Beijing became: "I don't care if you cut down the most efficient
ones, so be it."[135] The IMF, as well, has suggested that Beijing relies
too heavily on administrative measures, such as limiting working
days and company mergers. Instead, it suggests, Chinese officials
should concentrate more on enforcing environmental and other
regulatory standards and eliminating subsidies.[136] This is the type of
structural reform the sector needs.

The Party in the State

In October 2016, Xi put to rest the notion that the party would reduce
its role in the management of SOEs. In a speech on the role of the
party, he stated: "Party leadership and building the role of the party are

the root and soul for state-owned enterprises . . . . The party's leadership in state-owned enterprises is a major political principle, and that principle must be insisted on."[137]

In its initial incarnation, Chinese SOE reform appeared designed to limit the role of the state and the party in managing the SOEs in a few respects. The first was to ensure that SASAC shifted from supervising the SOEs directly to supervising capital.[138] As Chen Qingtai, deputy director of the Development Research Center of the State Council, noted in an interview with *Caijing* in 2015: "SASAC and investor-operators need to become financial, rather than industrial, entities. Policy goals cannot be confused with investment goals."[139] This reform would remove SASAC from the direct intervention into SOE's day-to-day operations and would have it instead oversee the party leadership within the SOEs and, in some cases, the allocation of state funds to SOEs. However, as University of California, San Diego, economics professor Barry Naughton has detailed, in the battle over SOE oversight between the Ministry of Finance—which favored a model of SOE management in which all SOEs would be listed and managed by professional management companies—and SASAC—which favored a process that would restructure SOEs into a number of large, internationally competitive firms, thereby ensuring SASAC's continued leadership role— SASAC and its less transformative reform prevailed.

A second equally (if not more) important reform is the divorce of the party from SOE management within the firm. Evidence suggests, however, that the party is becoming more deeply involved in SOE management. In June 2016, SASAC announced that the Communist Party committees within the SOEs should study and approve all major decisions *before any decision by the board of directors of company management*.[140] And as Xu Baoli, a senior SASAC researcher commented in summer 2016, "Communist Party officials are stepping up intervention in day-to-day operations of state-owned corporations . . . there were cases in the past where the board would reject a proposal that had gone through the party. I doubt whether that will happen in the future."[141] According to the European director of a large Sino-European joint venture based in China, a newly established party cell attempted to interfere with investment decisions before he explained that they had no legal standing to do so.[142] In another case, a rising star who headed a listed subsidiary of a central government SOE quit his job in the face of growing party intervention. In addition to oppressive demands for party study sessions, the party felt increasingly comfortable making business decisions but was unwilling to claim any responsibility if things went wrong. After more than twenty years, he left for a position in the private sector.[143] Anne Stevenson-Yang also points to Beijing's placement of discipline inspection committees within the business development office of SOEs to review contracts, cut costs, and approve reimbursements for travel as further party encroachment on SOE independence. The reimbursement structure, Stevenson-Yang notes, was particularly important to senior SOE managers because when their pay was cut by 20 percent as part of an earlier round of SOE reform, the reimbursements more than compensated.[144] Far from enhancing market-driven decision-making within SOEs, the party has enhanced its role in driving SOEs' decisions.

Taking Stock

Chinese and foreign economic analysts have largely voiced disappointment with the progress of SOE reform to date. The reform, in the eyes of many, is plagued with contradictory messages and impulses. He Qinglian suggests, for example, that the 2015 Guiding Opinions reflect a strong "Xi Jinping quality." She argues: "It tries to combine the governance characteristics of both Mao Zedong and Deng Xiaoping and gain some advantage from both sides, thereby introducing a whole bunch of mutually contradictory formulations."[145] Chinese University of Hong Kong's Liu Xin supports He's assessment, arguing that the opinions leave enough room for interpretation that they will likely result in a less than optimal reform effort, in which "the Chinese government will partially give up its ownership when SOEs are performing poorly, and regain its ownership when SOEs are becoming better. In any case, the government will hold ultimate control in substance." Moreover, as Liu points out, the ability of SOE heads to remain party officials (even if their firms privatize) defeats the principle of developing a more professional management system for SOEs.[146] According to one estimate, only 5 percent of SOE assets—those in the steel and coal sectors—are targeted for real reform.[147]

Others are even more critical. Unirule Institute's Sheng Hong argues that the reforms fail to target the essential issues of SOEs: "Reform is for solving problems but this time reforms fundamentally do not target the problems I'm talking about. These problems include: SOE monopolistic power; free and low-cost use of state assets; not handing over profits; and no internal restrictions on allocations. These issues still remain problems. In my view, more seriously, the existence of SOEs is itself a problem."[148] And China Europe International Business School's Liu Shengjun put it even more starkly arguing that the state needs to recognize that SOE strength is antithetical to reform and opening up: "For SOE reform to progress it must first pursue an ideology and consider a fundamental question: At the end of the day, what is the necessity of SOEs?"[149]

The Reform in Context

The seeming paradox in the Third Plenum statements between the claim that the market would play "a decisive role" and the pledge to "persist in the dominant position of public ownership" has apparently been resolved in favor of the state. Despite the early promise of radical reform, SOE reform has been distinguished by a deepening of the already robust role of the party and the state in SOEs and limited opportunities for efficiency gains through privatization, competition, or bankruptcy.

Many observers suggest that there is significant disagreement within China's political system over SOE and broader economic reform.[150] While political battles at the very top may be underway, the result to date is largely consistent with repeated statements by top leaders, and most crucially by Xi Jinping, who, after all, is responsible for the overall coordination of economic reform. Xi stated in a March 2014 meeting: "State-owned enterprises should be supported and not abandoned. The strengthening of these companies will come in course of the reforms from within. They are to rise like a phoenix from the ashes."[151]

More broadly, the evolution of SOE reform during the new leadership's first term suggests an unwillingness on the part of the government—alongside its actions during the stock market saga—to risk a diminution of the role of the Communist Party and the state in the state-owned sector or the role of SOEs in the economy.

The desire of the state to continue to play a dominant role and limit the impact of the market is also reflected in other initiatives throughout the Chinese economy. The most significant new economic initiative to emerge from the Xi government, "Made in China 2025," is an ambitious ten-year strategy that establishes ten priority sectors for the Chinese economy, including aerospace and aviation, high-end machinery and robotics, new energy vehicles, advanced information technology, and high-performance medical devices, among others. The strategy includes localizing and indigenizing technologies and brands, substituting foreign technologies, and capturing global market share. In particular, it seeks to raise the domestic content of products in these industries to 40 percent by 2020 and 70 percent by 2025. To achieve these objectives, the state will pour billions of RMB into these sectors, effectively distorting the market and preventing open competition with foreign firms. As we will see in the next chapter, however, for Xi Jinping, the upside of accepting less-than-optimal technologies and market efficiencies in the short term is made up by the long-term ability of the country to use its advantages in labor costs and market size to dominate these industries in the future.

Other big initiatives ostensibly designed to open the door to greater market competition, such as the establishment of free trade zones (FTZs), have fallen far short of expectations. In surveys conducted by the American Chamber of Commerce in Shanghai and the European Union Chamber of Commerce in China, 75 percent of the American companies reported that they found no tangible benefits to locating business in the Shanghai FTZ; while of the ninety-three European companies that have established a presence, only twelve indicated that they would consider expanding their involvement into another FTZ.[152]

Economic reforms have progressed in some areas, notably toward a market-driven currency, greater market openness in areas such as hospitality, increased access to the Chinese stock and bond markets for foreigners, and more discretion for banks to set interest rates based on the creditworthiness of the borrowers. Yet in the majority of these areas there has also been backsliding and the reintroduction of some state controls.[153]

Instead of pushing forward with the reforms necessary to realize greater efficiency, productivity, and rationality in the allocation of capital, Beijing has elected to chart a less ambitious course. The result after four years of economic reform is a state sector that continues to incur ever-higher levels of debt, consume valuable credit, and provide few new jobs. It is a course that favors mega-mergers to support SOEs' ability to compete abroad but not to open the door for greater competition at home. And the central role of both the Communist Party in managing SOEs and SOEs in core sectors of the economy has expanded. The situation is perhaps best summed up by Gao Xiqing: "We're always saying a little bit—you know, haphazardly saying, OK, let's allow the market to play a little bit of a role. Finally, the 18th Party Congress says let the market be the decisive force. Are we allowing [it] to be the decisive force? It doesn't look like it."[154]

5

Innovation Nation

JACK MA, FOUNDER OF the Chinese global online sales platform phe-
nomenon Alibaba, is a natural storyteller. Within the first minute of
his speech in June 2015 before the Economic Club of New York—
the august, mostly male club of New York financial and economic
luminaries—Ma has me (a one-time guest at the club) and everyone
else in the room in the palm of his hand.

Ma tells his story with appealing humility. After traveling to the
United States in the mid-1990s and witnessing the power of the
Internet, which had yet to be established widely in China, he returned
home determined to start a company called "The Internet." With a
$1,000 loan, he, his wife, and a schoolmate pursued their vision: an
online sales platform that would connect Chinese consumers to small
Chinese businesses. In the early days, there were no customers, and the
team simply bought all the goods themselves. By 1999, the venture was
a bust. But Ma was not done. He recruited eighteen friends to start a
new company named Alibaba.com. The name reflected Ma's belief that
the Internet was a treasure island and his company was going to be
the one to "open sesame." This time, China was ready. In short order,
Alibaba tapped into a Chinese middle class that was wired, ready to
buy, and big on convenience.

Today Alibaba connects 10 million businesses to more than
500 million active consumers and facilitates the delivery of 12 million
packages daily.[1] Ma's empire has also expanded to include Alipay, the
world's largest online payment platform, the Hong Kong newspaper

the *South China Morning Post*, stakes in an online gaming company, the financial media company China Business Network, and Steven Spielberg's Amblin Partners, among others. He made history in 2014, when the $21.8 billion IPO for Alibaba became the largest in history.[2] In addition, he has opened a series of brick-and-mortar supermarkets, where customers can shop, dine, order groceries for delivery from their smartphones, and pay seamlessly using Alipay.[3] Now Ma is moving Alibaba into the United States. His message: Don't be afraid. I am not here to gobble up eBay or go toe to toe with Amazon.[4] I want to bring opportunity to American small businesses to sell in China. Already, he points out, Alibaba helps bring Alaskan seafood and Washington state cherries to China. In January 2017, Ma backed his optimism with real numbers, pledging that Alibaba would create one million jobs for American small businesses through the Alibaba platform by 2022. According to Credit Suisse's head of technology, media, and telecom David Wah, at the heart of the company's success is its continued focus on how to make it easier to do business everywhere—whether it is understanding how consumers want to interact with merchants or using all the infrastructure they have in place to create a cloud service business. Alibaba, Wah argues, is always positioned for the future.[5]

Ma's story is a universal one, particularly in the world of technology start-ups. He saw something that no one else did. Most of his friends and colleagues questioned his sanity. But he persisted. Ma even has the requisite set of failures: he failed his primary school test twice, his middle school test once, and the famed college admissions exam, the *gaokao*, two times. He was even rejected for a job at Kentucky Fried Chicken. His independent spirit and drive, however, made him a standout. At one point, he relates, he spent nine years showing foreigners around his hometown of Hangzhou for free simply to learn English.[6] In just a decade, he has become a household name not only in China but also throughout much of the world.

If China's leaders could clone Ma, no doubt they would. Ma is a poster child for the type of innovative and entrepreneurial spirit that the Chinese leadership is desperate to incubate throughout the country. In a series of speeches, Chinese President Xi Jinping has made clear his unhappiness with the current state of Chinese innovation, decrying China's laggard status in stark terms: "Generally speaking, the foundation of our scientific and technological innovation is not solid enough; our independent innovation ability, especially in the area of original creativity is not strong. . . . We cannot always decorate our tomorrows with others' yesterdays. We cannot afford to lag behind in this important race. We must catch up and then try to surpass others."[7]

China's leaders believe innovation is the key to their economic future. The desire to see China at the forefront of global scientific and technological development permeates their speeches. It is a point of national pride, as well as an economic necessity. The country's strategy to overcome its innovation gap is simple: spend on talent, spend on infrastructure, spend on research and development (R&D), and spend on others' technology. And on one level, the strategy is working. Over the past decade, China has surpassed Japan to become the world's second-largest investor in R&D (although China's investment is still exceeded by that of the United States, which poured more than $462 billion into R&D in 2015 compared to China's $376 billion).[8]

In 2016, Premier Li Keqiang announced a national R&D program to support critical areas such as clean energy, big data, a new arctic observatory, national cyberspace security, deep space exploration, brain research, and quantum communications and computation, among others. In Li's speech before the March 2016 NPC, he used the word "innovation" sixty-one times—almost twice the mentions he gave it in 2015. Overall investment in R&D is slated to increase incrementally from 2.05 percent of GDP in 2015 to 2.5 percent in 2020.[9] Money is also flowing into the world of technology start-ups. In 2016, venture capital firms invested $31 billion in Chinese start-ups and early stage companies, an increase of $5 billion over 2015.[10] China also surpassed the United States and Japan to become the top filer of patents.[11]

Behind these numbers, however, is a different story, one that is told by those most deeply engaged in China's innovation world—the Chinese scientists, investors, and officials tasked with making China's innovation dream a reality, as well as the international community, which competes with and also invests deeply in Chinese innovation. To begin with, the story hinges on the definition of innovation.

Innovation Chinese Style

To wrap my arms around this question of what constitutes innovation, I sat down with my colleague Adam Segal, the author of *Advantage*, a compelling study that compares innovation in China with that in other countries, including the United States. Segal proposes a definition of innovation that makes sense to me: innovation is science-based research that delivers a new product to the world and might even create a whole new industry. This is innovation U.S.-style, from Thomas Edison to Alexander Graham Bell to the Wright brothers.

Others offer a less ambitious understanding. Daniel Breznitz, a professor at Georgia Tech, argues that innovation doesn't necessarily have to lead to a fundamental scientific or industrial breakthrough. He notes, "Chinese technology companies shine by developing quickly enough to remain at the cusp of the global technology frontier without actually advancing the frontier itself."[12] Certainly Breznitz's analysis fits Chinese facts on the ground. China's patents have generally been seen as incremental improvements on previous, more innovative work of others or are process driven—making something work faster, better, or more cheaply.

Like Breznitz, a number of industry experts support the idea of China innovating differently from the United States. Kevin Wale, who headed the China office of General Motors during 2005–2012, describes the Chinese as innovating through commercialization. Rather than adopting the traditional, and often time-consuming, Western method of research, testing, and validation, the Chinese will bring something to market and innovate based on consumer wants.[13] Michael Dunne, one of the world's top experts on the Chinese car industry, agrees, noting that what most often passes for innovation in the Chinese auto industry is R&D geared to adjusting products to suit local tastes. When it comes to cars, he says, this means more chrome and longer wheelbases, along with Chinese-language dashboard instructions and GPS systems.[14]

Joanna Lewis, the author of a path-breaking study on the evolution of China's wind power industry, sees merit in China's unique path. China begins by licensing foreign technology or pursuing mergers and acquisitions to acquire desired technologies, and then innovating jointly with their new foreign partners. According to Lewis, China has been quite successful in taking Western intellectual property and innovating on the business side, enabling China to take Western technology to markets where the West is more reluctant to go, such as Africa.[15]

Summing up China's innovation strengths, professor George Yip, who codirected the Centre on China Innovation at the China Europe International Business School, highlights cost, process, supply chain, and finding new markets, among others.[16] A study by the American consulting firm McKinsey & Co. suggests Yip is on to something. Its authors found that China's large and flexible manufacturing force of 150 million, roughly ten times the size of that in the United States, allows it to scale up production faster than anyone else. It has an extensive supplier base that enables companies to adapt to changing customer needs with new or lower cost components, coupled with a fast turnaround.[17] The electronics manufacturer Xiaomi is one example of a company that practices customer-based innovation. The largest provider of smartphones in China, Xiaomi rapidly refines and adjusts its offerings based on online feedback using China's massive consumer market as a collaborator,[18] a concept it calls "design as you build."[19] In 2014, Xiaomi updated its smartphone operating system fifty-two times.[20]

Gary Rieschel, cofounder of Beijing-based Qiming Venture Partners, which invests in Chinese technology start-ups, including Xiaomi, finally squares the circle for me by distinguishing between innovation and invention. Sitting in the lobby of the Rosewood hotel in Palo Alto, part of California's famed Silicon Valley, Rieschel explains that the Chinese are great innovators, along the lines described by Breznitz, Lewis, and Yip. Invention—the type of breakthrough idea that revolutionizes a product line or industry—however, requires intellectual property rights protection, a long timeframe for investment, an appetite for risk, and a willingness to fail. None of these, he suggests, is, as of yet, well developed in China. This does not mean that Chinese scientists and engineers will never "invent" but rather that the system incentivizes innovation. Xi Jinping may yearn for invention, but he and the Chinese state are already deeply invested in the current model of innovation.

It is a model with both significant strengths and weaknesses. China's effort to innovate and assume a leading place in the global race to develop and deploy the electric car demonstrates both the advantages and limitations of this model. It is one that marries a strong role for the state in investing in and shaping the development of an innovative technology, as well as protecting it from foreign competition. The result is enormous inefficiency, waste, and fraud—and the largest electric car market in the world.

Full Speed Ahead

Spend a day in most of China's well-populated cities, and you are likely to notice two things almost immediately—the quality of the air—poor—and the density of cars—high. Every year, the relationship between the two becomes clearer as efforts to move or close heavy polluting industries and coal-fired power plants fail to yield the desired improvement in air quality. The culprit is most often China's expanding car market.

The Chinese government has a love-hate relationship with cars. Even as it encourages the Chinese people to take public transportation, it has pushed the development of a world-class domestic car industry. The Chinese car market is now the world's largest, having surpassed that of the United States: In 2016, China sold more than 28 million cars, while auto makers in the United States topped out at 17.6 million.[21] Moreover, China now manufactures over 24 million cars, more than any other country in the world.[22] By 2030, RAND and the Institute for Mobility Research estimate that the number of automobiles produced in China could reach 50 million annually.[23]

China's leaders would like to have all these automobiles run on clean energy—for reasons of both energy security and environmental protection. In September 2017, following in the footsteps of France and the United Kingdom, the government announced plans to ban fossil-fuel cars at some point in the future. This desire for clean-energy vehicles is not new. The Chinese government established the foundation for such an effort in the late 1990s. In 1999, it developed a Clean Vehicle Action Program that called for 10 percent of all taxis and 20 percent of all buses in twelve cities to run on alternative fuels such as natural gas or liquefied petroleum gas. The city of Beijing went even further, promising that the city's 3,600 buses and 14,000 taxis would all run on alternative fuels; Shanghai adopted the same policy for its 20,000 taxis.[24] Weak monitoring and enforcement, however, meant that many of the vehicles likely did not actually use the cleaner fuels.[25] As a next step, in 2001, Beijing included the electric vehicle as one of its twelve key "science and technology projects."[26] Funds flowed from a number of different sources, including the National High Tech R&D program (known as the 863 Program). By the eleventh Five-Year Plan (2006–2010), China was devoting approximately $7 billion to this research, much of which went to large, state-owned firms.[27]

The selection of former Audi engineer Wan Gang in 2007 to head the Ministry of Science and Technology (MOST) provided an important boost to the clean car effort. With a PhD in engineering from Clausthal University of Technology in Germany, Wan had spent almost a decade as part of Audi's R&D team, where he worked on fuel cells. He left Germany in 2000 to return to China to head Tongji University's R&D program in hydrogen cell and electric automobiles, eventually becoming the president of the university in 2004 before being appointed minister of science and technology. A voluble technocrat and reportedly one of the most popular ministers in the cabinet, Wan is also one of the very few non–Communist Party members in the upper echelons of the Chinese government—in fact, he was the first to be appointed minister in more than a half a century.[28]

Wan quickly became a missionary for electric car adoption in China, arguing in 2009 that electric vehicles were a particularly strategic area of interest for China and offered an opportunity to "catch up with and exceed developed countries" in the automobile industry.[29] That year, Chinese leaders adopted a plan to make China one of the leading producers of hybrid-electric and electric vehicles by 2012 and become the leading producer thereafter. Beijing established targets for pure electric and hybrid electric vehicles of 500,000 by 2015 and 5 million by 2020.[30] The following year it announced that sixteen SOEs would form an alliance to conduct R&D with government support totaling $15 billion behind it.[31] And the government embedded the alternative fuel and electric vehicle industry in China's five-year economic plan, the twelfth Five-Year Plan, as one of seven strategic emerging industries.

Wan also spearheaded the "ten cities, thousand vehicles" program beginning in 2009, which was overseen by four ministries: MOST, the Ministry of Information Industry Technology (MIIT), the Ministry of Finance (MOF), and the NDRC. The program identified ten cities that would produce one thousand electric vehicles each; with each city permitted to select its own standards and technologies. By 2011, the government had expanded the list of cities to twenty-five.[32] Everyone wanted a piece of the electric car boom. The government offered subsidies of 50,000–60,000 yuan ($8,000–9,000) to consumers who purchased the cars and instructed local electricity grids to set up charging stations for electric cars in Beijing, Shanghai, and Tianjin.[33]

Included in the government's plan was a mandate that foreign automakers who wanted to manufacture cars in China transfer their core electric battery or high-powered electric motor technology. For an electric vehicle to be sold in China, regardless of where it was produced, the MIIT required that a domestic Chinese firm be capable of "displaying mastery" of the vehicle's essential components.[34] But foreign automakers were not persuaded. GM, which sought to introduce its electric-battery powered Volt to China, refused to transfer the technology. As a result, it was ineligible for the Chinese government's $19,000 subsidy for electric cars—almost half the cost of the Volt itself.[35] Generous government rebates were available only for Chinese- made all-electric passenger vehicles or plug-in hybrids.[36]

The results were underwhelming. By one count, only 4,400 vehicles were purchased during the three years of the program; by another, only seven of the twenty-five cities had achieved their target of 1,000 cars.[37] Rather than produce a healthy competition, in which the best technologies triumphed and were adopted countrywide, the government's segmented approach and lack of coordination ensured that each province or region adopted a zero-sum outlook. Local companies and grids developed compatibility that was not shared through the rest of the country. Cars that were purchased in one city often could not use a charging station in another. And charging stations were located without consideration for where they were most needed: one contractor noted that charging stations were built "where politicians wanted them" and that there was "no real planning."[38] Local governments also inflated their success in order to increase the chance that Beijing would select them as a model.[39]

Competition and conflict between the central government ministries overseeing the program contributed to its poor start. While MIIT was responsible for the regulation and development of major industries and in charge of managing the electric vehicle supply chain once it matured, MOST was in charge of nationwide R&D and therefore responsible for battery technology. In one case, MIIT named Nissan its strategic partner at a global forum in 2009, while homegrown BYD (an acronym for the company's Chinese name Bi Ya Di and also for the English "Build Your Dreams"), which fell under MOST's supervision, was not even invited to the forum.[40]

While Chinese consumer interest in electric cars was weak, the country had a few strong advocates within its auto industry, most notably, Wang Chuanfu, the founder of BYD. Wang may not possess as compelling a personality or personal history as Jack Ma, but his vision and perseverance are equally impressive. Like Ma, Wang came from a poor background. Both his parents were rice farmers who passed away by the time he was fifteen years old. When he was in his late 20s, however, he managed to raise $300,000 from his relatives to start a phone battery company in 1995 in Shenzhen. His objective was to compete with Sony and Sanyo in the rechargeable battery market. Within seven years, BYD had become one of the world's largest manufacturers of cell phone batteries in each of the three major battery technologies.[41]

Wang decided to transfer his battery production capacity to the automobile business in 2003, when he purchased a near-defunct state-owned car company. Within two years, Wang had released the F3DM, a plug-in hybrid model that soon became one of the best-selling sedans in China. He followed several years later in 2011 with BYD's first all-electric car, the E6.[42] Wang benefited significantly from government support, partnering with the Shenzhen local government in the ten cities program, and receiving an estimated $435 million in subsidies from the Shenzhen government during 2010–2015.[43] Wang also attracted investment from American investment guru Warren Buffet,[44] which sent an important signal of BYD's promise to the international business community.

Despite Wang's initial success with the F3DM, the E6 struggled. Reviews of the car were not positive: one reviewer called it clunky and reminiscent of a "late-stage East German Wartburg car."[45] Accused of copying other automakers' designs, Wang seemed to acknowledge a deficit in innovation, stating that "60 percent of a new product is taken from publicly available information, 30 percent from existing products, 5 percent from the materials that are available, and only 5 percent from our original research."[46] According to auto expert Michael Dunne:

> I cannot think of a single example of Chinese innovation aside from this: Sometimes companies like BYD innovate by replacing expensive machinery with lots of inexpensive labor to arrive at the same product result while saving money. Or they jam down wages and make people work harder. Or the executives at a $100 million parts company have a simple rice and veggies and pork lunch together every day for $20 instead of eating out for $200. The Chinese are good innovators when it comes to finding ways to reduce costs, although this often leads to "quality fade."[47]

Tsinghua engineering professor Song Jian agrees with the quality concern, noting "huge design defects in BYD's electric cars could lead to many safety problems."[48] A number of Chinese scientists also highlighted the potential dangers of BYD's technology, including the battery casing, the method used to connect the battery modules, and even the heaviness of the batteries, which was roughly three times that of the foreign electric cars such as the Nissan Leaf or Chevrolet Volt, making the BYD electric cars energy wasters rather than savers compared with traditional combustion-engine vehicles.[49] After a BYD E6 burst into flames in 2012, the Guangdong propaganda authorities forbade local media from reporting anything critical on electric cars or BYD.

Round Two

Still both the Chinese government and Wang continued to push forward with their effort to make China and BYD a world-class leader in electric cars. Despite flagging sales, in November 2013, twenty-eight cities signed on to begin another round of city-based electric vehicle promotion. In some cases, the targets were wildly optimistic. Tianjin set a target for 2015 that was ten times its 2012 target.[50] By early 2013, China was still almost 480,000 vehicles away from meeting its first stated target of 500,000.[51] But the electric car dream team—NDRC, MOF,

MOST, MIIT, and the National Government Offices Administration—added new incentives, mandating that "new energy vehicles"—vehicles that do not rely exclusively on fossil fuels—account for 30 percent or more of new cars purchased by state organs every year.[52] They continued subsidies for vehicles priced less than $29,000 and offered new energy vehicle users preferential access to the license plate lottery[53]—a system by which local governments grant licenses to only a select number of applicants in order to limit the number of vehicles on the road. In September 2014, Beijing's decision to eliminate the 10 percent tax on Chinese electric vehicles contributed to a significant jump in electric car sales. In December, sales of passenger and electric vehicles reached 27,000.[54] (Foreign companies, however, were excluded from the benefits of the tax elimination and, as one foreign observer noted, this move, combined with preexisting subsidies, stacked the deck even further against foreign-made models.[55]) The Chinese government continued to try to incentivize the purchase of electric cars. In spring 2015, officials declared that electric vehicles would be exempt from the city's traffic restrictions and promised to address the problem of incompatible charging stations among provinces by providing charging interfaces for new energy vehicles. The result was yet another uptick in electric car purchases.[56]

BYD's fortunes soared along with the broader growing interest in electric cars. The company's batteries for electric vehicles command 9 percent of the global market,[57] and In 2015, BYD became the largest new energy vehicle manufacturer in the world; its electric buses run in more than 160 cities, fifty of which are in China.[58] In 2017, it expanded a small manufacturing plant it had opened in Los Angeles in 2013; eventually the company plans to build electric trucks and as many as 1,500 electric buses in the United States annually. Its electric car continues to sputter along. Although the E6 has won contracts with Opoli, a car-sharing service in San Francisco and San Diego, as well as with Uber in Chicago,[59] its numbers remain limited—only eighty BYD E6 electric vehicles have been exported to the United States.[60] Its price point and size make it attractive to taxi drivers; however, its efficiency—how far it can drive on the same amount of energy contained in one gallon of gasoline—is far lower than any other electric car on the international market and only one-fourth that of top-ranked Tesla. As of

November 2017, BYD senior management promises only that the E6 will find its way to American consumers sometime before 2020.

Back in China, a team of American and Chinese researchers, reviewing the progress of China's electric car development, found some reasons to cheer and some areas of concern.[61] Several of the local experiments appeared to be thriving. Shenzhen's partnership with Potevio New Energy, China Southern Grid, and BYD enabled a successful battery-leasing effort for electric buses. And in Hangzhou, the Kandi electric car-sharing service, which was modeled on the city's already successful bicycle rental program, also produced a win.[62]

Nonetheless, the team also found a number of ongoing challenges, chief among them that the Chinese government's practice of subsidies and closed government procurement has not stimulated innovation. In addition, too much local competition has translated into city pilots "losing sight of overarching goals" and developing standards that are not broadly used.[63] Moving forward with a single standard is now a significant challenge for China's EV market.[64] The internal trade barriers created by the city competition, as well as the lack of genuine foreign competition, has hindered Beijing's efforts to build a world-classs electric car industry. In addition, a report produced by a Harvard University economics scholar determined that government efforts to grant market access in exchange for technology transfer have not succeeded.[65]

The electric and new energy vehicle market has also come under scrutiny in the context of the anticorruption campaign. In 2016, Beijing fined five automakers a total of $225 million, an amount equal to the $150 million in subsidies the companies had received for promoting electric vehicles and half that sum in fines, for reporting false production and sales.[66] Inspectors have discovered cases where electric car manufacturers received subsidies for production and then sold the cars to their own rental subsidiaries and received subsidies for purchasing electric cars. Kandi, the successful electric car-sharing company, for example, received as much as $130 million in subsidies from the government of Hangzhou between 2013 and 2016 and then was paid as much as $12 per month for every car that was leased. The lure of subsidies—which were set to be reduced in December 2015—also led to an absurd increase in the number of electric buses produced in that year: from January to November, 90,100 electric-powered commercial vehicles were produced; in December alone, almost 58,000 were produced, some without seats or other parts,[67] even without batteries.[68] In addition, some companies claimed to have produced EVs when none was actually produced.[69] Gemsea Bus made no electric buses but collected $40 million in subsidies.[70] As one analyst Yang Zhiting noted, "To some extent, last year's EV boom is built on a pile of sand."[71]

As in many other sectors, such as clean energy, steel, coal, and cement, the electric car market has become oversaturated—the result of the distortions that government intervention and subsidies have produced. China currently has about 4,000 new energy vehicle models in development. MIIT is attempting to develop standards to ensure the companies have the necessary high-quality technology to make them competitive and pledged to grant permits to only fifteen companies to manufacture new energy vehicles in 2017.[72] MIIT has suggested that companies intending to sell electric cars must possess seventeen technologies, such as a process for recycling or reusing batteries, to get a permit. According to the *Economic Daily*, 90 percent of companies developing electric vehicles are unlikely to meet the standards within the next few years.[73]

The Chinese government is also trying to protect itself from foreign competition, to the detriment of the quality and level of advanced technology that its cars will possess. MIIT has carefully crafted regulations in the electric battery sphere that effectively prevent foreign multinationals from competing. In January 2016 MIIT banned electric buses from using one type of battery, of which the Korean companies Samsung SDI and LG Chem were major producers. This was followed by a regulation that required battery makers to have established their manufacturing plants for over a year to make the government-approved list of suppliers. This again effectively closed out Samsung SDI and LG Chem as suppliers for Chinese EV companies. Of the fifty-seven battery makers on the government list, none was a foreign company, despite the fact that Korean and Japanese batteries provide larger energy storage capacity and are preferred by a number of Chinese EV manufacturers.[74]

China's deep pockets combined with its ability to limit foreign competition mean that it has the wherewithal to forge ahead despite the waste, inefficiency, and seeming weaknesses in innovative capacity. The

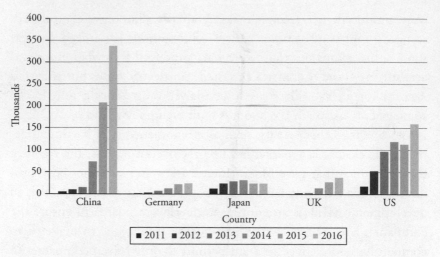

FIGURE 5.1 Total Electric Car Vehicle Registrations from 2011 to 2016 in Select Countries

Source: International Energy Agency; https://www.iea.org/publications/freepublications/publication/Global_EV_Outlook_2017.pdf

Chinese government and car companies have already put in motion investments that will yield an electric-car manufacturing capacity of 2.9 million per year.[75] Electric cars may well follow the trajectory of renewable energy technologies in China: plagued with issues of over-capacity and quality control but nonetheless ultimately able to produce world-class products and capture significant, if not the majority of, market share globally. In 2015, China surpassed the United States to emerge as the world's biggest market for all new energy vehicles, including electric, plug-in hybrid, and fuel-cell cars (see figure 5.1).

Yet Xi's statements suggest that he wants something more. He wants China to be not simply an innovation powerhouse but also a driver of global invention. Realizing this goal will require overcoming a number of significant obstacles, beginning with a history in which politics and culture have often impeded innovation.

A Slow Start

Innovation is central to Xi Jinping's notion of the rejuvenation of the great Chinese nation, but he is certainly not the first Chinese leader to stake out innovation as an essential element of China's economic rise.

Former Chinese president Hu Jintao also delivered a lengthy speech in 2007, calling innovation "the core of our national development strategy and a crucial link in enhancing the overall national strength."[76] Innovation is a matter of both economic imperative and national pride. Ancient China, after all, was the source of the "four great inventions" (*sidafaming*, 四大发明): printing, gunpowder, the magnetic compass, and papermaking. During the Zhou dynasty (1046–256 BCE), China also developed a highly sophisticated system of irrigation projects with canals that stretched hundreds of miles and enormous dams that changed the course of rivers. At the same time, Chinese agriculture, according to one account, produced "the highest yields in the world."[77] Even Chinese mythology valued invention. The epic feats of inventor-heroes with supernatural powers are remembered in legends: Fu Xi, who invented writing, music, marriage, and more; Sui Ren, who invented fire; Shen Nong, who invented medicine and farming techniques; and Huangdi, who invented the wheel, calendar, and compass, among other things.[78] Yet after 1300, China's innovative spirit appears to have evaporated.[79] The great chronicler of ancient Chinese science and innovation Joseph Needham suggests that a form of bureaucratic feudalism impeded the rise of modern capitalism and science in China.[80] Chinese scholars also pointed to the lack of tradition in inductive reasoning in science and the rigidity of the imperial examinations.[81]

The end of imperial China and its successor republican government did little to foster entrepreneurship and innovation, however, and during the first decades of CCP rule, entrepreneurship was shunned and viewed as an occupation for individuals who had a criminal record or were unable to find other jobs.[82] Scientific and other innovation was also stifled. Under the leadership of Mao Zedong, the government closed universities and scientific institutions and punished intellectuals for their "elitist, bourgeois inclinations."[83] It was a period in which "red" triumphed over expert. Dissenting ideas often resulted in harsh punishment. Millions of educated Chinese and businesspeople were sent to work in factories or down to the countryside to be reeducated.[84] During the particularly harsh reign of the Gang of Four, scientists were punished and tortured.[85] With the exception of security-related research on issues such as nuclear weapons and ballistic missiles or disease-prevention, advanced scientific research went dark.[86]

Only with the advent of the Four Modernizations in the mid-1970s, the reintroduction of exams and academic study in universities in the late 1970s, and Deng Xiaoping's reform and opening up in the early 1980s, did scientific innovation become a priority for the Communist Party. As the government began to allow scientists to take a stake in their innovations, universities spun off start-up technology companies. One of China's most well-known computer companies, Lenovo (originally named Legend), was founded in 1984 by Liu Chuanzhi, a computer scientist, and ten engineers, all of whom were members of the Institute of Computing Technology attached to the Chinese Academy of Sciences (CAS). They began their business with a loan of 200,000 yuan ($30,000) from CAS, and their first major success was a circuit board that enabled IBM-compatible personal computers to process Chinese characters.[87] Few observers could anticipate that twenty years after the founding of the company, the company would purchase IBM's PC business and a decade later its server business.

The mid-1980s was also a fertile period for the development of the legal and bureaucratic infrastructure to support science and innovation in China. Chinese physicist Chen Chunxian returned from a trip to the United States in 1980 and christened Zhongguancun, an area in Beijing near both Peking and Tsinghua Universities, "China's Silicon Valley."[88] Between 1984 and 1986, not only Legend but also Founder Group and Stone Group—two high-profile Chinese technology companies—were birthed in Zhongguancun.[89] China enacted its first patent law in 1984, and a year later, the Chinese Intellectual Property Press began keeping a database of patents.[90] In 1986, building on the success of the country's special economic zones, the government launched the 863 Program to encourage special market-based zones for technological development and entrepreneurship outside the centrally planned economy.[91] Still, starting a business was considered more risky and less prestigious than garnering a government job or one with an SOE.

Innovation and entrepreneurship got an important boost from Deng Xiaoping's daughter Deng Nan. Deng was trained in physics at Peking University and served as vice-minister of the State Science and Technology Commission from 1998 to 2004. During visits to the United States, she paid particular attention to MIT, a university renowned for fostering innovation and entrepreneurialism.[92] At the same time, under her leadership, the government began taking steps to encourage scientific innovation in the private sector, granting preferential policies such as reducing the sales tax on technology transfer, R&D expenditures, services, and consulting.[93]

Simultaneously, views on private entrepreneurship began to shift. President Jiang Zemin, in particular, viewed Chinese entrepreneurs as valuable to the economic success of the country and to China's international image. As noted in chapter 1, under his leadership, in 2002, the Communist Party changed its rules to allow entrepreneurs to become members.[94] By 2006, 70 percent of Chinese polled believed that "entrepreneurship was a good career choice."[95]

The 1990s and 2000s thus marked a period of significant evolution in China's approach to innovation and entrepreneurialism: the government began to reverse decades of political opposition to entrepreneurs and place a new priority on investing in research and development. Yet additional impediments remain. Weaknesses in talent, the culture of innovation, education, and intellectual property all impede Xi Jinping's drive to transform China into a global center of innovation.

The Talent Gap

Speaking at a general assembly of members from the Chinese Academy of Sciences and Academy of Engineering in 2014, Xi Jinping spoke forcefully about the need to address the technology gap and even more pressingly about the need to foster and retain the country's top talent.[96] It is surprising, but in a country with more than 1.3 billion people, one of the greatest challenges China faces is nurturing creative thinkers and developing and retaining the talented people necessary to meet its innovation needs for the twenty-first century. Out of 137 countries surveyed, the 2017–2018 World Economic Forum's Global Competitiveness Report ranked China twenty-eighth in innovation, forty-seventh in higher education and training, and seventy-third in technological readiness.[97]

One critical issue is China's continued brain drain. Since 1987, of the 4 million Chinese students that have studied abroad, only 2.2 million have returned home.[98] Xi has made it a priority to get these students back to China, arguing that "students and scholars studying abroad have a broad vision, and they ought to take the lead in making innovations."[99] So China has opened its borders and its pocketbooks to attract the world's most talented minds. Li Yuanchao, China's former vice-president, played a small but important role in that process. As head of the party's Organization Department, he advanced the "1,000 Global Talents" program in 2008 to attract the best and brightest from around the globe.[100] He worked hard to attract top scientists and other creative thinkers from the United States and Europe, with significant financial incentives, as well as preferential treatment in housing, education for their children, and other support for their research.[101] The financial incentives for institutions recruiting the scholars were also significant: some local Talents programs offered as much as 8 million yuan ($1.2 million) to universities or even more if they recruited someone recognized as part of the national-level 1,000 Talents program.[102] In just the first five years, three thousand returnees were recruited.[103]

However, a review of the program in 2013 raised a number of concerns. Some of the returnees had actually returned earlier and were now simply being grandfathered in.[104] While the program was designed to lure full-time, top-flight researchers, slots were also being filled by MBAs or other Chinese graduates who were not likely to spearhead China's technological innovation effort. In addition, a significant portion of the researchers wanted to maintain their positions in the West, while simultaneously directing research in China.[105] Corruption also plagued the system: in some instances, host institutions were apparently keeping the incentive funds for themselves.[106]

Moreover, as Beijing seeks to take advantage of this global talent, it is finding that the transition to living and working in China is not always smooth even for Chinese returnees. An editorial in the state-supported *Global Times* written by associate professor of law at the Beijing Institute of Technology Liu Guofu pointed out, "Currently, what China can offer is far less than the conditions they [foreign experts] enjoy in developed countries and regions."[107] Keeping foreign and returnee talent happy will depend less on housing and more on the overall work environment. Brown University physics professor Gang Xiao, who was educated in China, points to the difference in academic environment:

Scholars fresh from abroad can experience cultural shock in dealing with the established hierarchy in the research community . . . . Subjective factors often trump objective standards in internal and local evaluation processes, resource allocation and grant application . . . . Developing a research environment conducive to discovery and innovation also takes more than modern research facilities and money. Scholars need to be able to think independently, form collaboration networks without interference and distribute and access information freely. The internet is one of the most productive tools for scholars. Though the government has no intention to block web access for scientific research, the lack of full internet service will limit Chinese scientists' research efforts.[108]

Deans from two of China's most prestigious universities, Tsinghua University and Peking University, penned an article in *Science* in 2010 that publicly denounced China's research culture, arguing that top-down control of funding agencies by a small number of bureaucrats "stifles innovation." They further argued that it was an "open secret" that obtaining major grants is more contingent on "schmoozing with powerful bureaucrats and their favorite experts" than on doing good research.[109] One of the two deans, Peking University Dean Rao Yi was a returnee, having resigned his position at Northwestern University to accept the position in Beijing, where he was the first dean that Peking University had recruited internationally. (In the wake of the article, Rao was not selected as an academician at the Chinese Academy of Sciences. Other Chinese scholars suggest that he was "punished" for his outspokenness against the system.[110] He later left his position at Peking University to start an independent research university modeled on Caltech.) Professor of Chinese Studies Cong Cao, who left China for graduate training at Columbia University and now teaches at the University of Nottingham's campus in Ningbo, also suggests that the structure of China's reward system for innovation is skewed. The emphasis on prizes and academic honors rather than basic scientific inquiry and peer review contributes to widespread scientific fraud, plagiarism, and falsification of data. Cao reports that even conservative estimates suggest as much as one-third of Chinese researchers has engaged in some sort of scientific misconduct.[111]

The Numbers Game

Innovation is also impeded by the Chinese government's reliance on top-down campaigns to achieve markers of innovation, without necessarily paying enough attention to the actual content. Beijing set a national goal for 2 million patents by 2015, for example, and surpassed it ahead of schedule. But in 2014, more than 60 percent of patent applications were "utility and design" patents that "typically do not represent significant innovation."[112] The misguided focus on quantity as opposed to quality is also reflected in how little Chinese intellectual property is actually adopted by others outside the country. In 2013, China paid $21 billion for the use of foreign intellectual property but received only $887 million from other countries for use of its intellectual property. In 2015, the situation was even slightly worse. China paid $22.6 billion for foreign intellectual property use and received $676 million for its intellectual property.[113] Other Asian countries received much more: Japan for example received $37 billion, while even tiny Singapore received nearly $4 billion. The United States led the pack with $130 billion.[114] Senior Chinese officials recognize the problem. They believe that their country is losing out to others, such as the United States and Japan, by licensing rather than innovating new technologies.

Educated but Not Liberated

For many who operate in the world of Chinese innovation, the country's educational system is at the heart of the problem. Simply obtaining a university education can be difficult. In China, university tuition fees are the equivalent of 13.6 years of a farmer's income, while in a wealthier urban area, a parent might pay slightly more than four years of his or her salary.[115] A college education remains out of reach for the vast majority of young Chinese both for reasons of cost and access. Chinese students have only one main channel to achieve higher education, and from kindergarten through high school, children must focus on gaining access to a university. Parents and educators, alike, bemoan the strict, regimented, and narrowly defined path to college. Only 5 percent of Chinese have received higher education.[116]

The nature of the education is also a concern. Liu Daoyu, former president of Wuhan University, remains unimpressed by his country's fundamentals: "China boasts the biggest college population, the largest campuses and is the second biggest academic paper generator in the world, but it can barely foster a world-class scholar or school of thought."[117] According to Liu and other Chinese educators, innovation needs both fertile ideas from multiple sources and the freedom of expression to state one's views and make one's case. The point is made as well by China's artistic community. As the renowned artist Ai Weiwei argues, when the government talks about making Chinese culture strong and creative, it is bound to run into trouble:

> If a person has never had the right to choose their information, freely associate with any kind of ideology, and develop an individual character with some passion and imagination—how can they become creative? It is against human nature. If you are against every essential value of individualism and independent thinking, and the willingness to take risks and bear consequences, and have a sense of responsibility—what kind of creativity do you expect? . . . It would be impossible to design an iPhone in China because it's not a product; it's an understanding of human nature.[118]

Yet Xi Jinping seems distinctly uninterested in liberating education from the constraints of the party's thinking. During a tour of leading universities in June 2012, he called for the party to play an increased role in supervising higher education.[119] A number of Western observers argue that this system of parallel governance with both educators and CCP officials "limits rather than enhances the flow of ideas." The problem in their view is with the bounded "political world" in which Chinese schools, universities, and businesses exist, rather than with the innovative or intellectual capacity of the Chinese people.[120]

Stolen Property

Protection of intellectual property is a foundational principle of innovation and certainly of invention. Yet China has been much slower to move forward in a meaningful way to protect intellectual property than many in the international community had hoped. A 2013 report, published by a consortium made up of several governments and businesses, found that of 120 incidents of government-directed cyber-espionage of intellectual property, 96 percent came from China.[121] (Ironically, perhaps, Chinese historians date the first notions of copyright to the Tang dynasty [618–906 AD].[122])

Many American and European firms complain about intellectual property theft by Chinese companies; it registers near the top of every annual foreign chamber of commerce report ranking of challenges in doing business in China. While the Chinese government cannot be held responsible for every intellectual property infraction, it has often appeared to use its market power to try to force intellectual property transfer from multinationals to their Chinese partners or consumers rather than invest its political and financial capital in developing a more rigorous intellectual property protection system.[123] Since 2006, under the auspices of the "National Medium- and Long-Term Program for Science and Technology Development (2006–2020)," the government has advanced the idea of indigenous innovation: "enhancing original innovation, integrated innovation, and re-innovation based on the assimilation of imported technologies."[124] Most importantly, the plan stresses that importing technologies without attention to "assimilation, absorption and re-innovation" will weaken the country's indigenous research and development capacity.[125]

The results of this strategy can be seen in several different forms. The government strongly encourages multinationals to establish R&D centers in China to gain access to the Chinese market. The government also may require that foreign businesses transfer intellectual property to Chinese companies to gain access to the market or the company will be shut out, offering time and opportunity for a Chinese competitor to gain market access. As longtime business consultant and China resident James MacGregor has noted, "The belief by foreign companies that large financial investments, the sharing of expertise and significant technology transfers would lead to an ever-opening China market is being replaced by boardroom banter that win-win in China means China wins twice."[126]

Under Xi Jinping, the requirements for technology transfer have only expanded. Beginning in 2015, for example, the government put forth a new set of regulations under the guise of national security designed to force technology companies involved in providing computing and networking equipment to China to provide their source code.[127]

IBM reportedly acceded to Beijing's demands, while others, such as Microsoft, HP, and Cisco, found a middle ground by establishing joint ventures with Chinese companies and/or special products for the Beijing market that analysts believe allow the Chinese government a backdoor into the system.[128]

Build a Home for Innovation and Entrepreneurship

In his 2014 address before the World Economic Forum in Tianjin Premier Li Keqiang argued that the "key to realizing that [entrepreneurship and innovation] is to further liberate our mind, further liberate and develop productivity, and further liberate and increase social vitality, and remove all institutional obstacles."[129] Over the course of the next two years, the government followed through on its implicit pledge to improve the environment for entrepreneurs. It reduced both the amount of time and the number of permits necessary to start a new business. From 2012 to 2017, China rose in the World Bank's rankings in terms of "ease of doing business" and "ease of starting a business," from 91st to 78th and 151st to 127th, respectively.[130] In addition, in late 2015, the government established a $10 billion development fund to help small businesses; according to Li, over ten thousand new firms are registering in China every day.[131]

Beijing is not simply standing back and funneling money into research while it waits for the next Jack Ma. It is doing whatever it can to create the conditions in which he or she can emerge. Part of its effort centers on providing a home in which entrepreneurship can thrive. China is brimming with science and technology parks determined to duplicate the success of Silicon Valley, Route 128, and North Carolina's Research Triangle. The scale is mind-boggling. In Haidian Park, there are more than 5,000 "state-level" designated enterprises, 12,000 high-tech enterprises, and more than 330 publicly listed companies. They comprise 10 percent of all high-tech companies in the country, and in 2013, generated revenues of $273 billion.[132]

Many universities boast their own science and technology (S&T) parks. I dropped by to visit with Chen Hongbo, who helps oversee one of China's most prestigious S&T parks—the Tsinghua University Science Park. Chen is a tall, affable man who completed his

PhD studies in Australia and worked there for a number of years before returning to Beijing in 2002 to help oversee the park. Founded in 1994, the park is spread over 730,000 square meters and is home to four hundred companies, many of which put money into the university.[133] The majority of the science park's staff are graduates of the university. There is also a smaller affiliated Pioneer Park, particularly geared to engage students at the university and returning scholars.

Chen believes that the science park has the recipe for success: space; ties to the university; good tenants, including firms such as Microsoft, Google, and Deutsche Bank; and, most importantly, support from the government through financing and research. It has become a full-service enterprise with job fairs, a website for companies to become part of the network remotely, and a consultant team to help companies. What is still missing, according to Chen, is the service aspect. Chinese people are still in the early stages of developing a "service mentality": to take pride in their work, whether it is fixing an elevator or keeping the restaurant clean. He contrasts it with the West where people train for jobs as plumbers and take pride in their work. No one wants these types of service jobs. In his mind, this translates into a weaker business ecosystem in which a huge gap remains between China and the West in terms of things such as clean air, clean restaurants, and general maintenance of standards.[134] Nonetheless, Tsinghua University Science Park has become a brand throughout the country, establishing branches in Zhuhai, Nanjing, Kunshan, Guangzhou, and elsewhere.[135] It has also established InnoSpring, an incubator in Silicon Valley, as well as branches in Russia, Israel, and the United Kingdom.[136]

While the country's S&T parks boast government sponsorship and house some of the country's largest tech companies, such as Xiaomi, China is also developing a tech start-up culture that more closely approximates that of the rest of the world. In this world, private capital shapes the fortunes of young innovators, and start-ups are housed in young people's bedrooms or apartments or, if they are lucky, in spaces like 3Q, one of the eighteen or so shared workspaces created by SOHO China, the country's largest commercial real estate company. I got a tour of one of these workspaces from SOHO's CEO Zhang Xin during a trip to Beijing. It is a beautiful space in Beijing's central business district—a three-story glass aerie with a mix of different collaborative

FIGURE 5.2 Photo of a Workspace at the Guanghua Road SOHO 3Q in Beijing
Credit: Zhang Xin, SOHO China

workspaces spread throughout (see figure 5.2). Zhang designed the space, and different rooms offer different vibes: some have colorful prints, while others feature pictures of Albert Einstein and other great scientists. The start-ups that fill the more than three thousand desks range from Airbnb and college counseling to elevator maintenance and training to become a disc jockey. Zhang contrasts the energy present in the start-up sector with that in the company's more traditional real estate businesses. In 2016, she relays, the traditional commercial real estate market was flat, and the situation was even worse in 2017: already more space was being returned than rented. As a result, Zhang and her husband Pan Shiyi are investing more into the 3Q business with plans to open new workspaces in Hangzhou and Shenzhen.

For the true technology start-up in China, nothing beats a desk at Sinovation Ventures. The last stop on my tour to understand China's innovation ecosystem, Sinovation Ventures was founded as Innovation Works in 2009. It occupies the tenth floor of one of China's nondescript office buildings in the Haidian district, an area that many of

China's tech companies call home. The firm is the brainchild of Lee Kai-fu, onetime head of both Microsoft and Google China. Lee, who is in his mid-fifties, grew up in Taiwan and was educated at Columbia and Carnegie Mellon Universities. He left Google in 2009 to found Innovation Works, a firm devoted to incubating technology entrepreneurs in China.[137]

I first visited the firm in 2010 and had the opportunity to chat with Lee's number two, Ning Tao. Ning is just the type of person that China wants back. She hopped, skipped, and jumped her way through some of America's iconic tech firms—Microsoft, IBM, and Google, picking up a Yale MBA along the way, before following her mentor Lee back to Beijing to help him build Innovation Works. At the time, Ning described an ongoing challenge in recruiting young Chinese to the tech world. While many young Chinese are very smart and creative, she worried that they were risk averse—they want to join international companies or SOEs. She said, "Big talent joins big firms." Many young people are pressured by their families to take jobs that are more secure; Ning often had to get on the phone with parents to persuade them that their child was making a good choice. In fact, Ning pointed to something that I hear again and again from successful Chinese—many new firms are created by people who returned from the United States. She was hard-pressed to identify many successful examples of Chinese entrepreneur-based companies—Tencent, Alibaba, and Baidu were the ones that came to her mind—and she contrasted this with the United States, where she argued, there is a new batch of such firms every five years.[138] Lee also sees additional limitations, arguing: "The Chinese education system makes people hardworking, teaches people strong fundamentals, and makes them very good at rote learning. It doesn't make them creative, original thinkers." Out-of-the-box thinkers are either pushed toward conventional thinking or "become outcasts."[139]

Yet when I returned in 2017, there was no shortage of willing Chinese tech entrepreneurs, and confidence in China's future as a global tech power was at an all-time high. I met with Anita Huang, chief marketing officer for Sinovation. When I tried to ask about challenges to innovation in China, Huang cut me off: they are not looking for scientific breakthroughs, she said, they are looking for innovation tied to business. This is an area in which China excels. Huang pointed out that mobile Internet technology in China now far surpasses that in the United States. She uses her phone to order haircuts, food, and to arrange for movers for her home. Even food stall owners in China accept payment via smartphone. During a recent trip to the United States, she relayed, she forgot cash—because few people in China have need for it—and couldn't pay for a taxi ride using her phone.

It is an argument I have heard Lee Kai-Fu make. Speaking in New York before a packed audience of mostly Chinese and Chinese Americans in 2016, Lee argued that China is well positioned to surpass the United States as the world's "best breeding ground for internet startup companies" given the sheer density of its cities.[140] Lee noted that the urban migration process has led to fifty-four cities in China with over 2 million people, providing great opportunities for urban services such as nail salons, barbers, or food delivery. Baidu, China's leading search engine, created a "doctor Baidu" app that informs users of the best nearby physician and allows them to schedule appointments. Just six months after its launch, the app was available in six provinces and to 340 million citizens.[141] When asked by one audience member about the impact of the increasingly challenging Internet restrictions in China under Xi Jinping, Lee simply shrugged and said that now it is clearer what is allowed and what isn't.[142]

While support for digital technology start-ups had been the bread and butter for Sinovation, Huang told me that they are now most excited about the potential of artificial intelligence (AI). Sinovation has an AI Institute with about forty full-time staff and twenty interns. She believes that China has the potential to lead the world in AI because it generated so much more data than any other place and the government was much more pragmatic than in other countries. She used the example of driverless cars to illustrate her point. While in the United States, the government would require years of testing and develop reams of regulations, she argued, in China, the government would encourage companies to forge ahead. If there were a few accidents, that was okay. China would come out ahead.

Huang's compelling blend of optimism and pragmatism is widely shared, and when I sat down with Ming Lei, a cofounder of Baidu, I became a believer. Lei led the team that developed Baidu's search engine—the heart and soul of the company. An engineering graduate of Peking University, after his time at Baidu, Lei spent two years at Stanford Business School and was heavily recruited by top U.S. firms, such as Google. Yet Lei knew he would return to China; he considers himself a "Chinese nationalist" and didn't want to work for an American competitor. After he returned to China, he founded an online digital music company, Kuwo, spending eight tough years from 2005 until 2013 building the company. By 2010, Kuwo was the number one company in its space with more than 200 million users, but Lei wanted out. By 2012 he was looking to merge, first with China Music Corporation, which then eventually merged with Tencent's QQ music. Lei now sponsors research at Beijing Normal University, teaches a popular course on AI at Peking University, incubates a couple of AI companies with his own money, and is finishing a book on children's education.

Like Huang, Lei believes that China will be a leader in AI, and he sketched for me why. Part of his argument is unsurprising. Chinese excel in how to use and apply technology. The other part is more counterintuitive: the structural weaknesses in China's economy and social system provide opportunities to leapfrog over countries that provide more and better public goods. The weaknesses in China's healthcare system, for example, provide a gap which AI and entrepreneurs can fill. In the EU or the United States, the need and urgency are much less since the system is much better developed. Still, Lei argues that China remains well behind the United States in basic research and scientific innovation. "The smartest guys," he says, "go to the United States."

The Pot of Gold

While money continues to flow into the tech start-up sector, some of the inefficiencies and waste that plague the electric car sector are also emerging in venture capital (VC). Venture capital investment in China began during the 1990s and grew from "virtually nothing" to $858 million in 2000.[143] Most of the VC firms at that time were SOEs and had no experience in picking new technologies or good investments. Performance was underwhelming. Yet the Chinese government continues to play an active role in picking winners and losers, investing more than $16 billion in state-owned VC funds during the past almost two decades.[144]

Foreign VCs like Rieschel's Qiming bring both capital and knowledge. In 2015, VC firms invested $37 billion in China—more than double the previous year.[145] Qiming, alone, has more than $2.5 billion under management and receives almost one thousand pitches per month from start-ups.[146] Rieschel has frequently partnered with different parts of the Chinese government and reveals that different government actors play very differently. The NDRC, for example, which supported a Qiming RMB fund for healthcare in 2008, had no appetite for risk, telling the firm: "Do innovative stuff but don't lose any money." The Suzhou local government, which invests in all the top VC funds, in contrast, is not intrusive and unlike other regional governments doesn't require that deals are done locally.

Rieschel argues that while at one level the flood of government money is a good thing, too much money keeps companies alive that should die, and it muddies the water for the best ideas, making it harder for them to succeed. Over the long run, says Rieschel, the Chinese government cannot afford to keep pouring money into the sector and trying to pick winners and losers because only the truly innovative firms will generate the jobs that China needs moving forward. As he noted in an interview with the *Wall Street Journal*, "they [the government] have a fantasy that if they give everyone money they'll create entrepreneurs." What they are more likely to get, however are "inexperienced or corrupt managers" investing in regional copycats that are "unable to get big enough to be profitable," resulting in "catastrophic losses for the government."[147]

Whether money will continue to flood into the tech world is an open question. Investment by VC firms in 2016 was not quite half the $69 billion deployed in the United States. Some, however, wonder whether the reported numbers are accurate. According to Rui Ma, a Beijing-based venture capitalist, over 50 percent of start-ups typically engage in investment inflation, sometimes aided by the VC firms themselves that want to appear more robust than they actually are.[148] Moreover, according to Lee Kai-Fu, as Chinese economic growth has slowed, there is less money for start-ups as well. A small survey of thirty entrepreneurs by *China Daily* supports Lee's assessment. It found that 60 percent of them had problems attracting investment.[149]

Conclusion

Ming Lei may well be right that China lags behind the United States in invention—the breakthrough scientific discovery that disrupts an industry. It is in this arena that the limitations of China's political system become important. Constraints on education and the Internet, intellectual property theft, and a perverted system of rewards for research all hinder the development of an environment that fosters top-quality basic research.

Thus far Xi Jinping and the rest of the Chinese leadership, however, appear willing to forgo the structural reform that would enable China to lead in basic research and contribute to the development of breakthrough technologies in favor of the type of applied innovation that has made Jack Ma a household name. Chinese companies have become global leaders in mobile technology, and, if Lei and Huang have anything to say about it, are well on their way to becoming a powerhouse in AI. Innovation in China, as in most countries, now occurs in many different sectors of society, including businesses, universities, beautiful shared workspaces like 3Q, and incubators like Sinovation. And with an internal market of more than 1.3 billion people, Chinese technology companies can realize enormous success without casting their eyes abroad.

The experience of China's electric car sector represents yet another facet of China's innovation culture. It underscores the downside of China's refusal to reform and of the continued dominance of the Chinese state in the country's larger innovation ecosystem. Beijing identifies promising sectors and technologies for government investment, works through several different ministries and localities to promote the development and deployment of these technologies, and may constrain opportunities for competitive multinationals in the development of the country's domestic market, unless they are willing to part with their technologies. The costs are consequential. Even in the face of poor initial performance of Chinese indigenous technology and weak acceptance of it in the Chinese market, the government persists. Beijing's willingness to accept suboptimal technological outcomes in order for Chinese firms to capture the market—as in the case of battery technologies—leads to significant waste of resources and inefficiencies.

After more than a decade in development with billions of dollars of state funding, Chinese electric cars still compete only on a cost, not a quality, basis with the top international brands.

At the same time, while firms such as those of Rieschel and Lee help impose a market discipline on the world of start-ups in China, the government at all levels is eager to be a significant player in the investment arena. The result is a tech sector shaped not only by the quality of the innovation and the broader fortunes of the Chinese economy but also by the same inefficiencies and waste that infect state-driven innovation in sectors such as electric cars. As Rieschel states, it will only be harder for good companies to thrive in a world in which bad companies are not allowed to fail.

Underpinning much of the challenge in both China's SOE reform and the innovation sector, therefore, is a reluctance on the part of the Chinese leadership to relax the reins of state control and to allow the market to serve as a disciplining agent—helping to separate the best ideas from the weaker ones and the better companies from the poorer ones. The government is willing to tolerate a higher level of waste and inefficiency in the cause of capturing market share and fulfilling other developmental and strategic objectives. As the next chapter reveals, a similar pattern can also be found in China's efforts to address its air quality problem, where market forces—both economic and in the political realm of civil society—are taking a back seat to state-directed initiatives.

6

War on Pollution

IT ALL STARTED WITH a tweet. In 2008, the U.S. embassy in Beijing, concerned about the health of its employees, started tweeting hourly air quality reports from a rooftop monitor. The reports contained data on PM2.5, the smallest and most damaging particulates to people's health. When the air quality was particularly bad, the tweets alerted employees to stay indoors or to avoid strenuous exercise. The tweets were the only source of public information on the pollutant; the Chinese government did not have the capacity (or perhaps the desire) to make such real-time environmental information available.

As the tweets gained attention, Chinese officials asked the embassy to halt the Twitter feed, claiming the data were "not only confusing but also insulting." The embassy, however, continued to tweet the information. Chinese PM2.5 levels consistently measured well above those the United States would term safe: on one day in 2010 the embassy deemed a PM2.5 concentration "crazy bad."[1] Several prominent Chinese bloggers, including the children's author Zheng Yuanjie and real estate mogul and chairman of SOHO China Pan Shiyi, went online to press Beijing to take action. They asked their followers to respond to polls on the city's air quality. In November 2011, Zheng asked what Beijing residents thought about the quality of their air; of the almost seven thousand respondents, 89 percent replied that the air was "getting worse."[2]

The following month, in December 2011, smog led to the cancellation of almost seven hundred flights at the Beijing airport. This was not the first time that pollution had led officials to ground flights. However, the discrepancy between the Chinese government's claim that "fog" had caused the cancellations and the U.S. embassy tweets reporting on the traffic-stopping levels of air pollution resulted in an online uproar. Already in the previous month, Beijing netizens had criticized the local environmental protection bureau (EPB) when it had reported the city's air pollution as "light" while the embassy recorded the pollution as "beyond index." Following the December cover-up attempt, Pan Shiyi, who at the time had more than 7 million followers, launched an Internet poll in January 2012, seeking support to convince the Beijing government to publish PM2.5 data. More than 98 percent of the 38,000 total participants voted "yes" for public transparency.[3]

The government finally began to respond. In 2012, China began releasing its own PM2.5 statistics. Over the course of the year, it put in place as many as five hundred PM2.5 monitoring stations in over seventy cities around the country; and by the end of the year it had pledged hundreds of billions of dollars for air pollution reduction.[4]

Still the Chinese people were looking for results. When Beijing reported the city's air quality, for example, it characterized pollution levels in less alarmist ways than the United States: what constituted "good" in China was rated "unhealthy" by the United States. Chinese citizens were quick to pick up on the difference. As one Chinese netizen noted, "I never understand the Environmental Protection Ministry, especially this sentence: 'They [the United States] use their own country's air quality standards to evaluate ours, which is clearly unreasonable.' Does this mean Americans are higher human beings or lower human beings than Chinese?" At one point, the Chinese Ministry of Foreign Affairs tried to shut down the embassy tweets, arguing they contravened the Vienna Convention on Diplomatic Relations, in which "foreign diplomats are required to respect and follow local laws and cannot interfere in internal affairs."[5]

As the new Chinese leadership took power in late 2012, the salience of the issue remained high. In early 2013, PM2.5 levels soared above 800 on the 500-point scale, and Chinese netizens began referring to the situation as an "Airpocalypse."[6] The air quality was so bad that even state-run media took note of the problem. The Chinese people were bombarded by frightening information and images: breathing the air in Beijing was equivalent to smoking two packs of cigarettes per day; over 1 million Chinese were dying prematurely from air pollution–related respiratory diseases annually. The *People's Daily*, in particular, ran a front-page editorial titled "A Beautiful China Starts with Healthy Breathing" (*meili zhongguo, cong jiankang huxi kaishi,* 美丽中国，从健康呼吸开始) that described the dire state of the problem and emphasized the need to address the issue systemically rather than simply by crisis management.[7]

Despite the public outcry, the Chinese government begged for more time. Premier Li claimed in January 2013 that Beijing's air pollution represented "accumulated problems" that would take a long time to solve and would necessitate the "concerted effort of the whole society."[8] Yet societal pressure did not abate. Pan Shiyi launched a second poll that called for the creation of a "clean air act" in China, garnering 32,000 "yes" votes in just ten hours.[9] Pan's online environmental activism was cut short, however, when authorities accused him of being manipulated by "hostile foreign forces" and forced him to admit his "irresponsible social media usage" on CCTV.[10] Other environmental activists, however, took up the cause. That same year, well-known environmentalist Ma Jun, founder of the Beijing-based environmental nonprofit Institute for Public Environment, launched a social media pollution-mapping program that relied on Chinese netizens to locate, photograph, and report on polluting enterprises.[11] In early March, Premier Li relented, acknowledging that the government had failed to achieve much progress, and announcing that Beijing would meet China's environmental challenge with "an iron fist, firm resolution and tough measures."[12]

The Environment for Development

The Chinese leadership has its work cut out for it. The rapid and unfettered growth of the Chinese economy has contributed to an environmental disaster. Levels of air, water, and soil pollution are among the highest in the world. In 2015, none of the more than three hundred cities China monitors for air quality met the World Health Organization's air quality standards, and two-thirds of the country's cities could not even meet the country's own lower air quality standards. The country's overwhelming reliance on fossil fuel is one part of the problem. Coal accounts for more than 65 percent of the country's electricity use, and 62 percent of the country's energy overall. Moreover, as China's urban middle class expands, and income levels continue to rise, more energy is consumed: on average urban residents use as much as four times more energy than their rural counterparts.[13]

As the Chinese people have become wealthier, they have also taken to the road. As we saw in the previous chapter, China is now the world's largest car market. Levels of airborne particulates in Beijing are six times higher than in New York City; according to the Beijing Municipal Environmental Protection Bureau, about 20 percent of the fine particulate matter that is most damaging to human health (PM2.5) arises from automobile exhaust emissions.[14]

While air pollution may be the most visible and visceral of the country's environmental problems, water scarcity and pollution is in some respects a greater concern. Up to 40 percent of China's rivers are seriously polluted, and 20 percent are so polluted that their water quality is rated too toxic for physical contact.[15] China's Ministry of Environmental Protection (MEP) reported that in 2015, 280 million Chinese did not have access to safe drinking water.[16] The Yellow River, which traverses the country from west to east, is by one account, 10 percent sewage by volume.[17] Researchers at the Guangzhou Institute of Geochemistry at the Chinese Academy of Sciences have also revealed that one-third of the 162,000 tons of antibiotics consumed by China in 2013—more than half the global total—ended up in the country's water supply and soil.[18] Although the Chinese government assures their citizens that 80 percent of the water leaving treatment facilities meets government standards, by the time it travels through decaying infrastructure, it is generally no longer potable.

Rising water scarcity compounds the problem. Household and industrial demand for water is increasing dramatically, even as agriculture continues to account for the largest share of the country's water resources. From 2005 until 2015, agricultural demand for water increased from 358 to 385 billion m^3. At the same time, demand from industry jumped from 129 to 194 billion m^3; and municipal and household from 68 to 88 billion m^3. China is also notoriously water inefficient, losing up to 20 percent of its water to leaky pipes, and Chinese industry uses four to ten times the amount of water per unit of production than the average industrialized nation.[19] The consequences are grave. In the 1990s, China boasted 50,000 rivers; by 2013, that number had dropped precipitously to 23,000.[20] Cities such as Shanghai are sinking, as water is pumped out of underground aquifers to meet development demands. Ten provinces in China now rank below the World Bank's water poverty level of 1,000 m³ per person per year, and these provinces account for 45 percent of the mainland's GDP, 40 percent of its agricultural output, and more than half of its industrial production. According to vice-minister of Water Resources Jiao Yong, in 2012, China boasted more than 400 cities without sufficient water, and of those, 110 faced serious scarcity.[21] By 2030, the Chinese government anticipates a gap between demand and supply of water of 201 billion m³.[22] The United Nations ranks China one of thirteen countries in the world most affected by water scarcity.

China also must contend with high rates of land degradation and desertification. Deforestation, overgrazing of grasslands, and intensive agricultural practices have contributed to severe soil erosion and degradation in China's north and northwest regions. According to a survey by State Forestry Administration officials, well over 1 million square miles—roughly one-quarter of China's land—is now desert or facing desertification.[23]

At the same time, China's soil also suffers from serious contamination. In April 2014, the MEP released the broad outlines of its land pollution survey—which it had classified as secret one year earlier—and reported that 16.1 percent of the country's land was contaminated with heavy metal pollutants and nearly 20 percent of the farmland was heavily polluted. That same year, the National Environmental Monitoring Center produced a report that said that of five thousand vegetable plots sampled throughout the country, 25 percent were contaminated. While many of the contaminants, such as mercury, cadmium, and arsenic, are the result of pollution from coal-fired power plants or other heavy industries, there are other sources as well. In June 2015, the popular *Caixin* magazine reported that in one Beijing village, 45,000 cubic meters of garbage reached 5 meters into the ground and mixed with groundwater, contaminating both the water and soil. In and around Beijing, there are more than one thousand such unregulated landfills.[24]

These reports underscored once again the implications of the country's environmental practices for the health of its citizens.

The Air We Breathe, the Food We Eat, the Water We Drink

In a 2015 Pew Foundation poll, air pollution ranked second and water pollution third in a list of fifteen serious problems identified by the Chinese people. Only "corrupt officials" ranked higher.[25] Underlying the populace's concern is how the environment affects people's health. The most highly publicized health effect of Chinese pollution is the heightened risk of respiratory problems stemming from air pollution. In December 2016, for example, Beijing, along with twenty-one other cities in north and central China, issued a red alert in the face of a five-day period of dense smog. The cities ordered schools to close, imposed even-odd license restrictions for travel into the city, and called for thousands of factories to limit or stop production. There were reports of people with small children fleeing the city if they could. As a result, expensive private schools in Beijing put domes around their playing fields to try to protect the children from the poor air quality. And Chinese people walk around not only with air filtration masks but also with hand-held sensors so that they can determine whether any particular microenvironment is hazardous to their health. In a recent and widely publicized paper, scientists Robert Rohde and Richard Muller found that 1.6 million people in China die prematurely every year—or about four thousand per day—because of air pollution.[26]

While air pollution has long dominated the environment and health discourse, soil and water contamination are also of central concern to the Chinese people. Lee Liu, a geographer at the University of Central Missouri, has identified 459 cancer villages—villages in which cancer rates are significantly higher than normal—throughout the country. Most are clustered around rivers with the worst grade for pollution on the government's five-point scale. Some of these villages have cancer rates thirty times greater than the national average. In February 2013, the government-financed newspaper the *Global Times* took the unusual step of acknowledging the existences of these cancer villages and their link to pollution. Much like those who documented the ties between water pollution and the cancer villages,

Chinese public health experts are now exploring villages where rates of cadmium poisoning are excessive. Cadmium can enter the body in several ways, through direct contact with the metal or through consumption of contaminated soil, water, or food. *Caixin* reporter Liu Hongqiao completed a detailed study in 2014 of one town in Hunan Province and found that several hundred people demonstrated elevated levels of cadmium, over two hundred had been diagnosed with cadmium poisoning, and several deaths were attributed to poisoning as well.[27]

It's the Economy, Stupid

The economic losses from environmental pollution and degradation are another source of concern for both the Chinese government and people. There are no definitive numbers associated with the economic costs—they are notoriously difficult to calculate and different assessments incorporate different factors. However, economists have traditionally estimated that environmental degradation and pollution cost the Chinese economy the equivalent of anywhere from 3 to 10 percent of GDP annually from missed days of work due to pollution-related illness, crops lost to pollution, and decline in tourism due to air pollution, among other externalities.[28] More narrowly focused studies, for example a 2015 study by the U.S.-based RAND Corporation, have placed the cost of soil pollution to the Chinese economy at 1.1 percent of GDP,[29] and water pollution at 2.1 percent of GDP.[30] A recently published retrospective analysis by the Chinese Academy of Science that accounted for air and water pollution, as well as consumption of resources and ecological degradation, assessed environmental externalities as equivalent to 13.5 percent of GDP in 2005.[31]

While the macro numbers are astonishing, the real impact is felt on the ground, where jobs and livelihoods are at stake. And the detrimental health impacts of pollution themselves can further detract from economic well-being. For example, the international environmental NGO Greenpeace estimated that if Beijing, Shanghai, Guangzhou, and Xi'an could meet the World Health Organization's air quality guidelines, PM2.5-induced deaths would decrease by 81 percent and the cities could prevent up to $868 million of economic losses.[32]

Crop loss is an additional environment-induced economic burden. Investigative journalist He Guangwei revealed that farmers often know that their vegetables are contaminated with cadmium or mercury and therefore rarely eat local produce. Yet, if they acknowledge that the crops are contaminated, they will lose business and the local economy will suffer. When batches of rice from Hunan Province were discovered to have cadmium levels exceeding government limits, sales of all rice from the province plummeted.[33] He reported that this type of pollution decreases China's harvest by 11 million tons annually and that China produces as much as 12 million tons of heavy metal–contaminated grain every year, costing the Chinese economy more than $3.2 billion.

Water scarcity and pollution are particularly challenging. Water scarcity limits the development of industry: China's desire to develop its large reserves of shale gas to offset its planned reduction in coal consumption, for example, is hampered by the location of the reserves. Fracking is highly water intensive, and more than 60 percent of China's shale resources are located in water-scarce areas.[34] In addition, water scarcity and the encroaching desert have produced hundreds of thousands of internal environmental refugees. As the desert expands by more than 1,300 square miles annually, the *New York Times* reported in late 2016 that China faced the specter of over 325,000 internal "ecological migrants"—Chinese citizens who are forced to move largely because of shrinking water resources and the expanding desert.

Water pollution can be equally devastating. A team of Chinese and American scientists analyzed five decades of China's coastal marine ecosystem and found it had "steadily degraded to an almost irreversible point," with both the diversity and number of fish species falling steadily over time. Coral cover in the South China Sea, as well, has fallen to 15 percent of its 1978 level.[35] And over the past decades of economic growth, the prawn catch in China's Bohai Sea has fallen by 90 percent.[36]

China's reputation—and Beijing's in particular—also suffers as a result of its pollution problems, particularly because of the very visible air pollution. Pictures of runners wearing protective face masks to counter air pollution during the annual Beijing marathon undermine the city's allure, as do reports of multinationals offering hazard pay to their expat workers stationed in Beijing.[37] Surveys point to the environment as a leading cause of wealthy Chinese leaving the country and moving abroad and of fewer people visiting the country. Tourism in China from outside the country fell in each of three years between 2012 and 2014, with pollution cited as one of the top reasons. Beijing alone experienced a 50 percent drop in tourism in 2013 largely as a result of the air pollution.[38] One online Chinese tourism agency also estimated in 2016 that more than 1 million Chinese traveled abroad annually just to escape pollution.[39]

Taking It to the Streets

While the Chinese people worry about the health-related consequences of pollution, Chinese officials fear pollution-related social unrest. In 2013, a former senior party official acknowledged that the environment had surpassed illegal land expropriation as the largest source of social unrest in the country.[40] Protests around environmental issues stems overwhelmingly, but not exclusively, from "Not in my backyard" (NIMBY) considerations. Chinese citizens fear the health ramifications, as well as the potential loss of property values, when factories or waste incinerators are sited near their homes. The Chinese leaders' plan to develop the country's nuclear industry has become a new and significant source of concern for many Chinese people. The government has outlined plans to construct sixty nuclear power plants in China over the next decade and to become a global export powerhouse in the nuclear industry. Yet these plans are increasingly in doubt given growing popular unease. In one case, in August 2016, as many as ten thousand citizens in the coastal city of Lianyungang, about three hundred miles north of Shanghai, took to the streets for several days to protest plans to place a nuclear waste processing plant in their city. Residents complained that the local government had kept the project a secret and, in any case, the city already was home to a chemical industrial park. Local public security bureau officials attempted to bring the protests to a halt with an online warning that such protests were illegal. Hosts of online chat forums that spread news of the protests were "invited to tea" (a euphemism for an interrogation by public security bureau officials), and local officials tried to quell the protests by sending in riot police who dispersed the crowds, often violently. Yet the protestors were not deterred and returned the next day. In the end, local officials suspended plans for the $15 billion nuclear waste processing plant. At the same time, residents in Zhanjiang, Guangdong, a second possible site for the plant, also protested and forced local leaders there to withdraw the city from consideration for the plant's location.

The reaction of these local officials is increasingly the norm in China. Confronted with the specter of multiday, mass demonstrations that are fueled and amplified by social media, officials often try at first to threaten the protestors, then detain the protest leaders, and finally end the protests with a combination of violence and promises not to move forward with a planned project.

A 2016 editorial in *Caixin* suggested that officials need to change their behavior if they are to develop the public consensus necessary to move forward with such projects by promoting transparency about the project, educating the public, and setting a legal framework to guarantee the public's right to know about the projects. The editorial excoriated local officials for trying to hide plans and breeding distrust in the public by waiting until protests occurred before attempting to educate people.[41] Comments from domestic and foreign nuclear safety regulators to the effect that Chinese nuclear management standards "are not high enough" and that the National Nuclear Safety Administration is "overwhelmed" suggest there is reason for concern.[42]

The selection of Li Ganjie as Minister of Environmental Protection in June 2017 may help improve the situation. Li served for nine years as vice-minister in charge of nuclear safety within the Ministry of Environmental Protection and has pledged to improve transparency in environmental decision-making. As early as 2013 Li stated, "If the public doesn't participate in the process, and is unable to get explanations and timely answers to their questions, this generates mistrust and suspicion."[43] Moreover, draft regulations governing the approval process for nuclear power plants—reportedly eight years in development—include requirements that local governments hold debates among experts and public hearings about potential nuclear plants and radioactive waste-recycling centers before a site is selected.[44]

Yet such requirements for public transparency and debate have long been required under China's environmental regulations. The regulations will make little difference unless they are fully implemented.

As we will see, while Beijing can pass laws, the ability to enforce them remains an ongoing challenge.

The War on Pollution

Xi Jinping and the rest of the Chinese leadership recognize the range of economic, social, and political costs that environmental pollution inflicts on the Chinese people, as well as the price the leadership itself pays in terms of its legitimacy. Early in their tenure, they invoked the same dire language and military campaign rhetoric they used to describe the corruption challenge. In May 2013, Xi Jinping called for an ecological "red line" to prevent development from harming the environment and promised that officials who crossed the line would be punished. He also pledged that the environment would not be sacrificed for temporary economic growth and reinforced this point in a September 2013 speech before provincial leaders in Hebei—one of the country's most polluted provinces and, importantly, one frequently blamed for contributing to Beijing's air pollution—where he called for officials to be evaluated not only on the basis of how well they grew their GDP but also on how effectively they advanced environmental protection.[45] Six months later in March 2014, at the annual gathering of the NPC, Premier Li Keqiang called for a war on pollution,[46] noting that pollution was a significant problem and that the environment had sent a "red light warning" against the country's model of economic development.[47]

The Chinese leaders adopted air pollution as their first environmental priority. It was the most visible of the country's environmental challenges and, as the online campaign by Chinese netizens suggested, the most publicly discussed and debated. Tackling air pollution also had a secondary benefit of beginning to address complaints by the international community over the global impact of China's air pollution. Beijing was publicly embarrassed by reports that other countries could track toxic pollution clouds that affected their citizens back to Chinese factory emissions. In addition, as the world's largest contributor to climate change, China faced enormous international pressure to take action. Any meaningful response to local air pollution would simultaneously help reduce the country's emissions of the greenhouse gas carbon dioxide.

The leaders' approach reflected their newfound belief that, as Li Keqiang acknowledged in March 2013, the Chinese people were not prepared to wait for results. Over the next four years, the government passed a raft of impressive new environmental laws and regulations, adopted traditional state-directed campaigns with targets and time-tables for emissions, moved to centralize authority for environmental protection, and undertook a handful of legal and institutional reforms. Despite the new vigor demonstrated by the leadership to address the country's air pollution, however, the approach is overwhelmingly government centered and top-down in orientation. Input from the Chinese people and businesses remains highly constrained, depriving the government of important feedback and contributing to significant failures in policy implementation. Some regulations have been rolled back, raising questions over the sustainability of the government's commitment. And in a few critical respects, government policies continue to favor cheaper, dirtier growth over improved air quality.

Air Pollution's Dirty Past

Li Keqiang's assertion in January 2013 that air pollution in China had been a long time in the making and would therefore require time to address, while politically unpopular, was not without merit. The early decades of Communist Party rule caused dramatic new problems for the country's air quality. Mao's Third Front policy shifted factories to mountainous areas in China's interior to protect against potential foreign attacks, and the pollution they released became trapped in valley areas.[48] The Chinese government paid cursory attention to environmental issues in its planning, and the two decades spanning Mao's tumultuous campaigns, the Great Leap Forward and Cultural Revolution from 1958 to 1976, had devastating environmental ramifications. As Qu Geping, who was appointed China's first environmental agency head in the 1980s, described the period: "The environmental situation quickly deteriorated. A lot of places were polluted by either smog, sewage waters or rubbish . . . . There was extensive destruction of the natural environment of our country."[49] He described Beijing as transformed from a city that "did not produce even pencils" to one that boasted "700 factories and 2000 blast furnaces belching soot in the air."[50]

Little improved in the immediate aftermath of this period. British environmentalist Norman Myers described what he witnessed during his travels in the mid-1970s: "Many of China's urban areas contain a relatively low density of factories, due to the moderate degree of overall industrialization and a policy of dispersing light manufacturing and processing plants to communes in the countryside. But in Peking, on more days than not, atmospheric contamination cuts visibility substantially. In the lower Yangtze Valley, the city of Soochow is especially blighted with smoke from scores of exhaust stacks. Steel centers such as Anshan, and other industrial localities such as Wuhan, Tientsin, and Harbin, lie under smoke palls of varying intensities."[51]

Canadian geographer Vaclav Smil also documented the early signals of health-related consequences from pollution, focusing in particular on indoor air pollution from the burning of coal and biomass for cooking and heating. He pointed to high winter concentrations of particulate matter and sulfur dioxide as responsible for chronic respiratory diseases,[52] and Myers suggested that an "enlargement of the liver"[53] among school children in Beijing could have been caused by sulfur dioxide from a steel and iron factory.[54]

Yet the 1970s also marked the beginning of an environmental awakening in China. In the aftermath of the 1972 United Nations Conference on the Human Environment in Stockholm, China established a number of broad environmental guidelines, and in the following years codified more specific regulations regarding rare wild animals, industrial waste, and food safety, among other environment-related concerns.[55] In addition, in November 1978, the State Economic Commission and the State Council's Office for Environmental Protection ordered 167 of the country's largest industrial polluters, including those in the petroleum, coal, and building materials sectors, to install pollution controls or recycling processes within four years.[56] Implementation, however, was haphazard. The government also drafted the country's first comprehensive environmental law, the Environmental Protection Law for Trial Implementation of 1979 (in effect until the Environmental Protection Law of 1989 was passed). Throughout the 1980s China enacted a number of other "first-generation" environmental laws, including those to regulate marine systems, water pollution, forests, and grasslands.[57] The first major legal measure to address air quality was the 1987 Air Pollution

Prevention and Control Law (APPCL). Like many Chinese laws at the time, the APPCL—only eight pages long—was "broad, but vague," outlining responsibilities for various government agencies but lacking critical details for implementation and an understanding of the impact of the private economy on the environment.[58] It was, in the words of some China legal scholars, "aspirational" and prone to "highly general and exhortational terms" rather than specific and concrete language.[59] Certainly the APPCL—and its revised version in 1995—was no match for the surging coal consumption, double-digit economic growth, and quadrupling private automobile ownership that characterized China during the 1990s.[60] By the turn of the century, nearly all Chinese cities exceeded air quality standards for the major pollutants: TSP, NO_x, and SO_2,[61] and only 27.6 percent of over three hundred surveyed cities met the favorable Class II national standards for air quality. Beijing, Tianjin, and Shanghai topped the list for worst air overall.[62]

Further revisions to the APPCL in 2000 strengthened the law by developing a national system to collect emissions fees, shifting to total loading when calculating total pollutants emitted,[63] and strengthening vehicle emissions regulations. Additional legislation followed. In 2002 and 2003, China specifically targeted acid rain, sulfur dioxide (SO_2) emissions, and high-sulfur coal;[64] and in 2006, the State Environmental Protection Administration (elevated to a cabinet-level ministry and renamed the MEP in 2008) established five regional supervision centers to oversee local governments' implementation of environmental efforts.[65] Yet in this instance, as well, the government efforts fell short. The regulations failed to establish a system of penalties to discourage factories from polluting, to provide enough resources to the environmental protection bureaucracy to monitor and enforce the regulations, and to ensure that the standards themselves were stringent enough to protect the health of the Chinese people.

China's environment and its air quality continued to decline. Tens of thousands of small township and village enterprises polluted the air, water, and land without fear of regulatory enforcement or penalty. Even if government inspections yielded the closure of some factories, they frequently reopened after the inspectors had left.[66] Through the 1990s and 2000s, as China's economy continued to grow at a record-setting pace, so too did its environmental pollution and degradation; by the late 2000s, the country boasted ten of the world's fifteen most polluted cities. China's environmental challenges also began to receive international attention. In the lead-up to the 2008 Beijing Olympics, the environment became a contentious issue when international athletes raised concerns over the quality of the air. Beijing was forced to adopt a number of draconian measures to help ensure clean air, such as stopping construction, moving or shutting down heavily polluting factories, and cutting automobile usage in half.[67] Such stop-gap measures, however, failed to address the root causes of the problem. By 2010, only one city out of 113 surveyed by the MEP had air quality that met China's top-level standard.[68]

The Clean Air Challenge

In March 2017, three years after declaring "war on pollution," Li Keqiang stood before the NPC and pledged once more, "We will make our skies blue again."[69] For China's leaders, the environment, and air quality in particular, has become much more than a casualty of rapid economic development and weak political enforcement. There are serious costs to people's health, to the economy, to social stability, and to the country's reputation. It has become for Xi Jinping and the rest of the Chinese leadership an issue of political legitimacy.

On the face of it, the Chinese leadership has made some impressive strides toward addressing the challenge. According to official statistics, levels of PM2.5 have declined steadily over the past four years in a number of cities. Among the seventy-four cities under new air quality standards, the average PM2.5 concentration fell by 9.1 percent from 2015 to 2016, and that came on the heels of a 14.1 percent improvement over 2014. Beijing's average PM2.5 concentration, alone, has fallen from 89.5 in 2013 to 73 in 2016.[70] China also achieved a significant reduction in the percentage of coal in the country's overall energy mix to 62 percent in 2016—partly because of a slowing economy, partly because of measures to cut coal production and use, and partly because of the increased deployment of natural gas and renewables.[71]

Yet the sustainability of the improvement in air quality in at least part of the country remains in question. Several environmental experts suggest that the improvements in air quality have derived in significant measure from short-term, intensive campaign efforts, such as limited factory closures, as opposed to sustainable conservation, pricing reform, or energy-substitution policies. In addition, falsification of pollution data by government and industry officials is so rampant that emissions data cannot be fully trusted. In the first quarter of 2017, environmental inspections in the Beijing-Tianjin-Hebei area found 3,119 out of 8,500 factories had violated regulations through actions such as unrecorded emissions and data tampering and falsifying.[72] Moreover, the continued emphasis on infrastructure development, including highly polluting coal-to-chemical plants, as well as growing constraints on civil society actors involved in grassroots monitoring and organization, hamper efforts to improve the country's air quality. Finally, even as the government seeks to impose heavier fines on businesses for polluting, they offer few incentives for factories to undertake often costly measures to clean up their act. More than previous Chinese leaders, however, the current group has sought to use the legal system to support its enforcement efforts.

Weaving the Legal Web

Xi Jinping and the rest of the Chinese leadership have moved quickly to bolster the legal infrastructure underpinning environmental protection. Within their first year in office, they delivered a succession of increasingly stringent laws, regulations, and guidelines on air pollution. The twelfth Five-Year Plan on Air Pollution Prevention and Control in Key Regions in December 2012 (the drafting of which predated the new leadership), the Ten Measures of the State Council in June 2013, and the Action Plan for Air Pollution Prevention and Control in September 2013 all sought to establish priority areas for controlling pollution, set targets and timetables for reducing the most significant pollutants, and provide detailed guidance on specific projects for air pollution reduction.

The Action Plan set clear benchmarks for measuring the government's success or failure. Among the most salient elements of the final Action Plan was the focus on three priority regions: the Beijing-Tianjin-Hebei region, the Yangtze River delta, and the Pearl River delta, and the call for respective cuts of 25, 20, and 15 percent from 2012 PM2.5 levels in the three regions by 2017. (There are additional reductions for other pollutants, including SO_2, NO_2, and PM10.) Taken together these priority areas account for only 14 percent of China's land area but 48 percent of its population, 71 percent of GDP, and 52 percent of coal consumption.[73] In addition, the Action Plan stipulated that the consumption of coal nationwide was to drop below 65 percent of total energy consumption by 2017, and in the three priority areas, total coal consumption would achieve negative growth.

The price tag for the plan was high. A 125-page document associated with the twelfth Five-Year Plan on Air Pollution Prevention and Control detailed a list of projects to reduce emissions with a price tag of $55.6 billion. However, by the time the Action Plan was announced, the total cost of filling the government's air pollution control mandate had skyrocketed to $258 billion. To sweeten the pot, the central government promised financial incentives totaling $1.64 billion for cities that made significant progress in reducing concentrations of PM2.5 and other pollutants.[74] (The air pollution Action Plan was later followed by one for water [2015] and soil [2017].)

These initial efforts were reinforced by revisions to the APPCL, which were released to the public in September 2014, approved by the State Council that November, and adopted by the NPC in August 2015,[75] and by the passage of the thirteenth Five-Year Plan by the NPC in March 2016. One environmental law expert praised this round of revisions to the APPCL in particular for its "transparency and public participation" because the State Council's Legislative Affairs Office circulated the draft law for a month to field comments on the amendments. (Oftentimes, laws are first submitted to the NPC and then later circulated for comments, at which point it is more difficult to affect the final legislation.[76]) Some of the noteworthy revisions included requiring local governments to incorporate air pollution prevention and control into their economic and social development plans, strengthening air pollution control in specific areas based on coal burning, updating emissions permit systems, raising fuel standards, establishing heavy pollution alert systems, and increasing penalties for violating polluters.[77]

As one observer has noted, however, while the law includes many improvements, it also leaves other areas weak or fails to mention them at all. For example, the law still lacks health-based air quality standards, provisions for mandating information disclosure, and positive market-based incentives.[78] A former environmental inspector suggested that a small enterprise worth 1 million yuan ($147,000) cannot afford to spend 2 million yuan to address its pollution.[79] With Beijing still seeking economic growth targets upward of 6 percent, local officials cannot afford to close factories and put workers out of their jobs. In such a situation, collusion between officials and factory managers to evade regulations is certain to persist. A cap on coal use and new powers for local governments to limit vehicle traffic (as Beijing did during the Olympics and World War II victory anniversary parade) also failed to make it from draft versions into the final law.[80]

The Thirteenth Five-Year Plan (2016–2020) supports the same objectives as the APPCL and reinforces some of the elements of previous air pollution regulations, such as a real-time, online environmental monitoring system and the promotion of new energy vehicles, while attempting to fill in some of the holes. It includes quantifiable targets for decreasing energy consumption by 15 percent and a requirement that thirteen provinces suspend coal-fired power plant approvals and fifteen delay new construction. It also set an annual minimum purchase guarantee for wind and solar, as well as minimum electricity consumption quotas from non-hydro renewable sources for each province.[81]

Investing in Institutional Change

The new raft of laws, action plans, and regulations for air pollution reduction provides the framework for China's leaders to address the country's demands. Ensuring that the targets and standards are met, however, necessitates institutional change: restructuring the system of political and economic relationships, and of incentives and disincentives, that shape people's environmental choices. Amending the Environmental Protection Law (EPL) was a crucial first step. According to one author of the amendments, at the beginning of the revision process in 2011, prospects for shaping the document into a strong law were "grim." However, the MEP "catalyzed public dissent" by releasing a lengthy list of arguments against the first draft of the law and managed to obtain a much stronger second draft by mid-2013.[82] By 2014, the PBSC was drafting a final fourth version of the law; most legislative procedures are capped at three rounds of reviews.[83] The final version, which went into effect on January 1, 2015, represented the first time that the law had been amended in twenty-five years and introduced several important innovations to the process of environmental enforcement.

First, the amendments reform the system of environmental fines. Previously fines were a one-time payment that typically was small enough that polluters preferred to pay the fine and continue polluting. In the wake of the amendments, the environmental protection authorities can levy fines on a daily basis so that fines will accumulate for each day that the pollution violation continues. In one case, for example, a zipper company in the coastal city of Suzhou was fined 18,000 RMB ($2,772) per day and the costs climbed to 216,000 ($33,268) before being paid.[84] The MEP reports that in 2015, there were 715 daily penalty cases and the penalties totaled 569 million RMB ($83 million). There were also more than 97,000 administrative penalty cases, with fines totaling 4.25 billion RMB ($623 million). This represented a 34 percent increase over 2014.[85]

Second, the amended EPL includes a provision that protection of the environment will be one of the metrics used when evaluating local officials for promotion. Already the MEP has begun to publish a monthly list of the top ten most polluted cities, with the threat that promotion opportunities for the heads of those cities will be limited.[86] Whether the central organization department, which is responsible for personnel appointments, will actually use this information in its decision-making process, remains unclear. A similar regulation on the books since the mid-1990s failed to gain any significant traction.

In addition, the EPL allows the MEP to take tougher action against officials and others who corrupt the environmental impact assessment (EIA) process or otherwise fake data or improperly operate pollution prevention equipment. Yet violations continue apace. In one MEP survey, officials in several municipalities failed to include thirty or more polluting industrial sites in their lists of sites to be monitored and inspected. Even local environmental bureaus have participated in attempts to skew air pollution monitoring results. In Hanzhong in Shaanxi Province, EPB officials sprayed the air quality monitors with water from a fire hose, believing that this would ameliorate the sky-rocketing PM2.5 readings;[87] and in Xi'an, officials stuffed cotton into the air quality monitors.

Finally, the new EPL expands the ability of the public to bring environmental public interest lawsuits to court.[88] Seven hundred NGOs and government-organized NGOs earned the right to file environmental public interest lawsuits. (In an initial draft of the amendments, only one government-organized NGO had the right to launch a lawsuit.) In 2015, the country's courts heard forty-eight environmental public interest cases compared with a total of sixty-five in the previous eight years. Some of these cases are also being brought against EPBs. In Guizhou Province, for example, a court ruled against a local EPB for failing to enforce laws on water pollution.[89]

Still, challenges remain for NGOs and lawyers interested in bringing lawsuits against companies or officials for environmental wrongdoing. Some environmental activists note that high legal fees and the broader political crackdown on NGOs make their work more difficult. In one case, for example, the government-affiliated All-China Environment Federation (ACEF) sued the Jinghua Group Zhenhua Decoration Glass Limited Company in Shandong Province for emitting hundreds more tons of sulfur dioxide, nitrogen oxide, and smoke dust than stipulated by environmental regulations. The court ordered the company to pay nearly $3.3 million in fines and apologize publicly for its behavior.[90] Winning the Zhenhua case, however, cost the ACEF $75,000 in legal expenses and consultancy fees. While the ACEF has access to government funds, there are very few, if any, NGOs that can afford such fees.[91]

Even when the money can be raised and a court case won, there is no guarantee that the government will not intervene to contravene the decision. In one case, a citizen's group in Shenzhen used a crowd-sourcing campaign to raise almost $45,000 to hire lawyers to take the municipal government to court and force it to release all the information, including the environmental impact assessment, surrounding a hotly contested waste-to-energy plant. The group won its case in the Shenzhen Intermediate People's court, but the Shenzhen government appealed the decision. The case is now "in limbo" in a higher level court, even as construction of the project has begun.[92]

Chinese authorities also take a dim view of more sweeping indictments of official culpability, and courts can simply refuse to hear certain cases. In December 2016, a group of lawyers sued the Beijing, Hebei, and Tianjin governments for failing to address air quality issues effectively. For the lawyers, the broader principle at stake was clear: Is the government above the law? One lawyer noted, "If the government is not restricted by law, then what else can restrict it?" Thus far, a Beijing court has twice refused to hear the lawyers' case, and a court in Hebei has yet to acknowledge a case that was filed.[93]

Breaking the Ties That Bind Us

The 2015 appointment of Tsinghua University President Chen Jining, Li Ganjie's predecessor, as minister of environmental protection, gave credibility to the top leadership's pledge to take the environment seriously and heartened the country's environmental activists. Chen was the first environmental scientist to hold the most senior position in the ministry, and he was one of the few senior officials, along with his fellow technocrat in the Ministry of Science and Technology, Wan Gang, to have studied or had experience abroad. He also displayed a streak of independence rare in top government officials. In a January 2015 graduation speech he delivered for master's and PhD students at Tsinghua, for example, rather than draw on traditional Chinese philosophers or Xi Jinping for inspiration, Chen referenced Malcolm Gladwell's book *Outliers* and noted that he purchased the book during a trip to Taiwan.[94]

A lifelong scholar and political outsider, Chen used his new position to push hard for institutional reform of the environmental protection bureaucracy. In a potentially far-reaching reform, advocated by many Chinese environmental scholars, the government began to reduce the reliance of local EPBs on local governments. Local EPBs have long been crippled by their dependence on local governments and pollution fees from factories for funding.[95] Local officials often have close ties with or financial stakes in local factories, giving them an incentive to protect polluting firms. As a result, they may bring pressure to bear on or sometimes bribe local EPB officials to avoid fines or closing polluting factories. To break this corrupted system, Chen oversaw a number of pilots that delinked local EPBs from local governments and instead made the EPBs directly responsible to provincial environmental protection departments.[96]

A second reform, of equal significance, is the effort to disentangle the EIA process from the environmental protection bureaucracy. The process has long been deeply corrupted, and its mismanagement has had devastating repercussions. The case of the Tianjin warehouse explosion noted in chapter 3 contributed to an important growth in popular awareness of the importance of EIAs. On August 12, 2015, the Ruihai International Logistics chemical warehouse in Tianjin exploded, leaving 173 people dead, as many as 800 injured, over $1 billion in damages, and three hundred buildings destroyed. The warehouse had illegally stored hundreds of tons of dangerous chemicals, including seven hundred tons of highly toxic sodium cyanide. When it blew, it poisoned the groundwater and soil well beyond the area of the explosion. The investigation that followed concluded there had been a number of violations by Ruihai. It had, for example, begun handling hazardous chemicals before it obtained a permit and continued to handle chemicals after its temporary permit expired.

The accident also underscored one of the central weaknesses in China's environmental protection effort—public engagement. In the case of the Ruihai EIA, local officials allowed the company to pay for part of its own review. In addition, the EIA did not note that Ruihai, in direct violation of regulations, had placed a warehouse merely a half-mile from an apartment complex and a train station. Moreover, that 100 percent of the 128 residents surveyed as part of the EIA welcomed the warehouse into their neighborhood suggests that residents were not fully apprised of the dangers or were bribed to look the other way.

Corruption in the EIA process runs throughout the environmental protection bureaucracy. In 2016, the government's anticorruption drive netted, among others, former Vice-Minister of Environmental Protection Zhang Lijun, along with three of his subordinates. The charges were extensive: selling fake quality control certifications and monitoring equipment, interfering in the project approval process, allowing projects to move forward without EIA approval, and permitting changes to be made post-approval.[97] Chinese environmental NGOs undertook their own investigation of the EIA system as well and uncovered an extensive web of fraud in which businesses and local EPBs allowed unlicensed environmental impact assessment companies— even some without any qualified engineers—to undertake EIAs. In some cases, local environmental protection officials hired themselves as inspectors. To help rectify the situation, Minister Chen moved to decouple all the EIAs from the MEP so that departments could not be both "athletes" and "referees."[98] In March 2015, the Ministry announced it had punished sixty-three EIA firms for violating laws and regulations.[99]

Despite Chen's efforts, however, there was backsliding. In September 2016, proposed revisions to the Environmental Impact Assessment Law appeared to weaken the law. The review of the draft law did not engage the public, which was controversial, and removed the requirement that companies go through the EIA process before moving forward with any other parts of a project. In the revised law, companies can pursue permits simultaneously. Several environmental lawyers have asserted that this will lead to the failure of the EIA system:[100] if other permits are received first, the pressure for environmental inspectors to acquiesce to the entire project will be immense.[101] The challenge for the MEP is daunting. An inspection of nearly 20,000 firms in twenty-eight cities in the first half of 2017 found that approximately 14,000 failed to meet air pollution emission standards and more than 4,700 did not have the proper certification and/or were sited in unauthorized locations.[102]

Citizens United

Chinese officials will sometimes reference the horrible levels of air pollution in Los Angeles in the 1950s and 1960s as a means of excusing their own air quality problems as largely a symptom of economic development. Indeed many of the same issues were in play: parents kept their children out of school, and athletic events were cancelled when the pollution became too overwhelming. In the history of how Los Angeles improved its air quality, civil society played a central role. A women's activist group, Stamp Out Smog, for example, was one prominent group that held high-profile events, influenced public opinion, and drove political change. Other NGOs and the scientific community also provided hard evidence concerning the sources of pollution, in particular cars, that led California to advocate antismog controls on automobiles in the early 1960s.[103]

The Chinese government has suggested that it, too, would like the engagement of its people in advancing the cause of environmental protection. Li Keqiang's 2017 speech before the NPC was notable, among other things, for the environmental call to action he issued to the Chinese people: "Tackling smog is down to every last one of us, and success depends on action and commitment. As long as the whole of our society keeps trying we will have more and more blue skies with each passing year."[104] The actions of the Chinese leadership, however, do not always reflect such resolute words.

Under the Dome hit the Chinese Internet on February 28, 2015, and within days more than 200 million people had viewed it. During the nearly two-hour documentary, which many compared to U.S. Vice-President Al Gore's film *An Inconvenient Truth* and author Rachel Carson's *Silent Spring*, the former CCTV journalist Chai Jing, who financed and produced, as well as narrated, the film, reported on the country's struggle with air pollution through a mix of on-the-ground investigation and personal narrative. The personal touch struck a nerve with online audiences. Pan Shiyi posted online that Chai Jing was a hero: "My respect to the brave Chai Jing. She's a heroine."

Then Minister of Environmental Protection Chen called Chai personally to thank her for the video and stated publicly: "Chai Jing deserves our respect for drawing the public's attention to the environment from a unique public health perspective." Only one day later, however, the Shanghai Propaganda Department issued instructions to the Chinese media and websites to halt all coverage of Chai and the film, and the next day Beijing ordered its deletion from the Internet.[105] When asked about the documentary during a press conference, Premier Li Keqiang made no mention of the film in his response but did admit that the Chinese government's progress on air pollution fell short of the public's expectations, adding that the government was "determined to tackle smog and environmental pollution as a whole."[106]

Chai Jing's video, much like Pan Shiyi's tweets on air pollution, is emblematic of the contradiction in the Xi government's approach to civic engagement in environmental protection: the government welcomes public participation but only in support of government policy and as long as it doesn't challenge existing policy or appear to challenge the government's legitimacy. Particularly threatening in this regard are individuals who command large followings and speak out on issues in ways that move beyond a narrow technical complaint to address broader values.

Chai's crime may have been as simple as her call to the Chinese people to take individual action to protect the environment. Chai had a history of speaking out about individual rights. In a speech before the Beijing Journalists' Association in 2009, Chai spoke eloquently about citizens' rights: "A country is built upon individuals; she is constructed and determined by them. It is only if a country has people who seek truth, who are capable of independent thinking, who can record the truth, who build but do not take advantage of the land, who protect their constitutional rights, who know the world is imperfect but who do not slacken or give up—it is only if a country has this kind of mind and spirit that we can say we are proud of our country."[107] Or the video may have run afoul of senior Chinese officials as a result of the attention it generated and the connections it forged among netizens throughout the country. Indeed, the video sparked calls online for environmental protests, and at least two citizens who were part of a protest in Xi'an following the release of the video were arrested.[108] Chai Jing has gone underground with no public commentary or appearances since the video was deleted.

Still the Chinese people have carried Chai's call forward. Parents in several cities throughout China have asked schools to provide air-filtration systems for their children, although, outside Beijing, few cities have heeded their calls. The parents nonetheless press on, participating in popular protests or other demonstrations of opposition—such as placing masks on public statues.[109]

While Chai's video crossed the invisible line that demarcates the permissible from the impermissible, most seasoned environmental activists, such as Ma Jun and Wang Canfa, are careful to push for change in ways that Beijing deems helpful. Ma, a former journalist, focuses on greater transparency in environmental reporting and holding factories and officials accountable for their environmental practices. In the mid-2000s, Ma developed online maps of water and air pollution violations, focusing his energies on holding foreign firms accountable for the water and air pollution of the factories along their supply chain. As he explained to me at the time, targeting multinationals was politically safe. Later, as trust in his work grew, he expanded his scope to include both Chinese and foreign firms, although most of his work to raise firms' environmental practices continues to center on multinationals. By 2017, his NGO had publicized over 800,000 violations by more than 600,000 factories.

One of Ma's most successful endeavors is a Bluesky Map app launched in 2015 to engage the Chinese people in the air quality protection effort. The app allows the public to check on precise sources of local air pollution and take action. Speaking before the Chicago Council on Foreign Relations in November 2017, Ma described how a listed Shandong Province–based iron and steel company—with several polluting furnaces—initially refused to respond to Ma's call to clean up its pollution. Without recourse to the law, Ma said, he had the users of his app tweet the violations via Weibo and tag in the Weibo account of the local EPB. After a period of time, the EPB tweeted back to indicate that it had penalized the company and called on it to fix the violation. Yet the pollution continued; finally, after a few more months of citizen activism via the app, the company shut down three of its furnaces. Ma's work likely inspired a group of Beijing residents to create their own "sludge siege map" that identifies the locations of more than thirty sludge-dumping sites in the city.[110] Ma also has partnered closely with the U.S.-based Natural Resources Defense Council to pressure corporations to green their supply chain and to publish an annual Pollution Information Transparency Index that ranks over 120 Chinese cities on their transparency. Such work is politically sensitive for local officials but welcomed by leaders in Beijing.

Similarly, Wang Canfa, China's indefatigable and renowned environmental lawyer, began his efforts to hold local officials and factories accountable for their pollution by launching lawsuits on behalf of villagers, who had suffered negative health and/or economic consequences. In 1998, he established the Center for Legal Assistance to Pollution

Victims in Beijing, and by 2000 was receiving "over one hundred calls a month" from citizens seeking legal help in navigating China's environmental laws.[111] The work was challenging. Data were difficult to access from recalcitrant EPBs; financial support was limited and mostly came from outside China; and judges were often not trained to understand the environmental issues at stake. Yet Wang persisted and, using his position as a delegate to the local people's congress, eventually became the architect of an entire system of environmental courts, whose judges are required to be well-versed in environmental law. Now, he tells me, the challenge is getting enough cases to fill the courts.

While Ma and Wang are sophisticated political actors with strong connections to the Chinese government and the environmental protection bureaucracy, there are thousands of Chinese environmental NGOs without their experience and political cover. Two environmental activists in Ningde, for example, were arrested on the grounds of prostitution after investigating the link between nickel mining and wetland degradation.[112]

Moreover, the environment is not immune from the broader shifts underway in the political system in China under Xi Jinping. The 2017 Law on the Management of Foreign NGOs, discussed in chapter 2, makes support from foreign entities—traditionally the largest source of financial and capacity-building support for Chinese environmental NGOs—far more politically risky. At one point, Chinese environmental NGOs received 80 percent of their funding from sources outside China. As one activist noted in an interview with the *Guardian*, "The real purpose of the foreign NGO law is to restrict foreign NGOs' activities in China and to restrict domestic NGOs' rights in China by cutting the connection between [the two]."[113] Indeed thus far, the MEP has yet to agree to serve as the supervisory body for any foreign environmental NGO.

Some domestic Chinese NGOs will undoubtedly find alternative sources of support. Friends of Nature, the country's longest-operating environmental NGO, for example, established an environmental public interest fund to support litigation and received funding from Alibaba.[114] Yet, one longtime foreign environmental NGO head suggested to me, business brings a more results-oriented, short-time horizon approach to the funding process. Support for skills training, environmental law, and other forms of capacity building will undoubtedly suffer in such an environment.[115]

In addition, environmental NGOs, as well as environmental data, may be classified as issues of national security or entwined in the Xi government's concern over "hostile foreign forces." Nongovernmental organizations have become suspect because they are often advocates for greater transparency, official accountability, and the rule of law, all of which the Chinese government may view as subversive. As discussed in chapter 2, as of 2016, responsibility for managing foreign NGOs has shifted from the Ministry of Civil Affairs to the MPS. One Chinese citizen serving in the Beijing office of an American environmental NGO mentioned to me that negative comments about the work and the motives of his organization—long an important partner for both Chinese NGOs and the MEP on energy efficiency and climate change—had started appearing online as part of the broader "hostile foreign forces" narrative. The framing of environmental issues as issues of national security also extends to domestic NGOs. In one case in November 2016, for example, Liu Shu, the founder of the Hunan-based environmental NGO Shuguang, was arrested on charges of counterespionage, reportedly providing environmental information to an "unidentified contact." Her work involves defending victims of pollution, and she had been investigating the levels of heavy metals in a large lake.[116]

The Communist Party also called in 2016 for party committees to be established within domestic NGOs to "guide political thought."[117] According to one activist with whom I met in Beijing that year, these committees are unlikely to play a major role in determining the activities of the NGO: "For the most part," she argued, "the party committees will meet to discuss whatever new regulations or ideas the Party wants them to discuss. It won't affect those of us who are not Party members." Indeed, many Beijing-based environmental activists appear relatively sanguine about the narrowing political space. As one commented to me in mid-2017 during a conversation in Beijing, "We can still do our work. We just won't take any money from foreigners, and we will make sure that the work we do is in line with government priorities."[118] Such an outlook is unlikely to spur the type of disruptive activism that catalyzed Los Angeles' environmental transformation in the 1960s and 1970s.

The Campaign for Clean Air

Much like the leadership's effort to address corruption or to develop the electric car market, its plans for tackling air pollution include short- and long-term campaigns. In advance of the G20 summit in September 2016 in Hangzhou, which brought together all the leaders of the G20 countries, for example, local officials declared a week-long holiday, provided free travel vouchers worth $1.5 billion, and focused their energy on sweeping out any sign of pollution. They closed and relocated factories, stopped all construction, and removed diesel-consuming buses from the road. Powerhouse SOEs, including Baoshan Iron and Steel and Sinopec's Shanghai Petrochemical, either closed down for the duration or had production cut by 50 percent. Similar tactics were adopted in advance of the seventieth anniversary of the World War II Victory Parade in September 2015 and the APEC Summit in November 2014. For the parade, in addition to closing down factories and constructions sites, Beijing closed down nearly every steel mill, accounting for nearly 6.6 million tons in lost production.

Environmental experts are concerned that these short-term campaigns may take the place of more sustained efforts to address the air quality challenge. Polluting industries in Hebei, for example, were ordered to close down for forty-five days in fall 2016, likely contributing to a much improved PM2.5 average concentration for neighboring Beijing that year. The Chinese Academy of Engineering estimated that such short-term measures accounted for about 20 percent of the improvement in Beijing's air quality.[119] Plans are also in the works for provinces such as Henan, Shanxi, and Shandong to close as much as 30 percent of their aluminum-smelting capacity during November through March to reduce the smog around Beijing.

Forced factory closures in one province to benefit another, however, may contribute to political tensions. In March 2016 at the annual legislative session of the NPC, a number of officials complained about the pressures of a slowing economy and paying for environmental protection. Officials in Hebei, for example, reported that the effort to fight overcapacity in sectors such as steel and cement coupled with addressing pollution had cost the government $1.8 billion and 200,000 jobs.[120]

China's undeniable progress in advancing clean energy production and consumption may also face some headwinds in a campaign environment, in which impressive timetables and targets are often set without consideration for the actual conditions on the ground. Already, 40 percent of the world's new renewable power plants are in China,[121] and in 2016 China invested $78.3 billion in renewable energy—exceeding both Europe ($59.8 billion) and the United States ($46.5 billion).[122] Deputy Governor of the People's Bank of China Yi Gang has said that China must make between 2 and 4 trillion RMB ($300 to $600 billion) in "green investments" over the next five years, but the government can only cover 15 percent of that. So the private sector, he suggests, will have to do most of the financing.[123] Private sector interest, however, will depend heavily on whether China has put in place market incentives that make it financially worthwhile for the companies to invest. That may be difficult to find in China's current oversaturated clean energy environment. Already, much of China's clean energy capacity remains idle. In 2016, the levels of wind power curtailment (capacity not utilized) reached 43 percent in Gansu, 38 percent in Xinjiang, and 21 percent in Inner Mongolia—three of the most wind-power-rich provinces and regions. (In contrast, curtailment rates in the United States and Europe are generally between 0 and 5 percent.) And a study by Duke University researchers estimates that solar panels in China's coastal cities are likely suffering efficiency losses between 17 and 35 percent because of the air pollution.[124] Top-down political campaigns—whether to curtail pollution or to spur adoption of new technologies—are best in the early stages in which mobilization is the primary objective. Over time, however, as in the clean energy sphere, failure to pay attention to on-the-ground results and adopt policies in the face of new information yields suboptimal outcomes.

The West Is Not the Best: The Economic Imperative

Finally, the leaders' commitment to improved air quality is not uniform throughout the country: their primary focus is the wealthy coastal region. In 2013, Chinese leaders deliberately excluded the western provinces from mandated coal caps with the objective of continuing to develop coal capacity and transmitting the power to the eastern provinces. Li Haofeng, the deputy director general of the coal industry section of China's National Energy Administration stated, "We will create multi-function power supply centers in the west, where power plants will use clean coal to provide power to the coastal cities."[125] Local governments also continue to favor thermal power—even if it means wasting wind and solar—because it provides jobs and therefore income for the government.[126] Thus the Chinese government canceled eighty-five new coal-fired power plants in 2017 and pledged not to approve new projects in as many as thirteen provinces until 2018, but the other eighteen provinces and regions—primarily in the interior and western part of the country—presumably have greater latitude to consider new coal-fired power plants. Moreover, China boasts forty-six highly polluting coal-to-chemical plants, including coal-to-gas, in operation with another twenty-two under construction. (These are industrial processes by which coal is converted into other chemical properties, including formaldehyde, acetic acid, and methane, among others.) Coal-to-chemical projects are expensive and water intensive in regions that are water scarce. They are seen, however, as a way for coal-mines to stay operational. According to one estimate, overall, there are as many as 570 new coal-related projects slated for development.[127]

The results of this preferential policy are not surprising. Of ninety-one cities with rising average PM2.5 levels in 2015, sixty-nine were in central and western parts of the country.[128] In addition, the government is still committed to its growth target of doubling per capita GDP by 2020, a target that cannot be achieved with less than 6 percent growth. In 2016, data from 367 cities demonstrated that when credit loosened and investment kicked up again, so too did the levels of pollution. In Hebei, for example, there was a 24.2 percent increase in concrete and 7 percent increase in steel production, contributing to an increase in PM2.5 levels in thirteen cities in the Beijing-Tianjin-Hebei region. Thus, China's efforts to address its air pollution become much less coherent when demands of economic growth and the interior and western provinces are considered.

Do As I Say, Not As I Do

The Chinese leadership demonstrates little interest in considering the impact of its development on air quality outside its borders. As it looks to clean the air to meet the demands of the middle class, it is also encouraging firms—often the most polluting enterprises including coal-fired plants—to base production out of the country. Hebei Province plans to move 20 million tons of steel, 30 million tons of cement, as well as significant glass production outside of the country by 2023. It already has inked an agreement to export roughly 11 percent of its annual steel output to a new plant in South Africa.[129] And large Chinese-funded cement plants have been flooding into Tajikistan, increasing Tajik production fivefold between 2013 and 2015.[130]

An investigation by the online environmental site China Dialogue and the CEE Bankwatch Network, moreover, revealed that Chinese banks and companies are supporting at least seventy-nine coal-fired generation projects outside the country with a total capacity of more than 52 gigawatts. This exceeds the 46 gigawatts of planned closures in the United States by 2020.[131] Energy giant Huaneng has announced significant expansion plans for coal plants in South and Southeast Asia, Russia, and Eastern Europe. Importantly, China does not apply the same stringent standards for efficiency on its overseas plants that it does at home.[132] In Kenya, a consortium of Kenyan, South African, and Chinese energy firms is planning to build a large coal-fired power plant fifteen miles north of a UNESCO world heritage site. It is estimated that the new plant will be the country's largest source of pollution.[133] Thus, as China's leaders seek to ensure that wealthy coastal provinces and municipalities rein in their coal production and consumption to improve air quality, they are enabling the development of new coal capacity both in the western part of China and abroad.

These types of structural shifts suggest that Beijing's commitment is, in the first instance, to reduce air pollution in the wealthy areas, while relegating many of the poorer interior provinces, as well as other developing countries, to decades more of worsening air quality.

Clouds on the Horizon

In October 2017, Western news media heralded Xi Jinping's 19th Party Congress speech for its emphasis on the environment and qualitative growth as opposed to economic development, noting that Xi used the word "environment" eighty-nine times while mentioning the word "economy" only seventy times.[134] Yet speaking at a news conference at that same Party Congress, Minister of Environmental Protection Li Ganjie suggested that the government would fall short in meeting the country's 2017 air quality targets and asked that the Chinese people "be patient" as it would "take time to solve such a big problem."[135] Li's caution is well founded. In the midst of the Party Congress, the medical journal *The Lancet* revealed that in 2016 China ranked second only to India in deaths related to air pollution.

Separating real, sustainable progress in meeting Chinese air pollution reduction targets from apparent wins or short-term gains is challenging. Unlike its unwillingness to adopt institutional reforms in the SOE or innovation sectors, the new Chinese leadership has put in place a set of institutional changes that are likely to yield long-term benefits, such as removing oversight for local environmental bureaus from local governments, working to ensure the independence of the environmental impact assessment process, strengthening the legal system regarding environmental protection, and raising the limit on the amount of pollution fines that an enterprise pays. In addition, the government has begun to open the space for limited market forces to play a role in environmental protection by instituting an environmental tax that will incentivize polluters to reduce emissions beginning in 2018.

At the same time, Beijing is sharply constraining the role of civil society by silencing authoritative voices or activists who challenge government policy, invoking a national security overlay on environmental protection, embedding party committees within NGOs to supervise their activities, and limiting opportunities for cooperation with foreign counterparts. The result of such actions will be an NGO community that is less independent and capable of holding the government accountable in the ways that helped launch the movement to clean the air in the late 2000s.

The government's continued reliance on campaigns will also likely hinder the development of sustained change. While campaigns can be useful mechanisms for encouraging short-term, high-profile results, they are undermined in the long run by a failure to develop the incentives—political and economic—necessary to sustain them. Without providing incentives for businesses to adopt pollution control technology, local officials and business leaders will continue to find ways around the regulations—they are concerned about the dual pressures of economic growth and maintaining employment. There is also potential for the objectives of different campaigns to conflict. Thus, when the government decides to undertake another round of stimulus, pollution levels kick up.

Moreover, while the areas Beijing has targeted for improvement may demonstrate periods of improved air quality, much of this is achieved by shifting the country's pollution burden from the coastal provinces to the less developed parts of the country. This strategy raises questions about the government's overall commitment to rebalancing the nation away from fossil fuels, protecting the environment, and addressing the public health concerns of the Chinese people.

Finally, China's approach to the environment at home has significant ramifications for the role it plays in addressing global environmental challenges. Simply shifting its pollution from the eastern seaboard to the western provinces and other countries, without reducing overall fossil fuel use, for example, will not contribute to reducing the country's overall contribution to global climate change. China's plans to construct twenty-two additional coal-to-chemical plants, for example, will add 193 million tons of carbon emissions annually—more than the total carbon emissions of many countries. While China portrays itself as a leader in addressing climate change, as well as other global challenges, the reality of China's contribution, as we will see in the next chapter, is often quite different.

7

The Lion Awakens

Napoleon Bonaparte once said that China "is a sleeping lion," and "when China wakes up, the world will shake." In fact, the lion of China has awoken, but what the world sees now is a peaceful, amiable, civilized lion.
—Xi Jinping, March 2014[1]

SOME FOREIGN OBSERVERS MIGHT question Xi Jinping's description of China as peaceful and amiable, but none would doubt his assertion that the lion has awakened. China in the twenty-first century is a world power, ready to claim all the rights that such status confers. While in the past Chinese scholars and officials were careful to refer to China as an emerging or regional power, most now say simply: "China is a big power" (*Zhongguo shi yige daguo*, 中国是一个大国). Xi Jinping was among the first to signal China's new place in the global order. During a trip to Washington, DC, in 2012, while still vice-president, he proposed to define the relationship between the United States and China as a "new type of relationship among major countries" (*xinxing daguo guanxi*, 新型大国关系).[2]

By most any measure, China today is a global power. It is the world's first- or second-largest economy after the United States (depending on whether the economy is calculated in nominal or purchasing power parity terms), contributing 15 percent of global GDP in 2015[3] and 35 percent of global GDP growth during 2010–2015.[4] It exports its goods, capital, and labor around the world, earning the title of the world's largest trading power. It is also a significant and rising source of foreign direct investment (FDI), seeking natural resources to fuel the development of its industry and infrastructure and increasingly the technology and expertise that it believes will help raise its economy to the next level. China's military prowess also reflects its standing as a global power. One of only five designated nuclear weapons states under the Non-Proliferation Treaty,[5] China also boasts the world's largest standing army. With its investments in aircraft carriers, stealth fighter jets, and one of the world's few anti-ship ballistic missiles,[6] its ability to defend itself and to project power further afield is significant and growing. Its military spending ranks second only to that of the United States.[7]

Beyond these traditional measures of power and capabilities, however, Chinese President Xi Jinping has a stated and demonstrated desire to shape the international system, to use China's power to influence others, and to establish the global rules of the game. In this way, China distinguishes itself from global economic powers, such as Japan and Germany, and from other military powers such as Russia. Only the United States has the range of economic and military tools matched with global political aspirations that China now displays.

China's desire to have its opinion consulted, heard, and followed has an undeniable logic: it is an economic and military power with 20 percent of the world's population. An ambitious China offers the United States and the rest of the world the opportunity for greater partnership, cooperation, and burden sharing to support global growth and manage global challenges. At the same time, as we will see, China is using its newfound status to shape regional and global institutions in ways that better suit its interests and meet its objectives, in some cases supporting traditional norms, while in others supplanting them. Along with opportunities for greater cooperation has come the potential for significant new frictions between China and other international actors—most critically, the United States.

The Historical Legacy

Four character *chengyu* (成语), or idioms, are one of the delights of the Chinese language. Typically they reflect some nugget of wisdom or tale of morality derived from ancient Chinese myths or historical events. Chinese leaders use them often to enliven their policy pronouncements.

Former Chinese leader Deng Xiaoping popularized the aphorism *tao guang yang hui* (韬光养晦) or "hide one's capacities and bide one's time" in the early 1990s to sum up China's foreign policy. The *chengyu* dated to the mid-700s when Tang dynasty Emperor Xuanzong earned his throne in part because he hid his talents from potential competitors.[8] Deng also embedded the phrase in a much longer twenty-four character phrase: "Observe the situation calmly. Stand firm in our positions. Respond cautiously. Conceal our capabilities and await an opportune moment. Never claim leadership. Take some action." (*lengjing guancha, wenzhu zhenjiao, chenzhuo yingfu, taoguang yanghui, juebu dangtou, yousuo zuowei*, 冷静观察, 稳住阵脚, 沉着应付, 韬光养晦, 绝不当头, 有所作为).[9]

Throughout the 1990s and much of the 2000s, successive Chinese leaders followed Deng's lead. They referred to China as a developing country and emerging economy and stressed their desire for a peaceful external environment so that China could continue to grow. They called for "win-win" diplomacy and helped drive growth in the Asia-Pacific region. And, above all, attuned to the concerns of their neighbors, they cast their growing power as a "peaceful rise" (*heping jueqi,* 和平崛起), and when even that proved threatening, reframed it as "peaceful development" (*heping fazhan,* 和平发展).[10]

The 2008 global financial crisis, however, catalyzed a disparate group of economic and foreign affairs experts and officials who presented a different vision. As the United States fell into a deep recession and struggled to regain its economic footing, China appeared relatively unscathed, bolstered by a Chinese people who saved rather than spent, and trillions of dollars in foreign currency reserves. These officials believed that the financial crisis represented an inflection point in world history: the decline of the United States and the rise of China. China's central banker Zhou Xiaochuan captured the zeitgeist with his remark that perhaps it was time for the world to move away from the dollar as the world's reserve currency.[11] And China's official news service Xinhua underscored the belief that the United States' loss was China's gain: "The changing posture is related to the new reality. The depreciating U.S. dollar, sub-prime crisis, and financial market instability have weakened the American position when dealing with China. In the meantime, China's high-speed economic growth has massively increased the country's confidence."[12]

The moment also tapped into a deeply held desire within China for history to be righted. China's one hundred years of humiliation are deeply etched into the psyche of the Chinese people.[13] The revolutionary leader and president of China's first republic Sun Yat-sen described the sense of historical weakness felt by China during this period in a speech in 1924: "Today we are the poorest and weakest nation in the world, and occupy the lowest position in international affairs. Other men are the carving knife and serving dish; we are the fish and the meat."[14] The tumultuous history of the country through the half-century spanning the 1930s through the 1970s did little to address Sun's complaint about China's place in the world.

The desire to overcome this sense of weakness and humiliation permeated the writings of many contemporary Chinese thinkers during the 1990s and early 2000s. Renowned Tsinghua University professor Yan Xuetong, for example, argued in 2001 that the country had a historical mandate to regain its place as a global power: "The rise of China is granted by nature. In the last two thousand years, China has enjoyed superpower status several times . . . . Even as recently as 1820, just twenty years before the Opium War, China accounted for 30 percent of the world's GDP. This history of superpower status makes the Chinese people very proud of their country on the one hand, and on the other hand very sad about China's current international status. They believe China's decline to be a historical mistake, which they should correct."[15]

Not all Chinese foreign policy thinkers and officials, however, were entirely comfortable with this more openly ambitious foreign policy. The former president of China's Foreign Affairs University Wu Jianmin, for example, continued to favor Deng's lower key approach and believed that it would better serve China's need for economic development and domestic stability.[16] And Wang Jisi, former dean of Peking University's School of International Affairs, argued that it was unlikely that the significant gap in power between China and the United States could be closed in the near future.[17]

While scholarly debate continued, the late 2000s marked a period of increasing outward confidence in Chinese foreign policy. Chinese officials, including then Premier Wen Jiabao, lectured the United States on the American economy, instructing Washington to ensure that Chinese savings invested in U.S. Treasuries remained safe.[18] In China's backyard, Beijing began to assert more forcefully its claims in the East and South China Seas, both diplomatically and militarily. And as the host of the dramatic 2008 Summer Olympics, despite press attention to China's problematic human rights and environmental records, China got its first taste of the force of soft power.

The ascension of Xi Jinping confirmed the country's growing ambition. Xi's Chinese Dream seeks both the rejuvenation of the great Chinese nation, as well as a commitment to build a PLA capable of "fighting and winning wars."[19] In November 2014, Xi summoned the country's foreign policy and military elite to Beijing to hear him lay out his vision for China's foreign policy future. The speech, delivered at the Central Conference on Work Related to Foreign Affairs, cemented in the minds of those present Xi's intention to move the country from its status as an emerging or regional power to that of a global power. As one official present at the speech noted, it was a "diplomatic manifesto to secure the Chinese Dream."[20] For more than two decades, Chinese leaders had advanced the notion of China as a peacefully developing power. In Xi's words, it was now time for China to embrace "big country diplomacy" (*daguo waijiao,* 大国外交).[21] And in remarks before the Politburo the following month, Xi argued that he planned to "make China's voice heard, and inject more Chinese elements into international rules."[22] More than any post-revolution leader, Xi staked the legitimacy of the Communist Party at least in part on its ability to reclaim a leadership role on the global stage.

All Roads Lead to Beijing

Central to Xi's vision of a rejuvenated Chinese nation is a China that sits at the epicenter of Asia and beyond. In September 2013, Xi Jinping stood before officials, faculty, and students at Nazarbayev University in Astana, Kazakhstan, and laid out his vision for a "New Silk Road," or economic belt along the traditional Silk Road.[23] The following month while in Indonesia, Xi fleshed out his vision further, calling for a "Maritime Silk Road" that hearkened back to Chinese Admiral Zheng He's expeditions to the Red Sea and east coast of Africa.[24] With these two projects, he laid out a grand-scale initiative One Belt, One Road (OBOR) (*yidai yilu,* 一带一路) later renamed Belt and Road Initiative

(BRI) that, if successfully completed, could reshape the political and economic landscape of not only Asia but also much of the Middle East, Europe, and Africa.

Known now by its shorthand form, Belt and Road, Chinese officials initially described the initiative as an infrastructure plan to connect China to other parts of the world through ports, railroads, highways, and energy infrastructure. The plan gained urgency as China's economy continued to slow and Beijing was faced with significant production overcapacity in sectors such as steel, cement, and coal. The plan offered at least a partial way out. As one Chinese scholar described the leaders' intentions: "Many of China's production sectors have been facing over-capacity since 2006. The Chinese leadership hopes to solve the problem of overproduction by exploring new markets in neighboring coun-tries through OBOR."[25] It also served as a clear rebuttal to the United States, which, in 2011, had proposed its own New Silk Road initiative. The Chinese vision quickly eclipsed its U.S. counterpart, with com-mitments of tens of billions of dollars to the plan, compared with the $15 million earmarked by the U.S. administration (as a contribution to a larger World Bank project). The United States also incorporated its contributions to Afghan reconstruction, which increased the level of support by several billion U.S. dollars,[26] but it still fell far short of China's vision.

In March 2015, the Chinese Ministry of Foreign Affairs joined hands with the Ministry of Commerce and the NDRC to put this vision on paper in an ambitious plan to revitalize the Silk Road. The new BRI included sixty nations in Asia, the Middle East, Africa, and Europe,[27] encompassing up to 70 percent of the global pop-ulation and 55 percent of the world's GDP[28] (see figure 7.1.). By 2017, the BRI invited participation from all the countries in the world. The project design expands well beyond infrastructure to include connectivity through telecommunications and culture, the development of financial and free trade accords, and the opportu-nity for China to increase the use of its currency in global trade and investment. According to Chinese analysts, China has devel-oped a $40 billion fund solely to support BRI projects, alongside pledges of over $100 billion in project financing through its banks.[29] Almost nine hundred projects now fall under the BRI banner.[30] (Not

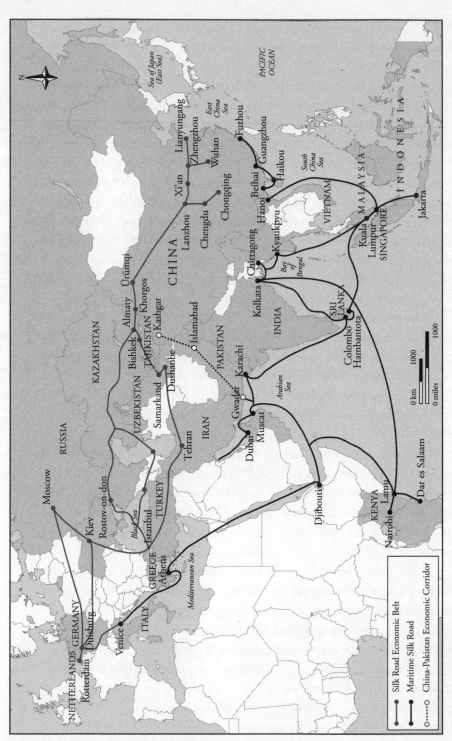

FIGURE 7.1 Map of China's Belt and Road Initiative

all BRI projects began after Xi's 2013 announcement. Ministry of Foreign Affairs official Shi Wei told me that projects that started before the announcement of the BRI may be included in the count.) One former Chinese official characterized the BRI as "the most significant and far-reaching initiative that China has ever put forward."[31]

The Chinese government has also fully integrated the BRI into its domestic planning process. The Leading Group for Advancing the Development of One Belt One Road was set up to oversee the coordination of the plan within the bureaucracy; and the thirteenth Five-Year Plan (2016–2020), which was ratified at the March 2016 NPC, formally embraced the initiative as one of the major pillars of China's economic development, along with Internet Plus (the government's plan to apply Internet technologies to traditional industries such as banking and commerce) and Made in China 2025.[32] More than half of the country's thirty-three provinces and autonomous regions have also incorporated BRI into their strategic plans, and it is viewed among Chinese officials as a mechanism for raising the standard of living for many of the country's poorer provinces.[33] Even SOEs have developed the BRI departments to ensure that the plan's mandate is considered in their investment decisions.

As with Xi Jinping's rejuvenation narrative, the BRI also carries with it memories of China's historical greatness. The term "Silk Road" did not come into being until the mid-1800s, when the German geologist and geographer Baron Ferdinand von Richthofen identified the trade and communication network as Die Seidenstrasse, or the Silk Road.[34] However, the earliest caravans traveling between China and Iran date back to as early as 106 BCE (although some historians argue that the origins of the Silk Road date back to 139 BCE when the Han Emperor Wudi sent one of his generals, Zhang Qian, on a diplomatic mission west to seek allies against the Han's enemies, the Xiongnu).[35] Over the next centuries, trade developed along several different routes between China and Central Asia, establishing what became known as the Silk Road, and the maritime routes that linked the East and West became known as the Spice Routes. While much of the trade was in goods—China traded silk for spices, grain, gems, vegetables, and fruit—a trade in ideas, including art, technology, and religion, also emerged.[36] In addition, the Chinese provided the security for the trade routes; during the Tang dynasty, for example, the army posted garrisons in Central Asia.[37]

Given the importance of its historical roots, the current incarnation of the Belt and Road has assumed almost mythical status among Chinese scholars and officials. I sat down with one of the most thoughtful and prolific scholars on the BRI, the head of the department of International Strategy within CASS's Institute of World Economics and Politics, Xue Li, and asked him about the significance of the initiative. Xue asserted it was "the top design" of Xi Jinping's foreign relations. It stemmed, he suggested, from Xi's desire to "do something big" and contribute to his historical legacy. Substantively, it represented an important shift in the self-identity of China from an East Asian country to a central country of Asia that included North, South, and West Asia. Xue decried the expansion of the BRI's mandate to the entire world, however, arguing, "If you put it everywhere, it becomes nothing." the BRI, he noted, also allows the Chinese economy to be "open outside but not inside."[38] Other Chinese scholars describe BRI as China's answer to the U.S. "pivot" or "rebalance to Asia." The pivot, which was articulated by President Obama in 2011, promised deeper U.S. security, political, and economic involvement in Asia—a greater commitment of U.S. forces, a formalized trade arrangement, and continued assistance to countries that sought to strengthen institutions of good governance. Zhang Yunling, director of international studies at CASS, has argued: "With its long-term interests in mind, China sees OBOR as a grand strategy. In my view, it can be considered China's 'pivot to the West.'"[39] Or as Major General Qiao Liang noted, the BRI is a "hedging strategy against the eastward move of the U.S. pivot to Asia."[40]

Many countries have welcomed the Chinese initiative and its promise of significant trade and investment opportunities, and several European countries jumped on board quickly to establish themselves as part of the BRI. The U.S. embassy in Beijing also has a special service to help American companies think through opportunities to do business via the BRI. Closer to home, the reception was less uniformly enthusiastic. The BRI is in many respects a traditional CCP top-down campaign; in this case, however, it is conducted not only through the Chinese system but also through the political and economic systems of others. In theory, participating countries will become tied to China through trade and investment, culture, finance, and potentially even security. Those geographically closer to China, such as India, have expressed concern about the degree of Chinese economic penetration or naval encirclement that the BRI may bring about.[41] Even in Pakistan, traditionally a close Chinese partner, citizens have expressed apprehension over a number of issues, such as the lack of transparency in the negotiations between their government and Beijing, concessions for Chinese companies, Chinese laborers taking Pakistani jobs, and the terms of repayment.[42]

Chinese scholars also are not wholly convinced that BRI is a sound strategy for their country. As Renmin University professor Shi Yinhong has commented with reference to the BRI, "The state of affairs can be described as 'China: unilateral fervour; others: little, if any, enthusiasm.' "[43] Shi has called on Beijing to ensure that BRI projects be undertaken collectively to avoid worrying other countries; he is sensitive to the potential for Chinese investment to raise hackles and provoke nationalist backlashes, particularly if environmental, health, and other social concerns are not addressed.[44] Shanghai Jiaotong University scholar Zhang Junhua echoes Shi's concerns, noting that the original Silk Road emerged from "bottom-up" trade that was initiated primarily by countries outside China. In contrast, he has argued, BRI is a "product of Chinese neomercantilist thinking." He has explained: "China's neomercantilism lacks sensitivity when addressing some issues in host countries, particularly regarding culture, environment and ethnicity. Beijing's authoritarian approach may also impede effective cooperation with democratic countries."[45]

University of Central Asia scholar Kemel Toktomushev has expressed reservations about the potential for elite corruption and rent-seeking in countries without strong institutions of transparency and accountability.[46] A study of the BRI's impact in Central Asia by Columbia University professor Alexander Cooley underscores such concerns. Cooley points to a backlash against Chinese investment, particularly in places such as Kazakhstan and Kyrgyzstan, where stories of Chinese corruption and scandals with infrastructure projects are contributing to rising Sinophobia. In one high-profile case, Kyrgyz Prime Minister Temir Sariyev was forced to resign in 2016 when a parliamentary commission reported that he had awarded a $100 million infrastructure contract to a Chinese firm, even though the firm reportedly lacked the proper license and had been underbid by Kyrgyz and Turkish competitors.[47]

Whether BRI projects will actually make money also remains an open question.[48] Zhang Junhua points to the China-Pakistan Economic Corridor (CPEC) as a prime example. The pledged investment totals $46 billion, which is equal to 17 percent of Pakistan's 2015 GDP, yet the projects associated with CPEC are plagued by security concerns and infighting within Pakistan. From Zhang's perspective, it is difficult to understand the economic rationale for such significant Chinese investment in such a poor and conflict-ridden environment. Pakistan itself decided to cancel a $14 billion CPEC dam project with Beijing because of the conditions Beijing placed on the deal including Chinese ownership of the dam, the high operation and maintenance costs, and a promise that Beijing could develop a second dam. Instead, Pakistan will pursue the project on its own. While some Chinese companies, such as the Industrial and Commercial Bank of China, have also expressed their doubts concerning the economics of the BRI, MOFA official Shi Wei suggests that the BRI is a fifty- to one-hundred-year project and believes that most Chinese companies will adopt a long-term perspective, using the BRI platform to get a foothold in a market that might not yet be developed.

China's Institutional Web

Alongside the BRI, Xi Jinping has also moved to cement China's leadership position in the Asia-Pacific region through the creation or support of a number of regional institutions. Most notably, during the same trip to Indonesia in which he put forth the Maritime Silk Road, he also proposed the establishment of an Asian Infrastructure Investment Bank (AIIB).[49] Laying claim to China's leadership in the region, Chinese Finance Minister Lou Jiwei said of the AIIB, "This is China assuming more international responsibility for the development of the Asian and global economies."[50] By most accounts, the infrastructure needs of the region are enormous—exceeding $8 trillion.[51] The two largest international banks committed to financing infrastructure globally—the World Bank and the Asian Development

Bank (ADB)—together support on average $50 billion in projects annually.

Xi Jinping did not conceive of the AIIB. A number of scholars and officials, including the eventual head of the AIIB, Jin Liqun, had floated the idea for a Chinese-led multinational bank for several years without success. Xi's support for the BRI, however, finally opened the door for such a proposal to be heard. Drafted by former Vice-Premier Zeng Peiyan, who now heads the China Center for International Economic Exchanges, the proposal was debated internally for several months. Some officials feared the AIIB would be a money loser or that China would be unable to run a multilateral bank given its inexperience. Support from Middle Eastern governments, who said they would participate and contribute financially to the bank, however, reportedly provided the Chinese leadership with the confidence to move forward.[52]

China's frustration with the inability of the international community—in particular the United States—to reform preexisting international economic institutions, such as the IMF and World Bank, to reflect more accurately China's standing in the global economy also contributed to its desire to forge ahead with the AIIB. In 2010, the IMF had promised a restructuring of shares that would increase China's voting weight, as well as that of other emerging economies. Three years later in 2013, however, the U.S. government, one of the IMF governors, had still not approved the reform.[53] (The shift to increase China's and other emerging economies voting rights within the IMF to reflect more accurately their contribution finally occurred in 2016.[54])

While many nations welcomed the Chinese initiative, a few, in particular the United States and Japan, expressed some concern. Within the United States, two questions arose: First, was China attempting to subvert traditional institutions such as the World Bank and ADB in favor of China-led institutions? Second, would the AIIB operate at substandard levels by not observing the environmental, social impact, transparency, and lending standards of the traditional banks? The administration's concerns were not without merit, as analysts such as Shi Yinhong and Zhang Junhua have pointed out. Obama officials urged their counterparts in other Western and Asian capitals to refrain from joining the AIIB, at least until there was greater clarity as to the structure, purpose, and governing principles of the bank were clear.[55]

The Chinese responded that the AIIB and any other Chinese-proposed institutions were not intended to challenge the existing international order but rather to complement it. Xi noted in an interview with the *Wall Street Journal* just prior to his September 2015 visit to the United States, "Many visionary people hold that as the global landscape evolves and major transnational and global challenges facing mankind increase, it is necessary to adjust and reform the global governance system and mechanism."[56] The Chinese ambassador to the United Kingdom further stated that the AIIB would act as "a supplement to existing multilateral development institutions," and would act "within the global economic and financial framework, and follow established international practices."[57] Blame for delayed reform of the international system was placed squarely at the feet of the United States by Zhang Yunling: "By delaying the restructuring of the IMF and opposing the establishment of the AIIB, the United States seems not to accept the changing demands of the international community."[58]

Many voices in the United States also urged the Obama administration to understand the AIIB as a Chinese contribution rather than a challenge to the global system, further noting that China's ability to use the AIIB as a means of advancing uniquely Chinese objectives or practices would be constrained by the fifty or more other countries participating. As Stanford University professor Phillip Lipscy argued: "The structural advantages that China enjoys in the AIIB will be beneficial only insofar as other players take the institution seriously and provide funding, skilled staff, and coordination. If the institution is perceived as being unfair or nontransparent, it will become nothing more than a shell organization through which China disburses bilateral foreign aid."[59]

Initially most Western nations refrained from joining the AIIB. In 2015, however, the United Kingdom broke rank, reportedly without any real consultation with Washington.[60] For the United States, it was an embarrassing diplomatic moment—one AIIB President Jin Liqun publicly likened to a Shakespearean drama in which Great Britain had long ago rejected the demands of the Roman Empire and was now rejecting those of the United States.[61] Other European and Asian countries quickly followed suit. Only Japan, concerned about the implications of the AIIB for its own leadership of the ADB, also remained outside the AIIB.

While it is too early to assess the implications of the AIIB, the bank has taken several steps to reassure potential critics that its standards meet those of traditional multinational banks. The Chinese relied on longtime World Bank lawyer Natalie Lichtenstein to help draft the AIIB's charter, and as the contours of the AIIB have taken shape, it appears to have adopted governance principles similar to those of the World Bank and ADB.[62] Moreover, three of the AIIB's four initial projects, announced in 2016, are cofinanced with other international banks, including the ADB and the European Bank for Reconstruction and Development.

China has a number of other institutional initiatives underway as well. It has become a driver of the Regional Comprehensive Economic Partnership (RCEP)—a sixteen-country trade negotiation initiated by the Association of Southeast Asian Nations (ASEAN) in 2011.[63] RCEP would result in the largest free trading bloc in the world.[64] Despite Xi's support for RCEP, however, he has already moved beyond it to propose a Free Trade Area of the Asia Pacific (FTAAP). The original FTAAP was proposed in 1994 by the United States at the Asia Pacific Economic Cooperation (APEC) summit in Bogor, Indonesia, as part of the Bogor Goals and was floated again at the 2006 APEC summit in Hanoi.[65] In 2014, Xi Jinping raised the prospect of such an agreement at the APEC summit, and the leaders endorsed what became known as the "Beijing Roadmap for APEC's Contribution to the Realization of the Free Trade Area of the Asia Pacific."[66]

Chinese Foreign Minister Wang Yi explained Beijing's adoption of FTAAP as an effort to "help to integrate regional bilateral and multilateral cooperation mechanisms and reduce the risk of overlap and fragmentation."[67] Other less charitable views suggest China was trying to draw attention away from the U.S.-backed trade agreement the Trans-Pacific Partnership (TPP) (now led by Japan and Australia) and to demonstrate that China can be an important actor in setting rules and standards for the global economy.[68]

China has won plaudits from the region and much of the rest of the world for its leadership in promoting economic integration in the

Asia-Pacific region and beyond. Its moves to assert regional leadership on the security front, however, have been less well received. In both the East and South China Seas, where Chinese claims of maritime sovereignty conflict with those of other states, Beijing's actions have been widely perceived as provocative and even destabilizing.

From Staking to Securing

In 2011, PLA Navy Commander Wu Shengli, responding to a question about the role of the United States in the South China Sea, made his view eminently clear: "How would you feel if I cut off your arms and legs? . . . That's how China feels about the South China Sea."[69] The South China Sea spans an area of 1,351,000 square miles and is rich in oil and gas, as well as stocks of fish, and as much as $5 trillion of trade passes through the Sea annually. Six nations in the region—China, Taiwan, Brunei, Malaysia, Vietnam, and the Philippines—lay claim to sovereignty over part or all the island chains within the Sea—the Spratlys and the Paracels—as well as small atolls. China's claims are the most expansive—almost 80 percent of the area—demarcated only by an ill-defined nine-dash line that dates to the 1930s and appeared in 1947 on an official Republic of China map.[70]

In defense of its claims, Chinese officials cite historical records. The Ministry of Foreign Affairs, for example, points to an 1868 Guide to the South China Sea that presents accounts of Chinese fisherman in the Nansha (Spratly) Islands, noting, "The footmarks of fishermen could be found in every isle of the Nansha Islands and some of the fishermen would even live there for a long period of time."[71] The Ministry also argues that China maintained administrative jurisdiction over the Spratlys during the Qing dynasty, based on maps issued between 1724 and 1817.[72] Chinese analysts argue that since the Chinese nine-dash line was portrayed on maps prior to the establishment of the modern international legal regime, current laws "should not negate China's prior rights in the South China Sea."[73] In their minds, China should enjoy "both the legal rights stipulated in the UNCLOS [United Nations Convention on the Law of the Sea], such as the EEZ [Exclusive Economic Zone] and continental shelf, as well as historical rights within the U-shaped line."[74]

Other governments dispute Chinese claims, noting that their own maps and those of other countries do not reflect the Chinese understanding.[75] In fact, some Chinese scholars have noted that their own country's claims are not airtight. To prevent any confusion, however, the Chinese government has made clear that the publication or display of maps that "do not comply with national standards" could potentially result in prosecution.[76]

U.S. Naval War College scholar Peter Dutton suggests that for China, realizing sovereignty over the islands would not only provide military and economic gain but also would offer "the healing of a sort of psychological wound in the collective Chinese mind."[77] The perceived loss of maritime sovereignty due to Chinese weakness in the past can now be rectified at a time of greater strength. Chinese Premier Zhou Enlai declared China's sovereignty over the Paracel and Spratly Islands during the Allied peace treaty negotiations in August 1951.[78] Throughout the ensuing decades, gaining sovereignty within the nine-dash line became a priority for Chinese military officials. China jockeyed with other claimants for control over various islands and reefs, all the while trying to balance its military assertiveness with diplomacy, including ratification of the United Nations Convention on the Law of the Sea in 1996 and signing a Declaration on the Conduct of Parties in the South China Sea with ASEAN nations in 2002.[79]

Chairman Xi at the Helm

Xi Jinping has made enforcement of Chinese claims in the South China Sea a priority. According to one source, even before assuming the presidency he reportedly served as chairman of the leading small group on the South China Sea beginning in 2010. During his tenure, Beijing broadened the definition of China's core interests—which traditionally had included only Taiwan, Tibet, and Xinjiang—to include maritime territory in the South China Sea.[80] During this same period, the PLA navy also conducted its first large exercise involving the South, North, and East Fleets to demonstrate its power projection capabilities.[81] At the same time, on the diplomatic front, China recommitted to the idea of trying to "shelve disputes and seek joint development" along the lines of Deng Xiaoping's approach.[82]

Xi's strategy involves both the strengthening of Chinese military capabilities and more consistent positioning of Chinese forces in the contested waters. Less than one month after assuming the position of general secretary of the Communist Party, Xi gave a speech on board the *Haikou*, a guided missile destroyer, which had previously patrolled the South China Sea, calling for unity between a prosperous country and strong military; and in early February 2013, a group of Chinese naval ships conducted a training and patrol mission in the South China Sea.[83] Xi also began to streamline the bureaucracy responsible for overseeing maritime domain issues to reduce competition and overlap.[84] His elevation of the air force and navy to a position equivalent to that of the army also serves his objectives in the South China Sea.[85]

Beginning in December 2013, China undertook a large-scale dredging and reef reclamation effort in the Spratly Islands. Over the following twenty months, China dredged and reclaimed seventeen times as much land as the other claimant states combined in the past four decades,[86] for a total of 2,900 acres.[87] Despite Xi Jinping's claim that China does not intend to pursue militarization of the islands, Chinese construction in the Spratlys has included airstrips, military buildings, and artillery[88] (see figure 7.2).

Chinese actions fueled tensions with several of the other claimants. Conflict flared with Vietnam in May 2014 over the Chinese placement of Haiyang Shiyou 981, an oil rig, 120 nautical miles off the coast of Vietnam. The oil platform prompted violent protests in Vietnam, and China withdrew the rig in July, several weeks ahead of schedule, ostensibly over concern about potential damage to the rig from typhoons.[89] China's relations with the Philippines also grew increasingly tense during this same period, as the two countries sparred over control of Scarborough Shoal. China levied trade bans on important goods from the Philippines; the Philippines, in turn, launched a two-and-a-half year suit over Chinese claims in a tribunal at the Permanent Court of Arbitration, which it won in July 2016: the court said that Chinese claims to the broad maritime swath within the nine-dash line had no historical or legal basis. Xi Jinping stated outright that China would not recognize the ruling, and Chinese officials maligned the judges as biased. Nonetheless, according to one Chinese think tank analyst who specializes in Chinese maritime issues, the

FIGURE 7.2 Photos Showing Chinese Development on Subi Reef in the South China Sea from July 2012 (*top*) to July 2016 (*bottom*)
Credit: CSIS Asia Maritime Transparency Initiative/DigitalGlobe

ruling gave strength to those in the government who were seeking a peaceful and legal basis for resolution of the conflict. Moreover, he claims that many in the Chinese foreign policy community were embarrassed by the official Chinese attacks on the judges.[90] International pressure on China to recognize the court's findings, however, abated with the election of Philippine President Rodrigo Duterte in March 2016. President Duterte stated that he would set aside the ruling in favor of improved economic relations with China.

Turning East

Even as China has found itself embroiled in conflict with several of its Southeast Asian neighbors in the South China Sea, it has also engaged in a similar conflict in the East China Sea with Japan over the Senkaku/ Diaoyu Islands. In the late 1970s, Deng Xiaoping had set aside the conflict between the two countries, asserting: "It does not matter if this question is shelved for some time, say, 10 years. Our generation is not wise enough to find common language on this question. Our next generation will certainly be wiser. They will certainly find a solution acceptable to all."[91]

In 2012, however, Shintaro Ishihara, the highly nationalistic and outspoken mayor of Tokyo, moved to purchase three of the contested islands from a private Japanese landowner. He pledged to develop the islands with port facilities and a typhoon shelter. In late August/early September, the Japanese government moved to purchase the islands to forestall Ishihara's provocative play.[92] Despite the underlying reason for the Japanese government initiative, the move prompted criticism from Beijing, as well as violent protests in several major Chinese cities, in which Japanese businesses and cars were attacked and destroyed.[93]

The Chinese government also followed up with an initiative of its own. In December 2012, China submitted claims to the UN Commission on the Limits of the Continental Shelf arguing that its EEZ in the area should be extended further than 200 nautical miles to the edge of the continental shelf.[94] Xi, himself, brought a strong background to the issue, having directed a special task force on the crisis in the Senkaku/Diaoyu Islands before becoming CCP General Secretary.[95] China also began referring to the Senkakau/

Diaoyu Islands as China's core interests. The Foreign Ministry noted, "The Diaoyu Islands are about sovereignty and territorial integrity. Of course, it's China core interests."[96] And in a further provocative move, on November 23, 2013, China declared an Air Defense Identification Zone (ADIZ) in the East China Sea. (An ADIZ requires that planes that want to fly through the area must notify the country claiming the ADIZ and ask permission.) China's claim overlapped with Japan's ADIZ, which it had held since 1968, as well as with that of South Korea. While commercial planes acknowledge the ADIZ, U.S., Japanese, and South Korean military flights all do not.[97]

Regional security tensions remain high between Japan and China. In 2016, hundreds of Chinese fishing boats and coast guard vessels sailed into areas near Japanese territorial waters, and China's PLA air force repeatedly flew their planes over contested waters. Diplomatic efforts to reduce tensions have been sporadic. President Xi and Prime Minister Abe met on the sidelines of the 2016 G20 Summit in Hangzhou, the first time they had met in a year and a half. The two leaders agreed to accelerate a mechanism for air and sea communications designed to avoid a military clash and also pledged to hold initial preparatory talks for a resumption of discussion on joint development of the gas deposits beneath the East China Sea.[98] Despite the positive tone of these talks, in late September 2016, Japan scrambled jets in response to a drill by China's PLA air force in which over forty planes passed through the East China Sea's Miyako Strait, which separates Miyako Island from Okinawa. And in 2017, Japan protested China's oil and gas activities in an area in which the two countries' EEZs overlap.

Fluid Politics

Beijing's actions in the South and East China Seas contributed to create a new security dynamic in the region. Regional actors flocked to the United States to provide a counterweight to the newly perceived threat from China. Washington strengthened ties with its formal allies, including Australia, Japan, South Korea, and the Philippines, and undertook new forms of defense cooperation with countries such as Vietnam and India. In 2016, after a two-year hiatus, the United States reintroduced freedom of navigation operations (FONOPS) that transited within 12 nautical miles of reefs on which China had constructed artificial islands to underscore the U.S. commitment to freedom of navigation.[99] And in 2017, the Trump administration signaled that it would establish a schedule for regular FONOPS in the South China Sea.

Regional naval powers such as Japan, Australia, and India also enhanced their security ties with each other, undertaking military exercises among themselves and in partnership with smaller regional actors, such as Vietnam and the Philippines. Even countries from outside the Asia-Pacific region, such as France, pledged deeper engagement in regional security to help uphold basic principles of freedom of navigation.

Political dynamics in the region remain fluid, however, as leaders seek the best path forward to realize their individual interests. Philippine President Rodrigo Duterte put aside the Permanent Court of Arbitration's decision on the South China Sea and traveled to China in October 2016 to mend ties and renew an emphasis on trade and investment. At the same time, he promised to downgrade military ties with the United States and threatened to cancel the bilateral agreement that permits U.S. use of five bases in the Philippines. (Some of Duterte's ire was likely due to the Obama administration's criticism of the indiscriminate nature of his war against drugs.) As a result of President Duterte's diplomacy, the Chinese coast guard has moved back from its occupation of Scarborough Shoal and allowed Philippine fisherman to resume their access. However, President Duterte's proposal to protect the shoal as a maritime conservancy has been met with little enthusiasm by Chinese officials, who do not believe he has the standing to determine the future of the Shoal. At the same time, President Duterte, along with Vietnam's President Tran Dai Quang and Prime Minister Abe, all issued joint statements with President Trump during the latter's November 2017 Asia trip denouncing the militarization of the South China Sea and calling for free and open access.

Chinese diplomatic initiatives have also made some progress. In August 2017, China and the Association of Southeast Asian Nations adopted a draft framework on a code of conduct for the South China Sea. While potentially a positive step forward to realizing a meaningful set of "rules of the road," some outside observers have questioned whether China is simply buying time as it completes its quest to assert de facto control over the South China Sea.[100]

Some countries appear to be looking for new economic and security partnerships with China, while others are becoming increasingly wary of the intentions behind Chinese actions. In particular, the dramatic acceleration of Chinese outward-bound investment under Xi's direction has raised concerns in a number of advanced economies.

China Goes Global

Long complacent, even welcoming of Chinese investment, some in the German government and business community began to see things differently in 2016. Within the first half of the year, Chinese investors made bids for twenty-four German companies, a rate of approximately one per week.[101] By November, Chinese firms had spent almost $11 billion for German companies; the previous record was $2.6 billion in 2014.[102] While the number and value of the deals alone were noteworthy, what drew scrutiny was the nature of the deals: they were heavily concentrated in the technology sector, a source of national pride and German leadership globally. One deal in particular, a bid by the Chinese appliance maker Midea Group for leading German robotics company Kuka AG drew attention from German officials. Midea already owned a 13 percent share in the company and was seeking an additional 25.1 percent from the German mechanical engineering company Voith.[103] Although the leadership of Kuka supported the Chinese bid, outside observers voiced concern over the loss of a technological lead in an area of core German strength. Others, such as Germany's economy minister, underscored Berlin's unhappiness with the lack of opportunity for German firms in China: "What we can't do is sacrifice German companies and German jobs on the altar of open markets when in reality there isn't a level playing field. Open markets require the same rules of the game."[104] And a few raised concern over the potential for some of Kuka's partners to drop them over the possibility that technologies might be transferred to China in the process.[105] By July, Midea had secured an almost 95 percent stake in Kuka. The fallout of the Kuka deal—as well as the many other Chinese acquisitions of German companies—however, has been significant. In October 2016, the German government withdrew its approval for the $741 million buyout by the German unit of China's Fujian Grand Chip

Investment Fund LP to acquire Aixtron SE, a German chipmaker, and subjected it to a new regulatory review. German officials and business leaders are worried about the hollowing out of their tech industry.

The German case is not unique. Countries everywhere grapple with how to manage both the enormous opportunities and the challenges presented by China's expanding international trade and investment.

The Resource Curse

Throughout many commodity-rich economies in Africa, Latin America, and Southeast Asia, China has long been a particularly important source of growth in infrastructure and resource-extraction industries. It ranks at the top of the world's charts for natural resource consumption: in 2015, it consumed 54 percent of the world's aluminum, 48 percent of the world's copper, 46 percent of the world's zinc, 28 percent of global soybeans, and 12 percent of the world's oil supply.[106] And even as Chinese economic growth slows, Beijing remains the largest trading partner for most of the world's commodity-rich countries.

Beginning in 1999, Chinese President Jiang Zemin and Premier Zhu Rongji articulated a "go out" strategy for Chinese companies, encouraging them to develop the resources necessary to fuel Chinese growth. Chinese companies, both SOEs and private enterprises, became leading investors in infrastructure throughout resource-rich economies to help ensure access to the copper, iron ore, and bauxite that the country needed for its own development.

For many countries, doing business with China held significant appeal. China's motto—"Don't mix business with politics"—often translated into a willingness to put aside environmental, labor, and governance concerns to accomplish the work more cheaply and quickly. Unlike the traditional development banks, such as the World Bank or Asian Development Bank, the Chinese Development Bank and Export-Import Bank of China did not insist on transparency in how loans or grant aid were distributed.

As several Chinese scholars have noted with reference to the country's BRI plan, however, this type of Chinese investment has drawn particular scrutiny in a number of countries. Chinese analyst He Jingjun has written that China's relations with "rogue states" and its disregard of international labor and environmental standards has contributed to a backlash from many developing countries.[107] Citizens in Peru, Zambia, and Vietnam, among many others, have protested against Chinese projects, pointing to weak corporate social responsibility. And some countries, such as Argentina and Mongolia, have passed laws to limit certain types of investment, in moves that while not solely targeted at China, nonetheless arose as a result of concerns over Chinese investment. Argentina, for example, passed a law that sharply limited the amount of rural land owned by foreign entities,[108] while Mongolia passed a highly restrictive regulation requiring government approval for foreign investments over $75 million or acquisitions of over 49 percent of shares in "business entities operating in sectors of strategic importance."[109]

While alarm bells have rung over the nature of Chinese investment, it is easy to overstate the impact of Chinese investment to date. China is an important, but rarely the lead investor in any region of the world. Chinese investment in Africa, for example, ranked third in the number of projects after the United Kingdom and United States, but first in monetary value (for the first time) in 2016.[110] In Latin America, China also ranked fourth in FDI after the Netherlands, the United States, and Spain.[111] Even in its own backyard, Southeast Asia, China ranked fourth in non-ASEAN foreign direct investment inflows into ASEAN in 2015 after the European Union, Japan, and the United States.[112]

Resource rich countries also recognize that overcapacity in many areas of Chinese industry may limit new Chinese investment in the near term. President Xi has called for Chinese companies to "go out" not in search of natural resources but for service and technology firms that will support China's rise as a competitive advanced economy. Chinese investment in the United States during 2000–2015, for example, totaled $62.9 billion, with the largest sectors being Internet and telecommunications, real estate and hospitality, and energy.[113] Chinese investment in Europe, which is also rising rapidly, mirrors that in the United States: real estate and hospitality, information and telecommunication technology, and financial services (although in 2015, investment in the automotive sector dominated as a result of ChemChina's purchase of Italian tire maker Pirelli).[114] In 2015, China's Ministry of Commerce reported that Beijing's investment in Africa had dropped by 40 percent.[115] At the same time, China's outward

FDI has increased from $60 billion in 2010 to over $200 billion in 2016,[116] for the first time approaching the level of U.S. outbound investment. However, even such investment may slow. In December 2016, the Chinese government became concerned over the rapidly increasing amounts of capital fleeing the country and began to place capital controls on outward-bound investment, as well as to inspect closely proposed deals to ensure that they were not simply a means of getting money out of the country. At the same time, FDI flows into China suffered a steep decline from 2013 to 2016 as many multinationals found the country's investment environment to be more challenging (see figure 7.3).

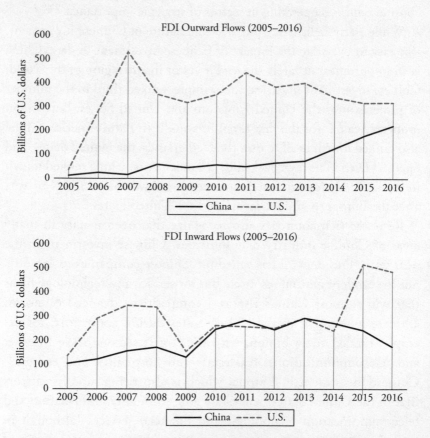

FIGURE 7.3 U.S. and Chinese FDI Inward and Outward Flows from 2005 to 2016

Source: World Bank, https://data.worldbank.org/indicator/BM.KLT.DINV.CD.WD?end=2016&locations=CN-US&start=2005&view=chart

Advanced economies, like their commodity-rich counterparts, generally welcome the influx of new capital, particularly during periods of slow global growth. However many countries' leaders are concerned over the lack of a level playing field when dealing with China: many sectors in China, such as energy, media, and telecommunications remain overwhelmingly closed to foreign merger and acquisition activity. In addition, for some countries, the close ties between the Chinese state and many enterprises introduces both economic and security concerns.

Uneven Playing Field

The significant presence of SOEs in China's overseas investment drive provokes widespread debate in host countries. State-owned enterprises are viewed as unfair competitors—receiving large government subsidies from Beijing. In addition, their links to the Chinese government raise concerns over the transfer of sensitive technology and corporate governance. While government reviews to prevent the transfer of defense-related technologies exist in all countries, the deepening engagement of Chinese companies in all sectors of the economy is likely to raise new issues. For example, Chinese investment in university labs may pose a new dilemma for universities in some countries. In the United States, controls exist for labs that receive federal funding, but there is no oversight for those that do not. This provides a new channel for defense-related technology to be developed and transferred from the United States to China. Issues of potential censorship or control over American cultural content also surround Chinese firms' purchase of entertainment and cultural assets, such as Getty Photos and Legend Entertainment.[117]

A 2016 Paulson Institute study by legal scholars Curtis J. Milhaupt and Wentong Zheng engenders a different but equally important set of questions regarding Chinese corporate governance. Milhaupt and Zheng suggest that private firms are not necessarily protected from state control and that ownership is not a significant determinant of firm engagement with the state. As Milhaupt and Zheng describe, managers of both private firms and SOEs benefit from close political and economic ties to the state.[118] They reviewed the government and party affiliations of the funders or heads of China's one hundred largest private firms (by revenue) and found close ties to the state: ninety-five out of the top one hundred private firms and eight out of the top ten Internet firms have founders who are current or former members of national or local people's congresses or the People's Political Consultative Conferences.[119]

In addition to the political linkages between the heads of China's most successful private firms and the state, the Chinese government also shapes the behavior of these firms by having significant shares in the firms, or, in some cases, even forcing mergers. In one case, the SOE Shandong Steel acquired a 67 percent stake in a private steel producer, Shandong Rizhao Steel, in the face of significant opposition by the owner of the private company.[120] Milhaupt and Zheng also note that many well-known Chinese companies considered private have mixed ownership, including Haier, TCL, and Lenovo.[121] While SOEs are more directly tied to the interests and demands of the state, nominally private firms are also bound to the state by an intricate web of political and financial ties. According to one European business official, it is well known that some deals, such as Alibaba's acquisition of the *South China Morning Post*, are undertaken in significant measure to support Beijing's broader strategic imperatives—in this case, its interest in shaping the media narrative outside the mainland.

The nature of Chinese state involvement in the country's economy produces several challenges for the international community. As we saw in chapter 5, in the case of the electric car market, the state may provide a protective web that prevents foreign firms from competing on an even playing field. At the same time, economic support from the state enables Chinese companies to access resources beyond those of their foreign competitors and to gain a potentially significant advantage when competing to acquire foreign firms abroad. Moreover, the political objectives of the Chinese state also drive foreign acquisitions in both natural resources and advanced technologies, which heighten national security concerns in some host countries.

The global nature of China's economic interests also contributes to Chinese efforts to protect the country's investments and trade routes, as well as safeguard the hundreds of thousands, if not millions, of Chinese workers living abroad. For example, the Chinese military was forced to evacuate tens of thousands of Chinese workers from Libya in 2011 and several hundred more from Yemen in 2015. As a consequence, Chinese scholars and officials are revisiting the country's historical reluctance to establish military bases overseas and formal alliances with other countries.

Allies and Bases or NOT

In 2010, renowned Fudan University scholar Shen Dingli published a little-noticed article arguing that China should consider establishing military bases overseas. Shen envisioned these bases as enabling China to respond to threats such as countries trying to block China's trade routes or secessionist efforts outside the mainland (presumably he is including Taiwan along with Hong Kong). He also suggested that they would afford China opportunities to retaliate against an attack from within the host country. Most important, Shen argues, these bases are essential to the Chinese navy's ability to restrict potential enemies' access to international waterways.[122]

Shen's view, at the time supported primarily by members of the Chinese military and dismissed by many in the government, represents a distinct break from deeply embedded foreign policy principles of noninterference in the domestic affairs of others and nonalignment. Afraid to have others meddle in China's affairs and to become entangled in military conflicts that do not directly affect China, Beijing has traditionally shied away from formal alliances and the establishment of any overseas bases.

In 2016, however, the Chinese military established its first overseas military logistics base in Djibouti. (Djibouti also hosts U.S., Italian, French, and Japanese troops.) According to Chinese officials, the base is designed to provide logistics and rest for Chinese troops and naval vessels, so they can participate in UN peacekeeping operations,[123] assist in noncombatant evacuation operations, and provide support for the BRI.[124] While Chinese officials stated that the Djibouti base does not represent a shift in China's traditional foreign policy principles, a precedent now exists. The Djibouti base could be the first step in developing Chinese bases in other places, such as Pakistan or Cambodia.

Bases represent in many respects a natural outgrowth of an increasingly robust, outward-facing PLA. The PLA has sixty-seven military academies and trains well over one thousand foreign officers annually.[125] Like American military academies, China's National Defense University offers a program for foreign officers; it was initiated in 2012. Latin America is particularly fertile ground: virtually all countries in the region that recognize China diplomatically send officers; it the National Defense University, and some also send military officials to the PLA Army and PLA Navy command schools.[126] China is also the third-largest source of global arms sales after the United States and Russia—thirty-seven nations buy arms from China, with the majority of sales in Asia—and maintains military-to-military relations with many, if not most of, its aid and investment recipient countries.[127] In September 2015 it pledged $100 million in military assistance to the African Union.[128]

Beijing also participates in a growing number of joint military exercises. From 2002 to 2012, China participated in twenty-eight exercises; in 2014 alone, China participated in thirty-one.[129] Roughly half of these exercises are with China's partners in the regional security organization, the Shanghai Cooperation Organization, that includes Russia, Kazakhstan, Tajikistan, Uzbekistan, and Kyrgyzstan.[130] It has also expanded into new partnerships, undertaking joint exercises with the Singaporean navy, Thai air force, and Malaysian military.[131] At the invitation of the United States, China also participated in the 2014 and 2016 RIMPAC exercises.

As China has taken the first step toward relaxing its stance against overseas bases, strategic thinkers have begun to debate the possibility of China establishing a formal system of allies. Yan Xuetong advocates that China needs both bases and military allies to maintain political balance in East Asia. Although Yan suggests the greatest opportunity for such allies rests with China's partners in the Shanghai Cooperation Organization, such as Russia and the Central Asian states, as well as with traditional Asian partners such as Laos and Cambodia, he also recommends that China actively seek to establish alliances with U.S. allies: "The more U.S. allies in this region become China's allies, the slighter chance for Washington's rebalancing strategy to achieve its goal."[132] As for some of the other nations of East and Southeast Asia—Japan, the Philippines, Vietnam, and South Korea—Yan advises that China will need "to be patient to wait for the domestic change in these four countries which will change their policy towards China."[133]

Russia also may provide a unique opportunity for Beijing to establish a more formal military alliance. The two countries were allied in the 1950s, although the relationship soon deteriorated and culminated in military skirmishes and a formal split in the early 1960s. Since that time, the two countries have had a relationship of convenience. Despite a deep reservoir of mutual suspicion, cross-border trade and investment from China into Russia soared during the 1990s and 2000s.[134] In addition, the two countries have a long history of voting together in the United Nations, particularly through the use of their veto power on the UN Security Council. (Over the past decade, they have joined hands to veto Security Council resolutions condemning political repression in Myanmar and Zimbabwe, and several resolutions on Syria.) Most often the two advocate noninterference and condemn overreach by the Security Council.[135] Russian President Vladimir Putin refers to Xi Jinping as a "very good friend and reliable partner" and uses the words "close ally" to describe China.[136] China also stood aside when Russia invaded Ukraine in 2013, electing not to criticize Moscow or join in the international sanctions for Russia's violation of Ukraine's sovereignty, and Russia has been noticeably silent on China's behavior in the latter's maritime disputes with its neighbors. The two countries have also made an effort to keep economic competition in Central Asia at a minimum by finding common ground between China's BRI and Russia's proposed Eurasian Economic Union.

Scholars such as Lingnan University's Zhang Baohui point to a more than decade-long strengthening of ties, including the two countries' first land, air, and sea joint military exercises in 2005, in which the Chinese PLA journal *People's Liberation Army Daily* (*jiefangjun bao*, 解放军报) stated that the military exercise signaled strategic intent.[137] Since then, the two countries have undertaken a number of naval exercises together, and in the context of a China that seeks more formal security partnerships, and a Russia that seeks to bolster its global standing, the two countries may form a closer strategic partnership, if not a formal alliance.

Still, Chinese officials routinely dismiss talk of an alliance with Russia, noting that the two countries differ on a few issues and that some Russians resent China's growing influence and distrust Chinese intentions.[138] Chinese scholars also have written dismissively of Russia's military prowess, arguing that Chinese military hardware is now, in some cases, more sophisticated. Zhou Bo, an honorary fellow at the PLA's Academy of Military Science, argues, "China doesn't need alliances for survival" since allies are only necessary to safeguard against potential aggression and "the non-alliance is one of China's highest moral grounds."[139] He also suggests that a Chinese alliance with Russia would only serve to increase tensions for both nations with the United States.

China's relationship with North Korea has most closely approximated a traditional alliance in the past. For decades, the Democratic People's Republic of Korea (DPRK) was considered China's closest partner, and the two countries have a mutual defense treaty. Beijing also remains Pyongyang's top trading partner, responsible for 70 to 80 percent of North Korea's trade, worth approximately $6.86 billion at its peak in 2014.[140] Since 2009 China has also been the only nation to continue to provide food aid,[141] and it is the source of an estimated 70 to 80 percent of North Korea's energy supplies.[142]

Since 2011, however, the belligerent and often erratic behavior of the DPRK leader Kim Jong-un, has strained relations. Chinese leaders were rattled by the execution in December 2013 of Kim Jong-un's uncle Jang Song-thaek, who was considered reform-oriented, a source of stability and maturity, and was trusted by the Chinese.[143] Kim Jong-un and Xi Jinping did not meet throughout Xi's first five-year term in office.

Moreover, during 2016 and 2017, the accelerated pace of North Korea's ballistic missile and nuclear weapons testing programs, including a nuclear test near China's border. This, along with the assassination of Kim Jong-un's half-brother, Kim Jong-nam (allegedly at Kim Jong-un's behest) and President Trump's more aggressive U.S. posture toward North Korea combined to persuade China to agree to progressively tougher UN Security Council sanctions on Pyongyang, including on North Korean coal, seafood, and iron ore exports.

Beijing also tried diplomacy to reduce tensions on the Korean Peninsula. In March 2017, Chinese Foreign Minister Wang Yi proposed a "freeze for freeze" in which the United States and South Korea would suspend their large-scale military exercises in exchange for North Korea halting the development of its missile and nuclear activities. The proposal failed to gain support from the relevant parties. However, Xi Jinping continues to advocate for a diplomatic solution.

There is an active debate among Chinese scholars over Beijing's policy toward the DPRK. Hu Bo, a senior fellow at the Pangoal Institution, for example, has argued that China has been too passive in the face of the deteriorating situation and should strengthen its deterrent capabilities and plan for the full range of eventualities. Hu implies that military action may even be necessary to keep the situation from deteriorating further.[144] In a highly unusual essay, Shi Yinhong argues that on the one hand, China should maintain openness to improving ties with the DPRK if the opportunity should present itself. Yet at the same time, Shi is critical of China's call for U.S.-DPRK negotiations for a peace treaty in the wake of the DPRK's nuclear tests. He argues that the proposal was based on number of "highly doubtful" premises including that the DPRK is developing nuclear weapons to deter security threats, that the DPRK will believe in U.S. commitments, and that the DPRK will not engage in strategic deception.[145]

According to a senior Chinese foreign ministry official, however, despite the North Korean refusal to cease its testing program and provocative behavior, there remains strong backing among conservative CCP officials for staying close to North Korea. For some, the primary driver is fear of instability across the border that might spill into China; for others, however, North Korea provides an important bulwark against democratic South Korea and its ally the United States.

Prospects for Beijing to establish formal alliances with some of its nominally closest security partners, Russia and North Korea, remain challenging—limited by mutual suspicion and/or competition. Perhaps in part, as a result, Xi Jinping has also articulated an alternative notion: a "Community of Common Destiny" or a "Community of Shared Future for Mankind."[146] Rooted in ideals of greater interdependence and integration among nations, such as that advanced by the BRI, Xi's vision calls for a new approach to international relations—one that is rooted in shared, as opposed to, national interest.[147] Chinese foreign policy analysts have been dispatched to expound on the idea in their writings and in meetings with foreigners, producing a wealth of discussion on the topic.

While Xi's proposal has been dismissed by some foreign analysts as merely another aspirational call for a better world,[148] it is, in fact, an attack on the traditional world order and U.S.-led system of alliances. Xi argues that international relations should be premised on "partnerships rather than alliances"—alliances are an outdated relic of the Cold War.[149] For Xi's idea to gain traction among countries wedded to their historical alliances, however, it will require that China itself be perceived as an actor that lives up to its own ideals: putting shared interests before its own, and providing an attractive model of partnership. China's difficulties in wielding soft power suggest that this will be a daunting task.

China's Not-So-Soft Soft Power

Central to Xi's rejuvenation narrative is the ability of China to attract other nations and people through its achievements, values, and culture. In many respects, it has proved a far more challenging effort than many in China had anticipated. The underlying cause of the leadership's difficulty in many instances is unavoidable—China's political system.

On June 1, 2016, Chinese Foreign Minister Wang Yi went viral. Standing before the Canadian press corps with Canadian Foreign Minister Stephane Dion, Wang answered a question that had been asked of and answered by Dion. The politically sensitive question concerned Chinese human rights and the case of a Canadian citizen detained in China since 2014 on espionage charges. Displaying distinctly undiplomatic behavior, Wang attacked the reporter, angrily stating: "Your question is full of prejudice and against China and arrogance . . . I don't know where that comes from. This is totally unacceptable . . . other people don't know better than the Chinese people about the human rights condition in China, and it is the Chinese people who are in the best situation, in the best position to have a say about China's human rights situation."[150]

Even as China's economy and military assume world-class status, its political system hinders its quest for soft power throughout much of the rest of the world. Wang's outburst speaks not to the question posed by the reporter, a form of which is asked at many official news conferences, but rather to the challenge China faces in moving the international narrative beyond its focus on issues of human rights and China's repressive political system. Despite China's best efforts, its quest for soft power remains elusive.

Chinese officials first began focusing on soft power in the early 1990s; Harvard University scholar Joseph Nye's book on the topic was translated into Chinese in 1992, sparking interest and discussion among Chinese scholars at the time.[151] It was not until 2007, at the 17th Party Congress, however, when President Hu Jintao linked the rejuvenation of China with the country's ability to project soft power, that it became a more formal component of Chinese foreign policy.[152] Soft power meant commanding the world's respect not only for China's economic and military achievements but also for its political and cultural accomplishments.

Xi Jinping adopted Hu's effort as his own. In 2014, he proclaimed, "We should increase China's soft power, give a good Chinese narrative, and better communicate China's message to the world."[153] Many of Xi's efforts have built on those of his predecessor—providing grant aid to developing countries, fostering Chinese language and culture through government-funded Confucius Institutes worldwide, positioning Chinese media in critical foreign markets, and supporting Chinese think tanks. In each of these areas, however, the very presence of the state and state priorities often undermine the government's efforts to improve its soft-power standing.

Cultural Conditioning

A central element of China's effort to promulgate soft power has been the establishment of more than four hundred Confucius Institutes— Chinese government-funded institutes to promote Chinese language instruction and cultural offerings worldwide. Yet the Confucius Institutes have also become lightning rods for controversy. Western university faculties have expressed concern that the Confucius Institutes compromise academic integrity, for example, by pressuring universities not to host controversial figures such as the Dalai Lama. In a few cases, such as that of the University of Chicago, faculty opposition has led an institution to close its Confucius Institute.[154]

As George Washington University professor David Shambaugh has detailed, China has also established an extensive global media presence to shape the image of China outside the country: Xinhua News Agency has 170 bureaus abroad; China Central Television broadcasts in six languages and has production operations in Nairobi, Kenya, and Washington, DC;[155] and China Radio International covertly controls more than thirty radio stations in fourteen countries, whose broadcasts are notable for their exclusion of commentary unfavorable to Beijing. A report on the widespread demonstrations in Hong Kong in support of free elections, for example, stated that the demonstrations had "failed without the support of the people in Hong Kong."[156]

Chinese scholars are well aware of the limitations of their government's efforts. Zheng Yongnian, now director of the East Asian Institute at the National University of Singapore, suggests that both Confucius Institutes and the Chinese media effort are "instrumental"—government-directed efforts at external publicity that "lack substance and are sometimes counterproductive." For Zheng, the only way for China to develop real soft power is for the country to liberalize its knowledge system by separating it from political control. He sums up the situation in stark terms: "The reality in China is: the wealthier the country, the more money the rulers control, the more severe the poverty of thought, and hence the more the civilization declines."[157]

President Xi's efforts to develop think tanks with "Chinese characteristics" to counter what he believes to be a narrative about China dominated by the West have encountered similar criticism. Xi originally proposed the idea in 2013, but by 2015, he acknowledged that the effort had not succeeded and announced a second initiative to create fifty to one hundred high-end think tanks and centers capable of competing internationally.[158] One such think tank based at Renmin University has received private funding of $50 million and is headed by a former *Global Times* editor. Yet far from welcoming debate and the competition of ideas between Chinese and Western think tanks, the former editor has called for Beijing to develop a blacklist of foreign scholars who write critically of the regime.[159]

Other Chinese scholars are also skeptical of Beijing's ability to deliver on Xi's ambition. Hong Kong University of Science and Technology professor Ding Xueliang offers a potent critique of Xi's initiative: "Think tanks exist to let scholars analyze, discuss about, and evaluate drawbacks and mistakes in senior-level decisions, and to criticize or come up with potential policy alternatives and improvements. What is the point of spending money and building think tanks if everyone simply 'unswervingly supports, agrees, and follows' the existing policy?"[160] Think tanks earn their international reputation by being independent of government influence, rooted in critical thinking, and open to discovery and debate; otherwise, their work will be discounted. As Ding suggests, limitations on public debate in China will almost certainly constrain the ability of these think tanks to achieve Xi's objective of conveying a convincingly attractive picture of China today.

At a fundamental level, China's efforts to promote soft power are hampered by the nature of its political system. At the 19th Party Congress, Xi Jinping proposed China as a model for other countries to emulate, for the first time directly challenging the United States and other liberal democracies as the political ideal. Yet it is not clear what precisely constitutes China's political model and whether other countries that are not led by a communist or otherwise authoritarian dictatorship can effectively follow China's example. Moreover, as Wang Jisi has argued, China's internal problems, including economic inequality, environmental pollution, and the lack of the rule of law, constrain the appeal of a China model. He notes that the best way for China to improve its soft power is to improve itself, and if China pushes too hard, it will trigger a backlash from other countries.[161]

China experienced such a backlash during summer 2017, when it was reported that the communist party's United Front Work Department had sought to influence Australian politicians and the overseas Chinese community to support Beijing's political objectives. As a result, the Australian government has begun consultations on how to develop laws to safeguard against CCP influence in local and national politics. Still, China is actively involved in training the next generation of political leaders in a number of developing countries. In Africa, for example, Beijing provides thousands of scholarships for African government officials to spend a period of time as short as two to three weeks or as long as a few years studying in China. In South Africa, Beijing even funds a party-building school to train members of the African National Congress in areas such as cadre development and media relations.

Underlying Wang's relatively negative assessment of China's soft power is also an understanding that soft power traditionally emerges organically—from values and ideals, from popular brands identified with a certain country, and from a nation's cultural achievements. To be persuasive, they also need to reflect the reality of the country. The repressive nature of China's current political system, as well as its societal problems, limits its appeal globally. Its contemporary culture is also constrained by political restrictions. The still underdeveloped and under-resourced civil society sector in China further means that China does not gain soft-power value from Chinese environmental, public health, or service-oriented international NGOs that operate in the developing world. And while, over time, Chinese brands may well hold global appeal, to date, only few, such as Alibaba and Haier, are recognizable names, and the nature of their businesses—online services and household appliances respectively—is unlikely to serve as a driver of Chinese soft power.

China is not yet a leading purveyor of soft power in the traditional sense. However, many countries celebrate China for its own brand of soft power: an ability to identify and address the developmental needs of other countries.

Bearing Gifts

One of Singapore's most senior foreign policy officials expressed his frustration as he explained to me why the United States was falling short in Southeast Asia when compared with China: "The Chinese sit down and go around the table and say, we will give you this, we will give you that. They always come with gifts. You [the United States] never do that." He is right. When Chinese leaders come calling, their visits are often heralded by a multibillion-dollar aid and investment package. Throughout the developing world, presidential palaces, soccer stadiums, bridges, and hospitals all bear a Chinese imprint. For China, such economic influence has long been an important element of its power. As Renmin University scholar Pang Zhongying has commented, *huairou* (怀柔)—which means pacifying and winning the hearts of foreigners through tributary trade—is an ancient Chinese ruling strategy and is better suited to China than the American concept of soft power.[162]

China does not publish project-level data or annual bilateral data concerning its financing activities abroad,[163] which makes it difficult to know precisely how much China is actually doing in terms of either FDI or overseas development assistance. It doesn't comply with the rules of the Organization for Economic Cooperation and Development, such as ensuring that overseas development assistance has a grant element of at least 25 percent. In addition, both Chinese and international media tend to conflate pledged aid and investment with realized aid and investment, contributing to an exaggerated sense of the level of Chinese investment throughout the developing world.

Lowy Institute scholar Philippa Grant notes that 80 percent of Chinese "aid" in the Pacific is in the form of concessional loans (loans granted with particularly low interest rates and/or with long grace periods for repayment) rather than grants or interest-free loans. Most of these loans are tied to Chinese goods and services.[164] Xi Jinping's $60 billion aid package for Africa, announced in December 2015, included an explicit commitment of $35 billion in export credits and loans and $5 billion in grant aid. Chinese largesse thus rarely comes without a price, but it generally results in projects that are completed far more quickly than otherwise would have been the case.

While Chinese and foreign media typically laud Chinese foreign investment and development assistance, Chinese citizens are not uniformly supportive of such largesse. In one instance, the Chinese public criticized Xi Jinping's support for a $2 billion South-South Cooperation Assistance Fund given that China boasted a per capita GDP that hovered around only $8,000. The government's response to the criticism stressed the political and economic benefits that China will receive from such assistance: an improved international image, stronger bilateral ties, and increased opportunities for Chinese exports.[165]

As measured by polling data, China's brand of soft-power engagement has seemingly had mixed results. Africa boasts the highest popular approval ratings for China, where roughly 70 percent have a favorable view of the country. Elsewhere in the world, however, support is less convincing. According to a 2016 Pew Foundation report, only 37 percent of Americans hold a favorable view of China, a slight decrease from the 2015 favorability rating of 38 percent. (Opinions in Europe, nonetheless, differ widely by country—with Greece posting a favorability rating of 57 percent and Spain only 28 percent. On average, however, European countries surveyed hold favorability ratings for China roughly at the same level as the United States.) Asia, like Europe, demonstrates widely disparate views: Australia reports a positive view of 52 percent, while Japan ranks at the bottom of the global survey with only 11 percent of Japanese viewing China favorably.[166] The mixed results reflect a variety of factors such as the level of security and economic threat perceived by people in the countries surveyed, as well as a fear of Chinese political influence. Near-term events, such as trade disputes, also shape people's perception of Beijing.[167] The results suggest that however positive China's intentions, other countries' citizens are persuaded more by the results of Beijing's engagement. This same gap between intentions and actions or rhetoric and reality emerges in China's efforts to establish itself as a leader in addressing global challenges.

The World Is China's Oyster

The year 2014 marked China's coming-out party in the world of global governance. Xi Jinping called for China to play a more significant role in contributing to meet global challenges, arguing that the country should be prepared not only to help write the rules of the game but also to construct the playground on which the game is played.[168] His statement marked another break from the Chinese tradition of assuming a low profile in international affairs and a departure from Beijing's oft-repeated assertion that as a developing country, it could not claim a leadership role in addressing global challenges. On issues as diverse as climate change, the Ebola epidemic, Internet governance, and management of the Arctic, China's role in responding to global challenges and establishing the norms that govern public goods is growing.

In November 2014, after years of rejecting any public commitment to reduce its greenhouse gas emissions, President Xi stood alongside President Obama and the two leaders jointly committed their countries to take action to reduce their contributions to climate change. The United States pledged to reduce its emissions by 26–28 percent below its 2005 level by 2025, and China pledged to achieve "peaking of CO_2 emissions" around 2030 and to increase the share of renewables in its energy mix to approximately 20 percent by 2030.[169] Together China and the United States, the world's first- and second-largest contributors of CO_2 emissions respectively, breathed new life into the sputtering climate negotiations. The following year, in the lead-up to the final round of climate negotiations in Paris, Washington and Beijing produced yet another declaration with side-by-side commitments, helping to bring the global negotiations to a successful conclusion.[170]

At the same time, China dramatically increased its contribution to the fight against the Ebola virus in West Africa. Traditionally, China has not been a major player in disaster relief or humanitarian concerns, putting just 0.4 percent of its foreign aid toward humanitarian relief.[171] And when the crisis broke in spring 2014, China's response was underwhelming. It pledged just $161,000 per country.[172] Criticism from the international community came quickly. China was among the largest trading partners and a significant investor in the three most affected countries: Guinea, Liberia, and Sierra Leone.[173] Yet other countries' assistance dwarfed that of China. The United States pledged $313 million,[174] the United Kingdom $202 million,[175] and the European Commission stepped forward with $192 million. Even Cuba pledged more financial assistance and twice the number of medical workers offered by China.[176] In the face of international pressure, particularly from the United States and United Nations, China rethought its response, stepping up to the plate with a more significant contribution— both financially and in terms of medical assistance to the relief effort. Eventually China provided a reported $120 million in aid to the affected countries,[177] as well as 170 medical workers to Liberia.[178]

China's cooperation and leadership were critical to meeting the threat of global climate change and Ebola. Yet its commitments did not come easily, and its efforts were not commensurate with its capabilities. China's climate change pledge represented only minimal new commitment over what the Chinese government had already planned to do; and in the case of Ebola, the Chinese contribution was only 3 percent of what the United States pledged. Nonetheless, both cases provide initial evidence that Xi's ambition for global leadership can be leveraged in positive ways for greater Chinese participation in addressing global threats.

China is less reticent about asserting its interests when it believes its economic or security needs are directly at stake. In areas such as Internet governance and overseeing the global commons, China is positioning itself to play a far more significant role than in years past. Unfortunately, its interests bring it directly into conflict with the United States.

Stalking the Cyber Realm

China's perspective on Internet governance is almost diametrically opposed to that of the United States and other liberal democracies. China supports a greater role for intergovernmental regulation of the Internet because it grants primacy to the state in determining norm setting. The United States and most other Western nations, in contrast, emphasize a "multistakeholder" model that includes governments, civil society, academia, business, and others.[179] China also uses the term "information security" rather than "cybersecurity" to signal its desire that a much wider range of online information should be regulated and controlled by the state.[180]

Unsurprisingly given its efforts to control the flow of information coming into China from abroad, China is very active in international negotiations on cyber-governance. During the UN cyber negotiations in 2015, China attempted—unsuccessfully—to advance its state-centered model of Internet governance and restrictive notion of Internet freedom.[181] According to some negotiators, China sought to ensure that state control over the Internet was enshrined in the final document, in particular pushing for the word "multilateral," which was considered code for states making the rules. In the end, many of the changes or points China wanted were not ultimately adopted, such as the addition of a phrase on "the sovereign right of states" and the elimination of phrases such as "freedom of expression" and "democratic."[182] The document did include a sentence advocated by China, which stated, "We recognize the leading role for governments in cybersecurity matters relating to national security," but this was followed by another line emphasizing the importance of the roles and contributions of all stakeholders.[183] At China's own World Internet Conference just days after the UN meeting, Xi reiterated his commitment to Chinese priorities, noting: "We should respect every country's own choice of their internet development path and management model, their internet public policy and the right to participate in managing international cyberspace . . . . There should be no cyber-hegemony, no interfering in others' internal affairs, no engaging, supporting or inciting cyber-activities that would harm the national security of other countries."[184] Xi's comments suggest little chance that he will accept the norms established in the nonbinding UN document, and, at the same time, he is forging agreements with Russia and other states, such as Cuba, that share his expansive understanding of the inherent dangers posed by a largely unregulated flow of information through cyberspace.

The Arctic Is China's Backyard

Heilongjiang, China's nothernmost province, is almost fifteen hundred miles away from the Arctic. Despite this, and while no part of China actually touches the Arctic, China has begun to insert its voice into the regime governing the fate of the region and its resources. The Arctic Council, which consists of the eight Arctic nations—Canada, Denmark, Finland, Iceland, Norway, Russia, Sweden, and the United States, as well as six indigenous peoples—was founded in 1996.[185] While China is not a member, in May 2013, it attained observer status, along with India, Italy, Japan, Singapore, and South Korea.[186]

China has quietly but insistently campaigned for a larger role in Arctic governance. It has argued that under the United Nations Convention on the Law of the Sea, the Arctic Ocean is a shipping commons.[187] Rear Admiral Yin Zhuo, for one, has stated that the "Arctic belongs to all the people around the world, as no nation has sovereignty over it . . . China must play an indispensable role in Arctic exploration as we have one-fifth of the world's population."[188] China also has established an extensive polar research effort: its Polar Research Institute of China in Shanghai has more than one thousand staff,[189] and cooperative research efforts are underway with research centers in at least five of the eight Arctic Council member states: Sweden, Finland, Norway, Denmark, and Iceland. The Polar Research Institute of China's objective is to participate in "relevant working group meetings of the Arctic Council and increase China's influence" in Arctic issues.[190] In addition, China has invested in resource-extraction projects in several of the Arctic countries; and Chinese government officials have stated that they plan to expand their cooperation with Nordic countries from research to ship building, shipping, and resource development.[191] Chinese scholars have also contributed to the campaign by routinely describing their country as a near-Arctic state or a polar power. Chinese scholar Tang Guoqiang goes so far to suggest that China could act as a spokesperson for the non-Arctic states, representing their views and interests in discussion with the Arctic Council.[192]

China's interest in the region is straightforward. The region is rich in resources: oil and gas, fish, and minerals, among them. According to one estimate, it holds one-third of the world's natural gas reserves,[193] as well as uranium and significant reserves of rare earths. Rare earths, in particular, are vital to Beijing's plans to become a world leader in clean technologies, and China is rapidly exhausting its own vast reserves. Greenland alone has the capacity to meet 25 percent of world demand for rare earths, and China has developed several natural resource investment projects with the country.[194] Smaller Arctic countries such as Iceland are excited to partner with China given Beijing's significant financial and research capacity. China is also interested in the Arctic for trade reasons. As the climate changes and the Arctic ice melts, three new trade routes may open that will dramatically reduce cargo transport time and help China avoid the security challenges of traditional routes such as the Strait of Malacca. Already, Denmark and China are discussing cooperation to explore these new routes. And Liu Cigui, the director of China's State Oceanic Administration, has linked China's policy toward the Arctic directly with its broader foreign policy goals, stressing its link with Beijing's objective of becoming a maritime power.[195]

The Chinese are aware that their involvement, particularly in resource extraction, will be viewed with some suspicion. Chinese scholar Jia Xiudong has tried to defuse tensions, noting, "China's interest and involvement in the Arctic are more for having options in case of emergency rather than resource plundering."[196] Moreover, while Greenland is resource rich but population poor, the country's deputy foreign minister has taken great pains to reassure the world of its political capacity: "We are, in mining terms, a frontier country. But we are not a frontier country like frontier countries in Africa or South America . . . . We have evolved over 300 years a solid legal framework, a well-educated population, rules, democratic institutions and a strong society."[197]

No single Chinese measure to enhance its economic, political, research, or security position in the Arctic provides Beijing a voice in

Arctic Council decision-making. Membership in the Arctic Council, moreover, is preordained by geography. Nonetheless, by becoming a major investor in the region, as well as a source of research capacity, China is attempting to change the facts on the ground in a manner that demands the other players take greater account of Chinese interests.

Conclusion

The question up for debate at New York University's Skirball center in mid-September 2017 centered on whether U.S. President Trump was "making China great again." My fellow debater Harvard Law School professor Noah Feldman supported the proposition, arguing that President Xi would fill the vacuum of global leadership left by President Trump's "America First" policy. Moreover, he argued, regional actors were looking for a degree of economic stability that only China could provide, again in the absence of U.S. leadership. For me, in contrast, the answer was an incontrovertible no. No country can *make* another great, and greatness is not a zero-sum game—when U.S. greatness diminishes, China's does not automatically increase. In addition, I argued, greatness has to be earned, and in the words of Winston Churchill, the price of greatness is responsibility.

Xi Jinping seeks greatness for China. It is embodied in his call for the rejuvenation of the great Chinese nation. The trappings are there: a world-class military, a game-changing economy with world-class technology, and a global footprint that matches—and perhaps even exceeds—that of any other country. Yet, Xi's quest remains largely unrealized. He has established institutions such as the AIIB and BRI with China in a position of leadership, but their value and import have yet to be realized. His efforts at soft power have largely fallen flat as a result of the inability of China's political system to present a set of social norms, political values, and cultural dynamism that attracts large segments of the world's population. Positive steps to build an economic community in Asia are undermined by aggressive military actions in the region. And, as this chapter has argued, true responsibility, along the lines Winston Churchill describes, largely eludes Xi Jinping's China.

Yet for the United States and the rest of the world, Beijing's more ambitious foreign policy, when coupled with its efforts to wall off its domestic polity, demands a fresh approach. There are new opportunities to leverage Xi's ambition for leadership and important new obstacles to forging a constructive relationship. Managing both requires an understanding of China's domestic and foreign policy dynamics and how they intersect and conflict with U.S. interests.

8

The Road Forward

SPEAKING AT THE APEC summit in Lima, Peru, in November 2016, Chinese President Xi Jinping assured the world that China would remain a standard-bearer for globalization. He stated: "Sealing off and excluding others is not the correct choice . . . China will not shut the door to the outside world but open more . . . . We're going to ensure the fruits of development are shared."[1] Xi's words were welcomed worldwide. If China were prepared to defend globalization against the seeming threats of protectionism and isolationism emerging in much of Europe and the United States, the rest of the world, or at least most of the nations of APEC, were prepared to stand behind it. And, if there had been any doubts concerning Xi's commitment, they were allayed two months later when Xi became the first Chinese president to travel to the epicenter of globalization, the World Economic Forum's annual January gathering in Davos, Switzerland, and deliver yet another rousing defense of globalization.

In several respects, China is already a leading pillar of the globalized world. It is the largest trading power in the world; tens of millions of Chinese travel abroad annually; and of the five permanent members of the UN Security Council, it deploys the largest number of peacekeeping troops in the world. Throughout the 2000s, China also became one of the world's top recipients of FDI, welcomed foreign universities and NGOs to assist in the country's development, and sent as many as half a million students to study abroad every year. China's military is also expanding its domain: it has established its first logistics base in Africa, enabling its military, for the first time, to boast a global presence, and Beijing is developing ports in strategic regions that serve not only commercial but also security interests. In addition, Xi Jinping's initiatives, such as BRI, the FTAAP, and the AIIB extend well-beyond the Asia-Pacific region and establish China as a creator of new institutions that promote a more globalized and integrated world through lower tariff barriers for trade and greater ease of investment. The current Chinese leadership has also assumed a greater role in organizations such as the IMF and hosted the G20, the annual conclave of twenty of the most important economies in the world.

Xi has also accelerated the drive of his predecessors to become a global power through soft power. He has used Confucius Institutes to spread Chinese language and culture throughout the world, initiated a program to develop world-class think tanks that will present a Chinese government perspective on the country's domestic and foreign policies, and supported an aggressive and well-funded state-run media campaign to advance Beijing's message.

Yet the China that has emerged under Xi Jinping is in equal measure a threat to the underlying principles of globalization and to the liberal world order. It demonstrates few of the attributes of a globalized country, much less a global leader in support of liberal political and economic values and institutions. Xi Jinping has sought to control the flow of capital leaving the country, to restrict opportunities for foreign firms to compete with domestic companies in critical areas such as clean energy, and to force multinationals to transfer core technology in order to do business in China. Contrary to the very essence of globalization, Xi has moved to reverse the trend of greater flows of information between China and the outside world. New regulations seek to restrict the ability of professors to use Western social science textbooks or to discuss Western ideas of governance and economics in the classroom. The party increasingly circumscribes the range of foreign television and other media content available to avoid the passive indoctrination of the Chinese people with Western values. And new restrictions on Internet content, as well technological advances, constrain the free flow of information in the cyber world. The Law on the Management of Foreign NGOs establishes new boundaries for interaction between Chinese civil society and their foreign partners, limiting the ability of foreign NGOs to support their Chinese counterparts financially and to undertake joint projects. China has demonstrated a willingness to ignore the tenets of international law by rejecting the unfavorable ruling it received regarding its sovereignty claims in the South China Sea.

Globalization implies the free flow of information, capital, and people, which, in turn, contributes to an increasingly interdependent and integrated world. The China that has emerged under Xi Jinping, however, is ambitious to lead but embraces globalization insofar as it controls the flow of ideas, as well as human and financial capital. While this rejection of an open market for ideas and capital brings with it inefficiencies and waste, these are costs that the Chinese leadership is willing to bear to realize a longer-term strategic vision. The United States needs to recognize that Xi Jinping's Third Revolution presents a new model of Chinese behavior at home and abroad and adjust its expectations and policies accordingly.

How the United States Looks at China

Xi Jinping's ambition for China to play a larger role in shaping the world's norms and institutions and to assert its presence more forcefully in its own neighborhood has provoked a rethinking in the United States (and elsewhere) about the nature of Chinese power and its implications for the rest of the world. There is, however, very little agreement among American scholars and policymakers as to China's ultimate objectives or the appropriate U.S. response. Some, such as American foreign policy scholars Robert Blackwill and Ashley Tellis, suggest that China's intention is to threaten U.S. national interests, weaken its alliance system, and replace the United States as Asia's dominant power.[2] They argue that a smart response would be for Washington to balance against China as it once did against the Soviet Union. Such balancing would include establishing preferential trading agreements with U.S. allies and friends that consciously exclude Beijing; levying economic sanctions on China if it does not reduce the level of state intervention in areas such as currency and trade; preventing China from acquiring military capabilities that would allow it to inflict "high-leverage strategic harm" on the United States; and strengthening the capacity of Washington's allies on China's periphery.

Others, such as China military experts Lyle Goldstein and Michael Swaine, argue that China does not seek to push the United States out of the region; instead, China desires only to carve out a space for its security commensurate with its rising capabilities.[3] Its assertiveness, they argue, stems from fears, uncertainties, and insecurities, as well as a certain amount of opportunism. In their eyes, Chinese actions are a natural outcome of the country's increasing capacity to meet the threat it believes it faces from the United States' long-standing dominance in the Asia-Pacific region. They fault U.S. policy on the grounds that it contributes to Chinese insecurity, which in turn, they argue, leads to greater Chinese assertiveness.

The answer these analysts posit, rests in a strategic reassessment by both the United States and China: Washington should "rethink its objective of primacy" and Beijing should "recalibrate its own sense of strength." In their eyes, a broader shift in military capabilities and economic power away from the United States and toward China, as well as other emerging markets, is underway, meaning it is unrealistic to think of the primacy of one nation. The United States should therefore find a way to accommodate China's rightful desire for a greater voice and role in international affairs and institutions, while China should find ways to reassure its neighbors. Such a recalibration of each side's baseline demands would then pave the way for a series of reciprocal actions that could reduce tensions and mistrust, and build confidence through mutual restraint.

A third camp, epitomized by China scholar Thomas Christensen, remains agnostic concerning Chinese intentions, claiming it is too early to understand clearly Xi's intended endgame; the United States thus needs to prepare for any eventuality.[4] As Christensen argues, U.S. policy should embrace the concept of a strong U.S. presence in the Asia-Pacific region but pursue a more deeply committed version: Washington needs to increase its diplomatic efforts to engage China in regional and global governance, but simultaneously maintain a strong military presence in the region. Any Chinese insecurity that might result from increased U.S. military activity would probably benefit the United States by encouraging Chinese officials to be more accommodating. At the same time, Washington should provide China's neighbors with the opportunity to cooperate with the United States in security, economic, and diplomatic relations without jealously begrudging their positive economic and diplomatic relations with China.

While each of these perspectives differs in its understanding of the nature of the U.S.-China relationship and its prescription for U.S. policy, together they offer a set of important reminders for U.S. policymakers as to how the United States should think about its policy toward China. First, U.S. interests should be placed front and center. It is easy for the United States to become reactive, formulating policy largely in response to the stream of initiatives that seems to pour out of China on a daily basis. Yet that gives every advantage to China and leaves the United States without a strategy or context for its policy. Second, the United States should constantly reevaluate its long-term interests and capabilities in light of those of other actors. China's rise as a global power, particularly in the Asia-Pacific region, has the potential to significantly reconfigure power relations over the coming decade or more. The United States must think now about the landscape of the Asia-Pacific region a decade out, the role the United States wants to play, and what it will take to get there. Finally, the "engage but hedge" approach, which has in one form or another been the dominant U.S. policy toward China since relations were established in 1979, has the virtue of orienting the relationship on a positive trajectory while nonetheless protecting U.S. interests in case China's intentions are malign.

This study adds a fourth consideration for U.S. policy toward China: a focus on China's foreign policy is not enough to guide U.S. policy. American policymakers must also pay close attention to and address the domestic changes underway in China, as well as their implications for Chinese foreign policy and for U.S. actors' opportunities in China. The policy of the United States toward China for over four decades has been premised on two assumptions: first, American values (and to a lesser extent, interests) are universal and thus worthy of promulgation; and second, notwithstanding some serious counter-indications, such as the 1989 Tiananmen Square massacre, as China's economy develops, its domestic and foreign policies will evolve in ways generally supportive of U.S. interests. For the foreseeable future, however, the opposite is true. Under Xi's leadership, China's domestic political and economic landscape does not reflect progress toward an open, transparent, or democratic system.

As such, China under Xi Jinping poses a set of distinct new challenges. First, Xi Jinping is not only more ambitious to lead in a globalized world but also seeks to project the current Chinese political and economic development model globally. This raises the specter of a far more difficult international environment for the United States in which free trade, the free flow of information, and principles of good governance are routinely challenged by an ever-expanding set of authoritarian nations.

Second, China's innovation strategy, the BRI, and SOE reform reflect non-market principles and behavior that pose a challenge to U.S. economic interests at home, in China, and globally. The United States is ill-prepared to compete against a China that has the political and economic wherewithal to accept the suboptimal economic and efficiency outcomes generated by non-market practices in the near term to try to ensure market dominance over the long term.

And third, while China takes advantage of the openness of the United States and other market-based liberal democracies to further its economic interests and advance its political and cultural influence, it increasingly constrains opportunities for foreign actors to participate in China's political and economic development. This has direct costs for U.S. business, as well as for the ability of civil society, including American cultural representatives, NGOs, and universities, to develop relations with their counterparts in China—historically an essential pillar of the U.S.–China relationship.

Working with and managing the relationship with Beijing, therefore, requires not only consistent assertion of U.S. interests and priorities and attention to China's foreign policy interests but also equal consideration of the country's domestic political and economic evolution. In some cases, the United States will need to reinforce traditional approaches to managing its relationship with China; in others, it will need to adopt new measures, some of which have traditionally been rejected as not conducive to a robust U.S.–China relationship.

A Workable U.S.–China Policy

The policy of the United States toward China has been remarkably consistent over the past four decades. From one administration to the next, American presidents have sought to expand and deepen relations with their Chinese counterparts, while at the same time advancing U.S. principles of free trade, freedom of navigation, and democracy, both in China and more broadly throughout Asia. In the 2000s, for example, President George W. Bush's effort to promote China as a "responsible stakeholder" sought to ensure that China's rise would support rather than undermine the international institutions that had been established and underpinned by these principles. President Obama's pivot or rebalance toward Asia also projected these same U.S. interests within Asia through an increased military presence and security cooperation with allies and partners; a proposed multilateral trade agreement, the TPP; and political-capacity building in authoritarian countries, including China, and nascent democracies, such as Myanmar. All of these efforts—whatever form they assumed—rested on the assumption that U.S. political, economic, and security interests were best served by the United States investing in institutions and initiatives abroad that reflected U.S. values and priorities at home.

President Trump and his administration have raised questions about whether this assumption is still relevant. The president's "America First" policy has translated into the withdrawal of the United States from several of its commitments to global and regional leadership, such as the Paris climate accord and the proposed TPP. President Trump has also called for other countries to share more of the burden of addressing global challenges, explicitly accusing them of not paying their fair share. His comments and initiatives suggest that he does not hold the same understanding of the intrinsic value of U.S. global leadership that his predecessors did. He offers a narrower conception of when and how the United States will lead, and he prioritizes immediate threats to the United States rather than the development and exercise of institutions to manage underlying challenges in security and trade.

Within the context of "America First," the Trump administration's China policy has rested primarily on the pursuit of two priorities: first, resolving the North Korea nuclear challenge, and second, leveling the playing field on trade. It has, for example, pressured Beijing to enforce sanctions on North Korea more effectively, initiated an investigation into Beijing's practices on intellectual property and forced technology transfer, attacked China's subsidies to robotics companies, and threatened to impose tariffs on Chinese steel imports. It also has pushed hard on short-term, transactional initiatives to try to yield quick wins, such as pressing Beijing for access to the Chinese market for U.S. beef.

Yet such an approach will not suffice to meet the larger and longer-term China challenge. The Trump administration needs a strategic framework for its relationship with China that establishes U.S. priorities and the diplomatic, economic, and military approaches necessary to realize them. Such a framework will support U.S. actors in advancing their business or other interests and, by extension, U.S. influence; provide a much-needed coherence and stability to U.S. policy that will help prevent minor misunderstandings or miscalculations between the United States and China from spiraling into much greater conflict; and offer U.S. allies the predictability and surety they require to coordinate with the United States on difficult China-related issues.

Go Long

The Trump administration has not entirely forsaken the policy framework of its predecessors. Despite the high-profile indications of a significant shift in U.S. policy toward China and Asia, there are also signals of underlying continuities in fundamental values and priorities. In his speech before the APEC Forum CEO Summit in November 2017 in Vietnam, President Trump called for a free and open Indo-Pacific, rooted in a rules-based order.[5] Implicitly, the president conceded that the United States benefits from its leadership and partnerships in the region. More than $1 trillion of U.S. trade flows through the South China Sea annually, making regional stability of paramount importance. Just a day later in the Philippines, representatives of Australia, India, the United States, and Japan revived the Quadrilateral Security Dialogue—a Japanese initiative that had been dormant for a decade—in support of common strategic and economic principles and objectives in the region. Other members of the Trump administration, most notably Secretary of Defense James Mattis and Secretary of State Rex Tillerson, have consistently offered support for a more multilateral, principles-based foreign policy, calling for the United States to retain its "enduring commitment to the security and prosperity of the region based on strategic interests, the shared values of free people, free markets, and a strong and vibrant economic partnership."[6]

Recognizing the changed context of both U.S. and Chinese political environments, the United States should retain what has worked well for its policy toward China while adapting to a new political reality. This requires adopting a set of approaches that reflect a mix of new and old. These include a renewed push in diplomacy that leverages Xi Jinping's ambition for global leadership, an enhanced effort toward multilateralism that nonetheless recognizes greater burden sharing, a greater willingness to adopt punitive measures when China flouts agreements or pursues unfair advantage, and a commitment to strengthen the capacity of the U.S. government to understand the ongoing and often rapid transformations in Chinese domestic and foreign policy. Informing and guiding all these efforts should be a continued U.S. commitment to its fundamental values, including democracy and respect for human rights, a market economy and free trade, and support for the international institutions that reflect these principles.

Diplomacy First

There are many examples of successful U.S. diplomatic efforts with China that have yielded important benefits globally. With U.S leadership, the two countries found common ground in advancing global cooperation on climate change, arresting the spread of Ebola, and preventing the development of nuclear weapons in Iran. Such cooperation is inevitably hard won. However, Xi Jinping's ambition for China to assume a position of leadership in a globalized world has the potential to provide the United States with greater leverage in encouraging China to do more on the global stage.

Two areas of pressing importance where both countries could exert significant leadership and bolster their bilateral relationship are the global refugee crisis and the North Korean nuclear threat. Although the

United States itself is less a leader in responding to refugee crises than previously—now seeking to limit the number of refugees it accepts—it continues to provide significant financial support globally for refugee support and relocation. China, however, has remained largely silent as millions flee conflict in the Middle East. Even more inexplicably, it has only reluctantly stepped up to help address the refugee crisis in its own backyard: the more than 650,000 Rohingya fleeing violence in Myanmar and seeking refuge in Bangladesh. It has limited its support to an offer to facilitate a bilateral dialogue between Bangladesh and Myanmar and a cautionary statement that the crisis should not slow down progress on the Bangladesh-China-India-Myanmar economic corridor—part of Beijing's BRI.[7] The United States, which has pledged tens of millions of dollars in aid for the refugees, threatened sanctions, and called for an investigation into the atrocities,[8] should call on China as a regional and global power to do more. Much as it did in the case of the Ebola epidemic, the United States should quietly draw attention to Beijing's limited response, press it to provide financial as well as other assistance, and encourage it to use its extensive economic leverage in Myanmar to help bring a halt to the violence. Moreover, a coordinated response by the United States and China to provide assistance for the Rohingya's safe passage back to Myanmar, assurances of citizenship, or resettlement elsewhere would send an important signal to Myanmar to resolve the crisis. As transpired in the case of climate change, it could also mark a first step in a broader international effort to address the global refugee crisis.

Cooperation between the United States and China is also essential in meeting the challenge of North Korea's ballistic missile and nuclear weapons program. Both countries have devoted significant attention to the issue and agree on the objective of denuclearization on the Korean Peninsula, but options are limited. The Trump administration has persuaded China to adopt increasingly tough trade and other sanctions on North Korea, but the sanctions have yet to bring North Korea to the negotiating table. A preemptive military strike on North Korea would engender retaliation and devastating human and economic losses in South Korea, along with the potential to draw both the United States and China into military conflict. Simply allowing North Korea to continue on its current path directly endangers the security of the United

States. And China's double freeze proposal—in which the United States and South Korea freeze their military exercises in exchange for North Korea freezing its development and testing program—failed to engage the relevant parties.

Nonetheless, a combination of diplomacy and sanctions led by the United States and China remains the most viable path forward. Full enforcement of current sanctions by China is a first and necessary step. For its part, the United States should commit in earnest to a variant of China's "freeze for freeze" proposal, agreeing to some "modest adjustment to conventional military exercises"[9] while the parameters and sequencing of a potential agreement are determined. The United States and China could also take a page from their own history of diplomatic opening and use sports or culture to open the door to North Korea. There is no clear path forward, but setting the stage for more formal negotiations would be a first step.

Most U.S.–China diplomatic engagement operates not at the level of grand bargains to address global challenges but at the more mundane level of technical cooperation around the big issues of global governance. The United States and China cooperate on a wide range of issues, including drug trafficking, cybercrimes and the dark web, counter-terrorism, and clean energy, among others. While these cooperative efforts do not often make headlines, they begin to build an institutional infrastructure for cooperation. And as one U.S. state department official mentioned to me, "when you take politics out of the equation, cooperation can be quite good."

As China's ambition and footprint expand, the need for technical cooperation will grow. Future areas could include developing rules of the road for limiting space debris or marine pollution in the Arctic, both of which are building blocks in a much larger area of potential conflict in global governance between the United States and China. Another issue of particular importance is coordinating standards for development finance. Working with Chinese development banks to ensure Chinese companies adopt best practices in the environment, regarding labor, and in transparency as they advance the BRI is essential to preserving the competitiveness of American companies. The United States could further its economic interests in this regard by joining the AIIB.

While advancing U.S. interests through diplomatic engagement with China represents the ideal in the Sino-American relationship, the often differing values, priorities, and policies of the two countries necessitates that the United States also maintains a range of alternatives in its toolbox. Partnering with allies and others in Asia, Europe, and elsewhere is an important element of U.S. policy toward China. President Trump's call for greater burden sharing does not need to be understood as a retreat by the United States from global leadership, but rather as an opportunity for other regional powers to assume a greater role in addressing shared challenges.

An Allied Front

One of America's greatest strengths in its relationship with China is its allies. Many countries in Europe and Asia share the United States' interest in finding an effective set of policies to manage the challenges posed by Xi's more walled-off domestic environment and ambitious foreign policy. The United States should seek to coordinate and cooperate with these countries to amplify its influence over Chinese policy. Such partnerships will not be one-size-fits-all. Different issues will engage different countries.

On the security front, China's military expansionism in the South China Sea and claim to sovereignty over Taiwan pose a significant threat to peace and stability in the Asia Pacific region. With regard to both issues, the U.S. priority must be to deter further efforts by China to realize its sovereignty claims through unilateral actions. This means developing a robust coalition of partners that includes not only the other claimants in the South China Sea but also the larger European military powers, such as France and Britain. These countries have already been outspoken in their calls for China to adhere to the 2015 Permanent Court of Arbitration ruling that rejected Beijing's expansive sovereignty claims. Along with the United States and Asian partners, these countries should form the basis of a more active military effort in the South China Sea to preserve freedom of navigation. In practice, this means consistent enforcement and equal treatment of all claimants through frequent and regular FONOPS. The Trump administration's decision to undertake such scheduled FONOPS is an important step, but it should be pursued in conjunction with others to signal not just a U.S. or even regional commitment to international law but a global one.

The United States should also support the decision of China and ASEAN to begin negotiations on a code of conduct for the South China Sea. However, the process of negotiation should not provide cover for Beijing to continue in the meantime to militarize the features it controls or otherwise expand its claims. If China resumes militarization of the features on which it has outposts, the United States should not try to dissuade other claimants from further developing military capabilities on the features they control.

The United States should also reiterate its commitments under the Taiwan Relations Act, such as providing Taiwan with adequate arms for self-defense. President Trump's early statements regarding the U.S. position on Taiwan—first threatening to revisit the One China policy, and later suggesting it could be a bargaining chip in a trade negotiation with Beijing—sowed confusion. Here, too, the United States should seek broader support among its Asian and European allies for upholding the basic principle of Taiwanese sovereignty and its freedom to develop without fear of Chinese coercion.

In the area of trade and investment, China's Made in China 2025 seeks to prevent foreign competition in a wide swath of cutting-edge technologies by absorbing leading technologies and technology firms from abroad and at the same time preventing international firms from competing in China. The first line of defense for the United States should be to strengthen its own innovation capacity through government-supported investment in basic research and the creation of an incentive system—market based and otherwise—that encourages the development and adoption of new technologies. The second line of defense should be to protect critical U.S. technology assets. In late 2017, the U.S. Congress proposed new legislation to expand the role of the Committee on Foreign Investment in the United States that would help prevent countries—in particular China—from gaining access to certain core U.S. technologies or sensitive information such as financial data. As the United States seeks to respond to China's increasingly coercive trade and investment policies in the technology sector, it should work with Germany, the United Kingdom, and other countries with strong technology sectors to develop common legislation on these issues, as well on related areas as investment by SOEs, or foreign investment in university labs. In areas of technology where national security is not at risk, the final line of defense should be to push China to open its market or risk the United States closing sectors of its market to Chinese technology firms.

A multilateral approach to China may also, in some instances, include China itself. The United States should approach the BRI as an opportunity as well as a challenge. Washington should explore the opportunities offered by China's BRI for partnership with China, as well as with others. There are also opportunities to hold China, as the creator of the BRI, accountable for upholding best practices. One possibility would be to host a multilateral summit on infrastructure.[10] The summit could focus on principles to guide social and environmental impact assessments, transparency in the bidding process and financing, and potential projects for multilateral cooperation. The BRI should not become a free pass for China to export its overcapacity in highly polluting industries or a means of employing its surplus construction labor to the detriment of other countries' labor interests.

For the United States, in particular, China's digital road presents a challenge. If fully realized, Chinese technologies will capture the full range of digital opportunities, such as fiber optic cables, satellite systems, and e-commerce throughout much of the developing world. The U.S. government should initiate a comprehensive review of the digital technology infrastructure needs of Asia and support U.S. companies' active engagement through trade delegations and Ex-Im Bank financing. The U.S. government and firms have experience working in India to develop smart cities that could be adapted to additional developing countries.

The Trump administration should also revisit U.S. participation in the TPP. The remaining eleven nations have pressed forward with a modified agreement without the United States. The White House should review the TPP in its new incarnation and ascertain whether there is the opportunity to join in or modify additional elements in ways that better preserve U.S. interests. While the Trump administration is focused on retaliatory measures against China, these have the potential to escalate into a trade war. The TPP remains, in principle, the best

economic leverage the United States can exert to advance economic reform in China and realize a level playing field for U.S. companies over
the long term.

The United States should also partner with its allies in the region to
support through both word and deed a commitment to good governance including the rule of law, transparency, and official accountability.
For Chinese civil society, the U.S. model, as well as U.S. partnership and
support through the nongovernmental sector, has been instrumental in
opening the political space where it can operate. The United States,
along with its allies, should also speak out in support of Chinese activists. Here, too, Xi Jinping's desire to be a leader on the global stage and
export the China model offer a new opportunity for other countries to
hold China accountable for its human rights practices and to ensure
that it does not try to use its growing influence to subvert human rights
discourse internationally.

China under Xi Jinping also seeks to influence the domestic politics of
other countries as those politics relate to China. The Chinese government
mobilizes students and other citizens living abroad to represent the interests of the Chinese government by, for example, spying on other Chinese
students, denouncing professors who offer contrarian positions, and protesting against invited speakers who criticize China. It also seeks to use
its power to grant or withhold visas and project funding to shape how
foreign scholars portray China. The United States and other countries
should publicize Beijing's efforts to intimidate overseas Chinese, as well
as foreign scholars; transparency is an important antidote to Beijing's attempts to limit free expression outside its borders. Moreover, universities
and think tanks should resist undertaking joint projects with Chinese
institutions if any participant is denied entry to China. Otherwise China
will continue to use its leverage to divide and conquer.

The importance of publicly supporting the foundational values of
the United States and other democracies within the context of the
U.S.–China relationship extends well beyond the borders of the two
countries. China's expansionism via military, economic, and political
partnerships with other countries throughout the world provides Xi
Jinping with increasing opportunities to export the Chinese model of
authoritarian-led development. Such countries are likely to become
more natural allies of China on issues such as Internet governance and to

make less reliable economic and security partners for the United States over the long term. An important element of countering such a development is for the United States and its allies both in Asia and Europe to continue to support programs that build good governance capacity globally through the rule of law, development of property rights, and institutions that promote transparency, such as an open media.

When All Else Fails: Withhold, Sanction, and Reciprocate

American policymakers have long acted under the assumption that if the United States remains true to its democratic values and models best behavior—with an open and rules-based economy and political system—China will eventually follow suit. Xi Jinping's Third Revolution has largely upended this understanding. Instead, U.S. openness has become a vulnerability in the face of an increasingly ambitious but walled-off China. China is able to expand its political, economic, and cultural influence in the United States while not affording U.S. institutions and firms the same opportunities inside its borders. In this manner, China's domestic political and economic practices under Xi Jinping have become a far more significant impediment to the realization of U.S. interests than under previous Chinese leaders.

When American interests are directly and meaningfully undermined by Chinese actions, the United States should openly consider adopting punitive measures, making clear to China the costs of noncompliance with agreements or established norms. In some cases, the action may be relatively low cost. For example, the Trump administration signaled its unhappiness with a lack of Chinese progress in returning Americans held in China by canceling the participation of one U.S. bureaucracy in the cybersecurity and law dialogue, thereby depriving China of an important public win back home.

Economic retaliation is also an important option. In September 2015, President Obama threatened sanctions against Chinese firms over state-sponsored cyber-attacks on American companies. The result was a formal, bilateral cyber agreement, and, according to a number of experts, a noticeable diminution in the number of cyber-attacks on American companies in the wake of the agreement.

In the new era of Xi Jinping, the United States should also avail itself of reciprocal action. Reciprocity has long been resisted by U.S. policy-makers as precipitating a race to the bottom. However, when diplomatic and multilateral efforts fail, it should be a viable option. For example, the United States could consider constraining Chinese investment in areas where Chinese sectors are significantly closed, such as telecommunications, transportation, and media, among others. In particular, China is eager to bring its expertise in construction to the United States to gain access to significant infrastructure development opportunities. Washington should not open the door to partner with Beijing unless it receives similar access in China. China has also long insisted that foreign firms manufacture significant components in certain sectors to have access to the Chinese market. The United States could likewise demand that Chinese firms in these sectors manufacture within the United States as the price of access to the U.S. market.

Similarly, in the cultural arena, including education and media, the United States should adopt a policy of targeted reciprocity. The ability of the Chinese government to establish Confucius Institutes, for example, should be matched by a willingness on the part of China to accept American government-sponsored entities, such as American Centers in U.S. embassies that provide access to Western books, speakers, and other cultural experiences. If not, the United States should close the door to additional Confucius Institutes. Chinese visa denials for American journalists and scholars should also be reciprocated with denials for government-sponsored journalists and senior government media and propaganda officials.

Reciprocity may well emerge as a "lose-lose" proposition. However, there is little advantage to the United States in retaining its openness to Chinese influence, whether economic or political, if China is increasingly closing its door to the United States. Reciprocity should remain a tool in the U.S. toolkit, albeit one of last resort.

The Future Is Now

As the musical genius Tom Lehrer once proclaimed, "Be Prepared—that's the Boy Scout's solemn rule." When it comes to managing the U.S. relationship with China, the ability to think creatively, to adapt

U.S. policy quickly to new Chinese initiatives, and to see what might be coming next are essential. This means developing a significant coterie of China expertise throughout the government, both in Washington and on the ground in China, and providing adequate training and budgetary support. This includes continuing financial support for American students who seek to study in China. Despite the importance of China to the United States and the world more generally, China ranks a distant fifth in popularity as an overseas destination for American students after the United Kingdom, Italy, Spain, and France.[11]

While arguing for more China expertise in the U.S. government may seem axiomatic, it has special resonance for the leadership period of presidents Trump and Xi. At the top of President Trump's agenda are two issues directly related to China—North Korea and bilateral trade deficits—and China plays a role in virtually every issue of regional and global significance. Yet the Trump administration has been slow to fill positions with both direct and indirect China responsibility, leaving a few talented officials to bear the burden of managing an extraordinarily complicated and challenging set of issues.

A deep reservoir of China expertise is also particularly necessary in an era of Xi Jinping. Xi, more than other recent Chinese leaders, is prone to both bold pronouncements, such as the BRI, and surprising moves, such as the placement of an oil rig in waters contested with Vietnam or the takeover of Scarborough Shoal. The United States will be better positioned to keep up with or even counter such surprises if it has the ability to pay close attention to early warning signs. For example, a short piece by a prominent Chinese scholar floated the idea of a Chinese policy shift with regard to military bases several years in advance of Beijing's decision to develop the logistics base in Djibouti. Similarly, several Chinese scholars have suggested that in one form or another China should consider establishing alliances or work to undermine the U.S.-led alliance system by promoting Xi Jinping's vision of a "Community of Common Destiny." In either case, the United States should begin thinking strategically about its current alliance structure and what steps to take to address any vulnerabilities.

At the same time, the United States can gain leverage in negotiations with China by understanding domestic dynamics within the country around particular issues. On the issue of China's relationship with

North Korea, for example, the Chinese government has confronted substantial domestic pressure from Chinese foreign policy experts and officials to work more closely with the United States. Thus, President Trump might have avoided offering China trade concessions in exchange for greater Chinese pressure on North Korea in April 2017 had he recognized that prominent voices in China were already pushing the Chinese government to adopt a tougher stance toward Pyongyang.

Finally, while many Chinese revel in Xi's efforts to clamp down on corruption, propel economic growth, and expand China's role globally, his mass campaigns and regressive reforms have also produced significant pockets of discontent. Some segments of the Chinese public are frustrated by the government's inability to clean up the environment, restrictions on their ability to invest abroad, and constraints on the Internet. Technology entrepreneurs are unhappy about the government's increasing intrusion into their business decisions at home and abroad. Scholars are concerned about limitations on their freedom to publish, teach, and travel. Activists for change—whether labor, legal, or women's rights—are unnerved by the dramatic increase in political repression. Chinese officials complain about Xi's power grab and the arbitrary nature of many new regulations. And despite Xi's unprecedented centralization of power, there have been efforts by powerful officials to unseat him as the country's leader. With all of this, the United States must remain attuned to the potential—however unlikely—for China to experience significant social unrest.

The Future of U.S. and Chinese Leadership and Partnership

While President Trump preaches "America First" and withdraws from international accords, President Xi calls for win-win solutions and defends the shared benefits of globalization. The contrasting rhetoric of presidents Trump and Xi makes it easy to jump to the conclusion, as many analysts have, that as the United States withdraws from global leadership, China stands ready to take its place. Yet that would be a mistake. The United States may well be taking a step back from its willingness to lead the way on addressing the world's many challenges, but China is not prepared to replace it. Global leadership requires a willingness to subordinate one's own narrow interests for the benefit of the larger community. It also means stepping forward to forge an international consensus on thorny global issues such as terrorism or the Syrian refugee crisis.

When put to the test, however, China has not yet stepped up to the plate. The vacuum left by the Trump administration's step back from global leadership on refugees was filled by Canada and Germany; on regional trade, by Japan and Australia; and on family planning services, by the Netherlands. Even in China's own backyard—addressing North Korea's nuclear proliferation or managing the refugee crisis in Myanmar—China has not yet put forward a workable solution. China's leadership globally is largely confined to those issues where its interests are easily advanced, such as economic development through the BRI or security cooperation to prevent terrorist attacks or democratic revolutions through the Shanghai Cooperation Organization.

Nonetheless, with Xi Jinping at the helm, China has become a transformative power—reversing the previous thirty years of reform and opening at home and a low-profile foreign policy abroad. China can and should be an important U.S. partner whenever possible. The two countries found common ground on climate change, the Iran nuclear deal, and—to an important extent—North Korea. However, on a wide range of issues, such as Internet sovereignty, human rights, sovereignty claims over the South and East China Seas, as well as Taiwan, and trade and investment practices, among others, U.S. and Chinese priorities, policies, and values are not aligned. Moreover, China cannot be a leader in a globalized world while at the same time closing its borders to ideas, capital, and influences from the outside world. The United States, in partnership with its allies and other partners, must continue to seek opportunities for cooperation but at the same time be prepared to counter and confront China when Xi's Third Revolution spills over into the rest of the world, undermining the principles underpinning global security and prosperity it purports to uphold.

NOTES

Chapter 1

1. The World Economic Forum is a convening organization based in Switzerland that takes as its mission public-private partnership in service of addressing the world's transnational and global challenges. It is most well known for its annual January Davos retreat.

2. "Full Text of Xi's Address to the Media," *China Daily*, November 16, 2012, http://www.chinadaily.com.cn/china/2012cpc/2012-11/16/content_15934514.htm.

3. "Full Text of Xi's Address to the Media."

4. "Xi Pledges 'Great Renewal of Chinese Nation,'" *Xinhua*, November 29, 2012, http://china.org.cn/china/2012-11/30/content_27269821_3.htm.

5. "Profile: Xi Jinping: Pursuing Dream for 1.3 billion Chinese," *Xinhua*, March 17, 2013, http://english.cntv.cn/20130317/100246.shtml.

6. "Xi Jinping: To Follow the Past and Herald the Future, Continue to Work Courageously Towards the Great Rejuvenation of the Chinese Nation [*Xi Jinping: Cheng Qian Qi Hou Ji Wang Kai Lai Jixu Chao Zhe Zhonghua Minzu Weida Fuxing Mubiao Fenyong Qianjin*]," *Xinhua*, November 29, 2012, http://news.xinhuanet.com/politics/2012-11/29/c_113852724.htm.

7. "Background: Connotations of Chinese Dream," *China Daily*, March 5, 2014, http://www.chinadaily.com.cn/china/2014npcandcppcc/2014-03/05/content_17324203.htm.

8. Xiaoping Deng, "Reform and Opening to the Outside World Can Truly Invigorate China," in *Selected Works of Deng Xiaoping*, vol. 3 (Beijing: People's Publishing House, 1993), 232.

9. "Jiang Zemin's Speech at the Meeting Celebrating the 80th Anniversary of the Founding of the Communist Party of China," *China.org.cn*, July 1, 2001, http://www.china.org.cn/e-speech/a.htm; "Full Text of Hu Jintao's Speech at CPC Anniversary Gathering," *Xinhua*, July 1, 2011, http://cpcchina.chinadaily.com.cn/news/2011-07/01/content_12819337.htm.

10. Jiang Zemin succeeded Zhao Ziyang as general secretary. Zhao served only two years (1987–1989) before being ousted for his unwillingness to crack down on the student protestors during the Tiananmen Square demonstrations. His predecessor, Hu Yaobang served five years as general secretary before being forced out on the grounds that his policies had encouraged the 1987 student protests in support of democracy.

11. Xiaohuai Yang, "Xi Jinping: My Road into Politics," *Zhonghua Ernu* (Summer 2000), trans. Carsten Boyer Thagersen and Susanne Posborg, Nordic Institute of Asian Studies, http://www.nias.ku.dk/news/interview-2000-china%E2%80%99s-vice-president-xi-jinping-translated-western-language-first-time.

12. "Xi Leads Top Leadership, Meeting Press," *Xinhua*, November 15, 2012, http://www.china-embassy.org/eng/zt/18th_CPC_National_Congress_Eng/t989541.htm.

13. David Shambaugh, "The Chinese State in the Post-Mao Era," in *The Modern Chinese State*, ed. David Shambaugh (Cambridge: Cambridge University Press, 1994), 200.

14. Minxin Pei, "China's Return to Strongman Rule," *Foreign Affairs*, November 1, 2017, https://www.foreignaffairs.com/articles/china/2017-11-01/chinas-return-strongman-rule.

15. Full Text of Xi Jinping's Report at the 19th Party Congress delivered on October 18, 2017, Beijing, *PRC Xinhua*, November 3, 2017, http://news.xinhuanet.com/english/special/2017-11/03/c_136725942.htm.

Chapter 2

1. "Special Feature: *The Southern Weekly* Controversy," Freedom House, January 18, 2013, https://freedomhouse.org/cmb/2013_southern_weekly.

2. Teddy Ng, "Tuo Zhen, Crusading Journalist Turned Guangdong Propagandist," *South China Morning Post*, January 5, 2013, http://www.scmp.com/news/china/article/1120156/tuo-zhen-crusading-journalist-turned-guangdong-propagandist.

3. David Bandurski, "A New Year's Greeting Gets the Axe in China," China Media Project, January 3, 2013, http://cmp.hku.hk/2013/01/03/a-new-years-greeting-gets-the-axe-in-china/.

4. "[*Southern Weekend*]: A Comparison of the Two New Year's Greetings [<*Nanfang Zhoumo*> *Yuandan Xianci Liang Banben Bijiao*]," BBC Chinese, January 4, 2013, http://www.bbc.com/zhongwen/simp/chinese_news/2013/01/130104_nanfangzhoumo_newyear.shtml.

5. Ian Johnson, "Test for New Leaders as Chinese Paper Takes on Censors," *New York Times,* January 6, 2013, http://www.nytimes.com/2013/01/07/ world/asia/chinese-newspaper-challenges-the-censors.html.

6. "Special Feature: The *Southern Weekly* Controversy."

7. Annie Zhang, "China's Press Freedom Goes South," *Foreign Policy,* January 11, 2013, http://foreignpolicy.com/2013/01/11/chinas-press-freedom-goes-south/.

8. Malcolm Moore, "Two Liberal Chinese Media Outlets Targeted by Government," *Telegraph,* January 4, 2013, http://www.telegraph.co.uk/ news/worldnews/asia/china/9780220/Two-liberal-Chinese-media-outlets-targetted-by-government.html.

9. Verna Yu, "The Death of a Liberal Chinese Magazine," *Diplomat,* July 19, 2016, http://thediplomat.com/2016/07/the-death-of-a-liberal-chinese-magazine/.

10. Moore, "Two Liberal Chinese Media Outlets Targeted by Government."

11. Simon Denyer, "China's Xi Tells Grumbling Party Cadres: 'Don't Talk Back,'" *Washington Post,* December 29, 2015, https://www.washingtonpost. com/world/asia_pacific/chinas-xi-tells-grumbling-party-cadres-dont-talk-back/2015/12/27/a6b25d2c-a446-11e5-8318-bd8caed8c588_story.html.

12. Alice Miller, "More Already on the Central Committee's Leading Small Groups," *China Leadership Monitor* 44 (Summer 2014)1 6, http://www. hoover.org/sites/default/files/research/docs/clm44am.pdf.

13. Zachary Keck, "China Creates New Military Reform Leading Group," *Diplomat,* March 21, 2014, http://thediplomat.com/2014/03/china-creates-new-military-reform-leading-group/.

14. Kejin Zhao, "China's National Security Commission," Carnegie Endowment for International Peace, July 14, 2015, http:// carnegieendowment.org/2015/07/14/china-s-national-security-commission-pub-60637.

15. "A Very Chinese Coup," *Economist,* October 15, 2015, http://www. economist.com/news/china/21674793-li-keqiang-weakest-chinese-prime-minister-decades-very-chinese-coup.

16. Chris Buckley, "Xi Jinping Assuming New Status as China's 'Core' Leader," *New York Times,* February 4, 2016, http://www.nytimes.com/ 2016/02/05/world/asia/china-president-xi-jinping-core.html.

17. "Politburo of the Communist Party of China's Central Committee Convenes Meeting [*Zhonggong Zhongyang Zhengzhiju Zhaokai Huiyi*]," *Xinhua,* January 29, 2016, http://news.xinhuanet.com/politics/2016-01/ 29/c_1117940977.htm.

18. "Sichuan Provincial Party Committee Convenes Standing Committee Meeting, Wang Dongming Hosts the Meeting and Gives Speech [*Sichuan Shengwei Zhaokai Changwei Huiyi Wang Dongming Zhuchi Huiyi Jianghua*]," *Sichuan Daily,* January 12, 2016, http://cpc.people.com.cn/n1/ 2016/0112/c117005-28043373.html.

19. Jonathan Landreth, "Xi Jinping: A Cult of Personality?," *ChinaFile*, March 4, 2016, https://www.chinafile.com/conversation/xi-jinping-cult-personality.

20. Austin Ramzy, "Musical Ode to Xi Jinping and His Wife Goes Viral," *New York Times* (Sinosphere blog), November 25, 2014, http://sinosphere.blogs.nytimes.com/2014/11/25/musical-ode-to-xi-jinping-and-his-wife-goes-viral/.

21. "The Ideal Chinese Husband: Xi Dada and the Cult of Personality Growing around China's President," *South China Morning Post,* February 29, 2016, http://www.scmp.com/news/china/policies-politics/article/1918443/ideal-chinese-husband-xi-dada-and-cult-personality.

22. Chris Buckley, "Chinese President Returns to Mao's (and His) Roots in Yan'an," *New York Times* (Sinosphere blog), February 13, 2015, http://sinosphere.blogs.nytimes.com/2015/02/13/chinese-president-returns-to-maos-and-his-roots-in-yanan/?mtrref=www.google.com&gwh=9154F5945EBDB80C7CEA129899A5F487&gwt=pay&_r=0.

23. Ryan Mitchell, "Xi Jinping: A Cult of Personality?," *ChinaFile*, March 4, 2016, https://www.chinafile.com/conversation/xi-jinping-cult-personality.

24. Hannah Beech, "China's Chairman Builds a Cult of Personality," *Time,* March 31, 2016, http://time.com/4277504/chinas-chairman/.

25. Dingding Chen, "Sorry, There's NO 'Cult of Personality' in China," *The Diplomat*, April 4, 2016, http://thediplomat.com/2016/04/sorry-theres-no-cult-of-personality-in-china/.

26. Keyu Jin, "Xi Jinping Is Consolidating Power—But for a Higher Purpose," *South China Morning Post,* August 5, 2016, http://www.scmp.com/comment/insight-opinion/article/1999504/xi-jinping-consolidating-power-higher-purpose.

27. Cheng Li, "Xi's Reform Agenda: Promises and Risks," *China-U.S. Focus,* March 3, 2014, http://www.chinausfocus.com/political-social-development/xis-reform-agenda-promises-and-risks/.

28. Andrew Nathan, "Who Is Xi?," *The New York Review of Books*, May 12, 2016, https://www.nybooks.com/articles/2016/05/12/who-is-xi/.

29. Willy Lam, "The Eclipse of the Communist Youth League and the Rise of the Zhejiang Clique,'" Jamestown Foundation China Brief 16.8, May 11, 2016, http://www.jamestown.org/programs/chinabrief/single/?tx_ttnews%5Btt_news%5D=45422&#.V-1Xq_krK71.

30. Katsuji Nakazawa, "A Dark Horse Emerges in Chinese Succession Race," *Nikkei Asian Review,* July 8, 2016, http://asia.nikkei.com/Politics-Economy/Policy-Politics/A-dark-horse-emerges-in-Chinese-succession-race?page=1.

31. Nakazawa, "A Dark Horse Emerges in Chinese Succession Race."

32. Lam, "The Eclipse of the Communist Youth League."

33. Jeremy Page, "President Xi Jinping's Most Dangerous Venture Yet: Remaking China's Military," *Wall Street Journal,* April 24, 2016,

http://www.wsj.com/articles/president-xi-jinpings-most-dangerous-venture-yet-remaking-chinas-military-1461608795.

34. "Xi's New Model Army," *Economist*, January 16, 2016, http://www.economist.com/news/china/21688424-xi-jinping-reforms-chinas-armed-forcesto-his-own-advantage-xis-new-model-army.

35. Jerome Doyon, "Personnel Reshuffle in the PLA: The Two Promotions That Did Not Happen," European Council on Foreign Relations, March 2016, http://www.ecfr.eu/page/-/XIS_ARMY_-_REFORM_AND_LOYALTY_IN_THE_PLA_-_ECFR164.pdf.

36. "China's Xi Shakes Up Rival Power Base before Party Reshuffle," *Bloomberg*, April 24, 2016, http://www.bloomberg.com/news/articles/2016-04-24/shake-up-at-china-university-signals-political-shift-under-xi.

37. "China Slashes Influential Communist Youth League's Budget," *Reuters*, May 3, 2016, http://www.reuters.com/article/us-china-politics-league-idUSKCN0XU0OG.

38. Lam, "The Eclipse of the Communist Youth League."

39. "Xi Jinping: Solving China's Problems Requires China to Find Ways and Approaches That Are Suitable for Itself [*Xi Jinping: Jiejue Zhongguo de Wenti Zhineng Zai Zhongguo Dadi Shang Tanxun Shihe Ziji De Daolu He Fangfa*]," *Xinhua*, October 13, 2014, http://news.xinhuanet.com/politics/2014-10/13/c_1112807354.htm.

40. Jon S. T. Quah, "Minimizing Corruption in China: Is This an Impossible Dream?," *Maryland Series in Contemporary Asian Studies* 4 (2013): 13.

41. Song Ling, "Construction of Anti-Corruption Institutions and Culture in Traditional China and Its Implications for Modern China," *Social Sciences in China* 32, no. 4 (2011): 163.

42. Robert M. Marsh, "The Venality of Provincial Office in China and in Comparative Perspective," *Comparative Studies in Society and History* 4 (1962): 454–66, 454–55.

43. Ling, "Construction of Anti-Corruption Institutions and Culture in Traditional China," 168–69.

44. As quoted in Nancy Park, "Corruption in Eighteenth-Century China," *Journal of Asian Studies* 56, no. 4 (1997): 967–1005, 967.

45. Orville Schell, "Crackdown in China: Worse and Worse," *New York Review of Books*, April 21, 2016, http://www.nybooks.com/articles/2016/04/21/crackdown-in-china-worse-and-worse/.

46. Park, "Corruption in Eighteenth-Century China," 997.

47. Quah, "Minimizing Corruption in China," 51.

48. Quah, "Minimizing Corruption in China," 31, 67.

49. Quah, "Minimizing Corruption in China," 60.

50. Minxin Pei, *China's Crony Capitalism* (Cambridge, MA: Harvard University Press, 2016).

51. Jonathan Watts, "Chinese President Hu Jintao's Warning as Communist Party Celebrates 90 Years," *Guardian,* July 1, 2011, https://www.theguardian.com/world/2011/jul/01/chinese-president-corruption-communist-party.

52. Roderick MacFarquhar, "China: The Superpower of Mr. Xi," *New York Review of Books,* August 13, 2015, http://www.nybooks.com/articles/2015/08/13/china-superpower-mr-xi/.

53. "Xi Warns of Regime's Demise Unless China Tackles Graft," *Bloomberg News,* November 19, 2012, http://www.bloomberg.com/news/articles/2012-11-19/xi-jinping-warns-of-regime-s-demise-unless-china-tackles-graft.

54. Alice Miller, "The CCP Central Committee's Leading Small Groups," *China Leadership Monitor* 26 (Fall 2008): 6, http://www.hoover.org/sites/default/files/uploads/documents/CLM26AM.pdf.

55. "Portrait of Vice President Xi Jinping: 'Ambitious Survivor' of the Cultural Revolution," Wikileaks, November 16, 2009, https://wikileaks.org/plusd/cables/09BEIJING3128_a.html.

56. Xiaohuai Yang, "Xi Jinping: My Road into Politics."

57. "Xi Jinping Millionaire Relations Reveal Fortunes of Elite," *Bloomberg News,* June 29, 2012, http://www.bloomberg.com/news/articles/2012-06-29/xi-jinping-millionaire-relations-reveal-fortunes-of-elite.

58. Lynn T. White, "Political Mechanisms and Corruption," in *Routledge Handbook of the Chinese Economy,* ed. Gregory C. Chow and Dwight H. Perkins (New York City: Routledge, 2015), 296.

59. Schell, "Crackdown in China: Worse and Worse."

60. Didi Kirsten Tatlow, "Q. and A.: Ren Jianming on the Fight against Corruption in China, and His Own Solution," *New York Times* (Sinosphere blog), September 2, 2014, http://sinosphere.blogs.nytimes.com/2014/09/02/q-and-a-ren-jianming-on-the-fight-against-corruption-in-china-and-his-own-solution/.

61. "Central Authorities to Formulate Province and Ministry Level Cadre Lifestyle Treatment Regulations [*Zhongyang Zheng Zhiding Sheng Bu Ji Ganbu Shenghuo Daiyu Guiding*]," *People's Daily,* October 11, 2014, http://politics.people.com.cn/n/2014/1011/c1001-25808666.html.

62. "China Golf: Communist Party Bans Club Membership," *BBC,* October 22, 2015, http://www.bbc.com/news/world-asia-china-34600544.

63. "Catching Tigers and Flies," *ChinaFile,* January 21, 2016, https://anticorruption.chinafile.com/.

64. Zheping Huang, "China's Corruption Crackdown Is So Vast, Top Officials from Every Single Province Have Been Nabbed," *Quartz,* November 12, 2015, http://qz.com/547695/chinas-corruption-crackdown-is-so-vast-top-officials-from-every-single-province-have-been-nabbed/.

65. "Anti-corruption Drive Nets 70 SOE Top Executives," *China Daily,* January 9, 2015, http://www.china.org.cn/china/2015-01/09/content_34514533.htm.

66. "China Punishes Eight in Railway Corruption Case," *Reuters,* October 21, 2013, http://www.reuters.com/article/us-china-railways-corruption-idUSBRE99K02V20131021.

67. Jonathan Kaiman, "Liu Zhijun, China's Ex-railway Minister, Sentenced to Death for Corruption," *Guardian,* July 8, 2013, https://www.theguardian.com/world/2013/jul/08/liu-zhijun-sentenced-death-corruption.

68. Jun Mai, "China's Statistics Chief Wang Baoan Detained in Graft Investigation," January 26, 2016, *South China Morning Post,* http://www.scmp.com/news/china/policies-politics/article/1905778/chinas-statistics-chief-wang-baoan-detained-graft.

69. Xi Jinping, *The Governance of China* (Beijing: Foreign Languages Press, 2014), 426–27.

70. Jinping Xi, "Secure a Decisive Victory in Building a Moderately Prosperous Society in All Respects and Strive for the Great Success of Socialism with Chinese Characteristics for a New Era," speech delivered at the 19th National Congress of the Communist Party of China, October 18, 2017, http://www.xinhuanet.com/english/download/Xi_Jinping's_report_at_19th_CPC_National_Congress.pdf.

71. Elizabeth Economy, "China's Imperial President," *Foreign Affairs,* November/December 2014, https://www.foreignaffairs.com/articles/china/2014-10-20/chinas-imperial-president.

72. "Pure and Honest Healthy Atmosphere, a Bonus No Amount of Money Can Buy [*Qingfeng Zhengqi, Duoshao Qian Dou Maibulai De Hongli*]," *Central Commission for Disciplinary Inspection Magazine,* February 13, 2015, http://www.ccdi.gov.cn/yw/201502/t20150212_51324.html.

73. "China Corruption Crackdown 'Netted 300,000 In 2015,'" *BBC,* March 7, 2016, http://www.bbc.com/news/world-asia-china-35741357.

74. John Griffin, Clark Liu, and Tao Shu, "Is the Chinese Anti-Corruption Campaign Effective?," May 11, 2016, 7, http://www.cuhk.edu.hk/fin/event/symposium/SEFM_2016_paper_109.pdf.

75. Luisetta Mudie, "China's Anti-Corruption Dragnet Catches More Than Financial Criminals," *Radio Free Asia,* February 1, 2016, http://www.rfa.org/english/news/china/China-fugitives-02012016124112.html.

76. Keira Lu Huang, "China Ramps up Global Manhunt for Corrupt Officials with Operation 'Skynet,'" *South China Morning Post,* March 26, 2015, http://www.scmp.com/news/article/1748113/china-ramps-global-manhunt-fugitive-corrupt-officials-skynet.

77. "No Sand in Eyes: China's Top Graft-Buster Vows Strengthened Discipline," *Xinhua,* January 25, 2016, http://news.xinhuanet.com/english/2016-01/25/c_135041040.htm.

78. Philip Wen, "One of China's 'Most-Wanted' Fugitives Has Returned from the US to Surrender," *Reuters*, March 9, 2017, http://www.businessinsider.com/r-one-of-chinas-most-wanted-fugitives-returns-from-us-to-surrender-2017-3.

79. Xin Haiguang, "China's Great Swindle: How Public Officials Stole $120 Billion and Fled the Country," *Time*, June 26, 2011, http://content.time.com/time/world/article/0,8599,2079756,00.html.

80. Senmiao Qiu, "The Price of China's Anti-Corruption Campaign," *Waltham Economy of Asia Review*, October 11, 2014, https://brandeisear.wordpress.com/2014/10/11/the-price-of-chinas-anti-corruption-campaign/.

81. Ben Bland, "China Austerity Drive Hits Officials' Perks," *Financial Times*, April 20, 2016, https://www.ft.com/content/70ae4374-06d1-11e6-9b51-0fb5e65703ce.

82. Ray Kwong, "China at Corruption Crossroads," *EJInsight*, February 4, 2016, http://www.ejinsight.com/20160204-china-at-corruption-crossroads/.

83. Bruce Dickson, *The Dictator's Dilemma* (New York: Oxford University Press, 2016), 91.

84. Eric X. Li, "The Life of the Party," *Foreign Affairs*, January/February 2013, https://www.foreignaffairs.com/articles/china/2012-12-03/life-party.

85. Li, "The Life of the Party."

86. Yasheng Huang, "Why Democracy Still Wins: A Critique of Eric X. Li's 'A Tale of Two Political Systems,'" *Ted Blog*, July 1, 2013, http://blog.ted.com/why-democracy-still-wins-a-critique-of-eric-x-lis-a-tale-of-two-political-systems/?utm_source=feedburner&utm_medium=feed&utm_campaign=feed%3a+tedblog+%28tedblog%29.

87. Dickson, *The Dictator's Dilemma*, 91.

88. Yuxin Zhang, "Why Xi Jinping's Anti-Corruption Campaign Won't Legitimize the CCP," *Diplomat*, August 12, 2014, http://thediplomat.com/2014/08/why-xi-jinpings-anti-corruption-campaign-wont-legitimize-the-ccp/.

89. "The Battle at Zhongnanhai," *China Uncensored*, n.d., http://www.chinauncensored.com/index.php?option=com_content&view=article&id=759:the-battle-at-zhongnanhai&catid=25:real-china&Itemid=57.

90. Susan Jakes, "Interactive: Visualizing China's Massive Corruption Crackdown," *Foreign Policy*, January 21, 2016, http://foreignpolicy.com/2016/01/21/interactive-visualizing-chinas-massive-corruption-crackdown/.

91. Griffin, Liu, and Shu, "Is the Chinese Anti-Corruption Campaign Effective?," 3–4.

92. Keira Lu Huang, "Xi Jinping's Reforms Encounter 'Unimaginably Fierce Resistance,' Chinese State Media Says in 'Furious' Commentary," *South China Morning Post*, August 21, 2015, http://

www.scmp.com/news/china/policies-politics/article/1851314/
xi-jinpings-reforms-encountering-fierce-resistance?page=all.

93. "Anti-Corruption: Changing China," *Transparency International,* October
31, 2014, http://www.transparency.org/news/feature/anti_corruption_
changing_china.

94. Griffin, Liu, and Shu, "Is the Chinese Anti-Corruption Campaign
Effective?," 2, 4.

95. "The Devil, or Mr Wang," *Economist,* March 26, 2015, http://www.
economist.com/news/china/21647295-chinas-second-most-powerful-
leader-admired-and-feared-devil-or-mr-wang.

96. Conversation in Stockholm, Sweden, with Shanghai-based German
businessman, January 2016.

97. Banyue Tan, "Under High Anti-Corruption Pressure Government-
Business Relations Have Become a Little Prejudiced: Officials Hide from
Entrepreneurs, Won't Eat, Won't Take, Won't Interfere [*Fanfu Gaoya Xia
Zheng Shang Guanxi Youdian Pian: Guanyuan Duozhe Qiyejia, Bu Chi
Bu Na Ye Bu Gan*]," *The Paper,* May 6, 2015, http://www.thepaper.cn/
newsDetail_forward_1328261,

98. Duncan Hewitt, "How China's Anti-Corruption Campaign Is Putting
Pressure on a Slowing Economy," *International Business Times,* March 22,
2016, http://www.ibtimes.com/how-chinas-anti-corruption-campaign-
putting-pressure-slowing-economy-2308834.

99. Zhao Yinian, "Local Officials Neglect Duties, Premier Says," *China Daily,*
February 10, 2015, http://www.chinadaily.com.cn/china/2015-02/10/
content_19535745.htm.

100. Yinian, "Local Officials Neglect Duties."

101. Dan Steinbock, "Can We Blame the Anti-Graft Campaign for Hurting
China's Growth?," *EJInsight,* January 12, 2016, http://www.ejinsight.com/
20160112-can-we-blame-anti-graft-campaign-hurting-china-s-growth/.

102. Viola Zhou and Jun Mai, "A Kinder, Gentler New Anti-Corruption
System for China?," *South China Morning Post,* October 23, 2017,
http://www.scmp.com/news/china/policies-politics/article/2116151/
kinder-gentler-new-anti-graft-system-china.

103. Macabe Keliher and Hsinchao Wu, "How to Discipline 90 Million
People," *Atlantic,* April 7, 2015, http://www.theatlantic.com/international/
archive/2015/04/xi-jinping-china-corruption-political-culture/389787/.

104. Peter J. Seybolt, "Terror and Conformity: Counterespionage Campaigns,
Rectification, and Mass Movements, 1942–1943," *Modern China* 12, no. 1
(Jan. 1986): 39–73, 42–43.

105. Thomas B. Gold, "'Just in Time!': China Battles Spiritual Pollution on
the Eve of 1984," *Asian Survey* 24, no. 9 (1984): 947–74, 948.

106. Brendan Forde, "China's 'Mass Line' Campaign," *Diplomat,* September 9,
2013, http://thediplomat.com/2013/09/chinas-mass-line-campaign-2/.

107. Erik Eckholm, "Ideas & Trends; Repeat after Him: The Party Isn't Over," *New York Times,* May 2, 1999, http://www.nytimes.com/1999/05/02/weekinreview/ideas-trends-repeat-after-him-the-party-isn-t-over.html.

108. Commentary, "'Mass Line' Campaign Key to Consolidate CPC's Ruling Status," *Xinhua,* June 19, 2013, http://english.cntv.cn/20130619/100979.shtml

109. Jerome Doyon, "The End of the Road for Xi's Mass Line Campaign: An Assessment," *Jamestown China Brief* 14, no. 20 (Oct. 23, 2014), http://www.jamestown.org/programs/chinabrief/single/?tx_ttnews%5Btt_news%5D=42991&cHash=8b3cd141a264ddaa1b47d899074719f6#.V7xaSvkrK70.

110. "CPC Demands Officials Hear Public Views," *Xinhua,* March 26, 2014, http://www.globaltimes.cn/content/850950.shtml.

111. Forde, "China's 'Mass Line' Campaign."

112. "China Voice: 'Mass Line' Campaign another Long March for CPC," *Xinhua,* October 14, 2014, http://en.people.cn/n/2014/1015/c90785-8794990.html.

113. Meng Na, "Commentary: 'Mass Line' Campaign Key to Consolidate CPC's Ruling Status," *Xinhua,* June 18, 2013, http://english.cntv.cn/20130619/100979.shtml.

114. Doyon, "The End of the Road for Xi's Mass Line Campaign."

115. Doyon, "The End of the Road for Xi's Mass Line Campaign."

116. "'Mass Line' Campaign another Long March for CPC."

117. Heike Holbig, "Remaking the CCP's Ideology: Determinants, Progress, and Limits under Hu Jintao," *Journal of Current Chinese Affairs* 38, no. 3 (2009): 35–61, 44.

118. Li Haiqing, "Looking at the Mass Line from the Process of Modernization [*Li Haiqing: Cong Xiandaihua Jincheng Kan Qunzhong Luxian*]," *Study Times,* July 8, 2013, http://theory.people.com.cn/n/2013/0708/c49150-22112421.html.

119. Raymond Li, "Xi Looks to Legacy of Mao for Inspiration to Solve Corruption," *South China Morning Post,* June 19, 2013, http://www.scmp.com/news/china/article/1263927/xi-looks-legacy-mao-inspiration-solve-corruption.

120. Doyon, "The End of the Road for Xi's Mass Line Campaign."

121. "Document 9: A ChinaFile Translation," *ChinaFile,* November 8, 2013, http://www.chinafile.com/document-9-chinafile-translation.

122. Willy Lam, "China's Reform Summed Up: Politics, No; Economics, Yes (Sort of . . .)," *Jamestown China Brief* 13, no. 11 (May 23, 2013), http://www.jamestown.org/programs/chinabrief/single/?tx_ttnews%5Btt_news%5D=40913&cHash=f43af7a242ee9d4a62f82d39077eb69d#.V7SYcvkrK70.

123. Anne Henochowicz, "Slogan of the Week: Five Nos," *China Digital Times,* February 26, 2015, http://chinadigitaltimes.net/2015/02/slogan-week-five-nos/.

124. "Document 9: A ChinaFile Translation."

125. Zhao, "Xi Jinping's Maoist Revival," 87.
126. "Xi Urges Bigger Party Role in Education," *China Daily*, June 20, 2012, http://www.chinadaily.com.cn/china/2012-06/20/content_15515646. htm.
127. "Ministry of Education, Commenting on Strengthening the Improvement of Young Teachers' Ideological and Political Work in Colleges and Universities [*Jiaoyubu jiu jiaqiang gaijin gaoxiao qingnian jiaoshi sixiang zhengzhi gongzuo da jizhe wen*]," *People's Daily*, May 28, 2013, http://cpc.people.com.cn/n/2013/0528/c164113-21645402.html.
128. Michelle Florcruz, "China's Government Plans Old-Style Communist Ideological Education for Young Teachers," *International Business Times*, May 29, 2013, http://www.ibtimes.com/chinas-government-plans-old-style-communist-ideological-education-young-teachers-1282959.
129. Suisheng Zhao, "Xi Jinping's Maoist Revival," *Journal of Democracy* 27, no. 3 (July 2016): 90.
130. "Chinese President Signals Tightening of Control over Universities," *Guardian*, December 30, 2014, https://www.theguardian.com/world/2014/dec/30/chinese-president-signals-tightening-of-control-over-universities.
131. Zhao, "Xi Jinping's Maoist Revival," 90–91.
132. Interview with Chinese professor of political science, December 5, 2016, Council on Foreign Relations, New York, NY.
133. Zhao, "Xi Jinping's Maoist Revival," 92.
134. Adrian Wan, "Chinese Academy of Social Sciences Is 'Infiltrated by Foreign Forces': Anti-Graft Official," *South China Morning Post*, June 15, 2014, http://www.scmp.com/news/china/article/1533020/chinese-academy-social-sciences-infiltrated-foreign-forces-anti-graft.
135. "Chinese Academy of Social Sciences Party Leadership Group Notice on Status of Reforms from Special Inspection Group [*Zhonggong Zhongguo Shekeyuan Dangzu Guanyu Zhuanxiang Xunshi Zhenggai Qingkuang de Tongbao*]," Central Commission for Discipline Inspection, April 29, 2016, http://www.ccdi.gov.cn/yw/201604/t20160429_78300.html.
136. Chinese Academy of Social Sciences, "The Problem of Using Academic Resources to Seek Personal Gain Is Prominent [*Zhongguo Shekeyuan: Liyong Xueshu Ziyuan Youshi Mouqu Sili Wenti Tuchu*]," Central Commission for Discipline Inspection, February 4, 2016, http://m.ccdi.gov.cn/content/ab/ba/8284.html.
137. Discussion with Chinese scholar, Washington, DC, March 2016.
138. "CPC to Drill Members in Self-Discipline, Socialist Values," *Xinhua*, February 28, 2016, http://news.xinhuanet.com/english/2016-02/28/c_135138601.htm?mc_cid=91db808461&mc_eid=e8ed88c435.
139. "Who Draws the Party Line?," *Economist*, June 25, 2016, http://www.economist.com/news/china/21701169-xi-jinping-sends-his-spin-doctors-spinning-who-draws-party-line.

140. Chun Han Wong, "China's Xi Jinping Puts Loyalty to the Test at Congress," *Wall Street Journal,* March 1, 2016, http://www.wsj.com/articles/chinas-xi-jinping-puts-loyalty-to-the-test-at-congress-1456853257.

141. Sophia Yan, "Chinese Anti-Corruption Agency Warns of 'Major Problems' in Financial Sector," *CNN Money,* February 5, 2016, http://money.cnn.com/2016/02/05/news/economy/china-financial-sector-corruption-risks/.

142. Zhao, "Xi Jinping's Maoist Revival," 87.

143. "2017 World Press Freedom Index," Reporters without Borders, n.d., accessed November 25, 2017, https://rsf.org/en/ranking.

144. "2016 Prison Census: 259 Journalists Jailed Worldwide," Committee to Protect Journalists, December 1, 2016, https://cpj.org/imprisoned/2016.php.

145. Tom Phillips, " 'Love the Party, Protect the Party': How Xi Jinping Is Bringing China's Media to Heel," *Guardian,* February 27, 2016, https://www.theguardian.com/world/2016/feb/28/absolute-loyalty-how-xi-jinping-is-bringing-chinas-media-to-heel.

146. David Bandurski, "The Spirit of Control," *China Media Project,* February 24, 2016, https://medium.com/china-media-project/the-spirit-of-control-cf78fb585711#.8tj332wjq.

147. Josh Horwitz and Zheping Huang, "China's New Television Rules Ban Homosexuality, Drinking, and Vengeance," *Quartz,* March 3, 2016, http://qz.com/630159/chinas-new-television-rules-ban-homosexuality-drinking-and-vengeance/.

148. Holbig, "Remaking the CCP's Ideology," 42.

149. Rogier Creemers, "Xi Jinping's 19 August Speech Revealed?" (Translation), China Copyright and Media, November 12, 2013 (updated December 22, 2014), https://chinacopyrightandmedia.wordpress.com/2013/11/12/xi-jinpings-19-august-speech-revealed-translation/.

150. Zhao, "Xi Jinping's Maoist Revival," 85.

151. Kai Jin, "The Chinese Communist Party's Confucian Revival," *Diplomat,* September 30, 2014, http://thediplomat.com/2014/09/the-chinese-communist-partys-confucian-revival/.

152. Geremie R. Barmé, "Chinese Dreams [*Zhongguo meng,* 中国梦]," *China Story Yearbook 2013: Civilizing China,* Australia National University, October 2013, https://www.thechinastory.org/yearbooks/yearbook-2013/forum-dreams-and-power/chinese-dreams-zhongguo-meng-%E4%B8%AD%E5%9B%BD%E6%A2%A6/.

153. Jeremy Page, "President Xi Jinping's Most Dangerous Venture Yet: Remaking China's Military," *Wall Street Journal,* April 24, 2016, http://www.wsj.com/articles/president-xi-jinpings-most-dangerous-venture-yet-remaking-chinas-military-1461608795.

154. "China's Xi Jinping Unveils New 'Four Comprehensives' Slogans'," *BBC News,* February 25, 2015, http://www.bbc.com/news/world-asia-china-31622571.

155. Yifei Du, "24-Word Core Socialist Values Engraved on People's Mind," *People's Daily,* March 2, 2016, http://en.people.cn/n3/2016/0302/c98649-9023926.html; "Communist Party Leaders Introduce the 'System of Core Socialist Values' Drawing from the Shared Achievements of Human Civilization [*Zhonggong Shou Ti 'Shehuizhuyi Hexin Jiazhiguan' Jiqu Renlei Wenming Gongtong Chengguo*]," *Xinhua,* November 13, 2012, http://news.xinhuanet.com/18cpcnc/2012-11/13/c_113681008.htm.

156. Du, "24-Word Core Socialist Values Engraved on People's Mind."

157. "A Thousand Yes-Men Cannot Equal One Honest Advisor," *ChinaFile* translation, March 21, 2016, https://www.chinafile.com/reporting-opinion/features/thousand-yes-men-cannot-equal-one-honest-advisor; "Chairman of Everything," *Economist,* April 2, 2016, http://www.economist.com/news/china/21695923-his-exercise-power-home-xi-jinping-often-ruthless-there-are-limits-his.

158. Ansuya Harjani, "China's Fifth Plenum: 5 Things You Need to Know," *CNBC,* October 22, 2015, http://www.cnbc.com/2015/10/22/chinas-fifth-plenum-5-things-you-need-to-know-about-beijing-policy-meeting.html.

159. Merriden Varrall, " 'Rule by Law'? The Fourth Plenum of the 18th Party Congress," *Lowy Interpreter,* October 22, 2014, https://www.lowyinstitute.org/the-interpreter/rule-law-fourth-plenum-18th-party-congress.

160. Xi, *The Governance of China,* 152.

161. Xi, *The Governance of China,* 157.

162. Jiang Bixin, "Ruling in Accord with the Constitution to Open a New Era of Rule of Law [*Yi Xian Zhi Zheng Kaiqi Fazhi Xin Shidai*]," *People's Daily,* December 12, 2012, http://cpc.people.com.cn/n/2012/1212/c78779-19869633.html.

163. "Zhou Qiang Picked as Head of China's Supreme People's Court," *Bloomberg News,* March 15, 2013, http://www.bloomberg.com/news/articles/2013-03-15/zhou-qiang-picked-as-president-of-china-s-supreme-people-s-court.

164. Willy Lam, "CCP Tightens Control over Courts," *Jamestown China Brief* 11, no. 11 (June 17, 2011), http://www.jamestown.org/single/?tx_ttnews%5Btt_news%5D=38068&no_cache=1#.V7YNtvkrK70.

165. "Zhou Qiang Picked as Head of China's Supreme People's Court."

166. Peter Witherington, "The Impact of the Hunan Provincial Administrative Procedure Provisions," *Hastings International & Comparative Law Review* 36, no. 2 (2013): 632–33, http://heinonline.org/HOL/Page?handle=hein.journals/hasint36&g_sent=1&casa_token=&collection=journals&id=657.

167. Yongnian Zheng and Wei Shan, "Xi Jinping's 'Rule of Law' With Chinese Characteristics," *China Policy Institute Analysis* (University

of Nottingham), May 28, 2015, https://cpianalysis.org/2015/05/28/xi-jinpings-rule-of-law-with-chinese-characteristics/.

168. Josh Chin, "China Tries to Hold On to Judges by Offering Freer Hand," *Wall Street Journal,* October 21, 2014, http://www.wsj.com/articles/china-tries-to-hold-on-to-judges-by-offering-freer-hand-1413822462.

169. Neysun A. Mahboubi, "The Future of China's Legal System," *ChinaFile,* August 11, 2016, https://www.chinafile.com/viewpoint/future-of-chinas-legal-system.

170. Xi, *The Governance of China,* 163.

171. Xi, *The Governance of China,* 162.

172. Zheng and Shan, "Xi Jinping's 'Rule of Law' With Chinese Characteristics."

173. Yongnian Zheng, "How to Square Xi's 'Rule of Law' Campaign with China's Crackdown on Lawyers," *The World Post,* February 16, 2016, http://www.huffingtonpost.com/zheng-yongnian/rule-of-law-china-crackdown-lawyers_b_9238644.html.

174. Tom Mitchell, "Xi's China: Smothering Dissent," *Financial Times,* July 27, 2016, https://www.ft.com/content/ccd94b46-4db5-11e6-88c5-db83e98a590a.

175. "China: Detained Lawyers, Activists Denied Basic Rights," Human Rights Watch, April 3, 2016, https://www.hrw.org/news/2016/04/03/china-detained-lawyers-activists-denied-basic-rights.

176. "China Formally Arrests Top Rights Lawyers on Subversion Charges," *Radio Free Asia,* January 13, 2016, http://www.rfa.org/english/news/china/china-lawyers-01132016110726.html.

177. Javier C. Hernandez, "Zhou Shifeng, Chinese Lawyer, Is Sentenced to 7 Years for Subversion," *New York Times,* August 4, 2016, http://www.nytimes.com/2016/08/05/world/asia/china-zhou-shifeng-sentence.html.

178. Verna Yu, "Detained Human Rights Lawyer, Wang Yu, on Chinese State TV Informed of 'Failed Attempt to Smuggle Son Overseas,'" *South China Morning Post,* October 18, 2015, http://www.scmp.com/news/china/policies-politics/article/1869017/detained-human-rights-lawyer-wang-yu-chinese-state-tv.

179. "China: End Show Trials, Free Human Rights Lawyers & Other Defenders," *Chinese Human Rights Defenders*, August 8, 2016, https://www.nchrd.org/2016/08/china-end-show-trials-free-human-rights-lawyers-other-defenders/.

180. Javier C. Hernandez, "China Frees Wang Yu, Human Rights Lawyer, After Videotaped Confession," *New York Times,* August 1, 2016, http://www.nytimes.com/2016/08/02/world/asia/human-rights-lawyer-is-released-in-china-after-videotaped-confession.html.

181. Jun Mai and Nectar Gan, "Chinese Democracy Veteran Hu Shigen Jailed for Subversion," *South China Morning Post*, August 3, 2016,

http://www.scmp.com/news/china/policies-politics/article/1998638/
second-activist-sentenced-subversion-charges-after-huge.

182. Philip Wen, "In Lawyer Trials, China's Courts Have Done Away with Pretense of Due Process," *Sydney Morning Herald*, August 5, 2016, http://www.smh.com.au/world/in-lawyer-trials-chinas-courts-have-done-away-with-pretence-of-due-process-20160805-gqm3fl.html.

183. Eva Pils, "China, the Rule of Law, and the Question of Obedience: A Comment on Professor Peerenboom," *Hague Journal on the Rule of Law* (2015): 7, 83–90.

184. Pils, "China, the Rule of Law, and the Question of Obedience," 7, 83–90.

185. Eva Pils, "The Rise of Rule by Fear," *China Policy Institute: Analysis*, University of Nottingham, February 15, 2016, https://cpianalysis.org/2016/02/15/rule-of-law-vs-rule-by-fear/.

186. Pils, "The Rise of Rule by Fear."

187. Josh Chin, "Chinese Judge Criticizes Televised Confessions," *Wall Street Journal* (China Real Time Report), March 15, 2016, http://blogs.wsj.com/chinarealtime/2016/03/15/chinese-judge-criticizes-televised-confessions/.

188. Chin, "Chinese Judge Criticizes Televised Confessions."

189. Maria Repnikova and Kecheng Fang, "Behind the Fall of China's Greatest Newspaper," *Foreign Policy* (Tealeaf Nation), January 29, 2015, http://foreignpolicy.com/2015/01/29/southern-weekly-china-media-censorship/.

190. Chi-yuk Choi, "Writing on the Wall for Outspoken Chinese Magazine Two Years Ahead of Closure," *South China Morning Post*, July 29, 2016, http://www.scmp.com/news/china/policies-politics/article/1996017/writing-wall-outspoken-chinese-magazine-two-years-ahead.

191. E-mail on file with author, October 7, 2016.

192. Josh Horwitz, "Xi Jinping's Crackdown on Free Speech Is Being Criticized—by Advisers to China's Communist Party," *Quartz*, March 8, 2016, https://qz.com/633580/advisers-to-chinas-communist-party-are-openly-criticizing-xi-jinpings-crackdown-on-free-speech/.

193. "Jiang Hong: Only with Democracy Can We Cure Corruption [*Jiang Hong: Zhi You Minzhu Cai Neng Genzhi Fubai*]," *Caixin*, March 9, 2015, http://opinion.caixin.com/2015-03-09/100789438.html.

194. Interview with Jia Qingguo at the Council on Foreign Relations office in New York City, March 30, 2017.

195. Chun Han Wong, "Future of China's Wujie Media in Doubt after Letter Calling on Xi to Quit," *Wall Street Journal* (China Real Time Report), March 29, 2016, http://blogs.wsj.com/chinarealtime/2016/03/29/future-of-chinas-wujie-media-in-doubt-after-letter-calling-on-xi-to-quit/.

196. Charles Liu, "Open Letter Demanding Xi Jinping's Resignation Gets Censored from Chinese Website," *The Nanfang*, March 18, 2016, https://thenanfang.com/open-letter-demanding-xi-jinpings-resignation-gets-censored-website/.

197. John Sudworth, "China 'Detained 20 over Xi Resignation Letter,'" *BBC News,* March 25, 2016, http://www.bbc.com/news/blogs-china-blog-35897905.

198. Neil Connor, "Chinese Communist Party Members 'Plotted to Oust President Xi Jinping,'" *The Telegraph,* October 20, 2017, http://www.telegraph.co.uk/news/2017/10/20/chinese-communist-party-members-plotted-oust-president-xi-jinping/.

199. The '92 consensus is a reported agreement between Taiwan and the mainland that there is only one China, and both mainland China and Taiwan belong to the same China. The agreement makes no claim as to which side should govern China.

200. "Over Half of Taiwanese Favor Independence: Poll," *Taiwan News,* May 27, 2016, httpe://www.taiwannews.com.tw/en/news/2929335.

Chapter 3

1. "Michael Anti: China's Information War," YouTube, posted by Oslo Freedom Forum, January 7, 2015, https://www.youtube.com/watch?v=4gPoilBGwAs.

2. Emily Parker, *Now I Know Who My Comrades Are: Voices from the Internet Underground* (New York: Farrar, Straus, and Giroux, 2014), 13, 40.

3. "Michael Anti," *China File,* May 2, 2014, https://www.chinafile.com/contributors/michael-anti.

4. Michael Anti, "In China, Weak Ties Are Better Than Nothing," *New York Times* (Room for Debate), September 30, 2010, http://www.nytimes.com/roomfordebate/2010/09/29/can-twitter-lead-people-to-the-streets/in-china-weak-ties-are-better-than-nothing-6.

5. Jinping Xi, "Remarks by H.E. Xi Jinping President of the People's Republic of China At the Opening Ceremony of the Second World Internet Conference," Ministry of Foreign Affairs of the People's Republic of China, December 16, 2015, http://www.fmprc.gov.cn/mfa_eng/wjdt_665385/zyjh_665391/t1327570.shtml.

6. "China Poll: Are Chinese Officials Afraid of the Internet?," *The Economic Observer,* November 17, 2010, http://www.eeo.com.cn/ens/2010/1117/186143.shtml.

7. Elizabeth J. Perry, "Cultural Governance in Contemporary China: 'Re-Orienting' Party Propaganda," Harvard-Yenching Institute Working Paper Series, 2013, http://www.harvard-yenching.org/sites/harvard-yenching.org/files/featurefiles/Elizabeth%20Perry_Cultural%20Governance%20in%20Contemporary%20China_0.pdf, 9–10.

8. Evan Osnos, "China's Censored World," *New York Times,* May 2, 2014, http://www.nytimes.com/2014/05/03/opinion/sunday/chinas-censored-world.html?_r=0.

9. Frank Caso, *Global Issues: Censorship* (New York: Infobase, 2008), 56.

10. Jacques Gernet, *A History of Chinese Civilization*, 2nd ed., trans. J. R. Foster and Charles Hartman (Cambridge: Cambridge University Press, 1996), 244.

11. Caso, *Global Issues,* 58.

12. Caso, *Global Issues*, 59.

13. Susan Whitfield, "China (to 1912)," in *Censorship: A World Encyclopedia*, 4 vols., ed. Derek Jones (Oxon, UK: Routledge, 2001), 482–83.

14. Whitfield, "China (to 1912)," 4.

15. Osnos, "China's Censored World."

16. Jonathon Green and Nicholas J. Karolides, *Encyclopedia of Censorship* (New York: Facts on File, 2005), 103.

17. S. A. Smith, "Talking Toads and Chinless Ghosts: The Politics of 'Superstitious' Rumors in the People's Republic of China, 1961–1965," *American Historical Review* III, no. 2 (2006): 405–27, http://www.jstor.org/stable/10.1086/ahr.111.2.405?pq-origsite=summon#full_text_tab_contents.

18. Smith, "Talking Toads and Chinless Ghosts," 406–7.

19. David Bandurski, "Can China Conquer the Internet?," *ChinaFile*, December 3, 2014, http://www.chinafile.com/conversation/can-china-conquer-internet.

20. "Gun Power, Word Power, and Economic Power [*Qiang Gan Zi, Bi Gan Zi, Qian Dai Zi*]," Ding Dong Blog, February 17, 2011, http://history.people.com.cn/GB/198974/198977/13945969.html.

21. Caso, *Global Issues,* 63.

22. "May Fourth Movement," *Encyclopedia Britannica*, https://www.britannica.com/event/May-Fourth-Movement#ref274919.

23. "New Youth: Chen Duxiu," Asia Society (Wealth and Power), http://sites.asiasociety.org/chinawealthpower/chapters/chen-duxiu/.

24. "Open Doors Fact Sheet: China," Institute of International Education, 2011, http://www.iie.org/~/media/Files/Corporate/Open-Doors/Fact-Sheets-2011/Country/China%20Fact%20Sheet%20-%20Open%20Doors%202011.pdf?la=en.

25. David Houle, "Tiananmen Square and Technology," *Evolution Shift*, June 3, 2009, http://davidhoule.com/evolutionshift-blog/technology/cell-phones/2009/06/03/tiananmen-square-and-technology.

26. There is some controversy over when the first e-mail was sent, as it could have been sent in 1986, but the one in 1987 is confirmed to have been successful: https://www.thechinastory.org/lexicon/the-internet/.

27. "Ray Tomlinson, Who Sent the First E-mail, Has Died," *Economist*, March 7, 2016, http://www.economist.com/news/science-and-technology/21694354-raymond-samuel-tomlinson-died-march-5th-aged-74-email-pioneer.

28. "China's Internet: A Giant Cage," *Economist*, April 6, 2013, http://www.economist.com/news/special-report/

21574628-internet-was-expected-help-democratise-china-instead-it-has-enabled.

29. "Cat and Mouse," *Economist,* April 6, 2013, http://www.economist.com/news/special-report/21574629-how-china-makes-sure-its-internet-abides-rules-cat-and-mouse.

30. Geremie R. Barme and Sang Ye, "The Great Firewall of China," *Wired,* June 1, 1997, www.wired.com/1997/06/china-3.

31. Barme and Ye, "The Great Firewall of China."

32. Rogier Creemers, "Cyber-Leninism: History, Political Culture and the Internet in China," in *Speech and Society in Turbulent Times: Freedom of Expression in Comparative Perspective,* ed. Monroe Price and Nicole Stremlau (Cambridge: Cambridge University Press, 2017), 255–73.

33. Philip Sohmen, "Taming the Dragon: China's Efforts to Regulate the Internet," *Stanford Journal of East Asian Affairs* 1 (Spring 2001): 19.

34. "New PRC Internet Regulation: A January 1998 Report from U.S. Embassy Beijing," Federation of American Scientists, http://fas.org/irp/world/china/netreg.htm.

35. "Cat and Mouse."

36. "Cat and Mouse."

37. Creemers, "Cyber-Leninism," 10.

38. Jeremy Goldkorn, "China's Internet—A Civilising Process (Fang Binxing and the Great Firewall)," in *China Story Yearbook 2013: Civilising China* (Canberra: Australia National University, October 2013), www.thechinastory.org/yearbooks/yearbook-2013/chapter-6-chinas-internet-a-civilising-process/fang-binxing-and-the-great-firewall/.

39. Charles Clover and Yuan Yang, "Great Firewall Creator Caught Skirting China Censorship System," *Financial Times,* April 6, 2016, http://www.ft.com/cms/s/0/0055b090-fbc2-11e5-b3f6-11d5706b613b.html#axzz4ExxRobu7.

40. Goldkorn, "China's Internet."

41. David Pierson, "Father of China's 'Great Firewall' Is Unrepentant," *Los Angeles Times,* February 18, 2011, http://articles.latimes.com/2011/feb/18/business/la-fi-china-firewall-20110219.

42. Parker, *Now I Know Who My Comrades Are,* 38; "People's Republic of China State Council Order 292: Method of Managing Internet Information Services [*Zhonghua Renmin Gongheguo Guowuyuan Ling 292: Hulianwang Xinxi Fuwu Guanli Banfa*]," Gov.cn, September 25, 2000, http://www.gov.cn/gongbao/content/2000/content_60531.htm.

43. "The Art of Concealment," *Economist,* April 6, 2013, http://www.economist.com/news/special-report/21574631-chinese-screening-online-material-abroad-becoming-ever-more-sophisticated.

44. "Google in China: A Timeline," *Week,* March 22, 2010, http://theweek.com/articles/496058/google-china-timeline.

45. "Public Pledge of Self-Regulation and Professional Ethics for China Internet Industry," Internet Society of China, March 26, 2002, http://www.isc.org.cn/english/Specails/Self-regulation/listinfo-15321.html.

46. Anne Applebaum, "Let a Thousand Filters Bloom," *Washington Post,* July 20, 2005, http://www.washingtonpost.com/wp-dyn/content/article/2005/07/19/AR2005071901556.html.

47. "Interim Administrative Provisions on Internet Publishing," chinaitlaw.org, January 20, 2010, http://www.china.org.cn/business/2010-01/20/content_19275637.htm.

48. "Chinese Vocabulary: Internet Commentators or Wu Mao," *Home Is Where the Heart Dwells* (blog), July 17, 2008, https://blogs.harvard.edu/guorui/2008/07/17/chinese-internet-vocabulary-internet-commentators-or-wu-mao/.

49. Chi-Chu Tschang, "China Blacks out Tibet News," *Bloomberg,* March 17, 2008, http://www.bloomberg.com/bw/stories/2008-03-17/china-blacks-out-tibet-newsbusinessweek-business-news-stock-market-and-financial-advice.

50. "Cat and Mouse."

51. "Regulations on Administration of Internet News Information Services," World Intellectual Property Organization, September 25, 2005, http://www.wipo.int/wipolex/en/text.jsp?file_id=337975.

52. Andrew Jacobs, "China's Answer to a Crime Includes Amateur Sleuths," *New York Times,* February 24, 2009, http://www.nytimes.com/2009/02/25/world/asia/25china.html.

53. "Chinese Netizens and Police Play 'Hide and Seek,'" *NBC News,* March 2, 2009, http://worldblog.nbcnews.com/_news/2009/03/02/4376872-chinese-netizens-and-police-play-hide-and-seek. "Police and Internet Users Investigating Team Announcement on 'Duo Maomao' Incident [*Jingfang Xiang Wangyou Diaochatuan Tongbao 'Duo Maomao' Shijian*]" *Southern Weekly,* February 20, 2009, http://infzm.com/content/24156."

54. Jacobs, "China's Answer to a Crime Includes Amateur Sleuths."

55. "Police and Internet Users Investigating Team Announcement on 'Duo Maomao' Incident."

56. Rebecca MacKinnon, " 'Eluding the Cat'—Bloggers Investigate Yunnan Prison Death," RConversation blog, February 4, 2009, http://rconversation.blogs.com/rconversation/2009/02/eluding-the-cat---bloggers-investigate-yunnan-prison-death.html.

57. "Verdict in 'Duo Maomao' Case, Family Members of the Deceased Receive 60,000 RMB in Compensation ['*Duo Maomao' An Xuanpan Sizhe Jiashu Jieshou 6 Wan Yuan Peichang (Tu),*]," *Beijing Times,* August 15, 2009, http://news.sohu.com/20090815/n265973955.shtml.

58. Tania Branigan, "Chinese Woman Who Killed Official Bailed after Online Outcry," *Guardian,* May 27, 2009, https://www.theguardian.com/world/2009/may/27/china-bails-deng-yujiao.

59. Jessica Levine, "What Is a 'Human Flesh Search,' and How Is It Changing China?," *Atlantic,* October 5, 2012, http://www.theatlantic.com/international/archive/2012/10/what-is-a-human-flesh-search-and-how-is-it-changing-china/263258/.

60. Levine, "What Is a 'Human Flesh Search.'"

61. Michael Wines, "Civic-Minded Chinese Find a Voice Online," *New York Times,* June 16, 2009, http://www.nytimes.com/2009/06/17/world/asia/17china.html?hp&_r=0.

62. Wines, "Civic- Minded Chinese Find a Voice Online."

63. James T. Areddy, "China Blasts High Speed Rail System," *Wall Street Journal,* December 29, 2011, http://www.wsj.com/articles/SB10001424052970204632204577126121683353312.

64. Elizabeth C. Economy, "China's Policy Train Wreck," *Asia Unbound* (CFR blog), July 26, 2011, https://www.cfr.org/blog-post/chinas-policy-train-wreck.

65. Sophie Beach, "Poll: 98% Say Wenzhou Train Buried to Destroy Evidence," *China Digital Times,* July 25, 2011, http://chinadigitaltimes.net/2011/07/poll-98-say-wenzhou-train-buried-to-destroy-evidence/.

66. Economy, "China's Policy Train Wreck."

67. Areddy, "China Blasts High Speed Rail System."

68. Elizabeth C. Economy, "China's New Political Class: The People," *Asia Unbound* (CFR blog), July 26, 2012, http://blogs.cfr.org/asia/2012/07/26/chinas-new-political-class-the-people/.

69. Josh Ong, "Sina Weibo, China's Twitter, Comes to Rescue Amid Flooding in Beijing," Next Web, July 23, 2012, http://thenextweb.com/asia/2012/07/23/sina-Weibo-chinas-twitter-comes-to-rescue-amid-flooding-in-beijing/.

70. "The Internet in China (III. Guaranteeing Citizens' Freedom of Speech on the Internet)," Information Office of the State Council of the People's Republic of China, June 8, 2010, http://www.china.org.cn/government/whitepaper/2010-06/08/content_20207994.htm.

71. Laura Zhou, "Exposure via Internet Now China's Top Weapon in War on Graft," *South China Morning Post,* June 27, 2013, http://www.scmp.com/news/china/article/1269790/exposure-internet-now-countrys-top-weapon-war-graft.

72. Guobin Yang, "Social Dynamics in the Evolution of China's Internet Content Control Regime," in *Routledge Handbook of Media Law,* ed. Monroe E. Price, Stefaan Verhulst, and Libby Morgan (Oxon, UK: Routledge, 2013), 297.

73. "Chinese Leaders Intensify Propaganda Orders and Jargon of Control in Run-Up to 17th Congress," China Media Project, July 3, 2007, http://cmp.hku.hk/2007/07/03/chinese-leaders-intensify-propaganda-orders-and-jargon-of-control-in-run-up-to-17th-congress/.

74. Simon Denyer, "In China, Communist Party Takes Unprecedented Step: It Is Listening," *Washington Post,* August 2, 2013, https://www.

washingtonpost.com/world/in-china-government-mines-public-opinion/2013/08/02/33358026-f2b5-11e2-ae43-b31dc363c3bf_story.html.

75. Perry, "Cultural Governance in Contemporary China," 20–21.

76. Perry, "Cultural Governance in Contemporary China," 21.

77. Denyer, "In China, Communist Party Takes Unprecedented Step."

78. Yang, "Social Dynamics," 297.

79. Jennifer Pan, Gary King, and Margaret Roberts, "How Censorship in China Allows Government Criticism but Silences Collective Expression," *American Political Science Review* 107, no. 2 (May 2013): 1.

80. Elizabeth C. Economy, "China: The New Virtual Political System," Council on Foreign Relations Markets and Democracy Brief, April 2011, http://www.cfr.org/china/china-new-virtual-political-system/p24805.

81. Parker, *Now I Know Who My Comrades Are*, 100.

82. Ben Blanchard, "China Pollution Protest Ends, but Suspicion of Government High," *Reuters,* July 8, 2012, http://www.reuters.com/article/2012/07/08/us-china-pollution-idUSBRE8670HP20120708.

83. Stephen Junor, "Social Media Changing the Protest Landscape in China," Index on Censorship, January 15, 2014, https://www.indexoncensorship.org/2014/01/social-media-giving-rise-democratic-consciousness-china/.

84. Brian Spegele, "Planned China Metals Plant Scrapped," *Wall Street Journal,* July 3, 2012, http://www.wsj.com/articles/SB10001424052702304211804577504101311079594.

85. Spegele, "Planned China Metals Plant Scrapped."   86. Economy, "China's New Political Class: The People."

87. Chris Buckley, "China PLA Officers Call Internet Key Battleground," *Reuters,* June 3, 2011, http://www.reuters.com/article/2011/06/03/us-china-internet-google-idUSTRE7520OV20110603.

88. Eyder Peralta, "Chinese Military Scholars Accuse U.S. of Launching 'Internet War,'" *National Public Radio*, June 3, 2011, http://www.npr.org/sections/thetwo-way/2011/06/03/136923033/chinese-military-scholars-accuse-u-s-of-launching-internet-war.

89. David Bandurski, "Rumor Fever," *New York Times* (Latitude blog), December 12, 2011, http://latitude.blogs.nytimes.com/2011/12/12/rumor-fever/?_r=1.

90. Bandurski, "Rumor Fever."

91. Malcolm Moore, "China Moves to Control Sina Weibo Social Network with Real Names," *Telegraph,* March 16, 2012, http://www.telegraph.co.uk/technology/news/9147767/China-moves-to-control-Sina-Weibo-social-network.html?ncid=txtlnkusaolp00000618.

92. C. Custer, "Sina, Tencent Weibo Punished for Spreading Rumors," *Tech In Asia*, March 30, 2012, https://www.techinasia.com/sina-tencent-weibo-punished-spreading-rumors.

93. "Sina Weibo IPO Lays Bare Censorship Burden," *China Digital Times,* March 18, 2014, http://chinadigitaltimes.net/2014/03/sina-Weibo-ipo-lays-bare-censorship-burden/.

94. "Carnegie Mellon Performs First Large-Scale Analysis of 'Soft' Censorship on Social Media in China," Carnegie Mellon University, March 7, 2012, http://www.cmu.edu/news/stories/archives/2012/march/march7_censorshipinchina.html.

95. Osnos, "China's Censored World."

96. "Carnegie Mellon Performs First Large-Scale Analysis of 'Soft' Censorship on Social Media in China."

97. "WeChat, New Media Increasingly Used to Fight Graft," *South China Morning Post,* June 26, 2013, http://www.scmp.com/comment/blogs/article/1269473/weixin-new-media-increasingly-used-fight-graft.

98. Tom Phillips, "Has Xi Jinping Joined China's Equivalent of Twitter?," *Telegraph,* February 6, 2013, http://www.telegraph.co.uk/news/worldnews/asia/china/9851587/Has-Xi-Jinping-joined-Chinas-equivalent-of-Twitter.html.

99. David Cohen, "Xi Jinping: China's First Social Media President," *Diplomat,* January 8, 2013, http://thediplomat.com/2013/01/xi-jinping-chinas-first-social-media-president/.

100. Evan Osnos, "Born Red," *New Yorker,* April 6, 2015, http://www.newyorker.com/magazine/2015/04/06/born-red.

101. Sophia Yan, "Beijing Uses Banned Social Media to Promote Xi's U.S. Visit," *CNN Money,* September 27, 2015, http://money.cnn.com/2015/09/27/technology/china-facebook-xi-jinping-ban/.

102. "Xi's Visit," Facebook page, n.d., accessed July 19, 2016, https://www.facebook.com/xivisit.

103. Chun Han Wong, "Chinese President Xi Jinping's Extreme Makeover," *Wall Street Journal,* May 12, 2016, http://www.wsj.com/articles/xi-jinpings-extreme-makeover-1463069291.

104. "China Internet Users," Internet Live Stats, http://www.internetlivestats.com/internet-users/china/, accessed July 19, 2016.

105. Cecilia, "1/3 Leisure Time Spent on Mobile Phone in China," China Internet Watch, April 13, 2015, http://www.chinainternetwatch.com/13086/13-leisure-time-mobile-phone/.

106. Sabrina, "China Internet Users Spent Most Online Time Watching Videos and Social Networking," China Internet Watch, August 26, 2013, http://www.chinainternetwatch.com/3378/china-internet-users-online-time/.

107. Mélanie Vaast, "Chinese E-Commerce Market Growth Statistics' Report 2016," E-Commerce Nation, February 21, 2017, https://www.ecommerce-nation.co/chinese-ecommerce-market-growth-statistics-report-2016/.

108. Qiang Xiao, "Can China Conquer the Internet?" *ChinaFile,* December 3, 2014, http://www.chinafile.com/conversation/can-china-conquer-internet.

109. William Wan, "Chinese President Xi Jinping Takes Charge of New Cyber Effort," *Washington Post,* February 27, 2014, https://www.washingtonpost.com/world/chinese-president-takes-charge-of-new-cyber-effort/2014/02/27/a4bffaac-9fc9-11e3-b8d8-94577ff66b28_story.html.

110. Greg Austin, "How China's Ministry of Public Security Controls Cyber Policy," *Diplomat,* April 29, 2015, http://thediplomat.com/2015/04/how-chinas-ministry-of-public-security-controls-cyber-policy/.

111. "Lu Wei Will Apply 'China Model' to Internet Governance," *Oxford Analytica,* January 19, 2015, https://dailybrief.oxan.com/Analysis/DB197078.

112. Paul Mozur and Jane Perlez, "Gregarious and Direct: China's Web Doorkeeper," *New York Times,* December 1, 2014, http://www.nytimes.com/2014/12/02/world/asia/gregarious-and-direct-chinas-web-doorkeeper.html.

113. Mozur and Perlez, "Gregarious and Direct."

114. Josh Horwitz, "China's Feared 'Internet Czar' Lu Wei Is Unexpectedly Stepping Down," *Quartz,* June 29, 2016, http://qz.com/719808/chinas-feared-internet-czar-lu-wei-is-unexpectedly-stepping-down/.

115. "Mark Zuckerberg Snapped with Chinese President Xi Jinping's Book," *Sydney Morning Herald,* December 9, 2014, http://www.smh.com.au/it-pro/business-it/mark-zuckerberg-snapped-with-chinese-president-xi-jinpings-book-20141208-1233er.html.

116. Josh Horwitz, "The Only Way Facebook Enters China Is as a Tool of the Government," *Quartz,* March 23, 2016, http://qz.com/644588/the-only-way-facebook-enters-china-is-as-a-tool-of-the-government/.

117. David Bandurski, "Where Is China's Internet Headed?," *ChinaFile,* June 30, 2016, https://www.chinafile.com/conversation/where-chinas-internet-headed.

118. Austin Ramzy, "What You Need to Know about China's Draft Cybersecurity Law," *New York Times* (Sinosphere blog), July 9, 2015, http://sinosphere.blogs.nytimes.com/2015/07/09/what-you-need-to-know-about-chinas-draft-cybersecurity-law/?_r=0.

119. Gerry Shih, "China's Draft Cybersecurity Law Could up Censorship, Irk Business," *Reuters,* July 8, 2015, http://www.reuters.com/article/2015/07/08/us-china-cybersecurity-idUSKCN0PI09020150708.

120. Tania Branigan, "China Cut off Internet in Area of Tibetan Unrest," *Guardian,* February 3, 2012, https://www.theguardian.com/world/2012/feb/03/china-internet-links-tibetan-unrest.

121. Nectar Gan, "Why China's Draft Cybersecurity Law Has Chilling Implications for the Internet and Multinationals," *South China Morning Post,* July 8, 2015, http://www.scmp.com/news/china/policies-politics/article/1834506/chinas-publishes-draft-cybersecurity-law-implications.

122. Timothy Stratford and Yan Luo, "3 Ways Cybersecurity Law in China Is about to Change," *Law360,* May 2, 2016, http://www.law360.com/articles/791505/3-ways-cybersecurity-law-in-china-is-about-to-change.

123. Paul Carsten, Megha Rajagopalan, and Sui-Lee Wee, "In China, VPN Internet Access Tools Suffer Further Disruptions," *Reuters,*

January 23, 2015, http://www.reuters.com/article/2015/01/23/us-china-internet-vpn-idUSKBN0KW0WS20150123.

124. Siqi Cao, "Foreign VPN Service Unavailable in China," *Global Times,* January 23, 2015, http://www.globaltimes.cn/content/903542.shtml.

125. James Fallows, " 'The Connection Has Been Reset,' " *Atlantic,* March 2008, http://www.theatlantic.com/magazine/archive/2008/03/-the-connection-has-been-reset/306650/.

126. Nicholas Weaver, "How China's 'Great Cannon' Works—and Why We Should Be Worried," *CNN,* June 5, 2015, http://www.cnn.com/2015/06/04/opinions/china-great-cannon/.

127. Eva Dou, "U.S. Coding Website GitHub Hit with Cyberattack," *Wall Street Journal,* March 29, 2015, http://www.wsj.com/articles/u-s-coding-website-github-hit-with-cyberattack-1427638940.

128. Alex Hern, " 'Great Cannon of China' Turns Internet Users into Weapon of Cyberwar," *Guardian,* April 13, 2015, http://www.theguardian.com/technology/2015/apr/13/great-cannon-china-internet-users-weapon-cyberwar.

129. Bill Marczak et al., "China's Great Cannon," University of Toronto Research Brief, April 2015.

130. Catherine Shu, "China Tried to Get World Internet Conference Attendees to Ratify This Ridiculous Draft Declaration," *TechCrunch,* November 20, 2014, http://techcrunch.com/2014/11/20/worldinternetconference-declaration/.

131. "Mobile Chat App Line and Web Services Disrupted in China," *BBC,* July 4, 2014, http://www.bbc.com/news/world-asia-china-28156725.

132. Josh Chin and Eva Dou, "Hong Kong Protests Lead to Censorship on WeChat," *Wall Street Journal,* October 3, 2014, http://blogs.wsj.com/chinarealtime/2014/10/03/hong-kong-protests-lead-to-censorship-on-wechat/.

133. "Fresh China Media Crackdown Hits Popular Accounts on Tencent's WeChat," *South China Morning Post,* March 4, 2014, http://www.scmp.com/news/china/article/1448182/crackdown-hits-popular-accounts-tencents-wechat.

134. "Fresh China Media Crackdown Hits Popular Accounts on Tencent's WeChat.""

135. David Bandurski, "China's 'Seven Base Lines' for a Clean Internet," China Media Project, August 27, 2013, http://cmp.hku.hk/2013/08/27/33916/.

136. "Resisting Internet Rumors Is Every Citizen's Responsibility [*Dizhi Wangluo Yaoyan Shi Meiwei Gongmin De Zeren*]," *Nanfang Ribao,* August 27, 2013, http://news.163.com/13/0827/08/9796TBCU00014AED.html, translated by David Bandurski, "China's 'Seven Base Lines' for a Clean Internet."

137. Paul Mozur, "Crossing Lines: Sina Punishes More Than 100,000 Weibo Accounts," *Wall Street Journal,* November 13, 2013, http://blogs.wsj.com/

chinarealtime/2013/11/13/following-7-bottom-lines-sina-strikes-at-Weibo-accounts/?mod=e2tw.

138. Samuel Wade, "Lawyers Criticize 'Straitjacket' for Online Rumors," *China Digital Times,* September 10, 2013, http://chinadigitaltimes.net/2013/09/lawyers-criticize-new-straitjacket-online-rumors/.

139. "China Detains Three for Tweeting about Hebei Flooding Deaths," *Radio Free Asia,* July 27, 2016, http://www.rfa.org/english/news/china/china-floods-07272016123614.html.

140. Echo Huang and Zheping Huang, "The Chinese Government's Incompetence Caused Flooding Deaths in Hebei, Villagers Say," *Quartz,* July 27, 2016, http://qz.com/740803/floods-in-china-caused- xxx-deaths/.

141. "New Rules Create Online Rumor 'Straitjacket,'" *Xinhua,* September 9, 2013, http://www.globaltimes.cn/content/809958.shtml.

142. Josh Chin, "China Tightens Grip on Social Media," *Wall Street Journal,* September 9, 2013, http://www.wsj.com/articles/SB10001424127887324549004579065113098846226.

143. Jason Q. Ng, "China's Rumor Mill," *Foreign Affairs,* October 6, 2015, https://www.foreignaffairs.com/articles/china/2015-10-06/chinas-rumor-mill.

144. Simon Denyer, "China's 'Donald Trump' Is Latest Victim of Government Crackdown," *Washington Post,* February 29, 2016, https://www.washingtonpost.com/news/worldviews/wp/2016/02/29/chinas-donald-trump-silenced-latest-crackdown-sparks-fear-and-mockery/.

145. Samuel Wade, "Tycoon Driven Offline amid Party Unity Drive," *China Digital Times,* February 29, 2016, http://chinadigitaltimes.net/2016/02/tycoon-purged-from-social-media-amid-drive-for-party-unity/.

146. Su Ping, "News Background: Famous Internet Commentator Ren Zhiqiang and His Shocking Words [*Xinwen Beijing: Leiren Leiyu Ren Zhiqiang*]," *BBC* Chinese, February 28, 2016, http://www.bbc.com/zhongwen/simp/china/2016/02/160228_ren_zhiqiang_background.

147. Ping, "News Background."

148. Denyer, "China's 'Donald Trump.'"

149. Edward Wong, "China Puts a Tycoon, Ren Zhiqiang, on Probation for Criticizing Policies," *New York Times,* May 2, 2016, http://www.nytimes.com/2016/05/03/world/asia/china-ren-zhiqiang.html.

150. Chris Buckley, "Chinese Tycoon Criticizes Leader, and Wins Surprising Support," *New York Times,* March 18, 2016, http://www.nytimes.com/2016/03/19/world/asia/china-ren-zhiqiang-weibo.html.

151. Feng Wang, "Outspoken Chinese American Investor Charles Xue Detained in Beijing 'Prostitution Bust,'" *South China Morning Post,* August 25, 2013, http://www.scmp.com/news/china-insider/article/1299448/outspoken-chinese-american-investor-charles-xue-detained-beijing.

152. Mary Kay Magistad and David Wertime, "What Is China's Online Future?," *PRI,* September 22, 2015, http://www.pri.org/stories/2015-09-22/what-chinas-online-future.

153. Malcolm Moore, "China Kills Off Discussion on Weibo after Internet Crackdown," *Telegraph,* January 30, 2014, http://www.telegraph.co.uk/news/worldnews/asia/china/10608245/China-kills-off-discussion-on-Weibo-after-internet-crackdown.html.

154. Mirjam Meissner, "China's Social Credit Systems: A Big-Data Enabled Approach to Market Regulation with Broad Implications for Doing Business in China," MERICS, May 24, 2017, https://www.merics.org/fileadmin/user_upload/downloads/China-Monitor/merics_ChinaMonitor_39_englisch_Web.pdf.

155. Meissner, "China's Social Credit Systems."

156. Yuan Yang, "China Penalizes 6.7m Debtors with Travel Ban," *Financial Times,* February 15, 2017, https://www.ft.com/content/ceb2a7f0-f350-11e6-8758-687615821a6.

157. Simon Denyer, "China's Plan to Organize Its Society Relies on 'Big Data' to Rate Everyone," *Washington Post,* October 22, 2016, https://www.washingtonpost.com/world/asia_pacific/chinas-plan-to-organize-its-whole-society-around-big-data-a-rating-for-everyone/2016/10/20/1cd0dd9c-9516-11e6-ae9d-0030ac1899cd_story.html?utm_term=.2a476576c887.

158. Shu, "China Tried to Get World Internet Conference Attendees to Ratify This Ridiculous Draft Declaration."

159. Shu, "China Tried to Get World Internet Conference Attendees to Ratify This Ridiculous Draft Declaration."

160. "The Internet in China (V. Protecting Internet Security)," Information Office of the State Council of the People's Republic of China, June 8, 2010, http://unpan1.un.org/intradoc/groups/public/documents/UN-DPADM/UNPAN042565.pdf.

161. Bandurski, "Can China Conquer the Internet?"

162. David Bandurski, "Two Share a Boat," China Media Project, September 29, 2015, http://standiers.com/cmp/2015/09/29/two-share-a-boat/.

163. *Michael Anti: Behind the Great Firewall of China,* online video, July 30, 2012, https://archive.org/details/MichaelAnti_2012G.

164. Hardeep Matharu, "China Set to Ban All Foreign Media from Publishing Online," *The Independent,* February 19, 2016, http://www.independent.co.uk/news/world/asia/china-set-to-ban-all-foreign-media-from-publishing-online-a6883366.html.

165. "Cat and Mouse."

166. Katie Hunt and CY Xu, "China 'Employs 2 Million to Police Internet,'" *CNN,* October 7, 2013, http://www.cnn.com/2013/10/07/world/asia/china-internet-monitors/.

167. Gary King, Jennifer Pan, and Margaret E. Roberts, "How the Chinese Government Fabricates Social Media Posts for Strategic Distraction, Not Engaged Argument," June 1, 2016, Working Paper, http://gking.harvard.edu/files/gking/files/50c.pdf, 7–9.

168. "Cat and Mouse."

169. "Cat and Mouse."

170. Yang, "Social Dynamics in the Evolution of China's Internet Content Control Regime," 288.

171. Kathrin Hille, "How China Polices the Internet," *Financial Times*, July 18, 2009, http://www.ft.com/intl/cms/s/0/e716cfc6-71a1-11de-a821-00144feabdc0.html.

172. Edward Tse, *China's Disruptors* (New York: Portfolio/Penguin, 2015), 161.

173. Yang, "Social Dynamics in the Evolution of China's Internet Content Control Regime," 293.

174. Tse, *China's Disruptors*, 80–81.

175. Sophie Beach, "'Network Security Officers' to Monitor Work of Web Firms," *China Digital Times*, August 5, 2015, http://chinadigitaltimes.net/2015/08/network-security-officers-to-monitor-work-of-web-firms/.

176. "China Plans Security Offices Inside Internet Firms to Stop 'Illegal Behavior,'" *Reuters*, August 5, 2015, http://www.theguardian.com/world/2015/aug/05/china-security-offices-internet-firms-stop-illegal-behaviour.

177. Mukul Devichand, "The Women of the Chinese Internet Remain Defiant," *BBC News*, April 30, 3015, http://www.bbc.com/news/blogs-trending-32518852.

178. Sile Zhao, "The Inspirational Backstory of China's 'Feminist Five,'" *Foreign Policy*, April 17, 2015, http://foreignpolicy.com/2015/04/17/china-feminist-bail-interview-released-feminism-activist/.

179. Jinyan Zeng, "China's Feminist Five: 'This Is the Worst Crackdown on Lawyers, Activists and Scholars In Decades,'" *Guardian*, April 17, 2015, https://www.theguardian.com/lifeandstyle/2015/apr/17/chinas-feminist-five-this-is-the-worst-crackdown-on-lawyers-activists-and-scholars-in-decades.

180. Emily Rauhala, "Hillary Clinton Called Xi's Speech 'Shameless,' and the Web Went Wild," *Washington Post*, September 28, 2015, https://www.washingtonpost.com/news/worldviews/wp/2015/09/28/hillary-clinton-called-xis-speech-shameless-and-the-web-went-wild/?utm_term=.99dce9506305.

181. Enid Tsui, "China's Feminist Five Unbowed a Year after Detention, Says Activist in Hong Kong for Forum," *South China Morning Post*, May 1, 2016, http://www.scmp.com/lifestyle/article/1947133/chinas-feminist-five-unbowed-year-after-detention-says-activist-hong-kong.

182. Andrew Jacobs, "China Further Tightens Grip on the Internet," *New York Times*, January 29, 2015, http://www.nytimes.com/2015/01/30/world/asia/china-clamps-down-still-harder-on-internet-access.html.

183. Jacobs, "China Further Tightens Grip on the Internet."

184. Jacobs, "China Further Tightens Grip on the Internet."

185. Hui Gezi Yin Shui [Pseudonym], "Why Do Scientists Need Google? [*Weishenme Kexuejia Xuyao Google*]," January 12, 2015, http://bbs.tianya. cn/post-worldlook-1365940-1.shtml.

186. Zheng Wan, "China's Scientific Progress Hinges on Access to Data," *Nature*, April 28, 2015, http://www.nature.com/news/ china-s-scientific-progress-hinges-on-access-to-data-1.17426.

187. Edward Wong, "China's Internet Speed Ranks 91st in the World," *New York Times*, June 3, 2016, http://www.nytimes.com/2016/06/04/ world/asia/china-internet-speed.html.

188. Evan Osnos, "Born Red," *New Yorker*, April 6, 2015, http://www. newyorker.com/magazine/2015/04/06/born-red.

189. "Business Confidence Survey 2017," European Union Chamber of Commerce in China, May 31, 2017, http://www.europeanchamber.com. cn/en/publications-archive/516/Business_Confidence_Survey_2017.

190. Tse, *China's Disruptors*, 53.

191. Adam Pasick, "Sina Weibo's IPO Will Have a Government Censorship Discount," *Quartz*, March 17, 2014, http://qz.com/188747/sina-Weibos- ipo-will-have-a-government-censorship-discount/.

192. "Word of the Week: Wall Nation," *China Digital Times*, July 28, 2016, http://chinadigitaltimes.net/2016/07/word-week-wall-nation/.

193. Peter Foster, "Man Behind 'Great Firewall of China' Pelted with Eggs," *Telegraph*, May 19, 2011, www.telegraph.co.uk/news/worldnews/asia/ china/8523806/Man-behind-Great-Firewall-of-China-pelted-with-eggs. html.

194. Foster, "Man Behind 'Great Firewall of China' Pelted with Eggs."

195. Xiao Qiang, "Fang Binxing Shoegate: Responses within China," May 20, 2011, *China Digital Times*, https://chinadigitaltimes.net/2011/05/fang- binxing-shoegate-twitter-responses/.

196. Goldkorn, "China's Internet."

197. Goldkorn, "China's Internet."

198. Tim Dwyer and Weiwei Xu, "Tianjin Disaster Takes Social News Sharing to New Levels in China," *The Conversation*, August 24, 2015, http://theconversation.com/tianjin-disaster-takes-social-news-sharing- to-new-levels-in-china-46401.

199. Eva Dou, "China's Censors Scramble to Contain Online Fallout after Tianjin Blast," *Wall Street Journal*, August 14, 2015, http://blogs.wsj.com/ chinarealtime/2015/08/14/chinas-censors-scramble-to-contain-online- fallout-after-tianjin-blast/.

200. Nikhil Sonnad, "Chinese Censors Have Blocked 50 Websites for 'Spreading Rumors' about the Tianjin Explosion," *Quartz*, August 18, 2015, https://qz.com/481679/chinese-censors-have-blocked-50-websites- for-spreading-rumors-about-the-tianjin-explosions/.

201. "Life in Tianjin Returning to Normal, Repairs Underway One Year after
      Deadly Blasts," CCTV.com, August 12, 2016, http://english.cctv.com/
      2016/08/12/VIDE0I3Cxnqocd0UolXlXFkJ160812.shtml.

Chapter 4

1.   Tom Mitchell, Gabriel Wildau, and Josh Noble, "Equities: A Bull
     Market with Chinese Characteristics," *Financial Times*, July 10, 2015,
     http://www.ft.com/cms/s/0/082499ca-2658-11e5-9c4e-a775d2b173ca.
     htmlk#axzz4KKjZJFOk.

2.   Enda Curran, "State Companies: Back on China's To-Do List,"
     Bloomberg Businessweek, July 30, 2015, http://www.bloomberg.com/
     news/articles/2015-07-30/china-s-state-owned-companies-
     may-face-reform.

3.   Gwynn Guilford, "The Shadowy Trading behind China's Stock Market
     Boom," *Quartz*, December 8, 2014, http://qz.com/308153/the-shadowy-
     trading-behind-chinas-stock-market-boom/.

4.   James F. Peltz, "Chinese Stocks Surge, Halting Severe Drop for at Least
     One Day," *Los Angeles Times*, July 9, 2015, http://www.latimes.com/
     business/la-fi-china-stocks-explainer-20150708-story.html.

5.   "China Stocks Extend $3.4 Trillion Tumble as Turnover Plummets,"
     Bloomberg News, August 5, 2015, http://www.bloomberg.com/news/
     articles/2015-08-06/china-s-stock-index-futures-slump-as-traders-test-
     state-support.

6.   Heather Timmons and Lily Kuo, "A Complete List of the Chinese
     Government's Stock-Market Stimulus (That We Know About)," *Quartz*,
     July 28, 2015, http://qz.com/445454/a-complete-list-of-the-chinese-
     governments-stock-market-stimulus/.

7.   Mitchell, Wildau, and Noble, "Equities: A Bull Market with Chinese
     Characteristics."

8.   Arthur R. Kroeber, "Making Sense of China's Stock Market Mess,"
     Brookings, July 13, 2015, https://www.brookings.edu/opinions/making-
     sense-of-chinas-stock-market-mess/; Timmons and Kuo, "A Complete
     List of the Chinese Government's Stock-Market Stimulus."

9.   "China Has Spent $236-Billion So Far Rescuing Its Stocks as It Burns
     through Cash Like Never Before," *Financial Post*, September 8, 2015,
     http://business.financialpost.com/investing/global-investor/china-has-
     spent-236-billion-so-far-rescuing-its-stocks-as-it-burns-through-cash-like-
     never-before.

10. Jack Hu, "Conspiracy Theory Blaming China's Stock Market Plunge on
     Foreign Forces Finds Online Support," *Hong Kong Free Press*, July 28, 2015,
     https://www.hongkongfp.com/2015/07/28/conspiracy-theory-blaming-
     chinas-stock-market-plunge-on-foreign-forces-finds-online-support/.

11. "China Suspends Circuit Breaker," *BBC*, January 7, 2016, http://www.
     bbc.com/news/business-35253188; "China Removes Xiao as CSRC

Head after Stock Market Meltdown," *Bloomberg News*, February 19, 2016, http://www.bloomberg.com/news/articles/2016-02-19/head-of-china-s-securities-regulator-to-step-down-wsj-reports.

12. Keith Bradsher, "Xiao Gang, China's Top Securities Regulator, Ousted over Market Tumult," *New York Times*, February 19, 2016, http://www.nytimes.com/2016/02/20/business/dealbook/china-securities-regulatory-commission-xiao-gang-resigns.html.

13. Gabriel Wildau, "China's Renminbi Liberalisation Leaves Capital Controls Intact," *Financial Times*, June 22, 2015, https://www.ft.com/content/7727bfec-18a1-11e5-a130-2e7db721f996.

14. "China Rattles Markets with Yuan Devaluation," *Bloomberg News*, August 10, 2015, http://www.bloomberg.com/news/articles/2015-08-11/china-weakens-yuan-reference-rate-by-record-1-9-amid-slowdown.

15. "IMF Survey: Chinese Renminbi to Be Included in IMF's Special Drawing Right Basket," International Monetary Fund, December 1, 2015, https://www.imf.org/en/News/Articles/2015/09/28/04/53/sonew120115a.

16. "China Capital Outflows Rise to Estimated $1 Trillion in 2015," *Bloomberg News*, January 25, 2016 http://www.bloomberg.com/news/articles/2016-01-25/china-capital-outflows-climb-to-estimated-1-trillion-in-2015.

17. Grace Zhu, "China Caps Overseas Cash Withdrawals," *Wall Street Journal*, September 29, 2015, http://www.wsj.com/articles/china-caps-overseas-cash-withdrawals-1443520794.

18. Vicki Schmelzer, "Analysis: Eye on China FX Reserve Data; More Outflows Expected," MNI, February 4, 2016, https://www.marketnews.com/content/analysis-eye-china-fx-reserve-data-more-outflows-expected.

19. Lingling Wei, "A Rare Look Inside China's Central Bank Shows Slackening Resolve to Revamp Yuan," *Wall Street Journal*, May 23, 2016, http://www.wsj.com/articles/china-preferring-stability-to-free-markets-loses-resolve-to-revamp-currency-1464022378.

20. Jinping Xi, "Full Text from President Xi Jinping's Speech," National Committee on U.S. China Relations, September 22, 2015, https://www.ncuscr.org/content/full-text-president-xi-jinpings-speech.

21. Bruce J. Dickson, *The Dictator's Dilemma* (New York: Oxford University Press, 2016), 9.

22. Rakesh Kochhar, "6 Key Takeaways about the World's Emerging Middle Class," Pew Research Fact Tank, July 8, 2015, http://www.pewresearch.org/fact-tank/2015/07/08/6-key-takeaways-about-the-worlds-emerging-middle-class/.

23. Moran Zhang, "China's Local-Government Debt Doubles in 2 Years, May Roll Out Municipal Bonds in March," *International Business Times*, December 24, 2013, http://www.ibtimes.com/chinas-local-government-debt-doubles-2-years-may-roll-out-municipal-bonds-march-1519768.

24. Atif Ansar, Bent Flyvbjerg, Alexander Budzier, and Daniel Lunn, "Does Infrastructure Investment Lead to Economic Growth or Economic

Fragility? Evidence from China," *Oxford Review of Economic Policy* 32, no. 3 (2016): 360–90, https://arxiv.org/ftp/arxiv/papers/1609/1609.00415.pdf.

25. World Bank, "Household Final Consumption Expenditure, etc. (% of GDP)," n.d., accessed October 1, 2016, https://data.worldbank.org/indicator/NE.CON.PETC.ZS.

26. Spencer Sheehan, "China's Struggle with Demographic Change," *Diplomat*, June 20, 2017, http://thediplomat.com/2017/06/chinas-struggle-with-demographic-change/.

27. David Cohen, "Channeling Deng Xiaoping," *Diplomat*, December 12, 2012, http://thediplomat.com/2012/12/channeling-deng-xiaoping.

28. Willy Lam, "Xi Jinping's 'Southern Tour' Reignites Promise of Reform," *China Brief* 24, no. 12 (Dec. 14, 2012): 3, https://jamestown.org/wp-content/uploads/2012/12/cb_12_10.pdf.

29. Keqiang Li, Speech at Summer Davos Opening Ceremony, September 11, 2013, http://www3.weforum.org/docs/AMNC13/WEF_AMNC13_TranscriptLiKeqiang.pdf.

30. Keqiang Li, "Li Keqiang Expounds on Urbanization," translated from a 2012 *Qiushi* issue by He Shan and Chen Xia, China.org.cn, May 26, 2013, http://www.china.org.cn/china/2013-05/26/content_28934485.htm.

31. Gwynn Guilford, "Likonomics: Believe It When You See It," *Quartz*, July 5, 2013, http://qz.com/100304/likonomics-believe-it-when-you-see-it.

32. Cheng Li, "Preparing for the 18th Party Congress: Procedures and Mechanisms," *China Leadership Monitor*, 36 (Jan. 6, 2012): 2, http://www.hoover.org/research/preparing-18th-party-congress-procedures-and-mechanisms.

33. Arthur R. Kroeber, "Xi Jinping's Ambitious Agenda for Economic Reform in China," Brookings, November 17, 2013, https://www.brookings.edu/opinions/xi-jinpings-ambitious-agenda-for-economic-reform-in-china.

34. J.M., "The Party's New Blueprint," *Analects: Economist*, November 16, 2013, https://www.economist.com/blogs/analects/2013/11/reform-china.

35. "Decision of the Central Committee of the Communist Party of China on Some Major Issues Concerning Comprehensively Deepening the Reform," China.org.cn, January 16, 2014, http://www.china.org.cn/china/third_plenary_session/2014-01/16/content_31212602.htm; Nargiza Salidjanova and Iacob Koch-Weser, "Third Plenum Economic Reform Proposals: A Scorecard," U.S.-China Economic and Security Review Commission, November 19, 2013, https://www.uscc.gov/sites/default/files/Research/Backgrounder_Third%20Plenum%20Economic%20Reform%20Proposals--A%20Scorecard%20%282%29.pdf.

36. "Communiqué of the Third Plenary Session of the 18th Central Committee of the Communist Party of China," China.org.cn, January 15, 2014, http://www.china.org.cn/china/third_plenary_session/2014-01/15/content_31203056.htm.

37. "China's Emphasis on Market's 'Decisive' Role to Boost Economic Efficiency," *Xinhua*, November 14, 2013, http://np.china-embassy.org/eng/News/t1099172.htm.

38. Mamta Badkar, "7 Experts Identify the Best and Worst Things about China's Latest String of Reforms," *Business Insider*, November 19, 2013, http://www.businessinsider.com/7-china-experts-on-third-plenum-2013-11.

39. "Decision of the Central Committee of the Communist Party of China on Some Major Issues Concerning Comprehensively Deepening the Reform," China.org.cn, January 16, 2014, http://www.china.org.cn/china/third_plenary_session/2014-01/16/content_31212602_2.htm.

40. Bob Davis, "Beijing Endorses Market Role in Economy," *Wall Street Journal*, November 12, 2013, http://www.wsj.com/articles/SB10001424052702304644104579193202337104802.

41. Derek Scissors, "Shrink the State or Stagnate," *AEI Insight*, March 2, 2016, https://www.aei.org/publication/shrink-the-state-or-stagnate/.

42. Badkar, "7 Experts Identify the Best and Worst Things about China's Latest String of Reforms."

43. Lucy Hornby, "China Ends World's Oldest Monopoly," *Financial Times*, November 21, 2014, https://www.ft.com/content/a666643c-7150-11e4-818e-00144feabdc0; Elizabeth C. Economy and Michael Levi, *By All Means Necessary: How China's Resource Question Is Changing the World* (New York: Oxford University Press, 2015), 12.

44. Mark Elvin, *Pattern of the Chinese Past* (Stanford: Stanford University Press, 1973), 217.

45. Economy and Levi, *By All Means Necessary*, 11.

46. Elvin, *Pattern of the Chinese Past*, 217.

47. Jonathan D. Spence, *The Search for Modern China,* 2nd ed. (New York: W. W. Norton, 1999), 57–58.

48. Ramon H. Myers and Yeh-Chien Wang, "Economic Developments, 1644–1800," *Cambridge History of China*. Vol. 9: *Part One: The Ch'ing Dynasty to 1800*, ed. Willard J. Peterson (New York: Cambridge University Press, 2002), 592.

49. Arthur R. Kroeber, *China's Economy* (New York: Oxford University Press, 2016), 43–44.

50. Morris L. Bian, *The Making of the State Enterprise System in Modern China* (Cambridge, MA: Harvard University Press, 2005), 180–81.

51. Bian, *The Making of the State Enterprise System in Modern China*, 45.

52. Bian, *The Making of the State Enterprise System in Modern China*, 59.

53. Bian, *The Making of the State Enterprise System in Modern China*, 183.

54. Bian, *The Making of the State Enterprise System in Modern China*, 187–88.

55. Bian, *The Making of the State Enterprise System in Modern China*, 51.

56. Keping Yu, "China's Governance Reform from 1978 to 2008," *Duisburg Working Papers on East Asian Studies*, 76 (2008): 14.

57. "China: Communist China," *Oxford Encyclopedia of Economic History*, vol. 1, ed. Joel Mokyr (New York: Oxford University Press, 2003), 435.
58. Keping Yu, "China's Governance Reform from 1978 to 2008," 14.
59. Dwight H. Perkins, "The Centrally Planned Command Economy (1949–84)," in *Routledge Handbook of the Chinese Economy*, ed. Gregory C. Chow and Dwight H. Perkins (New York: Routledge, 2014), 51.
60. "China: Communist China," ed. Mokyr, 437–38.
61. Wayne M. Morrison, "China's Economic Rise: History, Trends, Challenges, and Implications for the United States," *Congressional Research Service Report*, October 21, 2015, 4, https://www.fas.org/sgp/crs/row/RL33534.pdf.
62. Barry Naughton, "A Political Economy of China's Economic Transition," in *China's Great Economic Transformation*, ed. Loren Brandt and Thomas G. Rawski (New York: Cambridge University Press, 2008), 119; David Zweig, "China's Stalled 'Fifth Wave': Zhu Rongji's Reform Package of 1998–2000," *Asian Survey* 41, no. 2 (Mar./Apr. 2001): 233.
63. Barry Naughton, "China's Economic Think Tanks: Their Changing Roles in the 1990s," *The China Quarterly*, 171 (Sept. 2002): 632.
64. World Bank, "GDP Growth (Annual %)," n.d., accessed October 1, 2016, http://data.worldbank.org/indicator/NY.GDP.MKTP.KD.ZG?locations=CN.
65. "China's 12th Five-Year Plan: Overview," KPMG China, March 2011, 2, http://climateobserver.org/wp-content/uploads/2014/10/China-12th-Five-Year-Plan-Overview-2011041.pdf.
66. Guangyu Li and Jonathan Woetzel, "What China's Five-Year Plan Means for Business," McKinsey & Company, July 2011, http://www.mckinsey.com/global-themes/china/what-chinas-five-year-plan-means-for-business.
67. "China: Impact of the Thirteenth Five-Year Plan," event at the Council on Foreign Relations, April 19, 2016, http://www.cfr.org/economics/china-impact-thirteenth-five-year-plan/p37772.
68. "Central Inspection Group and Others Point to SASAC: SOE Reform Progress Is Slow [*Zhongyang Xunshizu Deng Duofang Dianming Guoziwei: Guoqi Gaige Jinzhan Huanman*]," *China Economic Weekly*, July 18, 2016, http://finance.sina.com.cn/china/gncj/2016-07-18/doc-ifxuapvw2224854.shtml.
69. "State-Owned Enterprise (SOE) Reforms in China: A Decisive Role for the Market at Last?," European Parliamentary Research Service, May 2016, http://www.europarl.europa.eu/RegData/etudes/BRIE/2016/583796/EPRS_BRI(2016)583796_EN.pdf.
70. "Reform of State-Owned Enterprises in China," *China Labour Bulletin*, December 19, 2007, http://www.clb.org.hk/en/content/reform-state-owned-enterprises-china.
71. Richard B. Freeman, "A Labor Market with Chinese Characteristics," in *Routledge Handbook of the Chinese Economy*, ed. Gregory C. Chow and Dwight H. Perkins (New York: Routledge, 2015), 109.

72. Gabriel Wildau, "China's State-Owned Zombie Economy," *Financial Times*, February 29, 2016, http://www.ft.com/cms/s/0/253d7eb0-ca6c-11e5-84df-70594b99fc47.html#axzz4JBQFzTVe.

73. E-mail correspondence with Arthur Kroeber, Founding Partner, Gavekal Dragonomics, November 26, 2017.

74. Curtis J. Milhaupt and Wentong Zheng, "Why Mixed-Ownership Reforms Cannot Fix China's State Sector," Paulson Institute Policy Memorandum, January 2016, 7, http://www.paulsoninstitute.org/wp-content/uploads/2016/02/PPM_SOE-Ownership_Milhaupt-and-Zheng_English.pdf.

75. Yaqing Xiao, "Deepening the Reform of SOEs and State Assets: Strengthen, Optimize, and Expand SOEs," June 16, 2017, http://www.studytimes.cn/zydx/GCFT/2017-06-16/9723.html.

76. Kroeber, *China's Economy*, 89, 100.

77. Kroeber, *China's Economy*, 99.

78. Yuqian Wang, "Private Investors Elbowed out by High Borrowing Cost, Research Shows," *Caixin*, July 27, 2016, http://www.chinasme.org.cn/cms/news/100000/0000000375/2016/7/28/5794b47332f5434e8798af2cce7dbfa2.shtml.

79. "The Great Restructuring of Central SOEs: In 13 Years Number of Central SOEs Nearly Halved [*Zhongqi Da Chongzu: 13 Nian Yangqi Shuliang Jihu Jianban*]," *China Economic Weekly*, April 11, 2016 http://finance.sina.com.cn/china/gncj/2016-04-11/doc-ifxrcizs7245094.shtml.

80. Yuqian Wang, "Private Investors Elbowed Out."

81. Goldman Sachs Investment Strategy Group, "Walled In: China's Great Dilemma," *Goldman Sachs Insight*, January 2016, 26, http://www.goldmansachs.com/what-we-do/investment-management/private-wealth-management/intellectual-capital/isg-china-insight-2016.pdf.

82. Yuqian Wang, "Private Investors Elbowed Out."

83. "Self-Employed, Private Firms Create a Third of Jobs in China," *Xinhua*, February 8, 2016, http://news.xinhuanet.com/english/2016-02/08/c_135084962.htm.

84. Houze Song, Derek Scissors, and Yukon Huang, "Is China on a Path to Debt Ruin?," *Foreign Policy*, May 24, 2016, http://foreignpolicy.com/2016/05/24/is-china-on-a-path-to-debt-ruin-chinafile-conversation-economic-reform/.

85. Kamal Ahmed, "China's Debt Mountain: Should We Worry?," May 24, 2017, http://www.bbc.com/news/business-40029092.

86. Stijn Claessens, M. Ayhan Kose, Luc Laeven, and Fabián Valencia, "Understanding Financial Crises: Causes, Consequences, and Policy Responses," International Monetary Fund, 2, https://www.imf.org/external/np/seminars/eng/2012/fincrises/pdf/ck.pdf.

87. Ben Moshinsky, "Goldman Sachs: China's 7-Year Debt Boom Is One of the Biggest and Fastest in History," *Business Insider*, June 20, 2016, http://www.businessinsider.com/goldman-sachs-on-china-debt-boom-2016-6.

88. Lukas Brun, "Overcapacity in Steel: China's Role in a Global Problem," Duke University Center on Globalization, Governance & Competitiveness, September 2016, http://www.americanmanufacturing.org/page/-/uploads/resources/OvercapacityReport2016_R3.pdf.

89. "Latest Gov't Audit Finds State-Owned Enterprises Wasted 12.7 billion Yuan," *Caixin*, June 30, 2016, http://www.caixinglobal.com/2016-06-30/101011564.html.

90. "Opinion of the CPC Central Committee and the State Council on Deepening the Reform of State-Owned Enterprises [*Zhonggong Zhongyang, Guowuyuan Guanyu Shenhua Guo You Qiye Gaige de Zhidao Yijian*]," *Xinhua*, September 13, 2015, http://news.xinhuanet.com/politics/2015-09/13/c_1116547305.htm.

91. The opinions were followed shortly in early 2016 by the announcement of a set of ten pilot-project areas designed to breathe life into the guiding opinions. Announced by SASAC, NDRC, and the Ministry of Human Resources and Social Security (HRSS), the areas included pilots to enhance the quality and power of the board of directors, recruit managers on a market basis, adopt a system of professional management, merge and reorganize central SOEs, pursue mixed ownership in some SOE sectors, expand opportunities for employee stock ownership, improve information disclosure, and strip down remaining social welfare functions provided by SOEs. These would be tested at a handful of SOEs. "SOEs Reform to Deepen as Ten Pilots Reforms Unveiled," *Xinhua Finance*, February 26, 2016, http://en.xinfinance.com/html/In_depth/2016/199753.shtml.

92. In July 2016, the State Council released an additional set of guidelines for SOE optimization. This is Natixis Global Market Research's interpretation of the guidelines; the official document has classified them into four categories: "Consolidation and Strengthening of Security and Strategy," "Innovative Development," "Restructuring and Consolidation," and "Clean Up and Withdrawal." http://english.gov.cn/policies/policy_watch/2016/07/27/content_281475402813390.htm. (1) *Strategic:* These firms will remain state-owned or become part of a holding company. They include SOEs engaged in water conservancy, "grain, cotton, oil, natural gas," strategic mineral resources, "power grids, nuclear power, important public technology platforms, geological data, defense," and hydropower. (2) *Innovation:* These firms will seek private capital, and there will be mergers between firms associated with various central science institutes and other corporations. The focus will be on promoting the use of "Internet Plus" programs to improve manufacturing and other industries and to create a venture fund to advance financial technologies. (Not all explicitly said in the State

Council version.) (3) *Consolidation*: These firms will be merged to reduce competition, foster the development of national champions, and support the "going out" strategy. (The documents don't explicitly say this is in relation to "going out.") Sectors targeted include construction, electricity, equipment, steel, shipping, tourism, aviation, and building materials; integrating upstream and downstream production for synergy in coal, power, and metallurgy; as well as restructuring in communications, new energy, and automobiles. (4) *Cleanup*: These firms are subject to the tightest controls on investment, particularly in sectors such as steel and coal, and firms under SASAC's management that have a loss for three years or more should restructure or go bankrupt. This group, however, accounts for only 5 percent of SOE assets. Alicia Garcia Herrero and Gary Ng, "SOE Reform in China: Loud Thunder, Small Raindrops," *China Hot Topics*, Natixis, August 22, 2016, 2, https://www.research. natixis.com/GlobalResearchWeb/Main/GlobalResearch/GetDocument/ -qYhgNMiaS6S1xNtuvuyvg==.

93. Herrero and Ng, "SOE Reform in China," 3.
94. Wendy Leutert, "Challenges Ahead in China's Reform of State-Owned Enterprises," *Asia Policy* 21 (Jan. 2016): 85, https://www.brookings.edu/ wp-content/uploads/2016/07/Wendy-Leutert-Challenges-ahead-in-Chinas-reform-of-stateowned-enterprises.pdf; "SOE Reform: More Plans, More Pilots," China Policy Brief, September 23, 2015, http://policycn. com/15-09-23-soe-reform-more-plans-more-pilots/.
95. Lyu Chang, "345 'Zombie' Enterprises to Be Cleaned Up," *China Daily*, May 21, 2016, http://www.chinadaily.com.cn/china/2016-05/21/content_ 25398030.htm.
96. Scott Cendrowski, "Why China's SOE Reform Would Always Disappoint," *Fortune*, September 15, 2015, http://fortune.com/2015/09/15/ why-chinas-soe-reform-would-always-disappoint/.
97. Qinglian He, "China's SOE Reform: Privatization or Taking over the Private Sector?," ChinaChange.org, September 30, 2015, https:// chinachange.org/2015/09/30/chinas-soe-reform-privatization-or-taking-over-the-private-sector/.
98. World Bank, "Labor Force, Total (China)," n.d., accessed October 1, 2016, http://data.worldbank.org/indicator/SL.TLF.TOTL. IN?locations=CN.
99. "China Reality Check: SOE Reform," event at Center for Strategic and International Studies, June 8, 2016, https://www.csis.org/events/ china-reality-check-soe-reform.
100. "State Council Information Office Holds a Briefing on the State of Affairs of Employment and Social Security [*Guo Xin Ban Jiu Jiuye He Shehuibaozhang Youguan Qingkuang Juxing Fabuhui*]," China.org.cn, February 29, 2016, http://www.china.com.cn/zhibo/2016-02/29/content_ 37880605.htm?show=t.

101. Benjamin Kang Lim, Matthew Miller, and David Stanway, "Exclusive: China to Lay Off Five to Six Million Workers, Earmarks at Least 23 billion," *Reuters*, March 3, 2016, http://www.reuters.com/article/us-china-economy-layoffs-exclusive-idUSKCN0W33DS.

102. "China Labour Bulletin Strike Map," China Labour Bulletin, n.d., accessed November 27, 2017, http://maps.clb.org.hk/strikes/en#.

103. Yongqi Hu, "End Excess Capacity and Boost Quality, Li Tells SOEs," *China Daily*, May 24, 2016, http://www.chinadaily.com.cn/china/2016-05/24/content_25433838.htm.

104. "No Massive Layoffs Expected in SOE Reform: Official," *Xinhua*, March 12, 2016, http://english.gov.cn/news/photos/2016/03/12/content_281475306113321.htm.

105. "No Massive Layoffs Expected in SOE Reform: Official."

106. Xiao, "Deepening the Reform of SOEs and State Assets."

107. "China Reality Check: SOE Reform," event at Center for Strategic and International Studies, June 8, 2016, https://www.csis.org/events/china-reality-check-soe-reform.

108. "China Plans to Merge State Companies While Avoiding Job Cuts," *Bloomberg*, March 12, 2016, http://www.bloomberg.com/news/articles/2016-03-12/china-to-merge-more-soes-while-avoiding-layoffs-regulator-says.

109. Mirjam Meissner, Lea Shih, Luisa Kinzius, and Sandra Heep, "Like a Phoenix from the Ashes: Reforms Are to Bolster China's State-Owned Enterprises," MERICS Web Special, Mercator Institute for China Studies, June 2015, 7, http://merics.org/fileadmin/templates/download/aktuelles/SOE-Reform_Web-Spezial_EN_final.pdf.

110. "State-Owned Enterprise (SOE) Reforms in China: A Decisive Role for the Market at Last?," European Parliament, May 2016, http://www.europarl.europa.eu/RegData/etudes/BRIE/2016/583796/EPRS_BRI(2016)583796_EN.pdf.

111. Daniel Ren, "The Major Metals Deal Maker Now Keeping Watch on China's Biggest State Firms," *South China Morning Post*, February 3, 2016, http://www.scmp.com/news/china/policies-politics/article/1908833/major-metals-deal-maker-now-keeping-watch-chinas.

112. "China's State Construction Giants CNBM & Sinoma Plan to Merge," *Reuters*, August 23, 2016, https://www.dealstreetasia.com/stories/chinas-state-construction-giants-to-merge-51374/.

113. Curtis J. Milhaupt and Wentong Zheng, "Why Mixed-Ownership Reforms Cannot Fix China's State Sector," Paulson Institute Policy Memorandum, January 2016, 19–20, http://www.paulsoninstitute.org/wp-content/uploads/2016/02/PPM_SOE-Ownership_Milhaupt-and-Zheng_English.pdf.

114. Wendy Leutert, "Challenges Ahead in China's Reform of State-Owned Enterprises," *Asia Policy* 21 (Jan. 2016), 88.

115. Meissner et al., "Like a Phoenix from the Ashes," 9.
116. Keqiang Li, "Full Text: Report on the Work of the Government," National People's Congress of the People's Republic of China, March 17, 2015, http://www.npc.gov.cn/englishnpc/Special_12_3/2015-03/17/content_1909942.htm.
117. Thilo Hanemann and Daniel Rosen, "Lower for Longer: The New Normal of China's FDI Balance," Rhodium Group, June 17, 2016, http://rhg.com/notes/lower-for-longer-the-new-normal-of-chinas-fdi-balance.
118. "SOE Reform: More Plans, More Pilots," *China Policy Brief*, September 23, 2015, http://policycn.com/15-09-23-soe-reform-more-plans-more-pilots/; Sheng Hong, "Why I Oppose SOE Reform This Time [*Wo Weishenme Fouding Zheci 'Guoqi Gaige'*]," *Caijing*, September 14, 2015, http://blog.caijing.com.cn/expert_article-151259-86280.shtml.
119. "China Reality Check: SOE Reform," event at Center for Strategic and International Studies, June 8, 2016, https://www.csis.org/events/china-reality-check-soe-reform.
120. Qinglian He, "China's SOE Reform"; "Xinhua News Agency: We Must Unequivocally Oppose the Erroneous Viewpoint of Privatization [*Xinhua She: Xu Qizhixianming de Fandui gezhong Siyouhua deng cuowu guandian*]," *Xinhua*, September 17, 2015, http://www.guancha.cn/economy/2015_09_17_334684.shtml.
121. Qinglian He, "China's SOE Reform."
122. Meissner et al., "Like a Phoenix from the Ashes."
123. Interview with Anne Stevenson-Yang, Council on Foreign Relations, New York, NY, October 11, 2016.
124. Chen Long, "The Mixed-Up Case of Mixed Ownership Reform," *Ideas*, Gavekal Dragonomics, September 25, 2015, 4.
125. Yanmei Xie, "China Unicom's Mixed-Ownership Mixup," Gavekal Dragonomics, August 25, 2017, www.gavekal.com.
126. Meissner et al., "Like a Phoenix from the Ashes."
127. Qinglian He, "China's SOE Reform."
128. Xin Liu, "China's State-Owned Enterprises Reform: Will It Work?," China Business Knowledge @ CUHK, January 5, 2016, https://cbkcuhk.wordpress.com/2016/01/05/china-state-owned-enterprises-reform-will-this-time-work/.
129. Wildau, "China's State-Owned Zombie Economy."
130. W. Raphael Lam, Alfred Schipke, Yuyan Tan, and Zhibo Tan, "Resolving China's Zombies: Tackling Debt and Raising Productivity," IMF Working Paper November, 2017, p. 6.
131. Lyu Chang, "345 'Zombie' Enterprises to Be Cleaned Up."
132. "PRC Launches Information Website for Bankrupt Enterprises and Sets Up Bankruptcy Courts," Baker & McKenzie, October 2016, http://www.bakermckenzie.com/en/insight/publications/2016/10/prc-launches-information-website/.

133. Michael Lelyveld, "China Stalls on Steel Capacity Cuts," *Radio Free Asia*, July 25, 2016, http://www.rfa.org/english/commentaries/energy_watch/china-stalls-on-steel-capacity-cuts-07252016105858.html.

134. Ruby Lian and David Stanway, "China Admits Overcapacity Not Yet Falling in Bloated Steel Sector," *Reuters*, May 15, 2016, http://www.reuters.com/article/us-china-steel-overcapacity-idUSKCN0Y703A.

135. "China: Impact of the Thirteenth Five-Year Plan," event at the Council on Foreign Relations, April 19, 2016, https://www.cfr.org/event/china-impact-thirteenth-five-year-plan.

136. "IMF Urges China to Be Bolder on Steel, Coal Capacity Cuts," *Reuters*, August 15, 2017, https://www.reuters.com/article/china-economy-imf-steel/imf-urges-china-to-be-bolder-on-steel-coal-capacity-cuts-idUSL4N1LI2J3.

137. Emily Feng, "Xi Jinping Reminds China's State Companies of Who's the Boss," *New York Times* (Sinosphere blog), October 13, 2016, http://www.nytimes.com/2016/10/14/world/asia/china-soe-state-owned-enterprises.html?_r=0.

138. "SASAC Director: SOEs Need to Shift from Managing Enterprises to Managing Capital [*Guoziwei Zhuren: Guoqi Yao Cong Guan Qiye Weizhu Xiang Guan Ziben Weizhu Zhuanbian*]," *Sina Finance*, March 11, 2016, http://finance.sina.com/gb/chinamkt/sinacn/20160311/23581423931.html.

139. "SOE Reform: More Plans, More Pilots," *China Policy Brief*, September 23, 2015, http://policycn.com/15-09-23-soe-reform-more-plans-more-pilots/.

140. "Testimony of the Honorable Dennis C. Shea," July 14, 2016, Hearing on "Evaluating the Financial Risks of China," https://www.uscc.gov/sites/default/files/Shea_Senate%20Banking%20testimony_071416.pdf.

141. "Xi Boosts Party in China's $18 Trillion State Company Sector," *Bloomberg News*, July 7, 2016, http://www.bloomberg.com/news/articles/2016-07-07/xi-boosts-party-say-in-china-s-18-trillion-state-company-sector.

142. Interview with European businessman, Washington, DC, October 7, 2016.

143. Interview with Chinese SOE head, Beijing, China, June 19, 2016.

144. Interview with Anne Stevenson-Yang, New York, NY, October 11, 2016.

145. Qinglian He, "China's SOE Reform: Privatization or Taking over the Private Sector?," *ChinaChange*, September 30, 2015, https://chinachange.org/2015/09/30/chinas-soe-reform-privatization-or-taking-over-the-private-sector/.

146. Xin Liu, "China's State-Owned Enterprises Reform: Will It Work?," China Business Knowledge @ CUHK, January 5, 2016, https://cbkcuhk.wordpress.com/2016/01/05/china-state-owned-enterprises-reform-will-this-time-work/.

147. Alicia Garcia Herrero and Gary Ng, "SOE Reform in China: Loud Thunder, Small Raindrops," *China Hot Topics*, Natixis, August 22, 2016, 2, https://www.research.natixis.com/GlobalResearchWeb/Main/GlobalResearch/GetDocument/-qYhgNMiaS6SixNtuvuyvg==.

148. Sheng Hong, "*Wo Weishenme Fouding Zheci 'Guoqi Gaige'* [Why I Oppose SOE Reform This Time]," *Caijing*, September 14, 2015, http://blog. caijing.com.cn/expert_article-151259-86280.shtml.

149. Shengjun Liu, "China's SOE Reform: Looking Back, Highlights and Breakthroughs [*Zhongguo Guoqi Gaige: Huisu, Liangdian Yu Tupo*]," *Financial Times Chinese*, September 15, 2015, http://www.ftchinese.com/ story/001063950?full=y.

150. Lingling Wei and Jeremy Page, "Discord between China's Top Two Leaders Spills into the Open," *Wall Street Journal*, July 22, 2016, http://www.wsj.com/articles/discord-between-chinas-top-two-leaders-spills-into-the-open-1469134110.

151. Minwu Zhu and Yandeng Tan, "Xi Jinping: SOEs Should Not Only Not Weaken, But Should Be Strengthened [*Xi Jinping: Guoyouqiye Bujin Buneng Xueruo Erqie Hai Yao Jiaqiang*]," *Liberation Daily*, March 6, 2014, http://news.ifeng.com/mainland/special/2014lianghui/shengyin/detail_ 2014_03/06/34486701_0.shtml.

152. "2015 American Business in China White Paper," American Chamber of Commerce in Shanghai, September 28, 2015, https://www. amchamchina.org/policy-advocacy/white-paper/2015-american-business-in-china-white-paper; "Business Confidence Survey 2017," European Union Chamber of Commerce in China, May 31, 2017, http://www.europeanchamber.com.cn/en/publications-archive/516/ Business_Confidence_Survey_2017.

153. Maggie Zhang, "China's Tough Capital Controls Put the Brakes on Outbound Deals," *South China Morning Post*, April 5, 2017, http://www.scmp.com/business/global-economy/article/2085109/ chinas-tough-capital-controls-put-brakes-outbound-deals.

154. "China: Impact of the Thirteenth Five-Year Plan," event at the Council on Foreign Relations, April 19, 2016, https://www.cfr.org/event/ china-impact-thirteenth-five-year-plan.

Chapter 5

1. "Alibaba Group Announces March Quarter 2017 and Full Fiscal Year 2017 Results," Alibaba Group, May 18, 2017, http://www.alibabagroup.com/en/ news/press_pdf/p170518.pdf.

2. Kristina Zucchi, "Top 10 Largest Global IPOs of All Time," *Investopedia*, January 12, 2015, http://www.investopedia.com/articles/investing/011215/ top-10-largest-global-ipos-all-time.asp.

3. Saheli Roy Choudhury, "Jack Ma's Alibaba Is Doubling Down on Its Supermarket Strategy," CNBC, July 18, 2017, https://www.cnbc. com/2017/07/18/alibaba-hema-stores-blend-online-and-offline-retail. html.

4. Jason Del Rey, "Jack Ma Insists Alibaba Doesn't Want to Take on Amazon and eBay in U.S.," *Recode*, June

9, 2015, http://www.recode.net/2015/6/9/11563406/
jack-ma-insists-alibaba-doesnt-want-to-take-on-amazon-and-ebay-in-u-s.

5. E-mail exchange with David Wah, June 10, 2017.

6. Jack Ma, interview at the Davos World Economic Forum, January 23, 2015, https://www.youtube.com/watch?v=2kzGKVLslE0.

7. Jinping Xi, *The Governance of China* (Beijing: Foreign Languages Press, 2014), 135, 132.

8. "Gross Domestic Spending on R&D (Indicator)," OECD, n.d., accessed on November 21, 2017, https://data.oecd.org/rd/gross-domestic-spending-on-r-d.htm.

9. Kathleen McLaughlin, "Science Is a Major Plank in China's New Spending Plan," *Science*, March 7, 2016, http://www.sciencemag.org/news/2016/03/science-major-plank-china-s-new-spending-plan.

10. Zen Soo, "Venture Capital Investments in China Surge to Record US$31 Billion," *South China Morning Post*, January 13, 2017, http://www.scmp.com/business/china-business/article/2062011/venture-capital-investments-china-surge-record-us31-billion.

11. World Intellectual Property Organization, "World Intellectual Property Indicators 2014," 2014, 12, http://www.wipo.int/edocs/pubdocs/en/wipo_pub_941_2014.pdf.

12. Daniel Breznitz, "Testimony before the Congressional U.S.-China Economic and Security Review Commission," May 10, 2012, http://www.uscc.gov/sites/default/files/5.10.12breznitz.pdf.

13. "Three Snapshots of Chinese Innovation," *McKinsey Quarterly*, February 2012, http://www.mckinsey.com/global-themes/asia-pacific/three-snapshots-of-chinese-innovation.

14. Author phone interview with Michael Dunne, President of Dunne Automotive, Ltd., October 2016.

15. Joanna Lewis, *Green Innovation in China: China's Wind Power Industry and the Global Transition to a Low-Carbon Economy* (New York: Columbia University Press, 2013).

16. George Yip, "China's Many Types of Innovation," *Forbes*, September 19, 2014, http://www.forbes.com/sites/ceibs/2014/09/19/chinas-many-types-of-innovation/#99d22a66fd07.

17. McKinsey Global Institute, "The China Effect on Global Innovation," McKinsey & Company, July 2015, 16, http://www.mckinseychina.com/wp-content/uploads/2015/07/mckinsey-china-effect-on-global-innovation-2015.pdf.

18. Erik Roth, Jeongmin Seong, and Jonathan Woetzel, "Gauging the Strength of Chinese Innovation," *McKinsey Quarterly*, October 2015, http://www.mckinsey.com/business-functions/strategy-and-corporate-finance/our-insights/gauging-the-strength-of-chinese-innovation.

19. David Brabbins, "Lessons from China: What Western Brands Can Learn from Chinese Smartphone Giant Xiaomi," *The Drum*, September 18,

2014, http://www.thedrum.com/opinion/2014/09/18/lessons-china-what-western-brands-can-learn-chinese-smartphone-giant-xiaomi.

20. McKinsey Global Institute, "The China Effect on Global Innovation."

21. Douglas McIntyre, "Porsche Delivers 225,000 Cars in 2015, as China Sales Rise 24%," *24/7 Wall St.*, January 12, 2016, http://247wallst.com/autos/2016/01/12/porsche-delivers-225000-cars-in-2015-as-china-sales-rise-24/.

22. "2016 Q2 Production Statistics," International Organization of Motor Vehicle Manufacturers, 2016, http://www.oica.net/category/production-statistics/.

23. Liisa Ecola, Johanna Zmud, Kun Gu, Peter Phelps, and Irene Feige, "The Future of Mobility: Scenarios for China in 2030," RAND Corporation and Institute for Mobility Research, 2015, 62, https://www.rand.org/content/dam/rand/pubs/research_reports/RR900/RR991/RAND_RR991.pdf.

24. "Peering through the Smog: Can Cars Be Clean?," *Shanghai Star*, October 17, 2004, http://www.china.org.cn/english/environment/109607.htm.

25. Kelly Sims Gallagher, "Foreign Technology in China's Automobile Industry: Implications for Energy, Economic Development, and Environment," Woodrow Wilson International Center for Scholars, *China Environment Series* 6 (2003): 6, https://www.wilsoncenter.org/sites/default/files/CES%206%20Feature%20Article,%20pp.%201-18.pdf.

26. Hong Shi, Hewu Wang, Minggao Ouyang, and Fachao Jiang, "Analysis of Response of China New Energy Vehicle Markets to Government Policies," EVS28 International Electric Vehicle Symposium and Exhibition, May 3–6, 2015, 3, http://www.evs28.org/event_file/event_file/1/pfile/EVS28-Analysis%20of%20Response%20of%20China%20New%20Energy%20Vehicle%20Markets%20to%20Government%20Policies_2.pdf.

27. Sabrina Howell, Henry Lee, and Adam Heal, "Leapfrogging or Stalling Out? Electric Vehicles in China," HKS Faculty Research Working Papers, May 2014, 8, http://belfercenter.ksg.harvard.edu/publication/24335/leapfrogging_or_stalling_out_electric_vehicles_in_china.html.

28. Jan Stojaspal, "Electric Vehicles in China: An Industry Is Born," *TU-Automotive*, August 1, 2013, http://analysis.tu-auto.com/telematics-evs/electric-vehicles-china-industry-born.

29. Norihiko Shirouzu, "China Urged to Aid Green-Car Buyers," *Wall Street Journal*, September 8, 2009, http://www.wsj.com/articles/SB125224741297789219.

30. Keith Bradsher, "China Vies to Be World's Leader in Electric Cars," *New York Times*, April 1, 2009, http://www.nytimes.com/2009/04/02/business/global/02electric.html; "Notice on the State Council's Publishing of the Energy-Saving and New-Energy Automobiles Development Plan (2012–2020) [*Guowuyuan Guanyu Yinfa Jieneng yu Xinnengyuan Qiche Chanye Fazhan Guihua (2012–2020 nian) de Tongzhi*]," State Council of

the People's Republic of China, June 28, 2012, http://www.gov.cn/zwgk/2012-07/09/content_2179032.htm.

31. Michael A. Levi, Elizabeth C. Economy, Shannon K. O'Neil, and Adam Segal, "Energy Innovation: Driving Technology Competition and Cooperation among the United States, China, India, and Brazil," Council on Foreign Relations, November 2010, 73, http://www.cfr.org/innovation/energy-innovation/p23321.

32. Christopher Marquis, Hongyu Zhang, and Lixuan Zhou, "China's Quest to Adopt Electric Vehicles," *Stanford Social Innovation Review* (Spring 2013): 53, http://www.hbs.edu/faculty/Publication%20Files/Electric%20Vehicles_89176bc1-1aee-4c6e-829f-bd426beaf5d3.pdf.

33. Bradsher, "China Vies to Be World's Leader in Electric Cars."

34. Howell, Lee, and Heal, "Leapfrogging or Stalling Out?," 14–15.

35. Sharon Terlep, "Road Gets Bumpy for GM in China," *Wall Street Journal*, September 16, 2011, http://www.wsj.com/articles/SB100014240531119039272045765727920031401106.

36. Keith Bradsher, "G.M. Plans to Develop Electric Cars with China," *New York Times*, September 20, 2011, http://www.nytimes.com/2011/09/21/business/global/gm-plans-to-develop-electric-cars-with-chinese-automaker.html.

37. Jing Wu, Xuena Li, and Jing Ge, "China's Electric Car Market Refuses to Start," *Chinadialogue*, February 18, 2014, https://www.chinadialogue.net/article/show/single/en/6719-China-s-electric-car-market-refuses-to-start; Marquis, Zhang, and Zhou, "China's Quest to Adopt Electric Vehicles," 6.

38. Jing Wu, Xue'na Li, and Jing Ge, "China's Electric Car Market Refuses to Start."

39. Colum Murphy, "Electric Cars Get a Needed Jolt in China," *Wall Street Journal*, February 26, 2014, http://www.wsj.com/articles/SB10001424052702304071004579406791647975728.

40. Robert A. Burgelman and Andrew S. Grove, "Toward Electric Cars and Clean Coal: A Comparative Analysis of Strategies and Strategy-Making in the U.S. and China," *Stanford Graduate School of Business Research Paper Series* (September 2010): 51, http://www.emic-bg.org/files/Toward_Electric_Cars_and_Clean_Coal.pdf.

41. Marc Gunther, "Warren Buffett Takes Charge," *Fortune*, April 13, 2009, http://archive.fortune.com/2009/04/13/technology/gunther_electric.fortune/index.htm.

42. "First Pure-Electric Vehicle Now Available for Consumers in China," *Business Wire*, October 26, 2011, http://www.businesswire.com/news/home/20111026007004/en/Pure-Electric-Vehicle-Consumers-China.

43. Mark Clifford, "Chinese Government Subsidies Play Major Part in Electric Car Maker BYD's Rise," *Forbes*, July 26, 2016, http://www.

forbes.com/sites/mclifford/2016/07/26/with-a-little-help-from-its-friends-lavish-chinese-government-help-for-top-electric-car-maker-byd/#648c96515334.

44. Alex Crippen, "Warren Buffett Invests in Chinese Company Developing 'Green' Cars," CNBC, September 27, 2008, http://www.cnbc.com/id/26916857.

45. Stephan Richter, "China's BYD, Bury Your Dreams?," *The Globalist*, September 17, 2010, http://www.theglobalist.com/chinas-byd-bury-your-dreams/.

46. Malcolm Moore, "Warren Buffett's Support Helps Make Wang Chuanfu China's Richest Man," *Telegraph*, September 28, 2009, http://www.telegraph.co.uk/finance/newsbysector/banksandfinance/6240168/Warren-Buffetts-support-helps-make-Wang-Chuanfu-Chinas-richest-man.html.

47. Author phone interview with Michael Dunne, President of Dunne Automotive, Ltd., October 2016.

48. "Electric Cars: The BURNING QUESTION," *South China Morning Post*, July 4, 2012, www.scmp.com/article/1005808/electric-cars-burning-question.

49. "Electric Cars: The BURNING QUESTION."

50. "The China Greentech Report 2014: Greener, Smarter, More Productive," the China Greentech Initiative, 2014, 100, http://2312f278ecf8e6e09baf-90b1678a74a398972a33aefb8f73d8ec.r92.cf2.rackcdn.com/China%20Greentech%20Report%202014-Final%20Version%20-%208.2mb.pdf.

51. Howell, Lee, and Heal, "Leapfrogging or Stalling Out?," 17.

52. "China Requires 30% of State Cars Use Alternative Energy," *Bloomberg News*, July 13, 2014, http://www.bloomberg.com/news/articles/2014-07-13/china-targets-30-new-government-vehicles-use-alternative-energy.

53. "Gov't Organs in China to Buy More New Energy Vehicles," *Xinhua*, July 13, 2014, http://www.globaltimes.cn/content/870276.shtml.

54. Levi Tillemann, "China's Electric Car Boom: Should Tesla Motors Worry?," *Fortune*, February 19, 2015, http://fortune.com/2015/02/19/chinas-electric-car-boom-should-tesla-motors-worry/.

55. Rene Chun, "Attack of the Chinese Tesla Clones," *Wired*, October 13, 2015, http://www.wired.com/2015/10/attack-of-the-tesla-clones-from-china/.

56. Tillemann, "China's Electric Car Boom."

57. El Borromeo, "BYD Company Consumers Complain about Insufficient Electric Car Battery Life," *Yibada*, June 23, 2015, http://en.yibada.com/articles/40276/20150623/byd-company-consumers-complain-insufficient-electric-car-battery-life.htm.

58. Zachary Shahan, "BYD Takes #1 Electric Car Spot as Electric Car Sales Triple in China (Video Interview)," *CleanTechnica*, January 20, 2016, http://cleantechnica.com/2016/01/20/byd-takes-1-electric-car-spot-as-electric-car-sales-triple-in-china-video-interview/.

59. James Ayre, "San Francisco Ride-Share Opoli Gets 50 YBD e6 EVs," *EV Obsession*, July 28, 2015, http://evobsession.com/san-francisco-ride-share-opoli-gets-50-byd-e6-evs/; Clifford Atiyeh, "Chicago Uber Drivers Are Leasing China's BYD e6 for $800 a Month—the Question Is Why?," *Car and Driver*, March 16, 2015, http://blog.caranddriver.com/chicago-uber-drivers-are-leasing-chinas-byd-e6-for-800-a-month-the-question-is-why/.

60. Danny King, "BYD Plug In Sales Grow Globally, But US Future Remains Cloudy," *Autoblog*, February 27, 2016, http://www.autoblog.com/2016/02/27/byd-plug-in-sales-grow-globally-us-future-uncertain/.

61. Howell, Lee, and Heal, "Leapfrogging or Stalling Out?"

62. Anthony Ingram, "Kandi Chinese Electric-Car Sharing Service Expands to Larger Cities," *Green Car Reports*, March 2, 2014, http://www.greencarreports.com/news/1090634_kandi-chinese-electric-car-sharing-service-expands-to-larger-cities.

63. Marquis, Zhang, and Zhou, "China's Quest to Adopt Electric Vehicles," 6.

64. Howell, Lee, and Heal, "Leapfrogging or Stalling Out?," 26.

65. Sabrina Howell, "Incentives to Invest in New Technology: The Effect of Fuel Economy Standards on China's Automakers," *Harvard University Economics Department*, May 5, 2015, http://scholar.harvard.edu/files/showell/files/howell_china_auto_paper_march_24_2015.pdf.

66. Rose Yu, "China Fines Five Auto Makers for Electric-Vehicle Subsidy Fraud," *Wall Street Journal*, September 8, 2016, https://www.wsj.com/articles/china-fines-five-auto-makers-for-electric-vehicle-subsidy-fraud-1473337367.

67. Limin An and Zhiming Bao, "Double Dips on the 'New Energy' Vehicle Ride," *Caixin Online*, March 15, 2016, https://www.caixinglobal.com/2016-03-15/101011807.html.

68. Limin An, Xinyu Wang, and Na Chen, "Electric-Vehicle Makers Face Sanctions for False Claims," *Caixin*, September 8, 2016, https://www.caixinglobal.com/2016-09-08/100992398.html.

69. Limin An and Na Chen, "Beijing Overhauls Electric Vehicle Incentives to Weed Out Cheaters," *Caixin*, August 25, 2016, https://www.caixinglobal.com/2016-08-25/101011397.html.

70. Joe McDonald, "China's Electric Vehicle Industry Shaken by Scandal," *AP*, September 12, 2016, http://bigstory.ap.org/article/466f3f8a95594e6287af9a806c2ebf29/chinas-electric-vehicle-industry-shaken-scandal.

71. Laura He, "Crackdown on Electric-Vehicle Subsidy Cheats Expected to Favour Industry Leaders," *South China Morning Post*, September 14, 2016, http://www.scmp.com/business/companies/article/2019315/crackdown-electric-vehicle-subsidy-cheats-expected-favour.

72. "95% of China's Electric Vehicle Startups Face Wipeout," *Bloomberg News*, August 28, 2016, https://www.bloomberg.com/news/articles/2016-08-28/most-of-china-s-electric-car-startups-face-wipeout-by-new-rules.

73. "95% of China's Electric Vehicle Startups Face Wipeout."

74. Limin An, "Electric-Vehicle Makers Hit By Battery Troubles after Foreign Players Fail to Make Govt. List," *Caixin*, July 22, 2016, https://www.caixinglobal.com/2016-07-22/101011501.html.

75. "China Said to Halt New Electrical Car Permits on Glut Concern," *Bloomberg News*, June 5, 2017, https://www.bloomberg.com/news/articles/2017-06-05/china-said-to-halt-new-electric-vehicle-permits-on-policy-review.

76. Segal, *Advantage*, 21–22.

77. Yifu Lin, "The Needham Puzzle: Why the Industrial Revolution Did Not Originate in China," *Economic Development and Cultural Change* 43, no. 2 (1995): 270, https://www.jstor.org/stable/1154499.

78. Maurizio Scarpari, *Ancient China* (New York: Sterling, 2002), 28.

79. Mark Elvin, *The Pattern of the Chinese Past* (Stanford, CA: Stanford University Press, 1973), 203.

80. Joseph Needham, *Science and Civilisation in China.* Vol. 7:2: *General Conclusions and Reflections* (Cambridge: Cambridge University Press, 2004), 9.

81. Dun Liu, "A New Survey of the 'Needham Question,'" *Studies in the History of Natural Sciences* 19, no. 4 (2000): 293–305, http://www1.ihns.ac.cn/members/liu/doc/needq.htm.

82. Nir Kshetri, "Institutional Changes Affecting Entrepreneurship in China," *Journal of Developmental Entrepreneurship* 12, no. 4 (2007): 1, https://libres.uncg.edu/ir/uncg/f/N_Kshetri_Institutional_2007.pdf.

83. Darryl E. Brock, "Science Innovation during the Cultural Revolution: Notes from the *Peking Review*," *Southeast Review of Asian Studies* 31 (2009): 1, http://www.uky.edu/Centers/Asia/SECAAS/Seras/2009/16_Brock_2009.pdf.

84. Brock, "Science Innovation during the Cultural Revolution."

85. Darryl E. Brock, "The People's Landscape: Mr. Science and the Mass Line," in *Mr. Science and Chairman Mao's Cultural Revolution: Science and Technology in Modern China*, ed. Chunjuan Nancy Wei and Darryl E. Brock (Lanham, MD: Lexington Books, 2012), 74.

86. Segal, *Advantage*, 85–86.

87. "Liu Chuanzhi," Zhongguancun Science Park, n.d., accessed October 31, 2016, http://en.zhongguancun.gov.cn/2011-11/14/content_14025993.htm.

88. "Winding Entrepreneurship Experience [*Quzhe de Chuangye Jingli*]," ChenChunxian.com, n.d., accessed October 31, 2016, http://www.chenchunxian.com/career.htm.

89. Scott Kennedy, "The Stone Group: State Client or Market Pathbreaker?," *The China Quarterly* 152 (Dec. 1997): 751, http://chinatrack.typepad.com/files/Stone_Group_CQ_Dec%252097.pdf; "About Us," Founder Group, 2010, http://www.founder.com/index.html.

90. Charles E. Eesley, "Entrepreneurship and China: History of Policy Reforms and Institutional Development," n.d., accessed June 23, 2016, https://web.stanford.edu/~cee/Papers/Entrepreneurship%20and%20 China-7-10-09.pdf.

91. Eesley, "Entrepreneurship and China," 16.

92. Eesley, "Entrepreneurship and China," 9–10.

93. Eesley, "Entrepreneurship and China," 10–11, 14.

94. Kshetri, "Institutional Changes Affecting Entrepreneurship in China," 4–5.

95. Kshertri, "Institutional Changes Affecting Entrepreneurship in China," 9.

96. Xi, *The Governance of China*, 131–41.

97. "The Global Competitiveness Report 2017–2018: China," World Economic Forum, 2017, http://reports.weforum.org/pdf/gci-2017-2018/ WEF_GCI_2017_2018_Profile_CHN.pdf.

98. "Introducing the Circumstances Regarding the '2015 Official Report on Employment for Chinese Students Returning From Studying Abroad' [*Zhongguo Liuxue Huiguo Jiuye Lanpishu 2015' Qingkuang Jieshao*]," Chinese Ministry of Education Study Abroad Service Center, March 25, 2016, http://www.moe.edu.cn/jyb_xwfb/xw_fbh/ moe_2069/xwfbh_2016n/xwfb_160325_01/160325_sfclo1/201603/ t20160325_235214.html.

99. Xi, *The Governance of China*, 65.

100. David Zweig and Huiyao Wang, "Can China Bring Back the Best? The Communist Party Organizes China's Search for Talent," *China Quarterly* 13 (Sept. 12, 2013): 595, http://journals.cambridge.org/action/ displayFulltext?type=1&fid=9003917&jid=CQY&volumeId=215&issu eId=-1&aid=9003914.

101. "The Recruitment Program for Innovative Talents (Long Term)," Thousand Talents Program, n.d., accessed October 26, 2016, httpı// www.1000plan.org/en/.

102. Zweig and Wang, "Can China Bring Back the Best?," 21.

103. Yojana Sharma, "'Thousand Talents' Academic Return Scheme under Review," *University World News* 273 (May 25, 2013), http://www. universityworldnews.com/article.php?story=20130524153852829.

104. Zweig and Wang, "Can China Bring Back the Best?," 604.

105. Sharma, "'Thousand Talents' Academic Return Scheme under Review."

106. Mara Hvistendahl, "China's Programme for Recruiting Foreign Scientists Comes under Scrutiny," *South China Morning Post*, November 3, 2014, http://www.scmp.com/news/china/article/1631317/ chinas-programme-recruiting-foreign-scientists-comes-under-scrutiny.

107. Guofu Liu, "Outdated Barriers to Foreign Talent Hold Nation Back," *Global Times*, March 10, 2011, http://www.globaltimes.cn/content/631933. shtml.

108. "Room for Debate: Will China Achieve Science Supremacy?," *New York Times*, January 18, 2010, http://roomfordebate.blogs.nytimes.com/2010/01/18/will-china-achieve-science-supremacy/.

109. Yigong Shi and Yi Rao, "China's Research Culture," *Science* 329, no. 5996 (Sept. 3, 2010): 1128, http://science.sciencemag.org/content/329/5996/1128.full.

110. Yojana Sharma, "Cronyism Outrage after Science Title Is Denied," *University World News*, October 23, 2011, http://www.universityworldnews.com/article.php?story=20111021220014567.

111. Cong Cao, "The Universal Values of Science and China's Nobel Prize Pursuit," *Minerva* 52, no. 2 (June 2014): 141–60, https://link.springer.com/article/10.1007%2Fs11024-014-9249-y.

112. McKinsey Global Institute, "The China Effect on Global Innovation," McKinsey & Company (July 2015): 22, http://www.mckinseychina.com/wp-content/uploads/2015/07/mckinsey-china-effect-on-global-innovation-2015.pdf.

113. "Charges for the Use of Intellectual Property, Receipts," World Bank, accessed June 23, 2016, http://data.worldbank.org/indicator/BX.GSR.ROYL.CD; "Charges for the Use of Intellectual Property, Payments," World Bank, accessed June 23, 2016, http://data.worldbank.org/indicator/BM.GSR.ROYL.CD?locations=CN.

114. "Charges for the Use of Intellectual Property, Receipts," World Bank, n.d., accessed June 23, 2016, http://data.worldbank.org/indicator/BX.GSR.ROYL.CD.

115. Michelle Florcruz, "China's Steep University Tuition Costs the Average Farmer 13 Years of Income," *International Business Times*, February 23, 2013, http://www.ibtimes.com/chinas-steep-university-tuition-costs-average-farmer-13-years-income-1101434.

116. Le Li, "China's 7 Million Recent Graduates Compete in Toughest Job Market Ever," *NBC News*, September 15, 2013, http://www.nbcnews.com/news/other/chinas-7-million-recent-graduates-compete-toughest-job-market-ever-f8C11161546.

117. Segal, *Advantage*, 46.

118. Weiwei Ai, "China's Censorship Can Never Defeat the Internet," *Guardian*, April 15, 2012, https://www.theguardian.com/commentisfree/libertycentral/2012/apr/16/china-censorship-internet-freedom.

119. "More Party Influence in Higher Education Institutions Urged," *Xinhua*, June 20, 2012, http://www.gov.cn/english/2012-06/20/content_2166332.htm.

120. Regina M. Abrami, William C. Kirby, and F. Warren MacFarlan, "Why China Can't Innovate," *Harvard Business Review*, March 2014, https://hbr.org/2014/03/why-china-cant-innovate.

121. Craig Timberg, "Vast Majority of Global Cyber-Espionage Emanates from China, Report Finds," *Washington Post*, April 22, 2013, https://www.

washingtonpost.com/business/technology/vast-majority-of-global-cyber-espionage-emanates-from-china-report-finds/2013/04/22/61f52486-ab5f-11e2-b6fd-ba6f5f26d70e_story.html.

122. William Alford, *To Steal a Book Is an Elegant Offense* (Stanford, CA: Stanford University Press, 1995), 9.

123. Dennis Shea, "The Impact of International Technology Transfer on American Research and Development," testimony before the U.S. House of Representatives Committee on Science, Space, and Technology, and Subcommittee on Investigations and Oversight, December 5, 2012, https://science.house.gov/sites/republicans.science.house.gov/files/documents/HHRG-112-SY21-WState-DShea-20121205.pdf.

124. George Yip and Bruce McKern, *China's Next Strategic Advantage: From Imitation to Innovation* (Cambridge, MA: MIT Press, 2016), 29.

125. "Outline of the National Medium- and Long-Term Program on Scientific and Technological Development [*Guojia Zhongchangqi Kexue He Jishu Fazhan Guihua Gangyao*]," PRC State Council, February 9, 2006, http://www.gov.cn/jrzg/2006-02/09/content_183787_2.htm.

126. James MacGregor, "China's Drive for 'Indigenous Innovation': A Web of Industrial Policies," U.S. Chamber of Commerce Global Regulatory Cooperation Project, July 2010, 7, https://www.uschamber.com/sites/default/files/legacy/reports/100728chinareport_0.pdf.

127. Joshua Keating, "Why China's New Terrorism Law Is So Controversial," *Slate*, December 28, 2015, http://www.slate.com/blogs/the_slatest/2015/12/28/china_passes_controversial_new_counterterrorism_law.html.

128. Paul Mozur and Jane Perlez, "U.S. Tech Giants may Blur National Security Boundaries in China Deals," *New York Times*, October 30, 2015, https://www.nytimes.com/2015/10/31/technology/us-tech-giants-may-blur-national-security-boundaries-in-china-deals.html?_r=0.

129. Keqiang Li, "Creating New Dynamism through Reform and Innovation," address at the World Economic Forum Annual Meeting of the New Champions, 2014, 4, http://www3.weforum.org/docs/Media/AMNC14_China%20Premiere%20Speech.pdf.

130. "Doing Business 2012: Doing Business in a More Transparent World," World Bank Group, October 20, 2011, 96, http://www.doingbusiness.org/~/media/WBG/DoingBusiness/Documents/Annual-Reports/English/DB12-FullReport.pdf; "Doing Business 2017: Equal Opportunity for All," World Bank Group, October 25, 2016, 207, http://www.doingbusiness.org/~/media/WBG/DoingBusiness/Documents/Annual-Reports/English/DB17-Report.pdf.

131. Kun Li, "Overseas Views on NPC & CPPCC: China Kick-Starts Innovation-Driven Growth," CCTV.com, March 3, 2016, http://english.cntv.cn/2016/03/03/ARTIoqvOS3k2Px2pvSePVXaP160303.shtml.

132. "Haidian Park: The Birthplace of China's Most Innovative and Entrepreneurial Technology Companies," *PR Newswire*, January 22, 2015, http://www.prnewswire.com/news-releases/haidian-park-the-birthplace-of-chinas-most-innovative-and-entrepreneurial-technology-companies-300024231.html.

133. "National Science & Technology Park (NSTP) at NUST, Islamabad," *Business Recorder*, June 29, 2015, http://fp.brecorder.com/2015/06/201506291200953/.

134. Author interview with Hongbo Chen, Tsinghua Science Park, Beijing, China, June 2012.

135. "Beijing's Tsinghua Science Park [*Beijing Qinghua Kejiyuan*]," TusPark.com, 2013, http://www.tuspark.com/index.php?m=content&c=index&a=show&catid=24&id=1.

136. "TusPark: 20 Years of Innovation," Tsinghua University, 2011, http://www.tsinghua.edu.cn/publish/newthuen/9365/2015/20150417082714652616824/20150417082714652616824_.html.

137. Rob Hof, "Google China Head Kai-Fu Lee Leaves to Start New Venture," *Bloomberg News*, September 4, 2009, https://www.bloomberg.com/news/articles/2009-09-03/google-china-head-kai-fu-lee-leaves-to-start-new-venture.

138. Author interview with Ning Tao in Beijing, China, June 2012.

139. Anil Gupta and Haiyan Wang, "China Can't Be a Global Innovation Leader Unless It Does These Three Things," *Harvard Business Review*, November 8, 2013, https://hbr.org/2013/11/china-cant-be-a-global-innovation-leader-unless-it-does-these-three-things.

140. Niu Yue, "Kai-Fu Lee: Cities Power China's Internet Startups," *China Daily*, February 15, 2016, http://usa.chinadaily.com.cn/epaper/2016-02/15/content_23488837.htm.

141. McKinsey Global Institute, "The China Effect on Global Innovation," 10.

142. Lee Kai-Fu, presentation at China Institute, New York City, February 10, 2016.

143. Charles E. Eesley, "Entrepreneurship and China: History of Policy Reforms and Institutional Development," July 10, 2009, 29, https://web.stanford.edu/~cee/Papers/Entrepreneurship%20and%20China-7-10-09.pdf.

144. Eesley, "Entrepreneurship and China."

145. Shai Oster, "China Venture Firm Raises $648 Million from Princeton, Duke," *Bloomberg Technology*, February 7, 2016, http://www.bloomberg.com/news/articles/2016-02-08/china-venture-firm-raises-648-million-from-princeton-duke.

146. "Qiming Venture Partners," Crunchbase, n.d., accessed October 31, 2016, https://www.crunchbase.com/organization/qiming-venture-partners#/entity.

147. Shai Oster and Lulu Yilun Chen, "Inside China's Historic $338 Billion Tech Startup Experiment," *Bloomberg Technology*, March 8, 2016, https://sg.finance.yahoo.com/news/china-state-backed-venture-funds-220000045.html.

148. Paul Bischoff, "Series A Bullshit: Why China's Startups Are Peddling Lies," *Tech in Asia*, February 12, 2015, https://www.techinasia.com/china-startups-faking-funding-amounts.

149. "Funding Proves Major Problem for Startups," *China Daily*, September 7, 2015, http://usa.chinadaily.com.cn/epaper/2015-09/07/content_21810883.htm.

Chapter 6

1. Christina Larson, "Beijing Air: 'Crazy Bad,'" *Foreign Policy*, November 19, 2010, http://foreignpolicy.com/2010/11/19/beijing-air-crazy-bad/.

2. Xuyang Jingjing, "The Microparticles Debate," *Global Times*, December 4, 2011, http://www.globaltimes.cn/content/686994.shtml.

3. Jeremy Page, "Microbloggers Pressure Beijing to Improve Air Pollution Monitoring," *Wall Street Journal*, November 8, 2011, http://blogs.wsj.com/chinarealtime/2011/11/08/internet-puts-pressure-on-beijing-to-improve-air-pollution-monitoring/.

4. David Roberts, "Opinion: How the US Embassy Tweeted to Clear Beijing's Air," *Wired*, last modified March 6, 2015, https://www.wired.com/2015/03/opinion-us-embassy-beijing-tweeted-clear-air/.

5. Ben Blanchard, "China Says Only It Has Right to Monitor Air Pollution," *Reuters*, June 5, 2012, http://www.reuters.com/article/uk-china-environment-idUSLNE85400D20120605.

6. James Fallows, "How Air Pollution in China Has Hit Previously Unimaginable Levels," *Quartz*, January 14, 2013, https://qz.com/43284/china-smog-air-pollution-hit-previously-unimaginable-levels/; Louisa Lim, "Beijing's 'Airpocalypse' Spurs Pollution Controls, Public Pressure," NPR, January 14, 2013, http://www.npr.org/2013/01/14/169305324/beijings-air-quality-reaches-hazardous-levels.

7. Lillian Lin and Laurie Burkitt, "Extreme Pollution in Beijing Lights Fire under State Media," *Wall Street Journal*, January 14, 2013, https://blogs.wsj.com/chinarealtime/2013/01/14/extreme-pollution-in-beijing-lights-fire-under-state-media/; Weizheng Wu, "A Beautiful China Starts with Healthy Breathing [*Meili Zhongguo, Cong Jiankang Huxi Kaishi*]," *People's Daily*, January 14, 2013, http://opinion.people.com.cn/n/2013/0114/c1003-20185739.html.

8. Runze Yu, "Vice Premier Li Keqiang Vows to Combat Air Pollution," *Sina English*, January 15, 2013, http://english.sina.com/china/2013/0114/548935.html.

9. Shiyi Pan, "Calling for Creation of Clean Air Act [*Huyu Lifa Kongqi Qingjie Fa'an*]," Weibo, http://vote.weibo.com/poll/2228862.

10. Josh Chin, "China Internet Users Scream for Clean Air Act," *Wall Street Journal*, January 29, 2013, http://blogs.wsj.com/chinarealtime/2013/01/29/chinese-internet-users-scream-for-clean-air-act/; Johan van de Ven, "Air Pollution in Beijing, 2011–2013," *Tuwenba*, April 28, 2014, http://www.tuwenba.com/content/MDYzODE0N6zY2.html.

11. Kristie Lu Stout, "Can Social Media Clear Air over China?" *CNN*, April 19, 2013, http://www.cnn.com/2013/04/19/world/asia/lu-stout-china-pollution/.

12. Luna Lin, "Will China's New Premier Li Keqiang Improve the Environment?," *China Dialogue*, February 4, 2013, https://www.chinadialogue.net/article/show/single/en/5847-Will-China-s-new-premier-Li-Keqiang-improve-the-environment-.

13. Yingling Liu, "A Chinese Perspective on Climate and Energy," in *State of the World 2009: Into a Warming World*, by the Worldwatch Institute (Washington, DC: Island Press, 2015), 84–87.

14. Elizabeth C. Economy, "18. The Environment," in *Handbook of China's Governance and Domestic Politics*, ed. Chris Ogden (Oxford: Routledge, 2013).

15. Elizabeth C. Economy, "China's Water Pollution Crisis," *Diplomat*, January 22, 2013, http://thediplomat.com/2013/01/forget-air-pollution-chinas-has-a-water-problem/.

16. Duncan Hewitt, "China Announces Ambitious Plan to Clean Up Its Water, Close Down Polluting Factories," *International Business Times*, April 17, 2015, http://www.ibtimes.com/china-announces-ambitious-plan-clean-its-water-close-down-polluting-factories-1886320.

17. Christina Larson, "Growing Shortages of Water Threaten China's Development," *Yale Environment 360*, July 26, 2010, http://e360.yale.edu/feature/growing_shortages_of_water_threaten_chinas_development/2298/.

18. "Maps Reveal Extent of China's Antibiotics Pollution," Chinese Academy of Sciences, July 15, 2015, http://english.cas.cn/newsroom/news/201507/t20150715_150362.shtml.

19. Ji Beibei, "Vast Amount of Resources Are Being Lost to Leaky Pipes," *Global Times*, May 31, 2011, http://www.globaltimes.cn/content/660025.shtml; "China's Water Crisis Part II—Water Facts at a Glance," March 2010, http://chinawaterrisk.org/wp-content/uploads/2011/06/Chinas-Water-Crisis-Part-2.pdf.

20. Katy Yan, "Almost 28,000 Rivers Disappear in China," International Rivers, June 12, 2013, https://www.internationalrivers.org/resources/almost-28-000-rivers-disappear-in-china-8009.

21. Joshua Bateman, "China's Looming Water Crisis," *Ecologist*, February 25, 2014, http://www.theecologist.org/News/news_analysis/2291208/chinas_looming_water_crisis.html/.

22. "Choke Point China," Circle of Blue, December 25, 2015, www.circleofblue.org/waternews/featured-water-stories/choke-point-china/.

23. Jonathan Watts, "China Makes Gain in Battle Against Desertification but Has Long Fight Ahead," *Guardian*, January 4, 2011, https://www. theguardian.com/world/2011/jan/04/china-desertification.

24. Yifang Chen, "Land of 1,000 Landfills," *Slate*, June 29, 2015, http://www. slate.com/articles/life/caixin/2015/06/unregulated_landfill_epidemic_ china_s_capital_is_cleaning_up_more_than_1.html.

25. Richard Wike and Bridget Parker, "Corruption, Pollution, Inequality Are Top Concerns in China," Pew Research Center, September 24, 2015, http://www.pewglobal.org/2015/09/24/corruption-pollution-inequality- are-top-concerns-in-china/.

26. Berkeley Earth, "Air Pollution Overview," Berkeley Earth, 2015, http:// berkeleyearth.org/air-pollution-overview/.

27. Hongqiao Liu, "The Polluted Legacy of China's Largest Rice-Growing Province," *China Dialogue*, May 30, 2014, https://www.chinadialogue. net/article/show/single/en/7008-The-polluted-legacy-of-China-s-largest- rice-growing-province.

28. John Vidal, "Air Pollution Costs Trillions and Holds Back Poor Countries, Says World Bank," *Guardian*, September 8, 2016, https:// www.theguardian.com/global-development/2016/sep/08/air-pollution- costs-trillions-holds-back-poor-countries-world-bank/; "Cost of Pollution in China: Economic Estimate of Physical Damage," World Bank, February 2007, 12, http://siteresources.worldbank.org/ INTEAPREGTOPENVIRONMENT/Resources/China_Cost_of_ Pollution.pdf, 12.

29. Keith Crane and Zhimin Mao, "Costs of Selected Policies to Address Air Pollution in China," RAND Corporation 2015, http://www.rand.org/ content/dam/rand/pubs/research_reports/RR800/RR861/RAND_RR861.pdf.

30. Keith Crane and Zhimin Mao, "Costs of Selected Policies to Address Air Pollution in China."

31. Gabriel Domínguez, "How Much Is Pollution Costing China's Economy?," *Deutsche Welle*, March 18, 2015, http://www.dw.com/en/how- much-is-pollution-costing-chinas-economy/a-18323476.

32. "Dangerous Breathing: PM2.5: Measuring the Human Health and Economic Impacts on China's Largest Cities," Greenpeace, 2012, http:// www.greenpeace.org/eastasia/Global/eastasia/publications/reports/ climate-energy/2012/Briefing%20Dangerous%20Breathing%20- %20Greenpeace.pdf.

33. "Hunan Rice Sales Plunge as China Probes Cadmium Contamination," *Bloomberg News*, May 2013, https://www.bloomberg.com/news/articles/ 2013-05-21/hunan-rice-sales-plunge-as-china-probes-cadmium- contamination.

34. Gwynn Guilford, "China Has More Shale Gas than Any Other Country. But Getting It Out of the Ground Could Be Disastrous," *Quartz*, September 2, 2014, https://qz.com/258776/

china-has-more-shale-gas-than-any-other-country-but-getting-it-out-of-the-ground-could-be-disastrous/.

35. Henry Gass, "More Chinese on the Coast, Less Fish in the Sea," *Scientific American*, August 8, 2014, https://www.scientificamerican.com/article/more-chinese-on-the-coast-less-fish-in-the-sea/.

36. Jonathan S. Watts, *When a Billion Chinese Jump: How China will Save Mankind—or Destroy It* (New York: Scribner, 2010), https://books.google.com/books?id=GVchqYiZaBoC&pg=PA263&lpg=PA263&dq=bohai+sea+prawn+catch+90+percent&source=bl&ots=awjTGZxGjG&sig=ksxx65N6EwMMORDj9EQ72PgknRc&hl=en&sa=X&ved=0ahUKEwj5voGIkI3QAhXIWSYKHfDQAMQQ6AEIHTAB#v=onepage&q=bohai%20sea%20prawn%20catch%2090%20percent&f=false.

37. D. G. MuCullough, "Will Panasonic's 'Hazard Play' Make A Difference to Air Pollution in China," *Guardian*, April 14, 2014, https://www.theguardian.com/sustainable-business/panasonic-hazard-pay-air-pollution-china.

38. Chao Deng, "Pollution Halves Visitors to Beijing," *Wall Street Journal*, October 31, 2013, http://blogs.wsj.com/chinarealtime/2013/10/31/beijing-air-pollution-drives-50-drop-in-visitors/.

39. Zhuang Pinghui, "Beijing's 'Smog Refugees' Flee the Capital for Cleaner Air Down South," *South China Morning Post*, December 19, 2016, http://www.scmp.com/news/china/society/article/2055739/beijings-smog-refugees-flee-capital-cleaner-air-down-south.

40. "Chinese Anger over Pollution Becomes Main Cause of Social Unrest," *Bloomberg News*, March 6, 2013, http://www.bloomberg.com/news/articles/2013-03-06/pollution-passes-land-grievances-as-main-spark-of-china-protests.

41. Dongxu Zhou, "Closer Look: Nuclear Protests Offer a Teaching Moment," *Caixin*, August 12, 2016, http://www.caixinglobal.com/2016-08-12/101011451.html.

42. Steve Thomas, "China's Nuclear Power Plans Melting Down," *Diplomat*, October 29, 2016, http://thediplomat.com/2016/10/chinas-nuclear-power-plans-melting-down/.

43. Samuel Wade, "Lack of Transparency Fuels Environmental Protests," *China Digital Times*, June 11, 2014, https://chinadigitaltimes.net/2014/06/mep-official-lack-transparency-fuels-environmental-protests/.

44. Rongde Li, "China to Get Community Feedback on All Nuclear Projects," *Caixin*, September 19, 2016, http://www.caixinglobal.com/2016-09-20/100990743.html.

45. Chang Tan, "China's 13th Five-Year Plan Emphasizes 'Environmental Shortcomings,'" *China Dialogue*, February 3, 2016, https://www.chinadialogue.net/article/show/single/en/8673-China-s-13th-Five-Year-Plan-emphasises-environmental-shortcomings-.

46. "Li Keqiang: Like War on Poverty: War on Pollution [*Li Keqiang: Xiang dui Pinkun Xuanzhan Yiyang: Jianjue xiang Wuran Xuanzhan*]," *People's Daily*, March 5, 2014, http://lianghui.people.com.cn/2014npc/n/2014/0305/c376646-24533743.html.

47. "China's Premier Li Keqiang 'Declaring War' on Pollution," *CBS News*, March 5, 2014, http://www.cbsnews.com/news/chinas-premier-li-kequiang-declaring-war-on-pollution/.

48. Elizabeth C. Economy, *The River Runs Black* (Ithaca, NY: Cornell University Press, 2004), 54.

49. Qu Geping and Li Jinchan, "Environmental Management in China," Food and Agricultural Organization of the United Nations, September 1980, http://www.fao.org/docrep/p4150e/p4150e01.htm.

50. Economy, *The River Runs Black*, 52, note 136.

51. Norman Myers, "China's Approach to Environmental Conservation," *Boston College Environmental Affairs Law Review* 5, no. 1 (1976), http://lawdigitalcommons.bc.edu/ealr/vol5/iss1/7.

52. Vaclav Smil, "Environmental Degradation in China," *Asian Survey* 20, no. 8 (1980): 778–79.

53. Interestingly, some researchers found in September 2015 that PM2.5 can lead to liver fibrosis, which can cause cirrhosis that may lead to liver enlargement. See http://www.dbusiness.com/daily-news/Annual-2015/Wayne-State-Study-Air-Pollution-Exposure-Causes-Liver-Fibrosis/.

54. Myers, "China's Approach to Environmental Conservation."

55. Qu Geping and Li Jinchan, "Environmental Management in China."

56. Qu Geping and Li Jinchan, "Environmental Management in China."

57. William P. Alford and Benjamin L. Liebman, "Clean Air, Clear Processes: The Struggle over Air Pollution Law in the PRC," *Hastings Law Journal* 52, no. 3 (2001): 6, http://wcfia.harvard.edu/files/wcfia/files/676_clean_air_5_03.pdf.

58. Alford and Liebman, "Clean Air, Clear Processes."

59. William P. Alford and Yuanyuan Shen, "Limits of the Law in Addressing China's Environmental Dilemma," *Stanford Environmental Law Journal* 16, no. 1 (1996): 205.

60. "18–26: Private Vehicle Ownership [*18–26: Siren Qiche Yongyouliang*]," *China Statistical Yearbook*, 2014, http://www.stats.gov.cn/tjsj/ndsj/2014/zk/html/Z1826c.htm; Xiaoyan Tang, "The Characteristics of Urban Air Pollution in China," in *Urbanization, Energy and Air Pollution in China: The Challenges Abroad—Proceedings of a Symposium* (Washington, DC: National Academies Press, 2004), https://www.nap.edu/read/11192/chapter/5#53, 47–54.

61. "Environment and People's Health in China," World Health Organization and United Nations Development Programme, 2001, 14, http://www.wpro.who.int/environmental_health/documents/docs/CHNEnvironmentalHealth.pdf.

62. "Environment and People's Health in China," 70.

63. Total loading means regulations would now be based on the total volume of pollutants emitted and not just on the concentrations of pollutants in emissions (which has little to do with the actual effects of the pollution if low concentrations are released over a long period of time).

64. Sarath K. Guttikunda and Todd Johnson, "Programs to Control Air Pollution and Acid Rain," in *Urbanization, Energy, and Air Pollution in China: The Challenges Ahead: Proceedings of a Symposium* (Washington, DC: National Academies Press, 2004).

65. Barbara Finamore, "Cleaning China's Smoggy Skies: China Released Draft Air Pollution Law Amendments for Public Comment," NRDC, September 11, 2014, https://www.nrdc.org/experts/barbara-finamore/cleaning-chinas-smoggy-skies-china-released-draft-air-pollution-law; "Environment Supervision Centers to Open," China.org.cn, July 25, 2006, http://www.china.org.cn/english/2006/Jul/175744.htm.

66. Qingyi Wang, "Coal Industry in China: Evolvement and Prospects," 2001, http://nautilus.org/wp-content/uploads/2011/12/C5_final.pdf.

67. "Clean Skies Campaign Was a Success, Beijing Says," *New York Times,* September 1, 2008, http://www.nytimes.com/2008/09/01/world/asia/01iht-cleanup.1.15792247.html.

68. "Environment and Air Quality Situation of Environmental Protection Priority Cities in the First Half of 2010 [*2010 Nian Shangbannian Huanjing Baohu Zhongdian Chengshi Huanjing Kongqi Zhiliang Zhuangkuang*]," Ministry of Environmental Protection of the People's Republic of China, 2010, http://www.mep.gov.cn/gkml/hbb/bgg/201008/W020100819534691175950.pdf.

69. Keqiang Li, "Report on the Work of the Government," speech delivered at the 5th Session of the twelfth National People's Congress of the People's Republic of China, March 5, 2017, http://www.chinadaily.com.cn/china/2017twosession/2017-03/16/content_28583634.htm.

70. Chun Zhang, "Can China Meet Its 2017 Air Quality Goals?," *China Dialogue,* January 25, 2017, https://www.chinadialogue.net/article/show/single/en/9574-Can-China-meet-its-2-17-air-quality-goals-.

71. Edward Wong and Chris Buckley, "Fading Coal Industry in China May Offer Chance to Aid Climate," *New York Times,* September 21, 2015, https://www.nytimes.com/2015/09/22/world/asia/fading-coal-industry-in-china-may-offer-chance-to-aid-climate.html?ref=asia.

72. Yang Yi, "What Will It Take to Clean China's Air," *The Diplomat,* June 22, 2017, http://thediplomat.com/2017/06/what-will-it-take-to-clean-chinas-air/.

73. "China Clean Air Policy Briefings No. 1: 'Twelfth Five-Year Plan' on Air Pollution Prevention and Control in Key Regions," *Clean Air Alliance of China,* April 2013, 3–4, http://pollutedairs.weebly.com/uploads/4/5/6/5/45652937/air_pollution.pdf.

74. "China's Cabinet Stresses PM2.5 Control," *People's Daily*, February 13, 2014, http://en.people.cn/90785/8534253.html.

75. Brian Spegele, "China Moves to Bolster Air-Pollution-Control Law," *Wall Street Journal*, November 26, 2014, https://www.wsj.com/articles/china-moves-to-bolster-air-pollution-control-law-1417011241; "Xinhua Insight: China Passes Law to Control Air Pollution," *Xinhua*, August 29, 2015, http://news.xinhuanet.com/english/2015-08/29/c_134568483.htm.

76. Finamore, "Cleaning China's Smoggy Skies."

77. "CN-7: Air Pollution Prevention and Control Law (Revision)," Institute for Industrial Productivity (2014), http://iepd.iipnetwork.org/policy/air-pollution-prevention-and-control-law-revision; Finamore, "Cleaning China's Smoggy Skies."

78. Finamore, "Cleaning China's Smoggy Skies."

79. Tailai Zhou, Rongde Li, and Xinyue Jiang, "Former Environmental Inspector Calls on Ministry Teams to Work with Businesses to Control Pollution," *Caixin*, July 12, 2017, http://www.caixinglobal.com/2017-07-12/101114709.html.

80. Liu Qin, "China's New Air Pollution Law Omits Key Measures in War in Smog," *China Dialogue*, April 9, 2015, https://www.chinadialogue.net/article/show/single/en/8156-China-s-new-Air-Pollution-Law-omits-key-measures-in-war-on-smog.

81. "China Begins to Suspend Coal-Fired Power Plant Approvals, Greenpeace Response," Greenpeace, March 24, 2016, http://www.greenpeace.org/eastasia/press/releases/climate-energy/2016/China-begins-to-suspend-coal-fired-power-plant-approvals-Greenpeace-response/; Paul Davies and Andrew Westgate, "China Ramps up Renewables," Latham & Watkins LLP, June 1, 2016, http://www.latham.london/2016/06/china-ramps-up-renewables/.

82. "A Suggestion and Comment Letter Regarding the Submission of Amendment to Environmental Protection Law (draft) [*Guanyu Baosong Dui Huanjing Baohu Xiuzhengan (Cao An) Yijian He Jianyi de Han*]," Ministry of Environmental Protection of the People's Republic of China, October 29, 2012, http://www.mep.gov.cn/gkml/hbb/bh/201210/t20121031_240778.htm.

83. Jost Wubbeke, "The Three-Year Battle for China's New Environmental Law," *China Dialogue*, April 25, 2014, https://www.chinadialogue.net/article/show/single/en/6938-The-three-year-battle-for-China-s-new-environmental-law.

84. "China Begins Enforcing Newly Amended Environmental Protection Law,' *Jones Day*, January 2016, 3, http://www.jonesday.com/files/Publication/1d201d08-ddef-4bc9-b017-f04ec8821f0f/Presentation/PublicationAttachment/9bd6ed7d-86fa-4ce9-b12d-f66f150fcacd/China_Begins_Enforcing.pdf.

85. Barbara Finamore, "Tackling Pollution in China's 13th Five Year Plan: Emphasis on Enforcement," NRDC, March 11, 2016, https://www.nrdc. org/experts/barbara-finamore/tackling-pollution-chinas-13th-five-year-plan-emphasis-enforcement.

86. "MEP releases Air Quality Status of Key Regions and 74 Cities in August," Ministry of Environmental Protection of the People's Republic of China, September 19, 2016, http://english.sepa.gov.cn/News_service/ news_release/201609/t20160919_364328.shtml.

87. Natalie Wang, "Environmental Staff in China Spray Air Quality Monitors with Water to Make Readings More Acceptable," *Nanfang*, January 21, 2015, https://thenanfang.com/hanzhong-officials-sabotage-air-quality-monitors-by-spraying-them-with-a-fire-hose-2/.

88. Karl Bourdeau and Dan Schulson, "'Citizen Suits' under China's Revised Environmental Protection Law: A Watershed Moment in Chinese Environmental Litigation?," Beveridge & Diamond, March 9, 2016, http://www.bdlaw.com/news-1863.html.

89. Michael Lelyveld, "China Plans Shift in Environmental Powers," *Radio Free Asia*, April 11, 2016, http://www.rfa.org/english/commentaries/ energy_watch/china-plans-shift-in-environmental-powers-04112016110439.html.

90. "China Firm Fined for Pollution in Landmark Case," Phys.org, July 21, 2016, http://phys.org/news/2016-07-china-firm-fined-pollution-landmark.html.

91. Olivia Boyd, "Civil Society Needed to Enforce Environmental Law," *China Dialogue*, October 20, 2016, https://www.chinadialogue.net/article/ show/single/en/9324-Civil-society-needed-to-enforce-environmental-law.

92. Michael Standaert, "As China Pushes Waste-to-Energy Incinerators, Protests Are Mounting," *Yale Environment 360*, April 20, 2017, http://e360.yale.edu/features/as-china-pushes-waste-to-energy-incinerators-protests-are-mounting.

93. Louise Watt, "Lawyers Sue Chinese Authorities for Not Getting Rid of Smog," *AP News,* March 2, 2017, https://apnews.com/74c322aef89443deaa 926305d912c643/lawyers-sue-chinese-authorities-not-getting-rid-smog.

94. "2015 Tsinghua Graduates First Graduation Ceremony Chen Jining Speech: Choice and Perseverance [*Tsinghua 2015 Shouci Yanjiusheng Biye Dianli Chen Jining Yanjiang: Xuanze Yu Jianchi*]," Tsinghua University, January 29, 2015, http://edu.people.com.cn/n/2015/0129/c1053-26473152. html.

95. Andre Laliberte and Marc Lanteigne, *The Chinese Party-State in the 21st Century: Adaptation and the Reinvention of Legitimacy* (New York: Routledge, 2008), 61.

96. "Reforming Eco-Environmental Protection Institutional Setup and Upgrading Environmental Treatment Capacity Remarks Made at the 2015 Annual General Meeting of China Council for International Cooperation," Ministry of Environmental Protection of the People's

Republic of China, November 11, 2015, http://english.mep.gov.cn/About_SEPA/leaders_of_mep/chenjining/Speeches/201512/t20151210_318850.shtml.

97. China Dialogue, "China's Anti-Corruption Fight Turns toward Environmental Agency," *Diplomat*, August 5, 2015, http://thediplomat.com/2015/08/chinas-anti-corruption-fight-turns-toward-environmental-agency/.

98. Jining Chen, Transcript of Minister Chen Jining's Press Conference, March 9, 2016, http://www.cciced.net/cciceden/NEWSCENTER/LatestEnvironmentalandDevelopmentNews/201603/t20160309_82663.html.

99. "China Punishes Environmental Impact Assessment Agencies," *Xinhua*, March 6, 2015, http://news.xinhuanet.com/english/2015-03/06/c_134044673.htm.

100. Te Ping Chen and Yang Jie, "Pollution Documentary *Under the Dome* Blankets Chinese Internet," *Wall Street Journal*, March 2, 2015, http://blogs.wsj.com/chinarealtime/2015/03/02/pollution-documentary-under-the-dome-blankets-chinese-internet/.

101. Zhang Chun, "Has China's Impact Assessment Law Lost Its Teeth?," *China Dialogue*, July 20, 2016, https://www.chinadialogue.net/blog/9122-Has-China-s-impact-assessment-law-lost-its-teeth-/en.

102. Edward Wong, "Nearly 14,000 Companies in China Violate Pollution Rules," *New York Times*, June 13, 2017, https://www.nytimes.com/2017/06/13/world/asia/china-companies-air-pollution-paris-agreement.html.

103. Sarah Gardner, "LA Smog: The Battle against Air Pollution," *Marketplace*, July 14, 2014, https://www.marketplace.org/2014/07/14/sustainability/we-used-be-china/la-smog-battle-against-air-pollution.

104. Keqiang Li, "Full Text: Work Report of the Government," *China Daily*, March 16, 2017, http://www.chinadaily.com.cn/china/2017twosession/2017-03/16/content_28583634_10.htm.

105. Daniel K. Gardner, "China's 'Silent Spring' Moment?," *New York Times*, March 18, 2015, https://www.nytimes.com/2015/03/19/opinion/why-under-the-dome-found-a-ready-audience-in-china.html?_r=0.

106. Edward Wong and Chris Buckley, "Chinese Premier Vows Tougher Regulation on Air Pollution," *New York Times*, March 15, 2015, https://www.nytimes.com/2015/03/16/world/asia/chinese-premier-li-keqiang-vows-tougher-regulation-on-air-pollution.html?_r=0; "Li Keqiang: Reducing Air Pollutants Improving Oil standard and Quality," *Souhu*, March 5, 2015, http://business.sohu.com/20150305/n409357947.shtml.

107. Celia Hatton, "*Under the Dome*: The Smog Film Taking China by Storm," *BBC News*, March 2, 2015, http://www.bbc.com/news/blogs-china-blog-31689232.

108. Tom Phillips, "China Arrests Anti-Smog Campaigners," *Telegraph*, March 9, 2015, http://www.telegraph.co.uk/news/worldnews/asia/china/11458961/China-arrests-anti-smog-campaigners.html.

109. "China's Citizens Are Complaining More Loudly about Polluted Air," *Economist*, March 2, 2017, https://www.economist.com/news/china/21717975-government-wants-silence-them-chinas-citizens-are-complaining-more-loudly-about-polluted-air.

110. Hongli Liu and Siqi Han, "Infographic: Conquering China's Sludge Mountains," *New Security Beat*, April 9, 2015, https://www.newsecuritybeat.org/2015/04/chase-stink-conquering-chinas-sludge-mountains-infographic/.

111. Elisabeth Rosenthal, "Pollution Victims Start to Fight Back in China," *New York Times*, May 16, 2000, http://www.nytimes.com/2000/05/16/world/pollution-victims-start-to-fight-back-in-china.html?pagewanted=all&src=pm.

112. Sara Hsu, "China Wages War on Pollution While Censoring Activities," *Forbes*, August 4, 2016, https://www.forbes.com/sites/sarahsu/2016/08/04/china-wages-war-on-pollution-while-censoring-activists/#42d51a2e3e8d/.

113. Tom Phillips, "China Passes Law Imposing Security Controls on Foreign NGOs," *The Guardian*, April 28, 2016, https://www.theguardian.com/world/2016/apr/28/china-passes-law-imposing-security-controls-on-foreign-ngos.

114. "China Begins Enforcing Newly Amended Environmental Protection Law," *Jones Day*, January 2016, http://www.jonesday.com/china-begins-enforcing-newly-amended-environmental-protection-law-01-21-2016/.

115. Interview with China-based U.S. environmental NGO director, Council on Foreign Relations, New York, NY, January 2017.

116. "China Jails Environmental Activist for 'Revealing States Secrets,'" *Radio Free Asia*, October 11, 2016, http://www.rfa.org/english/news/china/activist-10112016122729.html.

117. "China to Strengthen Communist Party's Role in Non-govt Bodies," *Reuters*, August 21, 2016, http://www.businessinsider.com/r-china-to-strengthen-communist-partys-role-in-non-govt-bodies-2016-8.

118. Author interview with Chinese environmental NGO official, Beijing, China, June 8, 2017.

119. Chun Zhang, "Can China Meet its 2017 Air Quality Goals?," *China Dialogue*, January 25, 2017, https://www.chinadialogue.net/article/show/single/en/9574-Can-China-meet-its-2-17-air-quality-goals-.

120. Te-Ping Chen, "China's Anti-Pollution Push Brings Costs for Its Provinces," *Wall Street Journal*, March 11, 2016, http://www.wsj.com/articles/chinas-antipollution-push-brings-costs-for-its-provinces-1457688102.

121. Peter Dockrill, "Renewable Energy Now Exceeds All Other Forms of New Power Generation," *Science Alert*, October 26, 2016, http://www.sciencealert.com/renewable-energy-now-exceeds-all-other-forms-of-new-power-generation.

122. Tom Randall, "Solar and Wind Just Did the Unthinkable," *Bloomberg*, January 14, 2016, https://www.bloomberg.com/news/articles/2016-01-14/solar-and-wind-just-did-the-unthinkable.

123. "China Says Must Make $315 Billion–$630 Billion Green Investments per Year," *Reuters*, October 8, 2015, http://www.reuters.com/article/us-imf-china-climatechange-idUSKCN0S236B20151008.

124. Mike H. Bergin, Chinmay Ghoroi, Deepa Dixit, James J. Schauer, and Drew T. Shindell, "Large Reductions in Solar Energy Production Due to Dust and Particulate Air Pollution," *Environmental Science & Technology Letters*, June 15, 2017, http://pubs.acs.org/doi/abs/10.1021/acs.estlett.7b00197.

125. Richard Martin, "China's Great Coal Migration," *Fortune*, July 11, 2014, http://fortune.com/2014/07/11/coal-china/.

126. Hao Feng and Zhe Yao, "Urban Chinese Willing to Pay Extra for Green Electricity," *China Dialogue*, September 19, 2016, https://www.chinadialogue.net/article/show/single/en/9246-Urban-Chinese-willing-to-pay-extra-for-green-electricity.

127. Zachary Davies Boren, "China Stops Building New Coal-Fired Plants," Unearthed: Greenpeace, March 24, 2016, https://energydesk.greenpeace.org/2016/03/24/china-crackdown-new-coal-power-plants/.

128. Zheping Huang, "China Decreases Air Pollution in Big Cities, but Small Cities Are Left Behind," *Quartz*, April 22, 2016, http://www.huffingtonpost.com/entry/chinese-air-pollution-levels_us_5718ff98e4b0479c59d75165.

129. "Hebei Iron Blazes Trail for China's Industrial Outsourcing," *South China Morning Post*, January 3, 2015, http://www.scmp.com/business/commodities/article/1673151/hebei-iron-blazes-trail-chinas-industrial-outsourcing.

130. Dirk van der Kley, "China Shifts Polluting Cement to Tajikistan," August 8, 2016, https://www.chinadialogue.net/article/show/single/en/9174-China-shifts-polluting-cement-to-Tajikistan.

131. Beth Walker, "China Cuts Pollution at Home, Grows Coals Abroad," Climate Home, September 27, 2016, http://www.climatechangenews.com/2016/09/27/china-cuts-pollution-at-home-grows-coal-abroad/.

132. Walker, "China Cuts Pollution at Home, Grows Coals Abroad."

133. David Obura, "As China Has Boosted Renewable Energy It's Moved Dirty Coal Production to Africa," *Quartz Africa*, September 26, 2017, https://qz.com/1087050/china-moved-coal-production-to-kenya-with-risky-environmental-impact/.

134. "Xi's Speech Had 89 Mentions of the 'Environment,' Just 70 of the 'Economy,'" *Bloomberg News*, October 18, 2017, www.bloomberg.com/news/articles/2017-10-18/in-xi-s-vision-for-china-environment-edges-out-economy.

135. David Stanway and Muyu Xu, "China Aims to Meet Air Quality Standards by 2035: Minister," *Reuters*, October 23, 2017, www.reuters.com/article/us-china-congress-pollution-jobs/china-aims-to-meet-air-quality-standards-by-2035-minister-idUSKBN1CS0T6.

Chapter 7

1. "Xi Jinping Looks Ahead to New Era of China-France Ties," CCTV.com, March 28, 2014, http://english.cntv.cn/2014/03/28/VIDE1395981962032239.shtml.

2. Xi Jinping, "Work Together for a Bright Future of China-US Cooperative Partnership," Ministry of Foreign Affairs of the People's Republic of China, February 15, 2012, http://www.fmprc.gov.cn/mfa_eng/wjdt_665385/zyjh_665391/t910351.shtml.

3. "World Economic Outlook Database: April 2016 Edition," International Monetary Fund, April 2016, https://www.imf.org/external/pubs/ft/weo/2016/01/weodata/index.aspx.

4. Chen Boyuan, "How Does a Slowing Chinese Economy Contribute to the World?," China.org.cn, January 23, 2016, http://www.china.org.cn/business/2016-01/23/content_37642210.htm.

5. These are states that are either signatories or have ratified the Treaty on the Non-proliferation of Nuclear Weapons.

6. John Garnaut, "Xi's War Drums," *Foreign Policy*, April 29, 2013, http://foreignpolicy.com/2013/04/29/xis-war-drums/.

7. Charles Clover, "China Extends Run of Double-Digit Military Spending Increases," *Financial Times*, March 5, 2014, https://next.ft.com/content/5e0ce88e-a412-11e3-88b0-00144feab7de.

8. "Tao Guang Yang Hui," *Baidu*, n.d., accessed August 8, 2017, http://baike.baidu.com/view/88881.htm.

9. John Garver, *China and Iran* (Seattle: University of Washington Press, 2006), 98.

10. Esther Pan, "The Promise and Pitfalls of China's 'Peaceful Rise,'" Council on Foreign Relations, April 14, 2006, http://www.cfr.org/china/promise-pitfalls-chinas-peaceful-rise/p10446.

11. Tania Branigan, "China Calls for End to Dollar's Reign as Global Reserve Currency," *Guardian*, March 24, 2009, https://www.theguardian.com/business/2009/mar/24/china-reform-international-monetary-system.

12. "A Changing Posture for Sino-U.S. Economic Dialogue: Toward a Better Offense-Defense Balance [*Zhongmei Jingji Duihua Geju Shengbian Gongshou Geng Pingheng*]," *Xinhua*, June 19, 2009, https://www.scribd.com/document/215762502/Zhang-Baohui-2010-254-255-1-PB.

13. Alison A. Kaufman, "The 'Century of Humiliation' and China's National Narratives," testimony before the U.S.-China Economic and Security Review Commission, http://www.uscc.gov/sites/default/files/3.10.11Kaufman.pdf, 1.

14. Denny Roy, *China's Foreign Relations* (Lanham, MD: Rowman and Littlefield, 1998), 10.

15. Yan Xuetong, "The Rise of China in Chinese Eyes," *Journal of Contemporary China* 10, no. 26 (2001): 33, http://www3.nccu.edu.tw/~lorenzo/Yan%20Rise%20of%20China.pdf.

16. Elizabeth C. Economy, "The Game Changer: Coping with China's Foreign Policy Revolution," *Foreign Affairs*, November/December 2010, https://www.foreignaffairs.com/articles/china/2010-11-01/game-changer.

17. Baohui Zhang, "Chinese Foreign Policy in Transition: Trends and Implications," *Journal of Current Chinese Affairs* 39, no. 2 (2010): 44, http://journals.giga-hamburg.de/index.php/jcca/article/view/203/369.

18. Michael Wines, Keith Bradsher, and Mark Landler, "China's Leader Says He Is 'Worried' Over U.S. Treasuries," *New York Times*, March 13, 2009, http://www.nytimes.com/2009/03/14/world/asia/14china.html.

19. Jeremy Page, "President Xi Jinping's Most Dangerous Venture Yet: Remaking China's Military," *Wall Street Journal*, April 25, 2016, http://www.wsj.com/articles/president-xi-jinpings-most-dangerous-venture-yet-remaking-chinas-military-1461608795.

20. Chen Xiangyang, "A Diplomatic Manifesto to Secure the Chinese Dream," China-U.S. Focus, December 31, 2014, http://www.chinausfocus.com/foreign-policy/a-diplomatic-manifesto-to-secure-the-chinese-dream/.

21. "Xi Jinping Issues an Important Speech at the Central Work Conference on Foreign Affairs [*Xi Jinping Chuxi Zhongyang Waishi Gongzuo Huiyi Bing Fabiao Zhongyao Jianghua*]," *Xinhua*, November 29, 2014, http://news.xinhuanet.com/politics/2014-11/29/c_1113457723.htm.

22. Evan Osnos, "Born Red," *New Yorker*, April 6, 2015, http://www.newyorker.com/magazine/2015/04/06/born-red.

23. Xi Jinping, *The Governance of China* (Beijing: Foreign Languages Press, 2014), 315–19.

24. Xi Jinping, *The Governance of China*, 320–24.

25. Junhua Zhang, "What's Driving China's One Belt, One Road Initiative?" East Asia Forum, September 2, 2016, http://www.eastasiaforum.org/2016/09/02/whats-driving-chinas-one-belt-one-road-initiative/.

26. "U.S. Support for the New Silk Road," U.S. State Department Bureau of South and Central Asian Affairs, n.d., accessed July 8, 2017, https://2009-2017.state.gov/p/sca/ci/af/newsilkroad/index.htm.

27. Nayan Chanda, "The Silk Road: Old and New," *Global Asia* 10, no. 3 (Fall 2015): 13.

28. Jae Ho Chung, "Views from Northeast Asia: A Chinese-Style Pivot or a Mega-Opportunity?" *Global Asia* 10, no. 3 (Fall 2015): 23.

29. "U.S. Support for the New Silk Road."

30. "Our Bulldozers, Our Rules," *Economist*, July 2, 2016, http://www.economist.com/news/china/21701505-chinas-foreign-policy-could-reshape-good-part-world-economy-our-bulldozers-our-rules.

31. Wu Jianming, "'One Belt, One Road,' Far-Reaching Initiative," *China-U.S. Focus*, March 26, 2015, http://www.chinausfocus.com/finance-economy/one-belt-and-one-road-far-reaching-initiative/.

32. "The 13th Five Year Plan: Main Themes and Winning Sectors," China Go Abroad, n.d., accessed August 10, 2017, http://www.chinagoabroad.com/en/article/the-13th-five-year-plan-main-themes-and-winning-sectors.

33. Xiankun Lu, "China 'One Belt & One Road' (OBOR) Initiative: Background, Contents and Perspective," International Institute for Management Development, February 12, 2016, https://www.linkedin.com/pulse/china-one-belt-road-obor-initiative-background-contents-xiankun-lu.

34. Daniel C. Waugh, "Richthofen's 'Silk Roads': Toward the Archaeology of a Concept," University of Washington, Seattle, 2010, http://faculty.washington.edu/dwaugh/publications/waughrichthofen2010.pdf.

35. Joseph Needham, *Science and Civilisation in China*. Vol 1: *Introductory Orientations* (Cambridge: Cambridge University Press, 1954), 176.

36. "About the Silk Road," UNESCO, n.d., accessed July 2016, http://en.unesco.org/silkroad/about-silk-road.

37. Chanda, "The Silk Road," 14.

38. Interview with Xue Li, Chinese Academy of Social Sciences, Beijing, PRC, June 22, 2017.

39. Zhang Yunling, "One Belt, One Road: A Chinese View," *Global Asia* 10, no. 3 (Fall 2015): 8–10.

40. Quoted in Chanda, "The Silk Road," 14.

41. Gareth Price, "India's Take on China's Silk Road: Ambivalence with Lurking Worries," *Global Asia* 10, no. 3 (Fall 2015): 32–33.

42. Zahid Hussain, "The China-Pakistan Economic Corridor and the New Regional Geopolitics," *Asie. Visions,* no. 94, IFRI, June 2017, http://www.ifri.org/sites/default/files/atoms/files/hussain_china_pakistan_economic_corridor_2017.pdf.

43. Shi Yinhong, "China Must Tread Lightly with Its 'One Belt, One Road' Initiative," *South China Morning Post,* August 18, 2015, http://www.scmp.com/comment/insight-opinion/article/1850515/china-must-tread-lightly-its-one-belt-one-road-initiative.

44. Shi Yinhong, "China Must Tread Lightly with Its 'One Belt, One Road' Initiative."

45. Junhua Zhang, "What's Driving China's One Belt, One Road Initiative?"

46. Kemel Toktomushev, "One Belt, One Road: A New Source of Rent for Ruling Elites in Central Asia," China–US Focus, August 20, 2015, http://www.chinausfocus.com/finance-economy/one-belt-one-road-a-new-source-of-rent-for-ruling-elites-in-central-asia.

47. Alexander Cooley, "The Emerging Political Economy of OBOR: The Challenges of Promoting Connectivity in Central Asia and Beyond," A Report of the CSIS Simon Chair in Political Economy, October 2016,

7, https://csis-prod.s3.amazonaws.com/s3fs-public/publication/161021_Cooley_OBOR_Web.pdf.

48. James Kynge, "How the Silk Road Plans Will Be Financed," *Financial Times,* May 9, 2016, http://www.ft.com/cms/s/2/e83ced94-0bd8-11e6-9456-444ab5211a2f.html#axzz48gxKLU5b.

49. Xi, *The Governance of China,* 387.

50. Gabriel Wildau and Charles Clover, "AIIB Launch Signals China's New Ambition," *Financial Times,* June 29, 2015, http://www.ft.com/intl/cms/s/0/5ea61666-1e24-11e5-aa5a-398b2169cf79.html#axzz30TrMEfgX.

51. "Infrastructure in Asia," Asia Securities Industry & Financial Markets Association, November 5, 2014, http://www.asifma.org/uploadedFiles/Events/2014/Annual_Conference/Closed%20Door%20Regulator%20Meeting%201%20-%20Infrastructure%20Financing%20-%20Michael%20Cooper%20HSBC.pdf.

52. "How China Successfully Redrew the Global Financial Map with AIIB," *South China Morning Post,* September 18, 2015, http://www.scmp.com/news/china/policies-politics/article/1859315/how-china-successfully-redrew-global-financial-map-aiib.

53. Robin Harding, "US Fails to Approve IMF Reforms," *Financial Times,* January 14, 2014, http://www.ft.com/cms/s/0/8d4755ee-7d43-11e3-81dd-00144feabdco.html#axzz4Cyw7rTWK.

54. Andrew Mayeda, "Congress Approves IMF Change in Favor of Emerging Markets," *Bloomberg,* December 18, 2015, http://www.bloomberg.com/news/articles/2015-12-18/congress-approves-imf-changes-giving-emerging-markets-more-sway.

55. Finbarr Bermingham, "China Launches AIIB to Rival World Bank without US Allies after Pressure from Washington," *International Business Times,* October 24, 2014, http://www.ibtimes.co.uk/china-launches-aiib-rival-world-bank-without-us-allies-after-pressure-washington-1471582.

56. "Full Transcript: Interview with Chinese President Xi Jinping," *Wall Street Journal,* September 22, 2015, http://www.wsj.com/articles/full-transcript-interview-with-chinese-president-xi-jinping-1442894700.

57. Liu Xiaoming, "New Silk Road Is an Opportunity Not a Threat," *Financial Times,* May 24, 2015, http://www.ft.com/intl/cms/s/0/c8f58a7c-ffd6-11e4-bc30-00144feabdco.html#axzz4CnTtb8g3.

58. Zhang Yunling, "One Belt, One Road: A Chinese View," 11–12.

59. Phillip Y. Lipscy, "Who's Afraid of the AIIB," *Foreign Affairs,* May 7, 2015, https://www.foreignaffairs.com/articles/china/2015-05-07/whos-afraid-aiib.

60. George Parker, Anne-Sylvaine Chassany, and Geoff Dyer, "Europeans Defy US to Join China-led Development Bank," *Financial Times,* March 16, 2015, http://www.ft.com/cms/s/0/0655b342-cc29-11e4-beca-00144feab7de.html.

61. Jane Perlez, "China Creates a World Bank of Its Own, and the U.S. Balks," *New York Times,* December 4, 2015, http://www.nytimes.com/2015/12/05/business/international/china-creates-an-asian-bank-as-the-us-stands-aloof.html.

62. Nayan Chanda, "Can Beijing Make AIIB Transparent?," *YaleGlobal,* July 2, 2015, http://yaleglobal.yale.edu/content/can-beijing-make-aiib-transparent.

63. Rohit Sinha and Geethanjali Nataraj, "Regional Comprehensive Economic Partnership (RCEP): Issues and Way Forward," *Diplomat,* July 30, 2013, http://thediplomat.com/2013/07/regional-comprehensive-economic-partnership-rcep-issues-and-way-forward/.

64. Jack Kim, "China-Backed Trade Pact Playing Catch-Up after U.S.-led TPP Deal," *Reuters,* October 10, 2015, http://www.reuters.com/article/us-trade-tpp-rcep-idUSKCN0S50022015I011.

65. C. Fred Bergsten, Marcus Noland, and Jeffrey J. Schott, "The Free Trade Area of the Asia-Pacific: A Constructive Approach to Multilateralizing Asian Regionalism," ADB Institute Working Paper Series No. 336, December 2011, http://www.adb.org/sites/default/files/publication/156191/adbi-wp336.pdf.

66. "The Beijing Roadmap for APEC's Contribution to the Realization of the FTAAP," Asia-Pacific Economic Cooperation, November 2014, http://www.apec.org/meeting-papers/leaders-declarations/2014/2014_aelm/2014_aelm_annexa.aspx.

67. "China Eyes Asia-Pacific FTA at APEC Meeting, Says Foreign Minister," *Xinhua,* October 29, 2014, http://news.xinhuanet.com/english/china/2014-10/29/c_133751935.htm.

68. Mireya Solis, "China Flexes Its Muscles at APEC with the Revival of FTAAP," *East Asia Forum,* November 23, 2014, http://www.eastasiaforum.org/2014/11/23/china-flexes-its-muscles-at-apec-with-the-revival-of-ftaap/.

69. Quoted in Robert Kaplan, *Asia's Cauldron: The South China Sea and the End of a Stable Pacific* (New York: Random House, 2014), 41.

70. M. Taylor Fravel, "China's Strategy in the South China Sea," *Contemporary Southeast Asia* 33, no. 3 (2011): 294–95, https://taylorfravel.com/documents/research/fravel.2011.CSA.china.strategy.scs.pdf.

71. "Historical Evidence to Support China's Sovereignty over Nansha Islands," Ministry of Foreign Affairs of the People's Republic of China, November 17, 2000, http://www.fmprc.gov.cn/mfa_eng/topics_665678/3754_666060/t19231.shtml.

72. "Historical Evidence to Support China's Sovereignty over Nansha Islands."

73. Li Mingjiang, "Reconciling Assertiveness and Cooperation? China's Changing Approach to the South China Sea Dispute," *Security Challenges* 6, no. 2 (Winter 2010): 54, http://www.regionalsecurity.org.au/Resources/Documents/vol6no2Mingjiang.pdf.

74. Mingjiang, "Reconciling Assertiveness and Cooperation?," 54.

75. Mark E. Rosen, "Philippine Claims in the South China Sea: A Legal Analysis," Center for Naval Analyses, August 2014, https://www.cna.org/CNA_files/PDF/IOP-2014-U-008435.pdf, 12–13.

76. Natalie Thomas and Michael Martina, "China Tightens Rules on Maps amid Territorial Disputes," *Reuters,* December 16, 2015, http://www.reuters.com/article/us-china-maps-idUSKBN0TZ1AR20151216.

77. Peter Dutton, "China's Maritime Disputes in the East and South China Seas," Testimony before the House Foreign Affairs Committee, January 14, 2014, 9, https://www.usnwc.edu/getattachment/9edbcea9-8425-4b96-aa14-aac1f81532c2/China-s-Maritime-Disputes-in-the-East-and-South-Ch.aspx.

78. Fravel, "China's Strategy in the South China Sea," 293.

79. Fravel, "China's Strategy in the South China Sea," 299.

80. Elizabeth C. Economy, "China's Imperial President," *Foreign Affairs,* November/December 2014, https://www.foreignaffairs.com/articles/china/2014-10-20/chinas-imperial-president.

81. "Stirring Up the South China Sea (1) (Asia Report No. 233)," International Crisis Group, April 23, 2012, 6, https://d2071andvipowj.cloudfront.net/229-stirring-up-the-south-china-sea-ii-regional-responses.pdf.

82. "China's Peaceful Development," Information Office of the State Council, September 2011, 2, http://english.gov.cn/archive/white_paper/2014/09/09/content_281474986284646.htm.

83. Alistair D. B. Cook, "South China Sea Disputes in the Xi Era," in *China Entering the Xi Jinping Era,* ed. Zheng Yongnian and Lance L. P. Gore (Oxon: Routledge, 2015), 304.

84. "Stirring Up the South China Sea (1) (Asia Report No. 233)," 8–13.

85. Ben Lowsen, "The Chinese PLA's New 'Army,'" *Diplomat,* March 29, 2016, http://thediplomat.com/2016/03/the-chinese-plas-new-army/.

86. Ritchie B. Tongo, "China's Land Reclamation in South China Sea Grows: Pentagon Report," *Reuters,* August 21, 2015, http://www.reuters.com/article/us-southchinasea-china-pentagon-idUSKCN0QQ0S920150821.

87. Gordon Lubold, "Report Says China Has Stepped Up Land Reclamation in South China Sea," *Wall Street Journal,* August 20, 2015, http://www.wsj.com/articles/pentagon-says-china-has-stepped-up-land-reclamation-in-south-china-sea-1440120837.

88. "Remarks by President Obama and President Xi of the People's Republic of China in Joint Press Conference," White House, September 25, 2015, https://www.whitehouse.gov/the-press-office/2015/09/25/remarks-president-obama-and-president-xi-peoples-republic-china-joint.

89. Carl Thayer, "4 Reasons China Removed Oil Rig HYSY-981 Sooner than Planned," *Diplomat,* July 22, 2014, http://thediplomat.com/2014/07/4-reasons-china-removed-oil-rig-hysy-981-sooner-than-planned/.

90. Interview with China maritime expert at the Council on Foreign Relations office in New York, NY, February 9, 2016.

91. Unryu Suganuma, *Sovereign Rights and Territorial Space in Sino-Japanese Relations: Irredentism and the Diaoyu/Senkaku Islands* (Honolulu: University of Hawai'I Press, 2000), 138.

92. Julian Ryall, "Japan Agrees to Buy Disputed Senkaku Islands," *Telegraph,* September 5, 2012, http://www.telegraph.co.uk/news/worldnews/asia/japan/9521793/Japan-agrees-to-buy-disputed-Senkaku-islands.html.

93. Steven Jiang, "Anti-Japan Protests Erupt in China over Disputed Islands," *CNN,* September 16, 2012, http://www.cnn.com/2012/09/15/world/asia/china-japan-islands/.

94. "China Submits Oceanic Claims to United Nations," *South China Morning Post,* December 15, 2012, http://www.scmp.com/news/china/article/1105655/china-submits-oceanic-claims-united-nations.

95. Irene Chan and Minjiang Li, "Going Assertive? Chinese Foreign Policy under the New Leadership," in *China Entering the Xi Jinping Era*, ed. Zheng Yongnian and Lance L. P. Gore (Oxon: Routledge, 2015), 262.

96. Harry Kazianis, "Senkaku/Diaoyu Islands: A 'Core Interest' of China," *Diplomat,* April 29, 2013, http://thediplomat.com/2013/04/senkakudiaoyu-islands-a-core-interest-of-china/.

97. Madison Park, "Why China's New Air Zone Incensed Japan, U.S.," *CNN,* November 27, 2013, http://www.cnn.com/2013/11/25/world/asia/china-japan-island-explainer/.

98. Christopher Bodeen, "G-20 Summit Yields Hopes for Better China-Japan Relations," *AP,* September 7, 2016, http://bigstory.ap.org/article/46abc2c711ea44c081a714f082a3ecdb/g-20-summit-yields-hopes-better-china-japan-relations.

99. Joseph Chinyong Liow, "What the United States and India Can Do Together on the South China Sea," Brookings Institution, June 10, 2016, http://www.brookings.edu/blogs/order-from-chaos/posts/2016/06/10-us-india-south-china-sea-liow.

100. Prashanth Parameswaran, "Will a China-ASEAN South China Sea Code of Conduct Really Matter?," *The Diplomat*, August 5, 2017, https://thediplomat.com/2017/08/will-a-china-asean-south-china-sea-code-of-conduct-really-matter/.

101. William Wilkes, "China's Deal Makers Have German Tech Firms in Their Sights," *Wall Street Journal,* June 9, 2016, http://www.wsj.com/articles/chinas-deal-makers-have-germany-tech-firms-in-their-sights-1465394152.

102. William Wilkes, "Germany Withdraws Approval of Chinese Takeover of Aixtron," *Wall Street Journal,* October 24, 2016, http://www.wsj.com/articles/german-withdraws-approval-of-chinese-takeover-of-aixtron-1477297215.

103. "Voith Denies Reports to Sell Kuka Stake to Midea," *Deutsche Welle,* June 23, 2016, http://www.dw.com/en/voith-denies-reports-to-sell-kuka-stake-to-midea/a-19351004.

104. Madeline Chambers and Caroline Copley, "Germany, Eyeing China, Urges 'Level Playing Field' for Foreign Investment," *Reuters,* June 8, 2016, http://www.reuters.com/article/us-kuka-m-a-mideagroup-germany-idUSKCN0YU1KI.

105. "Midea Makes Bid for Robotics Maker Kuka Official," *Deutsche Welle,* June 16, 2016, http://www.dw.com/en/midea-makes-bid-for-robotics-maker-kuka-official/a-19335399.

106. Ese Erheriene and Biman Mukherji, "China Remains a Key Commodities Player, Despite Waning Appetites," *Wall Street Journal,* August 25, 2015, http://www.wsj.com/articles/china-remains-a-key-commodities-player-despite-waning-appetites-1440534872.

107. Baohui Zhang, "Chinese Foreign Policy in Transition: Trends and Implications," *Journal of Current Chinese Affairs* 39, no. 2 (2010): 57, https://journals.sub.uni-hamburg.de/giga/jcca/article/view/254/254.

108. "2015 Investment Climate Statement—Argentina," U.S. Department of State Bureau of Economic and Business Affairs, May 2015, http://www.state.gov/e/eb/rls/othr/ics/2015/241462.htm.

109. "2013 Investment Climate Statement—Mongolia," U.S. Department of State Bureau of Economic and Business Affairs, April 2013, http://www.state.gov/e/eb/rls/othr/ics/2013/204697.htm.

110. Courtney Fingar, "Western Countries Lead Foreign Direct Investment into Africa," *Financial Times,* October 6, 2015, https://next.ft.com/content/fea83f20-6c2d-11e5-aca9-d87542bf8673.

111. Shannon O'Neil, "Foreign Direct Investment in Latin America," *Latin America's Moment,* Council on Foreign Relations blog, June 4, 2015, http://blogs.cfr.org/oneil/2015/06/04/foreign-direct-investment-in-latin-america/.

112. "Top Ten Sources of Foreign Direct Investment Inflows in ASEAN," ASEAN, October 27, 2016, http://asean.org/storage/2015/09/Table-27_oct2016.pdf.

113. "China Investment Monitor," Rhodium Group LLC, n.d., accessed August 8, 2017, http://rhg.com/interactive/china-investment-monitor.

114. Thilo Hanemann and Mikko Huotari, "A New Record Year for Chinese Outbound Investment in Europe," Rhodium Group, February 2016, http://rhg.com/wp-content/uploads/2016/02/A_New_Record_Year_for_Chinese_Outbound_Investment_in_Europe.pdf.

115. Huang Hongxiang, Zander Rounds, and Xianshuang Zhang, "China's Africa Dream Isn't Dead," *Foreign Policy,* February 18, 2016, http://foreignpolicy.com/2016/02/18/africa-kenya-tanzania-china-business-economy-gdp-slowing-investment-chinese/.

116. "Foreign Direct Investment Net Outflows for China (2016)," World Bank, 2017, https://data.worldbank.org/indicator/BM.KLT.DINV. CD.WD?locations=CN.

117. Shu Zhang and Matthew Miller, "Wanda Goes to Hollywood: China Tycoon's Firm Buys Film Studio Legendary for $3.5 Billion," *Reuters*, January 12, 2016, http://www.reuters.com/article/us-china-wanda-cinema-m-a-idUSKCN0UQ08F20160112.

118. Curtis J. Milhaupt and Wentong Zheng, "Why Mixed-Ownership Reforms Cannot Fix China's State Sector," Paulson Institute Policy Memorandum, January 2016, 5, http://www.paulsoninstitute.org/wp-content/uploads/2016/02/PPM_SOE-Ownership_Milhaupt-and-Zheng_English.pdf.

119. Milhaupt and Zheng, "Why Mixed-Ownership Reforms Cannot Fix China's State Sector."

120. Milhaupt and Zheng, "Why Mixed-Ownership Reforms Cannot Fix China's State Sector."

121. Milhaupt and Zheng, "Why Mixed-Ownership Reforms Cannot Fix China's State Sector."

122. Shen Dingli, "Don't Shun the Idea of Setting up Overseas Military Bases," China.org.cn, January 28, 2010, http://www.china.org.cn/opinion/2010-01/28/content_19324522.htm.

123. Andrea Ghiselli, "China's First Overseas Base in Djibouti, an Enabler of Its Middle East Policy," Jamestown Foundation China Brief 16.2, January 25, 2016, http://www.jamestown.org/single/?tx_ttnews%5Btt_news%5D=45017#.V3vdx_krK70.

124. Ben Blanchard, "China Launches Charm Offensive for First Overseas Naval Base," *Reuters,* March 23, 2016, http://www.reuters.com/article/us-china-djibouti-idUSKCN0WP300.

125. David Shambaugh, *China Goes Global: The Partial Power* (New York: Oxford University Press, 2013), 300–1.

126. "Annual Report to Congress: Military and Security Developments Involving the People's Republic of China 2016," Office of the Secretary of Defense, April 2016, 50, http://www.defense.gov/Portals/1/Documents/pubs/2016%20China%20Military%20Power%20Report.pdf.

127. Aude Fleurant et al., "Trends in International Arms Transfers, 2015," Stockholm International Peace Research Institute, February 2016, 2–3, https://www.sipri.org/sites/default/files/SIPRIFS1602.pdf.

128. "China to Set up 8000 Permanent Troops for UN Peacekeeping: Xi," *China Daily*, September 29, 2015, http://www.chinadaily.com.cn/world/2015xivisitus/2015-09/29/content_22004597.htm.

129. Kenneth Allen, "The Top Trends in China's Military Diplomacy," Jamestown Foundation China Brief 15.9, May 1, 2015, http://www.jamestown.org/single/?tx_ttnews%5Btt_news%5D=43866&no_cache=1#.V2rU3_krK70.

130. "2015 Report to Congress," U.S.-China Economic and Security Review Commission, November 2015, http://origin.www.uscc.gov/sites/default/ files/annual_reports/2015%20Annual%20Report%20to%20Congress. PDF, 407.

131. "Annual Report to Congress: Military and Security Developments Involving the People's Republic of China 2016," 12.

132. Yan Xuetong, "Inside the China-U.S.-Competition for Strategic Partners," *World Post*, November 2, 2015, http://www.huffingtonpost.com/ yan-xuetong/china-us-competition-allies_b_8449178.html.

133. Yan, "Inside the China-U.S.-Competition for Strategic Partners."

134. Tsuneo Akaha and Anna Vassilieva, *Russia and East Asia: Informal and Gradual Integration* (Oxon, UK: Routledge, 2014), 95.

135. Emma McClean, "Hard Evidence: Who Uses Veto in the UN Security Council Most Often—And for What?," The Conversation, July 31, 2014, http://theconversation.com/hard-evidence-who-uses-veto-in-the-un- security-council-most-often-and-for-what-29907.

136. "'Shanghai Cooperation Organization Expands, Commands Respect Worldwide'—Putin to Xinhua," *RT*, June 23, 2016, https://www.rt.com/ politics/official-word/347878-putin-xinhua-interview-china/.

137. Baohui Zhang, "Chinese Foreign Policy in Transition: Trends and Implications," *Journal of Current Chinese Affairs* 39, no. 2 (2010): 44.

138. Fu Ying, "How China Sees Russia," *Foreign Affairs*, January/February 2016, https://www.foreignaffairs.com/articles/china/2015-12-14/ how-china-sees-russia.

139. Zhou Bo, "The US Is Right That China Has No Allies—Because It Doesn't Need Them," *South China Morning Post*, June 13, 2016, http://www.scmp.com/comment/insight-opinion/article/1974414/ us-right-china-has-no-allies-because-it-doesnt-need-them.

140. Julie Makinen and Carol J. Williams, "China Unveils High-Speed Rail Line to North Korean Border," *Los Angeles Times*, August 31, 2015, http://www. latimes.com/world/asia/la-fg-china-north-korea-rail-20150901-story.html.

141. Mark E. Manyin and Mary Beth D. Nikitin, "Foreign Assistance to North Korea," Congressional Research Service, April 2, 2014, https:// www.fas.org/sgp/crs/row/R40095.pdf.

142. Walter Diamana, "Strategic Alliance: China-North Korea," *International Policy Digest*, July 2, 2015, http://intpolicydigest.org/2015/07/02/strategic- alliance-china-north-korea/.

143. Jane Perlez and Choe Sang-hun, "Public Ouster in North Korea Unsettles China," *New York Times*, December 9, 2013, http://www.nytimes.com/ 2013/12/10/world/asia/a-gamble-for-north-korea-leader-kim-jong- un.html?ref=northkorea.

144. Hu Bo, "How Should China Change Its Policy toward the Korean Peninsula," *China-US Focus*, September 22, 2016, http://www. chinausfocus.com/foreign-policy/how-should-china-change-its-policy- toward-the-korean-peninsula.

145. Yinhong Shi, "Multiple Pressures & Strategic Balance: China, DPRK & the Peninsula Issue," *China-US Focus*, July 13, 2016, http://www. chinausfocus.com/foreign-policy/multiple-pressures-strategic-balance-china-dprk-the-peninsula-issue.

146. Jinping Xi, "Opening Ceremony of the 19th CPC National Congress," October 17, 2017, http://live.china.org.cn/2017/10/17/opening-ceremony-of-the-19th-cpc-national-congress/.

147. Yiwei Wang, *The Belt and Road: What Will China Offer the World in Its Rise* (Beijing: New World Press, 2016).

148. Jacob Mardell, "The 'Community of Common Destiny' in Xi Jinping's New Era," *Diplomat*, October 25, 2017, https://thediplomat.com/2017/10/the-community-of-common-destiny-in-xi-jinpings-new-era/.

149. Limin Zheng, "Xi's World Vision: A Community of Common Destiny, a Shared Home for Humanity," *Xinhua*, January 15, 2017, http://english.cctv.com/2017/01/15/ARTIjfECMGRxn4TrlI0UqAclr70115.shtml.

150. Chris Buckley, "China's Foreign Minister Castigates Canadian Reporter for Rights Question," *New York Times,* June 2, 2015, http://www.nytimes.com/2016/06/03/world/asia/canada-china-wang-yi.html.

151. Barthelemy Courmont, "Soft Power Debates in China," Academic Foresight no. 13, January–June 2015, http://www.academic-foresights.com/Soft_Power_Debates_in_China.html.

152. "Hu Calls for Enhancing 'Soft Power' of Chinese Culture," *Xinhua*, October 15, 2007, http://www.china.org.cn/english/congress/228142.htm.

153. "Xi Eyes More Enabling Int'l Environment for China's Peaceful Development," *Xinhua,* November 30, 2015, http://www.chinaconsulatechicago.org/eng//xw/t1216243.htm.

154. "Confucius Says," *Economist*, September 13, 2014, http://www.economist.com/news/china/21616988-decade-ago-china-began-opening-centres-abroad-promote-its-culture-some-people-are-pushing.

155. David Shambaugh, "China's Soft-Power Push," *Foreign Affairs*, July/August 2015, https://www.foreignaffairs.com/articles/china/2015-06-16/china-s-soft-power-push.

156. Koh Gui Qing and John Shiffman, "Beijing's Covert Radio Network Airs China-Friendly News across Washington, and the World," *Reuters,* November 2, 2015, http://www.reuters.com/investigates/special-report/china-radio/.

157. "Scholars and Media on China's Cultural Soft Power," Wilson Center, www.wilsoncenter.org/scholars-and-media-chinas-cultural-soft-power.

158. Yanzhong Huang and Elizabeth Economy, "Where China Can't Compete," *Foreign Affairs*, September 21, 2015, https://www.foreignaffairs.com/articles/china/2015-09-21/where-china-can-t-compete.

159. Wang Wen, "The End of the So-Called 'China Collapse Theory' [*Shi Zhongjie Suowei "Zhongguo Bengkui Lun" De Shihou Le*]," China Social

Science Network, March 27, 2015, http://www.cssn.cn/zx/201503/t20150327_1562879_2.shtml.

160. "Scholars and Media on China's Cultural Soft Power."

161. Baohui Zhang, "Chinese Foreign Policy in Transition: Trends and Implications," *Journal of Current Chinese Affairs* 39, no. 2 (2010): 60.

162. "Scholars and Media on China's Cultural Soft Power."

163. Axel Dreher et al., "Apples and Dragon Fruits: The Determinants of Aid and Other Forms of State Financing from China to Africa," AidData Working Paper 15, October 2015, http://aiddata.org/sites/default/files/wps15_apples_and_dragon_fruits.pdf, 6, 10.

164. Philippa Brant, "The Geopolitics of Chinese Aid," *Foreign Affairs*, March 4, 2015, https://www.foreignaffairs.com/articles/china/2015-03-04/geopolitics-chinese-aid.

165. Yun Sun, "The Domestic Controversy over China's Foreign Aid and the Implications for Africa," Brookings Institution: Africa in Focus, October 8, 2015, www.brookings.edu/blogs/africa-in-focus/posts/2015/10/08-domestic-controversy-china-foreign-aid-africa-sun.

166. "Opinion of China," Pew Research Center, June 2016, http://www.pewglobal.org/database/indicator/24/.

167. "How Are Global Views on China Trending?," China Power, Center for Strategic & International Studies, November 7, 2017, http://chinapower.csis.org/global-views/.

168. Xi, *The Governance of China*, 135–36.

169. "U.S.-China Joint Announcement on Climate Change," White House: Office of the Press Secretary, November 12, 2014, https://www.whitehouse.gov/the-press-office/2014/11/11/us-china-joint-announcement-climate-change.

170. "U.S.-China Joint Presidential Statement on Climate Change," White House: Office of the Press Secretary, September 25, 2015, https://www.whitehouse.gov/the-press-office/2015/09/25/us-china-joint-presidential-statement-climate-change.

171. Ankit Panda, "China's Evolving Role in the Fight against Ebola," *Diplomat*, September 16, 2014, http://thediplomat.com/2014/09/chinas-evolving-role-in-the-fight-against-ebola/.

172. "China Always Ready to Provide Immediate Help for Africa in Fight against Ebola," *Xinhua*, August 10, 2015, http://news.xinhuanet.com/english/2015-08/10/c_134501068.htm.

173. Ian Taylor, "China's Response to the Ebola Virus Disease in West Africa," *The Roundtable: The Commonwealth Journal of International Affairs* 104, no. 1, http://www.tandfonline.com/doi/pdf/10.1080/00358533.2015.1005362.

174. Denis Fitzgerald, "Slowdown in Ebola Cases as Funding Increases," UN Tribune, November 5, 2014, http://untribune.com/slowdown-ebola-cases-funding-increases/.

175. Molly Anders, "UK Pledges $249M to South Sudan and Somalia in Response to Famine," Devex, February 22, 2017, https://www.devex.com/news/uk-pledges-249m-to-south-sudan-and-somalia-in-response-to-famine-89693.

176. Chris Leins, "China's Evolving Ebola Response: Recognizing the Cost of Inaction," Atlantic Council, November 10, 2014, http://www.atlanticcouncil.org/blogs/new-atlanticist/china-s-evolving-ebola-response-recognizing-the-cost-of-inaction.

177. Megha Rajagopalan, "Ebola Crisis Highlights China's Philanthropic Shortfall," *Reuters,* November 3, 2014, http://www.reuters.com/article/us-health-ebola-china-philanthropy-idUSKBN0IN21E20141103.

178. Drew Hinshaw, "Cuban Doctors at the Forefront of the Ebola Battle," *Wall Street Journal,* October 9, 2014, http://www.wsj.com/articles/cuba-stands-at-forefront-of-ebola-battle-in-africa-1412904212.

179. Scott Warren Harold, Martin C. Libicki, and Astrid Cevallos, *Getting to Yes with China in Cyberspace* (Santa Monica, CA: RAND Corporation, 2016), http://www.rand.org/pubs/research_reports/RR1335.html.

180. Adam Segal, "Chinese Computer Games," *Foreign Affairs,* March/April 2012, https://www.foreignaffairs.com/articles/china/2012-03-01/chinese-computer-games.

181. Dan Levin, "At U.N., China Tries to Influence Fight over Internet Control," *New York Times,* December 16, 2015, http://www.nytimes.com/2015/12/17/technology/china-wins-battle-with-un-over-word-in-internet-control-document.html.

182. Levin, "At U.N., China Tries to Influence Fight over Internet Control."

183. WSIS+10, "Outcome Document of the High Level Meeting of the General Assembly on the Overall Review of the Implementation of WSIS Outcomes," 2016, 10, http://workspace.unpan.org/sites/internet/Documents/UNPAN95707.pdf.

184. "Xi Defends China's Great Firewall in Push for 'Cybersovereignty,'" *Bloomberg News,* December 15, 2015, http://www.bloomberg.com/news/articles/2015-12-16/china-s-xi-defends-web-controls-in-call-for-cybersovereignty-.

185. "History of the Arctic Council," Arctic Council, September 16, 2015, http://www.arctic-council.org/index.php/en/about-us/arctic-council.

186. Steven Lee Myers, "Arctic Council Adds 6 Nations as Observer States, Including China," *New York Times,* May 15, 2013, http://www.nytimes.com/2013/05/16/world/europe/arctic-council-adds-six-members-including-china.html.

187. Arthur Guschin, "Understanding China's Arctic Policies," *Diplomat,* November 14, 2013, http://thediplomat.com/2013/11/understanding-chinas-arctic-policies/.

188. Elizabeth Economy, "The Four Drivers of Beijing's Emerging Arctic Play and What the World Needs to Do," *Forbes*, April 4, 2014, http://www.forbes.com/sites/elizabetheconomy/2014/04/04/the-four-drivers-of-beijings-emerging-arctic-play-and-what-the-world-needs-to-do/#631f8cf70d8d.

189. Guschin, "Understanding China's Arctic Policies."

190. Bree Feng, "China Looks North: Carving out a Role in the Arctic," Asia Pacific Foundation of Canada, April 30, 2015, www.asiapacific.ca/canada-asia-agenda/china-looks-north-carving-out-role-arctic.

191. Feng, "China Looks North."

192. Tang Guoqiang, "Arctic Issues and China's Stance," China Institute of International Studies, March 4, 2013, http://www.ciis.org.cn/english/2013-03/04/content_5772842.htm.

193. Guoqiang, "Arctic Issues and China's Stance."

194. Sarah Johnson, "Greenland: Rare Earth in the Arctic," IISS Voices, March 3, 2012, https://www.iiss.org/en/iiss%20voices/blogsections/2012-6d11/march-2012-bf81/greenland-rare-earth-arctic-7197.

195. Feng, "China Looks North."

196. Zhou Wa, "Bigger Chinese Role Sought in the Arctic," *China Daily USA*, February 18, 2014, http://usa.chinadaily.com.cn/epaper/2014-02/18/content_17289222.htm.

197. "Greenland, a Frontier Market Unlike Any Other for China," *China Economic Review*, February 27, 2014, www.chinaeconomicreview.com/china-in-the-arctic-greenland-iron-mining.

Chapter 8

1. "China Pledges Further Opening as Xi Jinping Pushes China-Backed Trade Deals as APEC," *Straits Times*, November, 20, 2016, http://www.straitstimes.com/asia/east-asia/xi-jinping-pushes-for-asia-pacific-trade-deals-with-china-to-fill-us-void.

2. Robert Blackwill and Ashley Tellis, "Revising U.S. Grand Strategy toward China," Council on Foreign Relations, April 2015, https://www.cfr.org/report/revising-us-grand-strategy-toward-china.

3. Lyle Goldstein, "Is it Time to Meet China Halfway?," *National Interest*, May 12, 2015, http://nationalinterest.org/feature/it-time-meet-china-halfway-12863; and Michael Swaine, "The Real Challenge in the Pacific," *Foreign Affairs*, May/June 2015, https://www.foreignaffairs.com/articles/asia/2015-04-20/real-challenge-pacific.

4. Thomas Christensen, *The China Challenge* (New York: W.W. Norton, 2016).

5. "Remarks by President Trump at APEC CEO Summit, Da Nang, Vietnam," White House: Office of the Press Secretary, November 10, 2017, https://www.whitehouse.gov/the-press-office/2017/11/10/remarks-president-trump-apec-ceo-summit-da-nang-vietnam.

6. "Resources: Members of Congress Criticize President Trump's Starvation Budget," Global Progressive Hub, June 22, 2017, http://globalprogressivehub.org/resources-responses-statements-trumps-starvation-budget/.

7. Haroon Habib, "Chinese Foreign Minister Debates Rohingya Crisis with Myanmar Leaders," *The Hindu*, November 19, 2017, http://www.thehindu.com/news/international/chinese-foreign-minister-debates-rohingya-crisis-with-myanmar-leaders/article20555827.ece.

8. Antoni Slodkowski, "Tillerson, in Myanmar, Calls for Credible Probe of Atrocities," *Reuters*, November 14, 2017, https://www.reuters.com/article/us-myanmar-rohingya/tillerson-in-myanmar-calls-for-credible-probe-of-atrocities-idUSKBN1DF0GM.

9. Richard Haass, "There Are No Good Options Left on North Korea," *The Hill*, August 16, 2017, http://thehill.com/blogs/pundits-blog/foreign-policy/346724-opinion-richard-haass-there-are-no-good-options-left-on.

10. Evan Medeiros, presentation before the Foreign Policy Association, PWC, New York, NY, September 29, 2017.

11. Alexa Pipin, "The 20 Most Popular Destinations for Americans to Study Abroad," *Business Insider*, August 24, 2016, http://www.businessinsider.com/where-american-students-study-abroad-2016-7/#3-spain-18.

INDEX

Page numbers followed by *f* and *t* indicate figures and tables, respectively. Numbers followed by n indicate notes.